*Systematics Critical and
Constructive 2:
With Compendium Interactions*

Systematics Critical and Constructive 2: With Compendium Interactions

Biblical—Interpretive—Theological—Interdisciplinary

RONALD R. RAY

PICKWICK *Publications* • Eugene, Oregon

SYSTEMATICS CRITICAL AND CONSTRUCTIVE 2: WITH COMPENDIUM INTERACTIONS
Biblical—Interpretive—Theological—Interdisciplinary

Copyright © 2022 Ronald R. Ray. All rights reserved. Except for brief quotations in critical publications or reviews, no part of this book may be reproduced in any manner without prior written permission from the publisher. Write: Permissions, Wipf and Stock Publishers, 199 W. 8th Ave., Suite 3, Eugene, OR 97401.

Pickwick Publications
An Imprint of Wipf and Stock Publishers
199 W. 8th Ave., Suite 3
Eugene, OR 97401

www.wipfandstock.com

PAPERBACK ISBN: 978-1-6667-1694-8
HARDCOVER ISBN: 978-1-6667-1695-5
EBOOK ISBN: 978-1-6667-1696-2

Cataloguing-in-Publication data:

Names: Ray, Ronald R., author.

Title: Systematics critical and constructive 2 : with compendium interactions : biblical—interpretive—theological—interdisciplinary / Ronald R. Ray.

Description: Eugene, OR : Pickwick Publications, 2022 | Includes bibliographical references.

Identifiers: ISBN 978-1-6667-1694-8 (paperback) | ISBN 978-1-6667-1695-5 (hardcover) | ISBN 978-1-6667-1696-2 (ebook)

Subjects: Theology, Doctrinal. | Hermeneutics. | Theology—Study and teaching. | Bible—Theology.

Classification: BT75.3 .R39 2022 (print) | BT75.3 .R39 (ebook)

Scripture quotations are from Revised Standard Version of the Bible, copyright © 1946, 1952, and 1971 National Council of the Churches of Christ in the United States of America. Used by permission. All rights reserved worldwide.

Scripture quotations are from New Revised Standard Version Bible, copyright © 1989 National Council of the Churches of Christ in the United States of America. Used by permission. All rights reserved worldwide.

To the Christian intellectual giants who have much influenced this writing, as seen in the bibliography and expanded table of contents. To my dear wife Diane who diligently proofread this work and greatly improved it stylistically, and to all those who have fought the good fight against racism and the Covid-19 virus.
And to the Ukrainian Resistance to Oppression.

Condensed Contents

Preface and Introduction 1

Essential Themes That Impact Throughout

   1. Human Nature 9

   2. The Event of Jesus's Resurrection and Some of Its Effects 20

   3. Some New Testament Interpretations of the Meaning of Jesus's Resurrection 28

   4. Jesus's Resurrection Disclosures, Christian Hope, Agape Here and Beyond 41

   5. The Holy Spirit and Christian Vocation 46

Additional Christology

   6. Mainly on the Implicit Self-Understandings of the Historical Jesus 59

   7. Explicit Self-Understanding of the Historical Jesus 66

   8. Post-Resurrection Faith in Christ of the New Testament Church 74

   9. Interpretations and Misinterpretations concerning Who Jesus Christ Was and Is 85

   Appendix: Another Misinterpretation concerning Christ: Most New Testament Miracle Traditions 95

   10. Soteriological Christology 98

Doctrine of God

   11. God's Triune Being and Revelation 111

       Primarily Biblical Foundations 111

       Primarily Post-Biblical Theological Contributions 119

   12. God's Revealed Transcendence 124

   13. Attributes of Our Loving and Free Interacting God 129

   14. God's Creative and Transformative Suffering and Interaction with the World 146

God the Creator and Governor

   15. God's Creational Purpose for Humans (Covenant and Creation) 155

   16. The Evolution of Species and an Emergent Evolution Perspective 160

   17. Humans as Hereditarily Influenced by Other Members of the Animal Kingdom 167

CONDENSED CONTENTS

Reconciliation by God through Christ

18. God Reconciled Humankind to Himself and Thereby Demonstrated His Love 175

    Biblical Basis 175

    Historical Theories concerning Divine Reconciliation 180

19. Justification and the Righteousness of God 185

20. Sacrifice, Redemption 195

Appropriating Christian Faith

21. Grace to Appropriate Atonement and to Persevere in Christian Faith 203

22. Appropriational Themes Related to Becoming and Being a Christian 215

23. Christian Prayer and Worship, Jesus' Baptism and Believer Baptism Distinguished but Interrelated, the Lord's Supper/Communion 236

    Christian Prayer 236

    Christian Worship 242

    Jesus's Baptism and Believer Baptism Distinguished but Interrelated 245

    The Lord's Supper/Communion 251

The Christian Life

24. The Christian as Witness 261

25. Christian Witnessing Entails Suffering 265

26. A Mini Theology of Christian Ethics 272

Christian Hope

27. Bases for the Hope of Eternal Life and Considerations concerning Its Scope and Nature 281

    Death and Eternal Life 281

    Universal Salvation and Eschatological Peril Teachings 285

The Church and Christian Tradition; True Religion and Some Other Religions; Christian Freedom

28. The Church; Conflicting Ways of Understanding Christian Tradition 295

29. Christ the Source of True Religion with Six Comparisons 305

30. Freedom within Limitation 321

Bibliography 325

The Index is found in the Expanded Table of Contents, and authorial sources in the Bibliography

Expanded Contents

Preface and Introduction 1
Essential Themes That Impact Throughout 7
1 *Human Nature* 9
    1. Distinction between God's Intentional and Permissive Wills 9
    2. One Response to Heidegger's Temporal Philosophy 9
    3. Reinhold Niebuhr: "Doctrine of Humankind as Creature" 10
    4. General Comments concerning Christian Understanding of Sin and of Our Response to Divine Forgiveness 11
    5. Kierkegaard's Challenging of the Socratic and Platonic Understanding of Sin 12
    6. Kierkegaard Again: The Possibility of the Offense 13
    7. Against the Justifying Action of the Lord Become Servant: Pride 14
    8. Against the Sanctifying Action of the Servant Become Lord: Disobedience, Greed, Sensuality 16
    9. Against the Fulfilling of Christian Vocation: Passivity 18
    10. Against the Stupidity of Not Responding to What Is Divinely Fitting 18
    11. Conclusion 19
2 *The Event of Jesus's Resurrection and Some of Its Effects* 20
    1. Why Jesus Was Rejected and Crucified, the Events Involved 20
    2. Centrality of Jesus's Resurrection 21
    3. Risen Christ's Disclosures 22
    4. Present Reality of the Risen Lord 24
    5. Jesus's Resurrection Is without Historical Parallel, but Is Supported by Strong Historical Evidence 24
    6. Encounter with Risen Lord Engendered Faith 26
    7. Jesus's Resurrection Due Entirely to God's Action 27
3 *Some New Testament Interpretations of the Meaning of Jesus's Resurrection* 28
    1. Jesus's Resurrection as Interpreted 28
    2. Jesus's Representative Resurrection and the Delayed Eschaton 28
    3. Jesus's Resurrection Guarantees Resurrection of Those Who Take Confidence in Him 30
    4. Vindication of Jesus's Life and Teaching 31

5. New Testament Perceived and Interpreted Jesus's Earthly Life through His Resurrection   32
6. Jesus's Resurrection Validates Atoning Reality of His Life and Death   32
7. Jesus's Resurrection as His Enthronement, Followed by Spiritual Disclosures to Chosen Witnesses; Enthronement, Not Ascension; Meaning of Jesus's Enthronement   33
8. Enthroned King Pours Forth Holy Spirit   36
9. Jesus's Resurrection Established Confidence in His Person and Mission Despite Eschaton's Delay   36
10. Jesus's Resurrection Institutes Mission Mandate   37
11. Historical and Theological Interrelatedness of Jesus's Crucifixion and Resurrection   37
12. Dying and Rising with Christ   39

4 *Jesus's Resurrection Disclosures, Christian Hope, Agape Here and Beyond*   41
1. Paul's Early Calling-Related Understanding of Jesus's Resurrection in Contrast to Matthew and Luke's Later Reliance on Highly Variable Oral Traditions   41
2. Gospel Accounts of Christ's Resurrection Appearances   42
3. Hope of Personal Identity in Fellowship with the Living God and Others   44
4. Agape Love Here and Beyond   44
5. Conclusion   45

5 *The Holy Spirit and Christian Vocation*   46
1. Divinity of the Holy Spirit   46
2. Jesus as Uniquely Led by the Spirit and Our Need to Be Born of the Spirit   47
3. Paul's Experiential Understanding of the Spirit and of the Spirit Basis of Christian Hope; Attestings by Wesley and Kierkegaard   48
4. New Testament's Attesting of the Outpouring of Holy Spirit and of Some of Its Effects   49
5. God as Holy Spirit Is Personal and Has Attributes   50
6. Holy Spirit as Revelation in Its Inwardly Communicative Aspect   50
7. The Paraclete Is Holy Spirit as Bearing Witness to God's Revelation in Jesus   51
8. Some Aspects of Old Testament Understandings of Spirit of God   52
9. Barth's and Edwards's New Testament Interpretations of Spirit's Work   53
10. The Spirit's Leading concerning Christian Vocation   54
11. Attitudinal Implications   55

ADDITIONAL CHRISTOLOGY   57

6 *Mainly on the Implicit Self-Understandings of the Historical Jesus*   59
1. Nature of Sources   59
2. Living Encounter with God through Christ by Means of Different New Testament Witnesses   60
3. Jesus as Sinless, but as Having Limited Knowledge   60

4. Implicit Christological Attesting 61
5. Jesus as Kingship Manifestation and as Spirit Led 61
6. Divine Forgiveness through Jesus 63
7. Linguistic Manifestations of Jesus's Relationship with God 64
8. "But I Say unto You" 65

7 *Explicit Self-Understanding of the Historical Jesus* 66
1. New Quest for the Historical Jesus 66
2. Some of the Criteria for Perceiving the Historical Jesus, with Additional Criteria Exemplified and Identified in the Following Sections 67
3. Jesus's Use of Son of God Title 68
4. Jesus the Mediator and Reconciler 69
5. Jesus's Expectation of Divine Vindication 70
6. The Son of Man and Related Christ Title 71
7. Jesus's Consenting to Messiah Title 73

8 *Post-Resurrection Faith in Christ of the New Testament Church* 74
1. Spiritual Communion with Risen Christ and Father; Jesus Worshipped as Exalted Lord 74
2. Jesus Christ as Savior and Lord 75
3. Son of God 77
4. The Incarnation 78
5. Fourth Gospel's Docetism 79
6. Theological and Historical Analysis 80
7. The Son as God's Agent of Creation 81
8. Was Son of God Conceived by and Born of a Virgin? 82

9 *Interpretations and Misinterpretations Concerning Who Jesus Christ Was and Is* 85
1. New Testament's Attesting and Denial of Jesus's Humanity 85
2. Philosophical Docetism's More Entrenched Denial of Jesus's Humanity 86
3. Apparent and Real Docetism Today 88
4. Denials of Jesus's Divinity 89
5. The Nicene Creed's Challenging of Denials of Jesus's Humanity and Divinity 89
6. Separating the Two Natures 90
7. Patristic Christological Reasoning concerning Unity of Jesus in Time with God in Eternity; Athanasian and Chalcedonian Insights 92
8. Reformed Theology's Additional Insight 93
9. Modern "Degree Christology" in Contrast to Classical Christology 93
10. Conclusion 94

Appendix: Another Misinterpretation concerning Christ: Most New Testament Miracle Traditions 95
1. Kasemann's Critical Insights 95
2. Luke's Attitude toward Miracles in His Gospel and in Acts of the Apostles 96
3. Fourth Gospel's Interpretation 96
4. Conclusion 97

EXPANDED CONTENTS

10 *Soteriological Christology* 98
    1. Interrelatedness of Person and Work 98
    2. Threefold Offices of Priest, King, and Prophet: Structural Design of Barth's Volumes on Reconciliation 99
    3. Savior 101
    4. Once and For All 102
    5. Non-Participatory "Proof" Is Impossible 102
    6. Jesus's Perfect Faithfulness or Sinlessness 103
    7. Jesus's Experience of God's Leading: A Christological Clue 106
    8. The Lord Become Servant and the Servant as Revealing the Lord: A Critical and Constructive Conversation concerning Kenotic Christology 107

DOCTRINE OF GOD

11 *God's Triune Being and Revelation* 111
  Primarily Biblical Foundations 111
    1. Interrelating Differences between Christology and Triunity 111
    2. Kenotic Biblical and Theological Linkage to Triunity 111
    3. God Can Distinguish Himself from Himself; God Hidden and Revealed, Veiled and Unveiled 114
    4. The Father as Originator of Son's and Spirit's Work and as Creator 114
    5. Fourth Gospel Threesome Language Is Not Triunitarian 115
    6. The Father Truly Known Only in the Son 115
    7. By the Spirit 116
    8. The Spirit of God and of Christ Truly Divine 116
    9. Post-Resurrection Understanding that in Jesus God Has Come among Us 116
    10. Father, Son, and Spirit 117
    11. Necessity of Triunity Doctrine: God's Revelation of His Very Self 118
    12. Triunitarian Recognition of Oneness of the Revealed God and Resultant De-divinizing of World 118
    13. Highly Metaphorical Language Required for Referring to God's Inner Being; Time and Space within Eternal Dimension 118
  Primarily Post-Biblical Theological Contributions 119
    14. God's Eternal Decision 119
    15. Modes of Inner Relationship and Modes of Revelation 119
    16. Distinctions and Relationships between Various Modes That Become Apparent in Revelation 120
    17. Indivisibility of the Work of Father, Son, and Spirit 120
    18. Triunity and the Certainty of Salvation 120
    19. Avoiding One-Sided Theologies of Triune Modes 121
    20. Moral Implications 121
    21. A Critique of Feminist Critique of Trinity 122
    22. Eschatology and Triunity 123

12 *God's Revealed Transcendence* 124
    1. An Exposition and Critique of Natural Theology's Presumption That We Can Know God Apart from Revelation in Christ 124
    2. Otherness and Nearness of Living God 126
    3. God as Personal, Self-Giving, with Genuine Agency Capacity 126
    4. God's Living Word 128

13 *Attributes of Our Loving and Free Interacting God* 129
    1. Christocentric Norm for Biblical Selectivity 129
    2. He Who Loves in Freedom 130
    3. God's Self-Existent and Moral Transcendence and Renewing Effect of Our Bowing to His Opposition to Our Opposition 130
    4. God's Inherent Attributes (Love and Freedom) and Interrelating Ones 132
    5. God as Changeable in Some Respects (Partially Mutable) and Capable of Being Acted upon and of Having Feelings (Passible) 132
    6. Mutability as Flexible Faithfulness 134
    7 Prayer and Divine Mutability 135
    8. The Loving, Righteous, and Truthful God Faithfully Honors His Promises and Requires That We Keep Our Promises 136
    9. God's Patient and Persistent Faithfulness 136
    10. Divine Suffering through God-World Self-Limitation; Nothing Takes God by Complete Surprise; God's Knows That His Ultimate Salvific Goals Will Be Achieved 138
    11. God's Superior but Not All-Controlling Power 139
    12. God's Permissive Will 142
    13. God as Omnipresent Spirit 144
    14. God's Beauty 145

14 *God's Creative and Transformative Suffering and Interaction with the World* 146
    1. Calvary as a Consistent Development 146
    2. God Can Give Us over to Historical Results of Our Misdeeds 146
    3. Divine Power through Empathetic Suffering 147
    4. The God Who Suffers, Feels, and Interacts 147
    5. The Vulnerable yet Active Sufferer 148
    6. Old Testament Witness concerning Divine Suffering 148
    7. Divine Suffering and Future Glorification 149
    8. The Related Issue of God's Knowingness 149
    9. God's Healing Ministry with Reference to Our Temporality 150

GOD THE CREATOR AND GOVERNOR 153

15 *God's Creational Purpose for Humans (Covenant and Creation)* 155
    1. Why Does the World Exist? 155
    2. That God Created through the Word/Son Points to Interrelationship of God's Will in Creating and in Reconciling 155

EXPANDED CONTENTS

    3. The Father's Decision for Triunity Shows Linkage between Creation and Covenant and Expresses God's Nature as Love 156
    4. In Jesus Christ God Remained Faithful to His Creational Purpose for Humans 156
    5. Understanding "Sagas" 157
    6. Genesis 1:1—2:4a, Priestly Account: Creation as External Basis of Covenant 157
    7. Genesis 2:4b–25, Yahwist Account: Covenant as Internal Basis of Creation 158

16 *The Evolution of Species and an Emergent Evolution Perspective* 160
    1. Evaluating Darwin's Understanding of Evolution as Due to Random Variations, Overpopulation, and Natural Selection; Evolutionary Insights beyond Darwin 160
    2. Additional Evolutionary Thinking beyond Darwin 161
    3. Whitehead's Contribution 162
    4. Human Continuity and Discontinuity with the Rest of Creation: An "Emergent Evolution" Perspective 163

17 *Humans as Hereditarily Influenced by Other Members of the Animal Kingdom* 167
    1. Innate Tendencies Can Sometimes Reveal Evolutionary Background: An Example concerning Staring 167
    2. Other Characteristics Social Animals Have in Common 168
    3. From Social Animal Ancestors We Have Inherited Capacities for Interpreting and Communicating 168
    4. Struggle for Quality of Life and Related Need to Balance Conflicting Tendencies 170
    5. Comparison of Intellectual Abilities and Behavior Patterns between Non-Human and Human Animals 170
    6. Moral Responsibility to Other Animals 171

RECONCILIATION BY GOD THROUGH CHRIST 173

18 *God Reconciled Humankind to Himself and Thereby Demonstrated His Love* 175
    Biblical Basis 175
    1. God's Merciful Outreach to Sinners through Jesus's Life and Teaching 175
    2. Jesus's Dying on a Cross 176
    3. Jesus's Rejection and Crucifixion Did Not Take Him by Surprise 176
    4. Jesus's Crucifixion as World's Judgment 177
    5. Jesus's Death on the Cross as Lowest Point of Divine Concealment; the Father's Raising of the Faithful Son as Validating Son's Faithfulness; Covenant Thereby Being Representatively Fulfilled from Human and Divine Sides 177
    6. "Christ for Us" Citations and Christ's Representative History on Our Behalf 178
    7. New Testament's Specific "Reconciliation" Understanding and Its Linkage with Justification and Right-Wising 179
    8. Divine Love as Source of Reconciliation 180

Historical Theories concerning Divine Reconciliation 180
    9. Dissatisfaction with Anselm's Satisfaction Theory of Divine Reconciliation 180
    10. Evaluation of Representative Punishment Theory; Distinction between Expiation and Propitiation 181
    11. Peter Abelard in Contrast with Anselm and Socinus 182
    12. Ritschl's Abelardian Contribution 183
    13. Faith Involves Recognizing Objective Atoning Value of What God Has Done for Us in Christ 184

19 *Justification and the Righteousness of God* 185
    1. Challenging Boastfully Supposing We Can Gain Salvation through Works 185
    2. Jesus Proclaimed and Embodied Justification as Divine Forgiveness 186
    3. Paul and Pauline Writers Attest Divine Forgiveness, Sometimes with Linkage to Justification 186
    4. Substitutionary Understandings of Atonement in General and of Justification in Particular 187
    5. Justification as God's Faithfulness to His Purpose in Human Creation 188
    6. Justification as Received through Faith Leading toward Obedience 188
    7. Righteousness of God/Justification as Double-Sided Concept 189
    8. Justification as Received through Faith, Not Works 189
    9. Confidence in Justification by Grace Provides Sense of Security, Invulnerability, and Peace with God 191
    10. Some Theologically Based Social Implications of Divine Justifying/Rightwising 192

20 *Sacrifice, Redemption* 195
    1. Atonement as Sacrifice 195
    2. Jesus's Sacrifice Began with His Incarnation and Included His Entire Life—Not Merely His Death 195
    3. Additional New Testament Evidence for Atonement as Sacrifice 196
    4. Jesus's Sacrificial Self-Offering as Abolishing Cultic Sacrifices 196
    5. Christ Redeems and Delivers Us from Bondage to Sinfulness, from Condemning Power of the Law, and from Sense of Futility and Meaninglessness in Face of Fate 197
    6. Objective-Subjective, Reality-Realization, Victory-Awareness of Victory 197
    7. Summary of Some Permanent Elements in Understanding Christian Reconciliation 198

APPROPRIATING CHRISTIAN FAITH 201

21 *Grace to Appropriate Atonement and to Persevere in Christian Faith* 203
    1. Understanding Creational versus Appropriational Grace: A Prelude 203
    2. Prevenient Grace Teaching 204
    3. Historical Development of Prevenient Grace Teaching; Pietism 206

        4. Supernatural Grace as Evoking Faith: Primarily Biblical Evidence 207
        5. Supernatural Grace as Evoking Faith: Augustine, Luther, Chalmers, Edwards, Barth, Brunner 210
        6. Grace to Persevere in Christian Faith 211
        7. Belief in Election Correlates with Divine Perseverance of the Saints, whereas Belief in Prevenient Grace Correlates with Recognition that Genuine Christians Can Totally Fall from Faith 212
        8. Conclusion 214

22 *Appropriational Themes Related to Becoming and Being a Christian* 215
        1. Biblical Terminological Variations for Becoming Christians 215
        2. Rebirth/Regeneration 216
        3. Dying and Rising with Christ 217
        4. Indicative and Imperative: Ongoing Process of Receiving Holy Spirit and Continuing to Die to Sin and to Rise to New Life in Christ 218
        5. Repentance 220
        6. Paul's Conversion-Repentance and That of Others 222
        7. Challenging Pentecostals' Two-Stage Understanding of Becoming a Christian 224
        8. Relationship between Sanctification and the Ongoing Need for Pardon 224
        9. Sanctification as Grounded in God's Holiness and His Action in Christ and through Holy Spirit Issues in Moral Renewal 226
        10. Sanctification Involves Cross-Bearing 227
        11. Substitutionary Sanctification in Christ as Aspect of Objective Atonement 228
        12. Freedom from Bondage to Sin: Becoming Adult Children of God or Friends of God 229
        13. Teleological Understanding of Christian Life 230
        14. The Moral Growth Involved in Sanctification and the Struggle Sometimes Entailed 230
        15. Sanctification and Empirical Righteousness: Luther and Wesley Compared 231
        16. Biblical Teachings concerning Attainment of Perfection in this World 232
        17. Assessment of Wesley's Perfection Teaching 233

23 *Christian Prayer, Christian Worship, Jesus's Baptism and Believer Baptism Distinguished but Interrelated, the Lord's Supper/Communion* 236
    Christian Prayer 236
        1. Some Differing Kinds of Praying 236
        2. Jesus's Praying in Private 237
        3. Asking for God's Forgiveness 237
        4. Lord's Prayer 238
        5. Petitionary Prayer 239
        6. The Spirit Can Empower Us to Pray 241

7. Line between Prayer and God-Centered Reflection Is Very Thin 241
8. Christians Care about Relationship with God, Not the Mere Fulfilment of Petitions 241
9. Thanksgiving as an Essential Aspect of Prayer 242

Christian Worship 242
1. Worship as a Means of Grace 242
2. The New Testament Holy Day 243
3. Edification (Upbuilding in Love) as a Criterion of Church Worship 243
4. Offering Ourselves for Service to God and Further Meanings of Worship 244
5. Worship Variation and Stability 244

Jesus's Baptism and Believer Baptism Distinguished but Interrelated 245
1. Jesus's Baptism by John 245
2. Spirit Baptism and Its Relation to Believer Water Baptism 247
3. Barth's Agreement with Schleiermacher in Advocating Believer Water Baptism and Rejecting Infant Baptism 248
4. New Testament Writers' Believer Baptism Terminologies and Procedures 250
5. Christian Community's Role in Baptizing Believers 251

The Lord's Supper/Communion 251
1. Jesus's Last Meal with His Disciples as His Farewell 251
2. Exegetical Examination of Pre-Gospels' Attestings of Lord's Supper Passages 252
3. Mood of Penitence, Joy, and Thankful Rededication 253
4. Remembering God's Sacrifice in Jesus and Jesus's Self-Giving 253
5. Bread and Wine, Body and Blood Issue 254
6. Frequency of Early Eucharistic Celebrations 255
7. Zwingli and Zwinglian Understandings of the Lord's Supper 255
8. Catholic Eucharistic Understanding 255
9. Exegetical Examination of Fourth Gospel's Drastically Reinterpreted Lord's Supper Teachings 256

THE CHRISTIAN LIFE 259

24 *The Christian as Witness* 261
1. Witnessing to Jesus Christ through Word and Deed, Sometimes at Considerable Cost 261
2. Agents of Reconciliation 262
3. Witnesses as Servants: Beyond Egocentric Christianity 262
4. The Breadth of Verbal Christian Witnessing 263
5. Witnessing through Actions and Attitudes 263
6. God Gives Courage and Strength to His Witnesses 264

25 *Christian Witnessing Entails Suffering* 265
1. Our Non-Atoning but Responsive Suffering in Correspondence with Christ; Sharing in the Prophetic Work of the Risen Christ 265
2. Enduring World's Resistance 267

3. Human Defenselessness of Christian Witnesses 269
4. Fulfillment through the Suffering Discipleship of Christian Witnessing 270
5. Though Others Have Suffered for Their Testimonies, Why We Do We Suffer So Little for Ours? 271

26 *A Mini Theology of Christian Ethics* 272
1. Living from the Power of God's Grace in Christ and through the Spirit; Learning from Dialogue with Fellow-Hearers of God's Word 272
2. Triunitarian Understanding of Christian Ethic 273
3. The Living Commander Bestows Freedom 273
4. The Otherness of God's Living Command 274
5. Sinner's Misuse of Legitimate Biblical Law 274
6. Glorifying God by Corresponding to the Shape of His Reconciling Deed in Christ 275
7. Relationship of the Living Command of God to Study of Christian Ethics 275
8. Implications of Understanding Christian Ethics in Context of Belief in God as Living Commander 276
9. Summary of the Bases of Christian Love 276
10. Love as Forgiveness Helps to Capacitate Love of Neighbor and of Former Enemy 277

CHRISTIAN HOPE 279

27 *Bases for the Hope of Eternal Life and Considerations concerning Its Scope* and *Nature* 281

Death and Eternal Life 281
1. Various Reasons for Thinking Seriously about Death 281
2. Rejection of Utopianism and Affirmation of Social Realism 282
3. Jesus's Resurrection Presupposes Possibility of General Human Resurrection 283
4. Some Characteristics of Eternal Life 283

Universal Salvation and Eschatological Peril Teachings 285
5. Paul and Pauline-Influenced New Testament Writings Often Attest Universal Salvation 285
6. Eschatological Peril as Also Attested by Paul 286
7. First Peter as Also Teaching Both Universal Salvation and Eschatological Peril 288
8. Fourth Gospel's Basis of Christian Hope in Contrast with 1 John 288
9. Theological Thinking concerning Universal Salvation: Schleiermacher, Barth and Newbigin as Inclusivists 289
10. The Great Importance of the Hope of Eternal Life 290

THE CHURCH AND CHRISTIAN TRADITION; TRUE RELIGION AND SOME OTHER RELIGIONS; CHRISTIAN FREEDOM 293

28 *The Church; Conflicting Ways of Understanding Christian Tradition* 295
    1. Foundation of the Church: Jesus Christ and God's Eliciting of Our Responsive Entrance 295
    2. Necessity of Preaching and Teaching 296
    3. Paul's Leadership within Churches He Founded 297
    4. Spirit-Guided Ministries within Paul's Churches 297
    5 Criteria That Help Community to Evaluate Charismatic Contributions 298
    6. Ministry according to Post-Pauline Pastorals 299
    7. Pastoral Epistles Modifications of Pauline Understanding of Charisma 299
    8. The Twelve Apostles and the Others 301
    9. Hiddenness of Church 301
    10. Inward and Outward Church Growth 302
    11. Criticism of Church 302
    12. Conflicting Ways of Understanding Post-New Testament Christian Tradition 303

29 *Christ the Source of True Religion with Nine Comparisons* 305
    1. Brunner and Barth on Priority of Revelation over Religion 305
    2. Biblical Examples of Christian Unfaithfulness; Need for Focusing on Revelation in Christ and Deliverance through Christ 306
    3. God's Grace in Christ Contradicting Our Contradiction; The Christocentric Basis of Christian Religion 307
    4. Christian Faith in Contrast with Mysticism 308
    5. Evaluating Five Religions 308
    6. Evaluating the Jehovah's Witnesses and Noting Their Similarities with Other Sectarians 311
    7. Evaluating the Teachings of the Church of Jesus Christ of the Latter Day Saints (Mormons) 313
    8. Evaluating African Separatist "Churches" and Noting the Similarity with Western Prosperity Gospel "Churches" 318

30 *Freedom within Limitation* 321
    1. Our Unique Opportunity 321

Bibliography 325

PREFACE AND INTRODUCTION[1]

---

[1]. Some of what was said in vol. 1 needs to be repeated in this preface, since readers of this work may not have read the first volume. The last two chapters of *Systematics Critical and Constructive 1* also deal with the meaning of faith/belief, which directly links to this volume.

Preface

THIS WORK COMPLETES A considerable portion of a lifetime of reflection concerning the nature of Christian Faith. But it gives only hints of my understanding of Christian Ethics.[1] As with the first volume it is hoped that these works will contribute to the upbuilding of Christian Faith and to more faithful living.

Sometimes in the background but often in the foreground of this work is *biblical analysis and interpretation*. In its critical and constructive effort this volume is much indebted to the writings of a wide range of biblical and systematic theologians. At such points this work *does not just expound* the ideas of particular biblical and systematic theologians, but *utilizes them* where helpful for articulating Christian Faith.

This critical and constructive writing is primarily for students studying theology in universities and seminaries, for their teachers, for congregational preachers and teachers, and interested lay people. Especially for the sake of the latter, but perhaps also for others, technical terms are kept to a minimum. Where these are needed synonyms or definitions are offered in close proximity to their first usage and sometimes later also.

Topics appear in this book that are not usually dealt with in systematic theologies: "The Evolution of Species and an Emergent Evolution Perspective" (chap. 16), "Humans as Hereditarily Influenced by Other Members of the Animal Kingdom" (chap. 17), and the "Nine Comparisons" accompanying "Christ as the Source of True Religion" (second part of chap. 29).

Readers who want to find particular discussions that are more specific than indicated by chapter headings should look to the *expanded table of contents, which is the detailed subject index of the book, with page numbers for every heading and subheading.* For utilized authorial sources see the bibliography.

---

1. I hope to have *Ethic of Christian Freedom & Discipleship and Theology of Christian Ethics (approximate title)* published soon. Chap. 1 of that book expands beyond the human sinfulness discussions within this chapter.

Introduction

A CHRISTIAN SYSTEMATIC THEOLOGIAN should read widely, think deeply, and share ideas concerning the biblical meaning of Christian Faith (as do biblical theologians). But for systematics the decisive focus is on the normative significance of Christian faith for today, taking account of insights from various disciplines, from biblical and historical theology in particular, and from the systematic theologies that one finds helpful.

Perhaps the reader would be interested in my own theological pilgrimage, since that may shed some light on this writing. Having read William Hordern's *Layman's Guide to Protestant Theology* before heading to Yale Divinity School, I was well armed against fad theologies, such as Harvey Cox's *Secular City* that later emerged. Much was learned from James Gustafson's Christian Ethics course, but much more from his subsequent writings. However I was never an uncritical student of his or anyone else. Paul Holmer's Kierkegaard course was influential as was Robert Clyde Johnson's seminar readings course on the four volumes (!) of Barth's *Doctrine of Reconciliation*. By student pressure that biblical teachers do direct biblical exposition, Nils Dahl's introductory New Testament course was turned into a lecture course on Ephesians and Colossians. The New Testament introductory aspect came from PhD candidate-led seminars related to the broad range of interpretive issues. The one course became two.

Not to be brainwashed by only one institution, my second year of seminary study was at the Pacific School of Religion. The second term was across the bay at San Francisco Theological Seminary for two readings courses arranged with Theodore Gill, the President, who had done his PhD under Brunner. One course was on Brunner's writings, the other on Reinhold Niebuhr's. We met periodically to discuss questions and issues raised by massive amounts of reading. Back at PSR I discovered that Charles McCoy welcomed student-initiated seminar courses, so one was arranged on the writings of H. Richard Niebuhr and another on those of Bonhoeffer.

The next year and as recently married I was back at Yale Divinity School. After graduation we left for Edinburgh for me to complete my reading of the Church Dogmatics, and where we both sat in on some teaching at New College, including Tom Torrance's Dogmatics course. Robert Davidson's hermeneutic seminar inspired great interest in me for that field of study.

The next two years we were in Oregon, I as a United Methodist pastor near Portland. From there to St. Andrews, Scotland to do a PhD on Barth's Christian Ethic. But having become disillusioned with my advisor, I switched from the Theology Department to

Christian Ethics, and did the first PhD on Jacques Ellul's Christian Ethic.[1] My research on Barth and Kierkegaard (as having influenced Barth) was relevant for understanding Ellul. During that time in Scotland I sat in on Ernest Best's New Testament graduate student seminar on hermeneutics.

I learned much from Ellul and we corresponded, he with what to me was illegible French penmanship and I in typed English. Along with what has now become many others Ellul has much influenced my understanding of Christian Ethics, but unlike the Ellulians that later emerged I understand Ellul's theological and ethical thinking as highly influenced by Barth, as Ellul understood his own work.

From Scotland to Portland (UMC pastor for five years) and then our family of four moved to Bukuru, just outside of Jos, Nigeria. There I taught at the Theological College of Northern Nigeria for fifteen years, teaching everything under the sun. Which was a theological education for me, but at that busy time my concentration was as much as possible on Christian Ethics.

For eleven years (1994–2005) we worked at Saint Paul's United Theological College, in Limuru, Kenya, just outside of Nairobi, at a long-distance-runner high altitude not far from the edge of the Rift Valley. At that college (which became Saint Paul's University) my teaching was in Systematics, Christian Ethics, Kierkegaard, and Sexuality and Christian marriage; but my research centered in Systematics.

Since "retiring" we have lived in Wilderness, South Africa, on the southern coast near George, where my research and continues, but without the teaching aspect.

---

1. Entitled "A Critical Examination of Jacques Ellul's Christian Ethic."

ESSENTIAL THEMES
THAT IMPACT THROUGHOUT

Chapter 1

Human Nature

1. Distinction between God's Intentional and Permissive Wills

"Wickedness and evil have no doubt entered creation with God's knowledge and permission, but they are not objects of His will in the sense of reflecting His creative pleasure."[1] The use of the distinction between God's intentional and permissive wills protects against the accusation that the presence of evil demonstrates that God is powerless or unloving. Our supremely powerful but not omnipotent God permits evil and is able to accomplish good amid the evil He permits. But our loving Father did not create evil, does not will that it exists, is fighting against it, can accomplish His good purposes in spite of it, and in Christ has eschatologically defeated it.

2. One Response to Heidegger's Temporal Philosophy

Heiddeger interpreted human existence in terms of temporality. "What is particularly significant in Heidegger's analysis is his understanding that time as humanly experienced is not a featureless line of duration. . . . (1) To be human is . . . *to exist 'ahead-of-oneself'*—to make plans, to worry about coming dangers, to have hopes, in short, to have concern for the future. If one never gave a thought to what comes next, one would neither exist temporally nor be human. (2) But being human also . . . [involves] 'thrownness.'" We are in a situation that we did not sign up for because by the time we have nearly adult consciousness we already have a past behind us with "relationships established, good and bad memories, debts incurred, satisfactions and regrets. To exist humanly means . . . never to be starting with a completely clean slate. (3) Finally, being human means . . . being in the world with other humans [and] with a whole environment." "How are humans to live in the context

---

1. Pannenberg, *ST*, 2:169.

of such a temporal experience? Heidegger saw two options, which he called authentic and inauthentic existence."[2]

To exist authentically means acknowledging that in the future we will die and that every moment means less time left. It also involves taking responsibility for the past as *our* past. With respect to the present, authentic existence entails accepting responsibility for decisions, knowing that decisions matter because they are often irreversible and place limits on one's finite future.

Inauthentic existence involves hiding from the realities just mentioned. Pushing death's inevitability from the mind and not taking responsibility for our present and past. Uncritically accepting roles proposed by others, blending in with one's social surroundings, hardly accepting our own decisions as our own.[3]

Jesus integrated and to that extent overcame the differences between past, present and future. He obediently accepted his past as fully his own and yet a gift from God. "He trustingly moved toward a future that, whatever tragedies might befall, moved him ultimately toward God. Thus he . . . could live each moment to the full. 'There was in Him no opposition or competition or conflict, but peace between origin, movement and goal, between past, present and future.'"[4]

"In communion with Jesus Christ, Christians can begin to live their lives from, with and toward God, such that life's fleetingness is no longer a burden or a terror." Can "begin to have the temporal course of one's earthly life cohere, . . . looking back to one's origin as from God, and therefore purposed, and forward to God as one's goal. Therefore one's beginning becomes not a shadow but a promise, and 'death now wears a guise in which we can look it in the face'"[5]

"Such a life opens up possibilities for love and vulnerability. One can take the risks of love sustained by a vision of one's life as providentially originated, destined to God, and coherent. No longer need the past seem only a burden, the future a cause of anxiety, and the present a [transient] moment."[6]

3. Reinhold Niebuhr: "Doctrine of Humankind as Creature"

"In the biblical view the contrast between the created world and the Creator, between its dependent and insufficient existence and His freedom and self-sufficiency, is absolute. But this contrast never means that the created world is evil. . . . It is never [seen as] a corruption of an original divine unity and eternity, as in Neo-Platonism; nor is it evil because of the desire and pain that characterize all insufficient and dependent life, as in Buddhism."[7]

---

2. Placher, *Narratives/Vulnerable God*, 33, 34.
3. Ibid., 34.
4. Ibid., 37–38, quoting Barth, *CD* 2/1:612.
5. Ibid., 39–40, quoting Barth, *CD* 2/1.
6. Ibid., 40.
7. Niebuhr, *Nature and Destiny*, 169.

The Christian view understands humankind primarily from the standpoint of God, rather than the uniqueness of our rational faculties or our relation to nature. To truly understand ourselves means to begin with a faith that we are understood from beyond ourselves, that we are known and loved by God and must find ourselves in terms of obedience to God's will. The relation of God to humankind makes it possible for us to relate to God without pretending to be divine; and to accept our creational distance from God, without believing that our sinful nature is caused by our finiteness. Our finite existence in the body and in history can be essentially affirmed, as with naturalism. Yet while preserving a sharp distinction between the human and divine, our uniqueness can be appreciated even more than with philosophical idealism. Believing in a Creator who created both mind and body, the unity of mind and body can be emphasized.[8]

4. General Comments concerning Christian Understanding of Sin and of Our Response to Divine Forgiveness

Sin has to do with the will's perversion. Sin is autonomy, centering life in one's self and seeking to know good and evil on one's own (see Gen 3:1–7). Sin has its origin and being in that we want to be our own source and standard. Thinking and acting accordingly, we and all humans are in considerable conflict with God. "Not all people commit all sins, but [excluding Christ] all commit this sin which is the essence and root of all other sins. There is not one who can boast that he does not commit it."[9]

For this reason people have proceeded to construct their own moral systems. However helpful and important these can be, they are not the product of a higher nature. They are tied, rather, to the power sinners have taken upon themselves of knowing good and evil. Sin is not first of all a failure to obey a morality, but the desire to determine it independently of God.

We thereby lose our true being. For neither as individuals nor as societies were we created to rotate around ourselves. We were created to glorify God. With self-containment we miss the authentic life we seek. "If any person would come after me, let him deny himself and take up his cross and follow me" (Mark 8:35a).[10]

Sin affects our whole selves, including our feelings, wills and intellects; conversion and then ongoing divine guidance impacts all of these. God created us, but he did not create us as sinners! We sinners are responsible for our sin and thus are genuinely guilty and in need of divine forgiveness and empowerment.

If we have responded to divine forgiveness we will be grateful. Grace evokes gratitude, and ingratitude is a sign that one is not living from grace. Primitive Christianity knew that as a result of divine forgiveness pertaining to the guilt of sin, "people were also *redeemed from the rule of sin as a power*, as is clearly shown in the utterances of Paul.[11] Not

---

8. Ibid., 13, 15–16.
9. Barth, *CD* 4/1:220.
10. Ibid., 421.
11. Rom 6:2, 6, 11–12; 7:4, 6; 8:4, 9, 12–13; Gal 5:16, 24.

that Christians [in and through Christ] are made actually sinless;[12] rather, [our] struggle against... temptation [can even be] increased.[13] ... Thus within the church there is quite often mention of *repentance*."[14]

5. Kierkegaard's Challenging of the Socratic and Platonic Understanding of Sin

Socrates and Plato understood moral fault as due to ignorance, and regarded such ignorance as acquired, rather than inherent. But if moral fault is acquired it must have a basis in our obscuring of our wills, which neither Socrates nor Plato could account for. The determinant that Socrates lacked concerning what sin is was the awareness of defiant will. Greek intellectualism could not perceive that a rational person with knowledge of what is right, could do what is wrong.[15]

Against Platonic naiveté, when merely natural people sense what is right and do not do it "the knowledge stops boiling." That is, if such people do not like what is right they may decide to "see about that tomorrow."[16] The next day they may have no objection to doing what they earlier had good reason for thinking was wrong.

Because people cannot existentially understand sin as long as they are entrapped by it, Christianity insists that more than intellectual cognition is required for such learning. We sinners do not want to understand sin because our natural tendency is to follow our own wills, rather than allow ourselves to be open to God's judgment, correction, and guidance. But if by God's grace we become receptive to God in these ways, we can be led in the way of obedience.

"Socrates explains that he who does not do the right thing has not understood it; but Christianity goes... further back and says, it is because [one does not will] to understand it [that he does not do the right thing].... And in the next place, describing what properly is defiance, it teaches that a man does wrong although he understands what is [wrong], or forbears to do right although he understands what is right; in short, the Christian doctrine of sin is pure impertinence [rudeness, disrespect] against [others], accusation upon accusation; [this] is the charge that the Deity as prosecutor takes the liberty of lodging against man."

But can any merely natural person "comprehend this Christian doctrine? By no means—this too is Christian, and so is an offense.... How then does Christianity explain this incomprehensible? Quite consistently... by means of the fact that it is revealed." "So then, Christianly understood, sin lies in the will, not in the intellect; and this corruption of the will goes well beyond the [natural awareness] of the individual."[17]

---

12. 1 Cor 3:1–3; 10:12; Gal 5:17; 6:1; cf. Jas 3:2.

13. 1 Cor 7:5; 2 Cor 2:11; 11:3; Eph. 6:10–17; 1 Pet 5:8.

14. The source of this paragraph's quotation was lost.

15. Kierkegaard, *Sickness unto Death*, 142, 145. Having received this insight from Christianity, Kant, unlike the rationalists, recognized the role of the will in moral matters, but did not believe in moral empowerment and guidance from the Living God, nor did he speak of divine forgiveness.

16. Ibid., 152.

17. Ibid., 154–55.

Shifting slightly, sin is not due to Adam's fall, nor even to our sinning in the past, but to our continual succumbing. "The particular sins . . . are the expression of the continuation of sin; in the particular new sins the momentum of sin merely becomes more observable."[18] Here Kierkegaard combines an emphasis on sin as a state of being with the voluntariness of sin as one's giving ongoing consent to the act that exhibits the state of being.

6. Kierkegaard Again: The Possibility of the Offense

Kierkegaard writes that "the opposition sin/faith is the Christian [offense], which in a Christian way transforms the definition of all ethical concepts, giving them one distillation more. At the bottom of this opposition lies the decisive Christian concept 'before God,' a determinant which in turn stands in relation to the decisive criterion of Christianity: . . . the paradox, the possibility of offense. . . . The possibility of offense . . . lies in the fact that a [person], as a particular individual, should have such a reality as is implied by existing directly in the sight of God; and then again, as a consequence of this, that [one's] sin should concern God. This notion of the particular [person] . . . before God speculative philosophy never gets into its head; it can only universalize the particular [person extravagantly]."[19]

Another aspect of the offense is that this humbling God wants to be the guiding presence in our lives. The Holy God of love wills to meet us and forgive us at the level of our sinfulness, and thereby become not only our Savior, but our Lord.

"There is so much said now about people being offended at Christianity because it is so dark and gloomy, offended at it because it is so severe, etc. It is now high time to explain that the real reason why [people are] offended at Christianity is because . . . its goal is not [humankind's] goal, because it would make of a [person] something so extraordinary that [the natural person] is unable to get it into his head."

"Christianity teaches that . . . the individual exists *before God*, . . . can talk with God any moment, sure to be heard by Him, in short, [people are] invited to live on the most intimate terms with God! Furthermore, for [our] sake God came to the world, let himself be born, suffers and dies; and this suffering God . . . entreats [us] to accept the help which is offered! Verily, if there is anything that would make [people lose their prior resistance], it is surely this! Whosoever has not the humble courage to dare to believe it, must be offended at it. But why is he offended? Because it is too high for him, because he cannot get it into his head, because in the face of it he cannot acquire frank-heartedness, and therefore must have it done away with, brought to naught and nonsense, for it is as though it would stifle him. . . . The narrow-mindedness of the natural man cannot welcome for himself the extraordinary which God has intended for him; so he is offended."[20]

We gain experiential awareness of our sinfulness as we become aware of divine forgiveness through the Holy Spirit's presence. "The sickness is disclosed with the cure."[21]

---

18. Ibid., 173.
19. Ibid., 133.
20. Ibid., 134, 137–38.
21. Barth, *CD* 3/3:309.

Prefatory comments before next four sections. In dealing with disputes between those who emphasize justification and those who stress sanctification we should recognize that "sin manifests itself in different forms. Sin can have the form of *pride, phariseeism, and self-salvation*. Sin can also have the form of *slowness and quietism*." The first form brings us near to legalism; the second to irresponsibility. Approaches for dealing with these two forms of sinning "have to be understood as complementary."[22] Sin can also take other forms, as seen in section nine and ten.

7. Against the Justifying Action of the Lord Become Servant: Pride

Sin/evil is the reality on whose account and against which God willed to become a human being to draw us to Himself. It is thus the reality that opposes and resists God. Forces of evil brought Christ to the cross and were defeated there. "Only from the standpoint of Jesus Christ, His birth, [life], death, and resurrection, do we see [evil] in reality and truth, without the temptation to treat it . . . dialectically and thus render it innocuous. From this standpoint we see it with fear and trembling as the adversary with which God and God alone can cope."[23] Thus the power of evil should be rated as high as possible in relation to ourselves and as low as possible in relation to God.[24] The God of power and love can help us to struggle against the temptation and sin that we of ourselves cannot master.

As for three types of pride that reflect the sinful lack of God-centeredness: first, *intellectual pride* reflects more than ignorance of ignorance. It entails a conscious or subconscious effort to obscure a taint of interest. For example, though philosophers seek truth, they do not as completely possess truth as they often imagine. And such pretention is never simply ignorance of ignorance, but an effort to obscure the limits of human knowledge, lest they give way to skepticism.[25]

Second, *moral pride* makes one's sense of virtue a vehicle of sin, which is why the NT often criticizes self-righteous sinners in contrast to obvious ones. Biblical moral theory differs from simple moralisms, including Christian moralisms. Thus Jesus's struggle against the Pharisees and Paul's insistence that people cannot be saved by works, lest anyone should boast. Thus Luther's insistence that the unwillingness to be regarded as a sinner is the final form of sin. Those who think they can justify themselves do not know God as judge and Savior. The sin of self-righteousness is responsible for serious cruelties and injustices. The history of social struggles reflects the wickedness and miseries resulting from self-righteousness.[26]

The sin of moral pride often interrelates with *spiritual pride*. The latter makes the self-deification implied by moral pride explicit. A person may claim that Christ is his judge, but may also be uncritically confident that he and not an opponent—not even a Christian

---

22. Berkhof, *Doctrine of Holy Spirit*, 75.
23. Barth, *CD* 3/3:305.
24. Ibid., 295.
25. Niebuhr, *Nature and Destiny*, 195, 184–85.
26. Ibid., 199–200.

one—is on the Lord's side. The worst form of intolerance is religious intolerance in which the particular interests of contestants hide behind [supposed] religious absolutes.

"Christianity rightly regards itself . . . as a religion of revelation in which a holy and loving God is revealed as the source and goal of all finite existence against whom the self-will of man is shattered and his pride abased. But as soon as the Christian assumes that he is, by virtue of possessing this revelation, more righteous, because more contrite than other people, he increases the sin of self-righteousness and makes the form of a religion of contrition the tool of his pride."[27]

There are no guarantees against spiritual pride, since even the general recognition of sinfulness can be used as a vehicle of sin. "'Discourses on humility are a source of pride to the vain,' declares Pascal, 'and of humility to the humble'"[28] If sin as involving various forms of pride is not recognized, the Christian gospel will be poorly understood. "Even the most 'Christian' civilization and even the most pious church must be reminded that the true God can be known only where there is some awareness of a contradiction between divine and human purposes, even on the highest level of aspirations."[29]

Insofar as the power of sin is being broken, we can abandon our egocentric view of ourselves and become God-centered. As one's sense of autonomous independence diminishes, the meaning of God's self-revelation and self-giving in Jesus Christ can register, and self pride can begin to be broken down. Inasmuch as these events become vital realities the message of Christ ceases to be "folly' and 'scandal' (1 Cor 1:18).[30] A person can "become a bankrupt sinner, a proud person humbled."[31]

As for sinfulness in connection with the collective will-to-power: "Individuals [can] be moral in the sense that they are able to consider interests other than their own in determining problems of conduct, and are capable, on occasion, of preferring the advantages of others to their own. . . . But all these achievements are more difficult, if not impossible, for human societies and social groups. In every human group there is less reason to guide and check impulse, less capacity for self-transcendence, less ability to comprehend the needs of others, and therefore more unrestrained egoism than [many of] the individuals, who compose the group reveal in their personal relationships."[32]

Niebuhr argued that the collective pride of classes, races and nations (and I would add tribes) has been history's greatest source of injustice. He insisted that groups have weak moral capacities because they find it nearly impossible to use critical reason to subordinate their interests to the wider good (and individuals find doing so hard enough). Groups can even use individual unselfishness to further *collective will-to power*, as when they require people to fight in wars caused by national selfishness. Though group norms can help to elevate individual behavior, communal standards often have the opposite effect. As seen in *To Kill a Mockingbird*, even if only out of fear or shame, individuals often will not do what they are willing to do when they join a mob.

27. Ibid., 201.
28. Blaise Pascal, *Pensees*, 377, cited in Niebuhr, *Nature and Destiny*, 202.
29. Niebuhr, *Irony of American History*, 173.
30. Brunner, *Revelation and Reason*, 73.
31. Barth, *CD* 4/1:619.
32. Niebuhr, *Moral Man and Immoral Society*, xi.

Power is necessary to establish and preserve unity, order, and justice in communities. However, each such achievement is flawed because groups gaining predominant political power appropriate rewards and privileges to their members. Those successful in their quests for power seek to justify their standing—even if they have deprived and victimized others. In reaction those who lack power may forcibly attempt to seize it. In these ways the will-to-power results in violence: That involving callous indifference and oppression (such as structural violence), and that reflecting hatred and aggressive counter-violence (such as revolution).

The pride of nations consists in making unconditioned claims for their conditioned values. Nations often presume greater devotion to transcendent values than the facts warrant; they often regard the values to which they are loyal as more absolute than they really are. Even nations that claim to fight for liberty and democracy do so only when vital national interests are imperiled. The great Hebrew prophets challenged the linking of national interests with God's will. Only within a religion of revelation could the voice of God be heard beyond human majesties, a divine power in comparison with which the nations are as a drop in a bucket.[33]

8. Against the Sanctifying Action of the Servant Become Lord: Disobedience, Greed, Sensuality

Concerning *disobedience*, in a non-historical tale Adam and Eve are said to have hidden from the presence of the Lord (Gen 3:8). Also likely to be a literary construct, the prophet Jonah is said to have tried to run away from a divine call to go and preach repentance to Nineveh. And called to proclaim the word of the Lord to Pharaoh, Moses protested, "I have never been eloquent... I am slow of speech and slow of tongue.... O my Lord, please send someone else" (Exod 4:10, 13).

Greed involves refusing to be sanctified concerning the responsible use of wealth. It is well described in Jesus's parable of the rich fool who thought to himself "'Soul, you have ample goods laid up for many years; take your ease, eat, drink, be merry.' But God said to him, 'Fool! This night your soul is required of you; and the things you have prepared, whose will they be?' So is he who lays up treasures for himself, and is not rich toward God" (Luke 12:19–21). "'Take heed, and beware of all covetousness; for a man's life does not consist in the abundance of his possessions'" (Luke 12:15).

"Greed as a form of will-to-power is today a particularly flagrant sin because modern technology has tempted contemporary people to overestimate the possibility ... of eliminating all natural insecurity. Greed has thus become the besetting sin of a bourgeois culture. This culture is tempted to regard physical comfort and security as life's highest good and to hope for its attainment to a degree which is [generally] beyond human possibilities. 'Modern man,' said a cynical doctor, 'has forgotten that nature intends to kill man and will succeed in the end.'"[34]

---

33. Niebuhr, *Nature and Destiny*, 213–15.
34. Ibid., 191.

If selfishness is the attempt to center life around oneself, *sensuality* is the destruction of harmony within the self, by identification with and devotion to particular impulses and desires. The sins of sensuality, as expressed for instance in sexual license, gluttony, love of luxury, drunkenness, drug addiction and abandonment to physical desires, have traditionally been subject to stronger social disapproval than selfishness.[35]

Sin as "sensuality is always: (1) an extension of self-love to point where it defeats its own ends; (2) an effort to escape the prison house of self by finding a god in a process or person outside the self; and (3) finally an effort to escape from the confusion which sin has created into some form of subconscious existence."[36]

Having entered upon the irresponsible way that leads to death, the soul of a sensually overindulgent person no longer controls his body, nor does his body obey his soul.[37] Barth describes a famous biblical attesting of murderous and dissolute behavior, that of King David: "The whole point of the story . . . is to prove that David too shares in the unfaithfulness of Israel to Yahweh, and thus stands with Israel (although not destroying God's faithfulness) under the judgment of Yahweh"[38]

---

35. Ibid., 228.

36. Ibid., 240. "A modern psychoanalyst explains the twofold function of addiction to alcohol as follows: 'Alcoholics are almost invariably jolly, sociable, talkative [people]—who indeed seem obliged to make themselves well liked and are skilful in doing so. It takes very little penetration to discover, however, that this inordinate wish to be loved, which compels them to be at so much pains to be charming . . . bespeaks a great underlying feeling of insecurity, a feeling which must constantly be denied, compensated for or anesthetized'" (Karl A Menninger, *Man against Himself*, quoted in ibid., 234–35).

37. Barth, CD 4/2:454.

38. Ibid., 465. "'Thou shalt not covet thy neighbor's wife' (Exod 20:17). The gaping David covets the woman—Bathsheba, the wife of Uriah the Hittite—whom he there sees washing herself. 'Thou shalt not commit adultery' (Exod 20:14). David wills to commit adultery with this woman. He [had] only to command her as the king and he [did] so. Had he not already committed it in his heart (Matt 5:28) as he looked on her and lusted after her—the wife of another? . . . The king of Israel an adulterer? The consequences are incalculable. . . . Already he is his own prisoner. It is only by further wrong that he can avert the consequences of the wrong which he has already done. First, he tries to practice a clumsy deception. Uriah is recalled. The ostensible reason is that he should report to David on the campaign. The real purpose is to restore him to his own house and therefore to Bathsheba. He will therefore think and even at worst cannot prove a contrary opinion, that the expected child is his own. But this plan is defeated by an unexpected obstacle: 'Uriah said unto David, the ark, and Israel and Judah abide in tents; and my lord Joab, and the servants of my lord are encamped in the open fields; shall I then go into my house, to eat and to drink, and to lie with my wife? . . . I will not do this thing' (11:11a). . . . As king he has the power [to dispose of Uriah]. 'Thou shalt not kill' (Exod 20–13). He has the power to kill without having to admit it even to himself. And he does it by sending his famous directive to Joab, carried by the returning husband himself, to place him in the fiercest part of the battle against the besieged city of the Ammonites, and then to leave him in the lurch, so that he is killed by the enemies of Israel. His orders were obeyed, involving an unnecessary, imprudent and costly attack which in itself David could only have censured. But he was quite unable to do so. For the report sent by Joab concluded with the news which he desired: 'Thy servant, Uriah the Hittite, is dead also.' . . . Bathsheba mourns for her husband. 'And when the mourning was past, David sent and fetched her to his house, and she became his wife, and bare him a son' (11:27). He could now be born without a scandal. It all belonged to the past. It had been covered over."

"'But the thing that David had done displeased the Lord.' This was the message that the prophet Nathan had to give him. He had done what he should not and could not do as the elect of Yahweh. He had contradicted at every point himself, his election and calling, and therefore Yahweh. He had allowed himself to stray and fall into lust and adultery and intrigue and murderous treachery—the one following the other by an iron law—and therefore into the sphere of the wrath and judgment of God. 'As the Lord lives, the man

SYSTEMATICS CRITICAL AND CONSTRUCTIVE 2

9. Against the Fulfilling of Christian Vocation: Passivity

Though sin in relation to God and others can manifest itself in pride, disobedience, greed, sensuality and the will-to-power, it can also be seen in "*the slide-into-powerlessness, unquestioning passivity*, . . . lethargy [the absence of energy and enthusiasm], and the fear of taking initiative." "Distorted interpretations of sin can help to lock victims into their victimization by undermining their will to break free."

"Human life as created and reconciled by God is denied not only by brutal domination of others but also by . . . always letting the agenda be set by others, doing what everyone else wants you to do or tells you to do. Mere passivity is the breeding ground of totalitarianism and inhumanity no less than outrageous pride. Both men and women of all races and classes are to some extent vulnerable to both forms of sin. . . . Given the one-sided emphases of traditional theologies of sin, the major effort in any [expansion of the understanding] of the doctrine of sin today must be to dismantle those interpretations that serve as a religious ideology inculcating passivity in the face of injustice. The human freedom and maturity intended by God is destroyed both *where one lords it over another and where one fails to resist being lorded over*."[39]

"True Christianity cannot be a private Christianity. . . . Not without justice we usually complain from the Christian angle that the increasing disintegration of human society is connected with the great modern apostasy from faith. The counter-question has also to be put whether it may not be the great secularization and dehumanization of human life in society which, having been so successfully accomplished *without any serious or timely protest on the part of the church and Christianity*, necessarily involved the great apostasy from faith."[40]

10. Against the Stupidity of Not Responding to What Is Divinely Fitting

As stupidly oblivious to the enlightening work of the Holy Spirit, sin is in part the failure to listen to the Living God concerning the "fitting" thing required of us in specific situations. As a result we are often silent when we should speak, and speak when we should be silent. Furthermore, as in counseling or even in talking with a friend, timing can be very important. Sensitively seeking God's leading prior to and/or in the situation is vital.

More generally, we often tend to laugh when we should weep, and weep when we should be comforted and laugh. We often make exceptions where the rule should be kept, and hold ourselves to the rule when we should choose in freedom. We toil when we should pray, and pray when work is much needed. We devote ourselves to historical and psychological investigations when decisions are demanded, and we rush into decisions when historical and psychological investigation is required. We are contentious where it is

---

that had done this thing shall surely die,' is his own confession when his act is held up before him in the mirror of Nathan's parable. And it invites the crushing retort: 'Thou art the man' (12:5f.), though because of David's sincere repentance that did not happen" (Barth, *CD* 4/2:466-67).

39. Migliore, *Faith Seeking Understanding*, 132-33, my emphases.

40. Ibid., 442, my emphasis.

unnecessary and harmful, and speak of love and peace where we may confidently critique. We speak of faith and the Gospel where what is needed is commonsense, and commonsense where we can and should attest the faith and commit ourselves and others quietly into the hands of God.[41]

Ecclesiastes 3 provides us with "a list of different things for which there is a proper time—in accordance with the fact that God Himself does everything [at the appropriate] time. The genius of stupidity is to think everything at the wrong time, to say everything to the wrong people, . . . to lose no opportunity of misunderstanding and being misunderstood, always to omit the one simple and necessary thing which is demanded, and to have a sure instinct for choosing and willing and doing the complicated and superfluous thing which can only disrupt and obstruct."[42]

11. Conclusion

Christians believe that the evil that invades the world and the hearts of people is not stronger than the Creator, and that in spite of sin the Creator can still accomplish His good purposes. We may be out of relationship with God, but God is not out of relationship with us. "Even the lost sheep remains in the sphere of the shepherd who seeks, even the lost coin in that of the woman who seeks, even the lost son feeding with the swine in the same world as the distant house of his father."[43] God the creator remains faithful to His covenant with creation. As sinners we have not escaped from the sphere of God's gracious will, from the relationship of Creator and creature, and from the covenant that God has instituted between Himself and us. We can fall but we cannot escape from God (Ps 139:1–12).[44] "To believe means . . . in the knowledge of our own contradictions against grace to cleave to the grace of God which infinitely contradicts these contradictions."[45]

---

41. Barth, *CD* 4/2:413.
42. Ibid., 413–14.
43. Barth, *CD* 4/1:481.
44. Barth, *CD* 4/1:482.
45. Barth, *CD* 1/2:338.

Chapter 2

The Event of Jesus's Resurrection and Some of Its Effects[1]

1. Why Jesus Was Rejected and Crucified, and the Events Involved

THERE SEEMS TO HAVE been a variety of human reasons why Jesus was rejected and crucified. Probable factors were His implicit claim to divine authority in forgiving sin in God's name and in speaking on God's behalf ("but I say unto you," Matt 5:44a).[2] Also contributing were His outreach to tax collectors and sinners (Luke 15:1–2) in defiance of Jewish ritual purity concerns (Matt 15:1–20; Mark 7:1–23). And His relativizing of the law of Moses (Mark 10:2–12) and statements about the destruction of the Jerusalem temple (Mark 13:1–4 and par.). That He finally went to Jerusalem posed a threat to many Jewish leaders' authority. His act of cleansing the temple could have been the final act that convinced many such leaders that He threatened their standing. Jewish authorities likely convinced the Roman rulers that Jesus imperiled Roman law and order; thus He was crucified on the Roman charge that He was claiming to be the king of the Jews (Matt 27:11–14; Mark 15:2–5; Luke 23:2–5).

Jesus was arrested by the Sanhedrin leaders under the guidance of Judas Iscariot, "and *all forsook him and fled*" (Mark 14:50 par.).[3] There is nothing in the further course of Mark to contradict this *earliest* gospel report. At the cross Jesus's work seemed to have collapsed, and His claim that through Him God was achieving eschatological salvation appeared disproven. There is little doubt that *Jesus died forsaken by his disciples*. A story

---

1. However one organizes Systematic Theology topics, from the beginning one must assume Jesus's resurrection. I discuss the resurrection early and locate all christological discussion afterward. Some might argue that dealing with the "Jesus of history" aspects of Christology before considering Jesus's resurrection would have been better. Doing so would certainly have discussed the material in the order in which the events occurred, i.e., first Jesus, then His resurrection, then the church's Christology. Such a procedure, however, is not reflective of the way we come to faith in Jesus Christ, since *all present knowledge of Him is in the light of His resurrection. Had it not been for that, He who was condemned to death as a criminal would likely have been long since forgotten.*

2. See chap. 6, sec. 8.

3. Luke 23:49 softened the Mark 14:50 content by saying that in connection with Jesus's death "all his acquaintances... stood at a distance." John 19:26 softened differently by attesting that the "disciple whom Jesus loved" stood beneath the cross.

with such cowardly attribution concerning the disciples is unlikely to have been invented by later imagination.

A related issue is whether the disciples stayed for a while within the precincts of Jerusalem after Jesus's crucifixion. That the earliest references to disclosures of the risen Christ are in Galilee, rather than in Jerusalem (Matt 28:7; Mark 16:7), suggests that after Jesus's capture, trial, and crucifixion the disciples fled from Jerusalem.[4]

Like other non-Gospel NT authors, Paul had little interest in explaining particular reasons why Jesus was rejected, apparently because he believed that such events reflected a force of evil that explained what had happened. Paul tells us that, blinded and misled by evil, the onlookers and the rulers did not understand God's wisdom and grace and thus crucified the Lord of glory (1 Cor 2:8).[5]

Jesus suffered and died in humiliating circumstances. Prior to His crucifixion the crowd mocked Him and the religious leaders and Roman soldiers abused Him. Jesus's authority was thus scorned, yet was ironically attested by the "king of the Jews" inscription on the cross (Matt 27:11–14; Mark 15:2–5; Luke 23:2–5). He died the slow torture death of asphyxiation that the Roman Empire reserved for criminals.

The renouncing and crucifying of Jesus spurned the claims to authority His words and actions had implied and asserted. Only if God has challenged the human repudiation of Jesus—only if God did indeed raise Jesus from death—do the NT affirmations concerning Him make sense.

2. Centrality of Jesus's Resurrection

Though in Jesus's earthly life a number of disciples had begun to follow Him, uniquely Christian Faith in Christ emerged only after His resurrection. Jesus may or may not have foreseen His own rejection, death and vindication by God. And Gospel texts to the contrary, it is less probable that He instructed His disciples concerning His "fate." If the disciples had received such teaching they obviously did not take it to heart, since they were dismayed by His crucifixion and fled.[6] "Jesus's work seemed to have collapsed, and His claim that through Him God was achieving eschatological salvation appeared to [have been] proven false. This is the way the disciples must have felt."[7]

Unless something extraordinary had occurred to convince former disciples that God had vindicated Jesus, it is hard to imagine why they would later "have taken immense risks [by asserting] in public that a man who had been condemned and hanged was no less than God's Messiah. . . . Without the [belief that God raised Him from death] it is inconceivable that the first disciples could have entertained the idea themselves." The enthusiasm of the disciples arose primarily from the conviction that Jesus "was alive as Lord and Messiah,

---

4. Geering, *Resurrection*, 140.

5. Cousar, *Theology of the Cross*, 26.

6. Mark 14:50, 66–72, and par.; see also John 20:19. A member of the Jewish council, who had not consented to Jesus' death, offered to bury Him (Mark 15:42–47; Luke 23:50–53). Matthew likely introduced his own opinion by adding that Joseph of Arimathea was not just a good man who looked for the coming kingdom, but was a Christian disciple (27:57). See chap. 14, sec. 3.

7. Kummel, *Theology of the NT*, 96. Luke 24:20–21 portrays this mood of the disciples.

and [some of them] could testify from their experience of actual encounter with him that God had glorified him."

"The disciples did not seem to be expecting to meet Jesus as their Lord. In Paul's [considerably later] case this is obvious; he was persecuting the Christians because he thought that Jesus had been a false prophet or bogus messiah. It is hard to think that his experience on the road to Damascus was a piece of unconscious self-deception or wish-fulfillment. And it seems clear from what took place after the arrest of Jesus, that Peter and the other disciples had no hope [that Jesus would rise]. . . . The experience of encounter came to [former disciples] out of the blue when they were least expecting it. This tells to some extent against it being hallucinatory."[8] Because the human events of Jesus's story ended on such a downbeat, it's unlikely that He would have been remembered in ancient times or today had it all ended at Calvary.

Paul in his Jewish period had been extremely zealous for the traditions of his fathers (Gal 1:14), and according to the pharisaically interpreted law, had regarded himself as blameless in God's sight (Phil 3:6). That legal system taught that a crucified person is cursed by God (Deut 21:23c), but Christians were claiming that God had raised the crucified Messiah. The preaching of the crucified and risen Christ was an "object of indignation for the Jews" (1 Cor 1:23), and had prompted Paul to "persecute and oppress the church of God above measure" (Gal 1:13; cf. 1 Cor 15:9). In view of Paul's violent resistance to God's action in Christ, he came to regard as a sign of pure grace that it pleased God to reveal his Son to him (Gal 1:15-16) and to call him to be an apostle (1 Cor 15:9-10).[9]

The resurrection of Jesus is so foundational that if God had not raised Jesus from death everything else Christian Faith affirms would be groundless. This does not, however, mean that Jesus's resurrection as an isolated event could have had such meaning. His resurrection linked with the pre-resurrection traditions concerning His life and teaching that His resurrection inspired His disciples to preserve. In raising Jesus God did not raise a random individual, but one "whose life called for it in view of the purposes and promises of God."[10] And one who at His Jewish hearing/trial manifested considerable authority by implying or claiming that He was the Messiah (Mark 15:2-5; Luke 23:3). So central was the conviction that God had raised the crucified and exalted Him to God's right hand that the NT frequently summarizes its essential message by referring to the crucifixion and resurrection story and its meaning.[11]

3. Risen Christ's Disclosures

Prior to Jesus's risen disclosure to His brother James (1 Cor 15:7), he and his family had renounced Him (Mark 3:21; John 7:5). Because the remaining eleven "apostles" fled in

---

8. Lampe in Lampe and MacKinnon, *Resurrection*, 30-31, 38.

9. Kummel, *Theology of the NT*, 150-51. We only know of Paul's conversion encounter with the Risen Lord from allusions in his epistles (Gal 1:12-16; 1 Cor 9:1; 15:8; Phil 3:6-7; possibly 2 Cor 4:6), since the three accounts in the much later book of Acts widely contradict Paul's own evidence (see Acts 9:1-19; 22:4-16; 26:9-18), (ibid., 150).

10. Berkhof, *Christian Faith*, 308.

11. 1 Cor 15:3-8; see also Rom 1:4; 4:23-25; 8:34; 10:9; Phil 2:8-11.

despair after the crucifixion (1 Cor 15:5), they only again became apostles after the Risen Christ's disclosures. Paul certainly considered his own such encounter as authorizing his apostolic calling (1 Cor 9:1; 15:8–10; Gal 1:12, 15)—regarding himself as the last of the apostles (1 Cor 15:8). As for the five hundred brethren who met the Risen Lord (1 Cor 15:6), most of them before that event would not likely have continued to regard themselves as Jesus's disciples. Things changed for all of these people upon the Risen Christ's revelations.[12]

With Paul's testimony we are on much firmer ground than with the Gospel narratives, for not only does Paul provide the earliest written attestation confirming Jesus's resurrection (written about twenty to twenty-five years after Jesus's death)—but offers the only first-hand account. He also affirms that after three years he went up to Jerusalem to get to know Cephas (Peter) and stayed with him fifteen days and met James, the Lord's brother (who had become an apostle) (Gal 1:18–19). In 1 Corinthians 15 Paul enumerated all the people known to him who had encountered the Risen Christ, "in order to prove by means of this enumeration that all the witnesses named attested the fact of the resurrection of the crucified One *in the same way as he did*: 'Whether then it was I or they, so we preach and so you believed'" (vs. 11).[13]

Paul certified that "last of all, as one untimely born, he *appeared* to me" (1 Cor 15:8, my emphasis). In 1 Corinthians 15:5–8 Paul four times used the word "*opthe*," "appeared,"[14] to refer to Christ's risen disclosures, both those in close proximity to Christ's death and concerning his own experience some years later. "Most New Testament scholars believe that this word . . . refers to spiritual awareness rather than to ocular sighting. Hence it is very interesting that Paul should use this word in his 'official list' of Christ's appearances, as well as to describe what he himself experienced."[15] When using this term Paul likely meant a mental experience granted at the Lord's initiative. Likely never having seen Jesus, would Paul have recognized him had He reappeared physically?

Since Paul exhibits no familiarity with the idea of a corporeal presence of Jesus after His death, since Paul's accounts are the earliest and are alone written by one who encountered the Risen Christ, and since the apostles in Jerusalem apparently accepted Paul's account as similar to their own, "we would need good [historical] grounds for believing that any other appearances were different in nature from what [Paul described]. That [evidence] would be all the more [needed] if we can also show why [the far later] gospel writers may have wanted to describe the experiences differently." Luke, for instance, wished "to refute the suggestion that the risen Jesus was just a 'spirit,' meaning in this case a 'ghost' (24:37, 39). Luke was here presumably [also] trying to counter the suggestion of some that that was all that He [ever] was." Luke also tended "to describe events involving the Spirit, like

---

12. Kummel, *Theology of the NT*, 103.

13. Ibid., 97, my emphasis.

14. Apart from the use of this word here and in Luke 24:34 in connection with resurrection appearances it is used in the NT with reference to "visions" of *objects in heaven* (and thus out of the human sight) and concerning the return of Christ (Ruef, *Paul's First Letter to Corinth*, 160). That Luke uses this same word to refer to a resurrection appearance is odd in view of Luke-Acts common (but obviously not consistent) physical realism with reference to the Risen Christ's appearances.

15. Badham, "The Meaning of the Resurrection of Jesus," 31.

Jesus receiving the Spirit at his baptism or the first disciples receiving it at Pentecost, in surprisingly tangible, sense-perceptible terms."[16]

Though it is improbable that Paul had ever seen Jesus, the Risen Lord made known that He was none other than Jesus raised from death. Since Paul's experience of the Risen Christ caused him to become aware of the continuity between the Exalted Lord and Jesus who walked this earth, Paul's spiritual perception of the Risen Lord's reality and identity can well testify to the continuity between Jesus of Nazareth and the Risen Christ. Of course Paul did not know much concerning Jesus's life and teachings, since the Gospels were yet to be written.

As for Paul's specific apostolic calling by the Risen Lord, the emphasis was on the commission to take the Gospel to the Gentiles (1 Cor 9:1). "Here clearly is a key feature that distinguished the Damascus 'revelation of Jesus Christ' from his . . . subsequent particular experiences; none other . . . had this epochal and eschatological significance for Paul. *That one experience determined the rest of his life; from it everything else flowed.*"[17]

4. Present Reality of the Risen Lord

Because of Christ's resurrection and the outpouring of the Spirit of the Risen Lord the early Christians spoke of Him as immediately present. Where two or three are gathered together in His name there is He in our midst (Matt 18:20). The same one who once lived, who was raised to eternal existence, and who then appeared to chosen witnesses is alive and interacting with us. Faith in the spiritually present Christ cannot produce historical facts in the life of Jesus, but the Living Christ convicts and liberates us in part by drawing us to the Gospels' portraits of Jesus—so that as we critically compare and meditatively ponder the accounts of the One there portrayed He in this way and in others[18] continues to gain victory in our lives.

Luke 24:11 says that the disciples were *not* so gullible as to believe in Jesus's resurrection merely because others had so attested (see also John 20:24–25, 28). As with the early disciples, we too believe in Jesus's resurrection only as we share in the power of the Risen Lord. Without present encounter, belief in Jesus's resurrection involves mere intellectual assent and falls short of Christian Faith.

5. Jesus's Resurrection Is without Historical Parallel, but Is Supported by Strong Historical Evidence

If what is "humanly possible" is the measure of what is historically possible, the resurrection of Jesus and His post-resurrection encounters must be regarded as impossible, as must our encounters with the Risen Christ through the Spirit. "In the biblical view, what is historically possible is always weighed within the horizon of a world that is ever open to the activity of the Living God. Nature and history are not closed in on their own inherent

---

16. Wedderburn, *Beyond Resurrection*, 73.
17. Dunn, *Jesus and the Spirit*, 113.
18. As with the other NT writings.

possibilities." This does not mean that all purported miracles either in the Bible or today should be accepted at face value. It does mean that Christian theology must recognize that God is a free agent who can and does interact amid history. "In the face of denials of the resurrection of Jesus, it is necessary for theology to become critical of criticism, to free the mind and prepare the way for an unprejudiced hearing of the witnesses."[19]

The NT regards the resurrection of Jesus as *humanly impossible, yet as having occurred*. Jesus's resurrection demonstrates that God can call into existence what does not exist (Rom 4:17, 24). The NT considers Christ's risen disclosures as unique events that had never before happened. Because of such manifestations former followers were called to proclaim Jesus's resurrection as God's unique miracle, the beginning of the New Creation. The resurrection of Jesus provides one of those occasions that exposes the unjustified narrowness of a commonly assumed premise of historical method, that events cannot conflict with what is regarded as humanly possible.

Whether a past event happened and, if so, how it should be understood are questions whose answers require evidence. In the case of an allegation concerning a unique and unrepeatable event, such as the resurrection of Jesus and His risen encounter with chosen witnesses, more evidence than usual is needed to substantiate the claim. But this is what the NT provides, once we get past later embellishments and concentrate upon the oldest such source—Paul.[20]

The following factors constitute historical evidence for Jesus's risen self-disclosures: (A) Paul's firsthand accounts of his encounter with the Risen Christ (1 Cor 9:1a; 15:3–8; Gal 1:15–17) as well authenticated in documents written relatively close to the time of the events described. And in 1 Corinthians 15:1–9 Paul mentions disclosures to Cephas (Peter), the twelve (really eleven), five hundred brethren, James, all the apostles, and lastly to himself. Galatians and 1 Corinthians were probably written only twenty to thirty years after Jesus's death.

(B) It is a well-substantiated fact that the early Christians soon, though not initially, came to believe that God had raised Jesus from death (Luke 24:17–21, 38; John 20:2, 11–13). "The Gospels portray the arrest, trial and crucifixion of Jesus as leaving the disciples in disarray and dismay: they ran away (Mark 14:50 and par.); they denied him (Mark 14:66–72 and par.); an outsider had to assume responsibility for Jesus's burial (Mark 15:43); they skulked in fear behind closed doors (John 20:19); they reacted with skeptical incredulity to the first reports of resurrection appearances (Luke 14:11; John 20:25); they resumed their previous occupation as fishermen, as if trying to forget all about Jesus or that they had ever been commissioned by Jesus (John 21:3; contrast 20:21)."[21] Yet their mood quickly gave way to joy—and they boldly began to proclaim the Crucified and Risen Lord. They professed that their sudden change of attitude was caused by the Risen Lord's manifestations.

"The disciples were taken by surprise by the turn of events and nothing that Jesus had said had really . . . prepared them for what was to come."[22] A way in which Christianity differs from the origins of other religions is in the "dramatic recovery from what had

---

19. Braaten, "The Person of Jesus Christ," 550.
20. See chap. 4.
21. Wedderburn, *Beyond Resurrection*, 39.
22. Ibid., 46.

seemed like a crushing defeat. Hans Kung makes this contrast explicit: 'we are faced with the *historical enigma of the emergence of [Christian Faith]*. How different this was from the gradual, peaceful propagation of the teachings of the successful sages, Buddha and Confucius; how different also from the largely violent propagation of the teachings of the victorious Muhammad.... A truly world-transforming religion emerged from the gallows where a man was hanged in shame.' Something must surely have happened to effect this change, ... which in a short time not only provoked a complete reversal of [the former disciples'] attitudes, but also enabled them to engage in renewed activity and to found the primitive Christian community."[23]

(C) There is conclusive evidence that Jesus died on the cross and was buried. The NT uniformly speaks of a "full tomb" and none of the early opponents of Christianity ever argued that Jesus had not died. It was a long while before that heresy developed, and when it first did, it was based on the philosophically dualistic assumption that if Jesus were the Son of God He could not have been truly born nor have truly died. Also, regarding the material world as inherently evil, such gnostic denials of Jesus's death assumed that a genuine incarnation would have tainted God.

As for the theory that Jesus swooned and revived, it is just that—a mere theory—there being no historical evidence of any early claims of this type. The notion that Jesus did not die implies that in proclaiming His resurrection/enthronement the early Christians were deceivers. That they would risk their lives to proclaim what they knew to be a fraud is psychologically implausible. In addition, one wonders what became of Jesus revived? There is no evidence that following His crucifixion Jesus lived a human life and later died a natural death.[24]

Though not based on philosophical dualism, but on a rejection of Jesus's resurrection-confirmed divinity, Muslims claim that Jesus did not die. But from earthly existence directly ascended, as the OT asserts concerning Elijah (2 Kgs 2:11c). Such later fictional affirmations should not be granted the right to arbitrate concerning what occurred centuries earlier.

6. Encounter with Risen Lord Engendered Faith

Because Jesus's former disciples were dejected following His crucifixion, their faith could not have engendered their certainty that Jesus was alive. Because their faith and hopes had collapsed, they would not have conjured up encounters with the Risen Christ by means of wishful thoughts. "The belief in Jesus as the Savior . . . and the initiator of the kingdom of God perished at the cross. His followers fled in despair. It was only due to [encounters with] the Risen Lord that despair gave way to new and unusually strong faith. Therefore the resurrection may be called the decisive redemptive event."[25]

---

23. Ibid., 47, with a quotation from Hans Kung, *Being a Christian*, 345.

24. Bicknell, *Thirty-Nine Articles*, 104. The historical speculation found in Dan Brown's novel, *The Da Vinci Code*, counts for nothing and insults Christian Faith.

25. Berkhof, *Christian Faith*, 307.

The Risen Lord did not appear randomly to people, but to those whom God had chosen as witnesses (Acts 10:40–41). Since the eleven apostles forsook Him and fled, even when revealing Himself to them He encountered nonbelievers. In revealing Himself to Paul, the Risen Lord converted the Christian persecutor into becoming the leading apostle (Gal 1:13, 15–16). In disclosing Himself to His brother James (1 Cor 15:7) the Risen Christ encountered one who during His earthly life had also not even been a disciple (Mark 3:21; cf. John 7:5).[26] These encounters were thus capable of "turning the skeptical or downright hostile into devoted followers."[27]

7. Jesus's Resurrection Due Entirely to God's Action

God alone can give life to the dead and call into being what does not exist (Rom 4:17c). Though God was uniquely revealed in Jesus, Jesus was not inherently immortal, incapable of dying, and thus did not raise Himself. The NT frankly affirms that Jesus died and generally insists that *God* raised Him from death,[28] highly exalted Him and bestowed upon Him God's own name (Phil 2:9). Like Jesus's reconciling death on the cross, His resurrection was a genuine occurrence in space and time. Unlike the events of Jesus's life, His resurrection could not have included His will and activity as components, since He had died.

Though the NT gives accounts of how Jesus suffered and died, and though it describes encounters with the Risen Lord, Jesus's resurrection is never depicted. Not only did no one observe that, but as an act of God alone it took place outside the context of human decisions and actions. Like the initial act of creation, it was a sovereign act of God alone.[29]

Jesus's resurrection, along with the resulting resurrection disclosures and the outpouring of the Spirit, "are . . . decisive events in the history of the world, focal point[s] in God's dealings with His creation." (The Incarnation may be equally important, but without Jesus's resurrection we would not know of it.) Jesus's resurrection located His human life within the perspective of eternity. Thereafter Jesus "is forever contemporary as the Lord to whom 'all authority in heaven and earth' is given, who is with us always, to the close of the age."[30]

---

26. Mark 3:31–35, Matt 12:46–50, and Luke 8:19–21 indicate that Jesus's family members did not support His ministry.

27. Wedderburn, *Beyond Resurrection*, 67.

28. Rom 4:24; 8:11; 2 Cor 4:14; Gal 1:1; Col 2:12; 1 Pet 1:21. For the contrary and likely ahistorical minority viewpoint see John 2:19–22; 5:26 and especially 10:17–18: "For this reason the Father loves me, because I lay down my life, that I may take it again. No one takes it from me, but I lay it down of my own accord. I have power to lay it down, and I have power to take it up again; this charge I have received from my Father." Such attributing of resurrection capacities to Jesus Himself is a docetic denial of His earthly humanity as exhibited elsewhere in the Fourth Gospel.

29. Barth, *CD* 4/1:300–301, 334.

30. Lampe in Lampe and MacKinnon, *Resurrection*, 90.

Chapter 3

Some New Testament Interpretations of the Meaning of Jesus's Resurrection

1. Jesus's Resurrection as Interpreted

IT IS THE RESURRECTION of Jesus *as interpreted* that is of importance to Christian Faith. Apart from the well-founded interpretations the NT provides, Jesus's resurrection could be understood as a resuscitation or as establishing Jesus's status as only a prophet.

First, the NT attests that Jesus's resurrection was no resuscitation to mortal life in this world, but resurrection/exaltation to eternal life. Resuscitations are described several times in the Bible (Matt 9:18–25; Luke 7:11–16; John 11). Whether or not we regard none, some or all NT resuscitations as historical, we can agree that such miracles have *nothing in common* with Jesus's resurrection. Jesus was not restored to finite existence, in the future to face again the reality of death. He was raised to life immortal—to deathless life beyond finite existence.

Second, apart from the NT's interpretations, Jesus's resurrection could be regarded merely as evidence of His prophetic power, as with the Koran's interpretation of Jesus's supposed virginal conception and ascension. Jesus's resurrection has Christian meanings because the NT places it in the context of resurrection-inspired Christian beliefs concerning its meaning and pertaining to the unique identity and mission of Jesus in relation to God and His work.[1]

2. Jesus's Representative Resurrection and the Delayed Eschaton

It was the experience of encounter with the risen Christ that created the understanding of His risen being and of Christian eschatological hope. Such ideas were not generated from

---

1. Christian theology is not unique in interrelating facts and interpretations. "Apart from meaningless sense impressions there is no experience that abides as a 'fact' without an element of valid interpretation having been imparted to it. This is true even of the facts of everyday life, the nature of which depends on the accepted interpretation of events—whether magical, astrological, mythical, naturalistic, etc." (Polanyi, *Science*, 89).

prior OT beliefs that were then applied to create confidence that Jesus rose. That Jesus was raised and that He appeared was rather "an inference drawn from a series of experiences,"[2] which the recipients believed were by divine initiative.

Three distinct and entirely separate OT interpretive possibilities were *not* utilized: "The [mere] concept of the exaltation of one humiliated in suffering and death (cf. Isa 52:13–15); that of [a merely] exceptional individual taken to be with God at the end of his or her life (cf. Gen 5:24; 2 Kings 2:1–18); and that of the [beginning of the] general resurrection at the end (cf. Isa 26:19; Dan 12:2)"[3] Jesus's resurrection does not match any of these. To affirm, as the NT does, that a single individual had been raised and that His *representative resurrection* guarantees the resurrection of others, and yet that the consummation would not immediately occur, is a combination that had never previously been conceived.[4]

Because NT Christians were confident that the Risen Lord was already present in their midst, the delay of the consummation did not constitute a major problem.

Many NT critics have hypothesized that the hope of an early consummation quickly gave way to disillusionment and disappointment and adaptation to the existing status quo. Such scholars have thought that the opinion repudiated in 2 Peter 3:4 expressed a laboriously suppressed NT conviction. These thinkers failed to take account of the present reality of hope substantiated by Christians' relation to the Risen Christ as Holy Spirit. Because of such Spirit-sustained confidence, the delay of the eschaton did not pose the theological crisis that such scholars have supposed. "We must disabuse our minds of the notion that the NT community had only darkness and twilight behind it and only the brilliant light of the *parousia* [final revelation/consummation] before it. . . . We must never forget, its gaze is always on Him. It may look backwards to His past even as far as the eternal counsel of God. It may look to His present at the right hand of God, from which He rules today by His Spirit. Or it may look to the future and His general and conclusive revelation. But *in every case it looks only to Him*."[5]

Second generation NT writers, such as Luke, recognized that Jesus's resurrection would be temporally more widely separated from His return than early Christians had thought, making the necessary expectation adjustment without apparent difficulty. "The relation of the Christ event to the end of the world . . . is not [dependent on the shortness of] the interval between both events. It is bound only to the material analogy of what has already happened in and with Jesus and that for which the apocalyptic expectation hopes for the ultimate future." "The delay of the end events, which now amounts to [over] two thousand years, is not a refutation of the Christian hope and of the Christian perception

---

2. Wedderburn, *Beyond Resurrection*, 69.

3. Ibid., 68.

4. "Gerhard Friedrich concludes, against D. F. Strauss, that the belief in Christ's resurrection cannot simply be explained as a deduction from Jewish apocalyptic beliefs, for 'the concept of the eschatological raising from the dead of an individual is utterly unparalleled and not to be inferred from [OT] tradition.' And even if one argues for the belief in certain circles that Jewish martyrs would immediately rise, . . . this belief had no direct connection with a general resurrection or the eschatological consummation of all things, nor was it usually linked to appearances of those risen" (ibid., 68).

5. Barth, *CD* 3/2:509, 492.

of revelation as long as the unity between what happened in Jesus and the eschatological future is maintained."[6]

Though in all probability Jesus envisioned the end of the world within the generation of those then living (Mark 13:30), the world's consummation obviously did not occur as soon as He expected. However, because it occurred representatively in His own person on behalf of the world, Jesus's eschatological thinking was largely (though not entirely) correct.[7] To err is human and not of itself sinful. In regard to the question at issue, Jesus would have sinned only if He had failed to trust His and the world's future into God's care.

3. Jesus's Resurrection Guarantees Resurrection of Those Who Take Confidence in Him

Jesus's resurrection is the main (but not sole) basis for the Christian hope of life beyond life.[8] In raising Jesus from death God guaranteed the salvation of those who look to Him. Jesus Christ was not merely a person—but *the person whom God authorized to represent others*. What happened in Him happened on our behalf and for our sake. His resurrection is the promise and pledge of our resurrection (1 Cor 15:12-19; Rom 8:11; 1 Thess 4:14). In Christ the human race has in principle triumphed over sin and death. Paul makes this point by summarizing the human race both in terms of Adam and by reference to Christ. This categorizing points in the right direction even if we do not believe that a first ancestor introduced finiteness and capacitated us to sin.[9]

Though Paul regarded Jesus's resurrection as an event that occurred in history and that necessitates a belief in the resurrection of the dead, he insisted that were one to deny the resurrection of the dead one could not consistently affirm Jesus's resurrection (1 Cor 15:13, 16). "For if the dead are not raised, then Christ has not been raised. If Christ has not been raised, your faith is futile and you are still in your sins" (1 Cor 15:16-17). If Christ was not raised, Christians are not merely pursuing a figment of their imaginations, but embracing death. If Christ was not raised it would be better to eat and drink and enjoy present life to the full (15:32). "But in fact Christ has been raised from the dead, the first fruits of those who have fallen asleep."[10]

Paul even understood the Risen Christ's resurrection of personality without this-worldly materiality as paralleling the heavenly embodiment we will receive in eternity (1 Cor 15:42-50). What "is sown a physical body, is raised a spiritual body. . . . Flesh and

---

6. Pannenberg, *Jesus*, 107, 107-8.

7. As was common with prophetic hopes and expectations, anticipations often do not exactly match fulfillments (Pannenberg, *Apostles' Creed*, 52-53).

8. Jesus's resurrection was epistemologically foundational, with other factors being secondarily foundational, such as knowledge of God's purposes in creation and of His love.

9. "For since death came through a human being, the resurrection of the dead has also come through a human being; for as all die in Adam, so *all will be made alive in Christ*" (1 Cor 15:21-22 NRSV, my emphasis). The truth articulated by this typological comparison—fallen humankind's common sinfulness—does not depend on Adam having been the first human ancestor, which no one who recognizes the scientific validity of evolution can believe.

10. 1 Cor 15:20; see also Rom 8:23, 29; 11:16; Col 1:18.

blood cannot inherit the kingdom of God, nor does the perishable inherit the imperishable" (1 Cor 15:44, 50).

"Paul (with dependence on the OT) takes the words [first fruits] to mean the first installment of the crop which foreshadows and pledges the ultimate offering of the whole. Because Christ has been raised from the dead, the resurrection of the rest of mankind (or at least those who are in Christ) is assured."[11] So also the author of 1 Peter reasons: By the great mercy of God the Father "we have been born anew to a living hope through the resurrection of Jesus Christ from the dead" (1:3). By believing in Jesus's resurrection the early Christians affirmed the general resurrection of the dead.[12]

4. Vindication of Jesus's Life and Teaching

The whole of Jesus's ministry and His explicit and implicit manifestations of divine authority required future confirmation if their present validity were to be sustained. "*Everything depended upon the connection between Jesus's claim and its confirmation by God.*"[13] "It was only through Jesus's resurrection that it was possible to believe in him again at all after his death on the cross. That was already true of the first group that gathered together after the events in Jerusalem, and it applies equally . . . to those of us who have come later."[14] Jesus put his own person too much in the foreground and covered it too much with divine authority to be remembered as a mere example or teacher. Therefore the Christian faith stands or falls with Jesus's resurrection.[15] That Jesus has been raised "means that God himself has confirmed the pre-Easter activity of Jesus."[16]

Through Jesus's resurrection God vindicated, supported and upheld Jesus and His work. This vindication meant something first of all for Jesus, that the Father had not forsaken Him, but had confirmed His work, putting life forever in front of Him. All that people did in rejecting and crucifying Jesus was overturned by God's action. "The stone which was rejected by the builders . . . has become the head of the corner" (Acts 4:11). "This Jesus . . . you crucified and killed by the hands of lawless [people]. But God raised him up" (Acts 2:23–24). Through His resurrection God has attested that Jesus is Lord and Christ (Acts 2:36), Son of God in power (Acts 13:33; Rom 1:4), "Leader and Savior" (Acts 5:31), "judge and Lord of the living and the dead."[17] By raising Jesus God placed His seal of approval upon Him, highly exalting Him, and bestowing upon Him the name above every name (Phil 2:9).

Christians can affirm Jesus's authority only because God raised Him from death. Having begun with the latter insight, we are led to affirm that Jesus was God's unique disclosure prior to the human recognition of this. This being so, "Easter time is simply the time of the

---

11. Barrett, *First Epistle to the Corinthians*, 350–51.
12. 1 Cor 6:14; 15:20; 2 Cor 4:14; Col 1:18; Rev 1:5.
13. Pannenberg, *Jesus*, 66, my emphasis.
14. Pannenberg, *Apostles' Creed*, 53.
15. Berkhof, *Christian Faith*, 307.
16. Pannenberg, *Jesus*, 67.
17. Acts 10:42b; cf. Rom 14:9; 2 Tim 4:1.

revelation of the mystery of the preceding time of the life and death of the man Jesus. The two times are inseparably linked.... But this means that this whole time is the time of the appearance and presence of God."[18]

5. New Testament Perceived and Interpreted Jesus's Earthly Life through His Resurrection

"The event of Easter is... the [lens] through which the apostles and their communities saw the man Jesus in every aspect of His relation to them—as the One who 'was, and is, and is to come' (Rev. 4:8)." "The Easter history is the starting-point for the Evangelists' portrait[s] of the man Jesus."[19] The NT does not offer exact details concerning Jesus's daily life, but tells a history interpreted with the insight bestowed by Jesus's resurrection. The final purpose from which all of the Gospels were written was well summarized by the Fourth Gospel: "These things are written that you may believe that Jesus is the Christ, the Son of God, and that believing you may have life in his name" (Rev 20:31).

Against Barth's and Brunner's primary focus on the Christ of post-resurrection faith and their sometimes disinterest in historical questions concerning the pre-resurrection Jesus, it is important to analyze the various layers of Synoptic historical traditions to reach probable conclusions concerning what Jesus said and did and regarding His understanding of His own person and role.[20] Then we can compare what we regard as Jesus's perspective and self-understanding with what we consider to be the NT church's thinking about Him. We should not, however, succumb to a "Jesus of history" ideology that affirms that only the earliest layer of Synoptic tradition (thought to more truly reflect Jesus's own view) is of value. Such an ideology implicitly rejects the interpretive value of Jesus's resurrection and of the outpouring of the Holy Spirit.

6. Jesus's Resurrection Validates Atoning Reality of His Life and Death

Only because God raised Jesus from death are we able to perceive that Jesus's life and death involved the vicariously accomplished reconciliation of humankind (Rom 4:23–25). Had God not raised Jesus, He would have been long forgotten and no one could ascribe saving significance to Him. Jesus's resurrection represents the Father's "Amen" to the "it is finished" of the Son's atoning life and death, certifying that our Lord's life and death are of redemptive significance (Rom 4:25).[21]

"The resurrection is marked off from the death of Jesus Christ as a new and specific act of God by the fact that in it there is pronounced the verdict of God the Father on the obedience of the Son: [God's] gracious... approval of the Son's representing of the human race; the justification of the will of the Father who sent the Son into the world for this

---

18. Barth, *CD* 3/2:455; see also 4/2:151.
19. Barth, *CD* 3/2:442, 443.
20. See chaps. 6 and 7 below.
21. Bicknell, *Thirty-Nine Articles*, 98–99.

purpose, of the Son who willed to submit to this will, and of the totality of sinful [people] as brought to [reconciliation] by the [life and] death of this their Representative."[22]

7. Jesus's Resurrection as His Enthronement, Followed by Spiritual Disclosures to Chosen Witnesses; Enthronement, Not Ascension; Meaning of Jesus's Enthronement

Many NT scholars have concluded that in the earliest Christian tradition, as reflected in Paul, Christ's resurrection is understood as a direct exaltation to the divine realm, rather than as the Risen Christ on visible display prior to His exaltation. "Being found in human form he humbled himself and became obedient unto death, even death on a cross. Therefore God has highly exalted him and bestowed on him the name which is above every name" (Phil 2:8-9). Similarly, though slightly later and by another, Ephesians refers to God raising Christ from the dead and directly causing him to sit at God's right hand in the heavenly places (1:20).[23] Pauline and post-Pauline traditions differ from those generally reflected in the Gospels, but the Gospels were written later than most of these writings. And Paul's letters had an influence on most of the non-Gospel writings in the NT.

Many scholars think that the oldest Easter reports presume no distinction between the resurrection of Jesus and His transition to the Father's realm and rule. Jesus's resurrection seems originally to have been regarded as His non-physical exaltation from death to God's eternal realm, and from there revealing Himself as glorified and enthroned in Eternity.[24] Numerous NT texts seem to make this point, rather than exhibiting the more materialistic traditions seen in elements of the Gospel accounts and in some of the accounts in Acts. In quoting an early hymn Philippians 2:8-11 moves directly from speaking of Jesus's death to affirming His enthronement, as does 1 Peter (1:21). These passages attest that *Jesus's resurrection disclosures occurred after His enthronement.*

Though in conflict with Luke's Gospel's historicizing narrative that the Risen Lord had resurrection appearances for forty days before His enthronement, the book of Acts (by the same author!) is particularly explicit in referring to the earlier tradition that Jesus's resurrection was His enthronement. Acts 2:32-33a uses parallelism in speaking of Jesus's resurrection and of His exaltation, implying that these are two ways of referring to the same thing: "This Jesus God raised up . . . Being therefore exalted at the right hand of God." Acts 5:30-31b also attests Jesus's resurrection as His exaltation: "The God of our fathers raised Jesus whom you killed by hanging him on a tree. God exalted him [to] his right hand as Leader and Savior."

Contradicting the above direct resurrection to eternity account that the author of Luke-Acts shared with Pauline and other NT traditions, *the same author* twice narrates Jesus's "ascension"! One wonders how literally Luke wished his readers to take his ascension

22. Barth, *CD* 4/1:354.
23. See also Luke 24:4-7; Acts 2:23, 32-33, 36; 5:30-31a; 1 Tim 3:16; Heb 1:3b; 13:20.
24. After Jesus's death His body remained in the grave, but His spirit was re-enthroned in the triune Godhead. When we die our bodies also remain in graves, or our ashes in urns or scattered somewhere, but because of God's love disclosed in Christ we will share in the eternal fellowship with God and with one another.

accounts—since they not only conflict with his direct enthronement narratives, but with each other (Luke 24:50–51; Acts 1:9–11). Perhaps he was more interested in telling stories made interesting by visualizable events than in attesting history.[25] Similarly, one notices that he writes that at Jesus's baptism there was a descending dove ("in bodily form") apparent to all (Luke 3:22a). See also the accompanying details related to visibility in connection with three Acts's accounts of Paul's conversion (Acts 9:1–19; 22:4–16; 26:9–18), which much conflict with each other and drastically conflict with Paul's account in Galatians 1:11–17. It is unlikely that the writer of Luke-Acts had independent evidence concerning the historicity of such details, and so relied on his own artistic imagination.

Modern cosmological knowledge does not permit one to think of God as dwelling a modest distance from the earth—and thus Acts's visualizing of Jesus's supposed ascension journey is today a hindrance. Surely the author of Luke-Acts did not intend what his ascension accounts today imply, that Jesus began a long space voyage.

It is not only doubtful that Jesus physically ascended, but that the author of Luke-Acts or anyone else saw Him do so. The ascension references of Luke-Acts were written long after the events they supposedly narrate, and for that and other reasons could not have been written by an eyewitness. With these accounts Luke seems to have imaginatively utilized the scientific concepts of his day to narrate what he envisioned to have been outward aspects of the Son's return to the Father.

Though the exaltation of the Son and His sharing in God's power belong to the essence of the kerygma, today's church can in good conscience break with the ecclesiastical tradition that linked enthronement with physical ascension. The church can and should draw such critical distinctions not merely because we do not share the NT's cosmology concerning "heaven" as "up," but because (aside from Luke-Acts) the rest of the NT does not attempt to visualize Jesus's enthronement. To the contrary, major lines of NT tradition (including Luke 24:6–7) identify Jesus's resurrection with His enthronement, and thus attest that the enthronement occurred with His resurrection, not forty days later as part of a physical event.

Even Barth demythologized/deliteralized in interpreting the Acts account of Jesus ascension, and appealed to Calvin for so doing! "Ascension as visible exaltation—i.e. exaltation that is perceptible as vertical elevation in space—of Jesus Christ before the eyes of His disciples is obviously not the way to the right hand of God. For the right hand of God is . . . [not] to be reached by [a trip] through . . . astronomic space."[26] The eternal realm is not a locality in this universe, but a higher mode of existence.[27]

There is no need for us to abandon twenty-first-century scientific learning in order to be spiritual sisters and brothers with Christians of the first century. For the first century Christians' faith in God was not identical with their worldviews. When they utilized such notions they used them as broken and imperfect means for expressing (in categories

---

25. It may have been for literary reasons that he provided two ascension accounts. For the sake of theological unity he may have wished to end his Gospel on the same note with which he began his Acts narrative concerning the work of the Holy Spirit in the early church.

26. Barth, *Credo*, 113; see 106 for the Calvin reference.

27. Bicknell, *Thirty-Nine Articles*, 110.

meaningful to them) a faith that transcends any worldly knowledge, as we also must do, though in ways very different from theirs.

Consider an imperfect analogy: The highway signboard that asked "*Where* will you spend Eternity?" phrased the question wrongly. A theological question was put as a scientific one. The genuine theological question is different and much more important. The issue is not *where* we will spend Eternity, but *with whom*? Christians believe that Eternity is to be spent with the God known in Christ, and with those raised from death.

If you had come to know a friend from a foreign country, and if he or she would be there to meet you and to be with you in that new and strange place, you could feel comfortable about going there. God is shown to be our Friend in Jesus, and when we die we go to meet this Friend. God's eternal realm will be transcendently different from this world, but because we have come to trust this Friend we can face the future with confidence, though we do not know "where" that will be.

Though still reflecting the human dimension, the enthroned Son belongs to the divine life of the God who has freedom and power in relationship with this world. Being at "God's right hand" is a figurative way of saying that the Risen Christ shares in God's kingly rule and authority (see Ps 110:1). God "made him to sit at his right hand in the heavenly places far above all rule and authority and power and dominion and above every name that is named, not only in this age but also in that which is to come, and he has put all things under his feet and has made him the head over all things."[28]

"Worthy is the Lamb that was slain to receive power, and riches, and wisdom, and strength, and honor, and glory, and blessing (Rev 5:12)." That "*all* power is given unto [Christ] in heaven and on earth" (Matt 28:18) does not mean—the figure must not be pressed to the point of . . . [absurdity]—that the eternal Father has now renounced this power and its exercise."[29]

As a figurative expression, Christ's sitting at God's right hand in no way indicates that Christ is no longer engaged in conflict with the powers of evil. "Our Lord's victory over the world in the days of His flesh was but a [pledge] of the longer warfare and the more complete conquest that are the work of His ascended life."[30]

Though the Son's enthronement was not a visualizable event, and though the Risen Christ's manifestations were spiritual, rather than material—as risen, exalted, and enthroned Jesus laid aside nothing that pertains to the fulfillment of human nature. Jesus is our forerunner, whose human personality has preceded us into the eternal realm.

Jesus's atoning life, death and entry into the eternal dimension took place once-and-for-all. As historical events these lie in the past and can never be repeated (Heb 7:27; 9:28; 10:12). Yet as our High Priest the Risen Lord provides us with abiding access to the throne of grace (Eph 2:13; Heb 4:14–16), and does so because His completed self-offering on our behalf stands forever (Heb 10:19–22).[31]

---

28. Eph 1:20b–22b; cf. Heb 12:2; Rev 3:21.
29. Barth, *Credo*, 107.
30. Bicknell, *Thirty-Nine Articles*, 114.
31. Ibid., 113.

8. Enthroned King Pours Forth Holy Spirit

Jesus's enthronement resulted in the sending of the Spirit. Ascended to the Father the Risen Lord has poured forth the promised Spirit (John 20:17, 22). "Having received the Spirit, each member of the church is empowered to do the works of the Spirit, each work being a sign that points back to [Jesus's] resurrection and forward to the parousia [final revelation or consummation]."[32] It is to our advantage that Jesus is no longer physically present because He now comes to us as the Continuator (John 16:7; see also Acts 2:32–33).

Jesus could work with His disciples only as restricted to a particular locale. The Risen Lord as Holy Spirit is not spatially restricted and has intimate access to the centers of our lives—and thus enables believers to do great deeds.[33] Through the ministry of the Holy Spirit Christ is present with us forever (Matt 28:20).

The enthroned Christ claims our lives. "If then you have been raised with Christ, seek the things that are above, where Christ is, seated at the right hand of God. Set your minds on things that are above, not on things that are on earth. For you have died, and your life is hid with Christ in God" (Col 3:1–3). Morally and spiritually the Christian can be raised up with Christ.

9. Jesus's Resurrection Established Confidence in His Person and Mission Despite Eschaton's Delay

Though the consummation did not occur before Jesus's generation passed away (Mark 9:11; 13:30; cf. Matt 10:23), nor even yet, the Easter event confirmed the message of Jesus by representatively anticipating our salvation. Even though the first generation, including Paul (1 Thess 4:15–17), expected the end shortly (cf. 1 Cor 15:51; Rom 13:11), the delay of the parousia was not a disappointment that shattered faith's foundations. With Christ as risen and the Spirit as manifested, eschatological salvation became a certainty for believers; thus the remaining span of time before the consummation became a secondary matter.

The resurrection of Jesus is the basis of Pannenberg's understanding of His divinity.

He argues that everything depends upon the connection between Jesus's claim to authority and its ratification by God through Jesus's resurrection.[34] Expounding this thesis: Firstly: "If Jesus is raised, then for a Jew it can only mean that God himself has confirmed the pre-resurrection ministry of Jesus." Secondly: "By being raised from the dead, Jesus was so closely associated with the Son of man [hope] that the inference was obvious: the Son of man is none other than Jesus who is to come again." Thirdly: "If Jesus, being raised from the dead, has been exalted to God, . . . then God is [decisively] revealed in Jesus"[35]

---

32. Minear, *To Die and Live*, 56.

33. Sinners that we are and remain and sinner that Christ was not, I disagree with John 14:12, that we through the Spirit of the enthroned Christ are able to do even greater deeds than Jesus.

34. Geyer "The Resurrection of Jesus Christ," 126, depicting Pannenberg's *Grundzuger der Christologie* (1964), 61. I cite only three of the four Geyer translated points, not agreeing that "If Jesus is raised then the end of the world has begun" (Geyer, "The Resurrection of Jesus Christ," 130, referencing Pannenberg, *Grundzuger der Christologie*, 62).

35. Ibid., 130, quoting Pannenberg, *Grundzuger der Christologie*, 62, 63, 64.

10. Jesus's Resurrection Institutes Mission Mandate

There is no evidence that when Jesus died anyone was still with him. Only after His resurrection did the work of mission begin in earnest. Through Paul's late encounter with the Risen Christ he came to realize that Jesus Christ, not the law, is the way of salvation. Paul sensed that an implication of that awareness is the mission mandate, in his case that of proclaiming Christ to the gentiles (Gal 1:16). In the Gospels, which were written later than Paul's letters, the resurrection appearances require mission outreach.[36] Though the details of those disclosure accounts are highly contradicting, they testify to the church's awareness of both the Risen Christ's presence in their midst and the mission mandate. Acts's 1:8 considerably later statement accurately reflects both of these: "You shall receive power when the Holy Spirit has come upon you; and you shall be my witnesses in Jerusalem and in all Judea and Samaria and to the ends of the earth" (1:8).

11. Historical and Theological Interrelatedness of Jesus's Crucifixion and Resurrection

It is essential that Christians regard the Crucified Christ as the Risen One and Risen Christ as the Crucified One. Failing to emphasize both Jesus's cross and His resurrection results in serious misunderstandings of Christian Faith. With the first distortion, which is much rarer, a theology of the cross that abstracts from the power of the Risen Christ can foster discouragement, defeatism, joylessness, and lead toward abandoning the Faith. With the second distortion, a theology of the resurrection that does not regard the Christian life as cruciform, optimistically misunderstands Jesus's resurrection as a mere fact that only requires enthusiastic consent. The result can be to turn aside from cross-bearing discipleship toward the "prosperity gospel" divinizing of "success." Such a pragmatic utilization of Christian Faith to achieve worldly goals has more in common with Traditional Religion than with genuine Christianity. For we are to seek first Christ's kingship and righteousness (Matt 6:33).

A theology that rings loudly the joyful note of Easter without the sobering, dissonant sounds of Good Friday inevitably tends toward triumphalism. The cries of human pain, rejection, and death exposed in Jesus's passion are modulated by the exuberant "He is risen!" To summarize each problem and each effect: *Without the resurrection, the cross becomes a cause of despair and without the cross, the resurrection becomes an escape from reality*.[37]

Paul emphasized both the (resurrection-inspired) charismatic energizing of the Christian life in faithfulness to the Risen Lord, and the (crucifixion-mirroring) importance of suffering, especially in connection with pursuing Christian purposes. Crucial to Paul's paradoxical interrelating of resurrection and crucifixion, victory and cross-bearing was his understanding that we sinners live amid the conflict between God's kingship and the ways of the world. Thus though we already share in the power of the coming kingdom we must continue to die to sin. We do this by taking up the particular crosses that Christ calls us

---

36. Matt 28:19–20; Luke 24:49; John 20:21–23; 21:15–19.
37. Dunn, *Theology of Paul*, 235.

to bear, and finding that we can faithfully proceed only by living in and from the power of the Risen Christ.[38]

Unlike the author of Luke-Acts, Paul had a genuine theology of the cross: He did not understand Jesus's suffering and dying as merely a stage toward His resurrection glory. For Paul the cross is the decisive atoning event, validated and made known by Jesus's resurrection, but never minimized or effaced by the latter. According to Paul it was on the cross that the decisive exchange occurred whereby God in His Son offered Himself in place of sinners. "Certainly for Paul too the [Risen] Christ . . . has entered upon his lordship. But the cross does not become just the way to lordship or the price paid for it. Rather, *it remains the signature of the risen Lord. He possesses no other visage except the countenance of the Crucified*, and only under this countenance can we take our stand (as a common Christian [hymn] expresses it)."[39]

Paul's Jewish religion had centered upon the performance of the law. Before his conversion he had believed Deuteronomy 21:23, that whoever dies on a cross is cursed by God, and hence Paul persecuted the Christians (Gal 1:13; 3:13; cf. 1 Cor 12:3). Having encountered the Risen Christ, Paul came to believe that Jesus Christ—not the law—is the way of salvation. He came to affirm that Jesus Christ not only was *not cursed by God*, but is loved and approved by Him and shows forth God's love. God's atoning action climaxed when Jesus "was put to death for our trespasses and raised for our justification" (Rom 4:25). Having become cursed according to Jewish legal standards and rejected by humans, God vindicated Jesus by raising Him from death.

Paul's vision of the Risen Christ overturned his thinking by overcoming his stumbling block concerning a crucified Messiah (1 Cor 1:23), convincing him of the messianic and vicarious value of Jesus's life and of His death on the cross. "Paul saw Christ Jesus taking upon himself the law's curse and transforming it into its opposite, so that he became the means of freeing humanity."[40] The cross became in Paul's eyes the 'power and the wisdom of God' (1 Cor 1:24) manifested amid apparent weakness. He henceforth understood that the crucified one is "Lord of Glory" (1 Cor 2:8).

The facing and overcoming of the paradox of the cross is at the center of Paul's theology. Part of the offensiveness of the cross to first-century Jews (1 Cor 1:23) and to many people since has been that they have expected to use *the law and/or moral attainments* to climb toward God. The offensiveness of the cross to first-century Gentiles (1 Cor 1:23)

---

38. "*For Paul the distinctive characteristic of the religious experience of the disciple of Christ is the experience of sharing in Christ's sufferings as well as of sharing in His life* (Rom 8:17; 2 Cor 1:5; 4:10; Phil 3:10ff.; Col 1:24). Against the enthusiasts of Second Corinthians Paul insists that the experience of the Spirit is not of power alone, nor of power that transcends and leaves weakness behind, but of *power in weakness* (4:7; 12:9ff.; 13:3ff.). To put it another way, religious experience for Paul is characterized by *eschatological tension* between the new life which he shares as being 'in Christ' and the old life which is 'in the flesh' (2 Cor 10:3ff.; Gal 2:20; Eph 4:20–24; Phil 1:21–24; Col 3:9ff.), by warfare between Spirit and flesh (Rom 7:14–23; Gal 5:16ff.), by the frustration of having to live out the life of the Spirit through the 'body of death' (Rom 7:24ff.; 8:10f., 22f.; 2 Cor 4:16–5:5). No religious experience however profound or spiritual or inspired or glorious sets the believer free from the limitations of his present existence." On the contrary what is to be recognized as typically Christian "*is precisely that experience which most clearly manifests the paradox of power in weakness, of life through death, of greatness as serving*" (Dunn, *Unity and Diversity*, 195).

39. Kasemann, "Pauline Theology of the Cross," 174–75.

40. Fitzmyer, "Pauline Theology," 1386.

and to many since is slightly different. They have expected they could gain their standing before God by means of intellectual understanding, speculation, and spiritual and/or moral attainments. Against both self-salvation schemes and any others, God in His wisdom manifested His love in the deep concealment of humility, suffering and rejection. Jesus's resurrection validates His cross as reflecting God's will to love sinners such as us.

Paul does nothing to soften the ongoing offensiveness of the cross, which must continually be faced even by Christians. Many of our ways of thinking must be repeatedly challenged and overturned by the "Cruciform God." "At the cross of Jesus despair ends because boasting ends there, and so [ends not only] the [contemptuousness] of the rebel, [but] the self-conceit of the pious, . . . [and] the illusions of those who think too highly of themselves. . . . *God . . . glorifies by deeply humiliating, enlightens by confronting [us] with the inescapable truth about ourselves, and makes us whole by including us among those to whom the first Beatitude is addressed.*"[41]

That the crucifixion and resurrection belong together in Paul's theology does not mean that he always mentions them together. But Paul never talks about one of these as though the other had not happened or was not essential. "The juxtaposition between 'Christ died for our sins' ([1 Cor] 15:3) and 'if Christ has not been raised, you are still in your sins' (1 Cor 15:17) leaves no doubt about the indispensable role of both [Jesus's] crucifixion and resurrection for salvation." "*What makes the message of the crucified Christ offensive is not simply the manner of his death once, but that [even with] the resurrection Christ is still known to the church as the crucified one.*"[42]

12. Dying and Rising with Christ

The reality of Jesus's dying and rising is reflected in the lives of believers: "We have this treasure in earthen vessels, to show that the transcendent power belongs to God and not to us. We are afflicted in every way, but not crushed; perplexed, but not driven to despair; persecuted, but not forsaken; struck down, but not destroyed; always carrying in the body the death of Jesus, so that the life of Jesus may also be manifested in our bodies" (2 Cor 4:7–9). "We know that our old self was crucified with [Christ], so that . . . we may no longer be enslaved to sin" (Rom 6:6). Having been crucified with Christ "the life we now live in the flesh we live by faith in the Son of God, who loved us and who gave himself for us" (Gal 2:20b, my pluralizing).

Our discipleship suffering and persecution as participating in our Lord's dying and rising (2 Cor 4:7–10) parallels Paul's experience. "For we do not want you to be ignorant, brethren, of the affliction we experienced in Asia; for we were so utterly, unbearably crushed that we despaired of life itself. . . . We felt that we had received the sentence of death; but that was to make us rely not on ourselves but on God who raises the dead" (2 Cor 1:8–9).

As we shoulder our crosses we experience the Risen Lord who meets us amid our trials and tribulations, wipes our brows and gives us the courage to take our next trembling

---

41. Kasemann, "Pauline Theology of the Cross," 164.
42. Cousar, *Theology of the Cross*, 96, 104.

steps trusting Him who goes before us. God is the Lord of the future and will use our lives and our witnessing as He sees fit. Many times God may utilize events to whittle us down to size, through suffering teaching us to depend more on Him and less on ourselves. In this sinful world, faithfulness to God will often meet with rejection and persecution—as the OT prophets continually remind us and as Jesus's rejection and crucifixion impress upon us. But the Easter Faith teaches us not to be unduly concerned about our suffering and persecution. God can bring victory from human defeat. We can hope for the eventual resurrected good use of our witnessing, but we must be content to walk by faith and not by sight, and must never trust in visible accomplishments.

Chapter 4

Jesus's Resurrection Disclosures, Christian Hope, Agape Here and Beyond

1. Paul's Early Calling-Related Understanding of Jesus's Resurrection in Contrast to Matthew and Luke's Later Reliance on Highly Variable Oral Traditions

IN 1 CORINTHIANS 15:3–8 Paul referred not only to his own encounter with the Risen Lord and thereby to his apostolic calling, but also to those of others. "For I delivered to you as of first importance what I also received, that Christ died for our sins in accordance with the Scriptures, that he was buried, that he was raised on the third day in accordance with the Scriptures, and that he appeared to Cephas, then to the twelve. Then he appeared to more than five hundred brethren at one time, most of whom are still alive, though some have fallen asleep. Then he appeared to James, then to all the apostles. Last of all, as one untimely born, He appeared also to me. For I am the least of the apostles, unfit to be called an apostle, because I persecuted the church of God" (1 Cor 15:3–10).

"The other apostles must have accepted [Paul's] calling, otherwise the agreement of Galatians 2:7–10 (cf. 1 Cor 15:9–11) would have been impossible."[1] "Those of repute . . . saw that I had been entrusted with the gospel to the uncircumcised, just as Peter had been entrusted with the gospel to the circumcised (for He who worked through Peter for the mission to the circumcised worked through me also for the Gentiles), . . . only [that] they would have us remember the poor, which very thing I was eager to do" (Gal 2:7–8, 10).

Since Paul wrote 1 Corinthians only twenty to thirty years after Jesus's resurrection, many of the witnesses he cited would still have been alive, and thus could have confirmed or denied his testimony. Of the resurrection encounters Paul referred to, only those of Peter and of "the twelve" are mentioned in the Gospels.

In contrast with Paul's accounts that derive from one who had himself encountered the risen Lord, the Synoptic testimonies passed through earlier oral stages, and Matthew and Luke also employed Mark, Q, and possibly other written and even oral sources. Whether or

---

1. Dunn, *Theology of Paul*, 239.

not the Fourth Gospel used earlier written sources is debatable, but either way the Fourth Gospel is a highly imaginative narrative construction. Also, all of the Gospels were written considerably later than Paul's epistles. If for only these reasons Paul's descriptions are likely to be more accurate.

2. Gospel Accounts of Christ's Resurrection Appearances

The apologetic pressures to stress the bodily reality of the Risen One was increasingly emphasized in the development of post-Marcan Gospel traditions. Accommodation to Pharisaic apocalyptic expectations of bodily resurrection may largely account for the claims that Matthew, Luke and John make concerning bodily resurrection appearances.[2] In contrast, Mark 16:1–8 exhibits a high degree of restraint, describing no resurrection appearance, and mentioning only a "young man's" promise that the Risen Lord would appear in Galilee (16:5–7).[3]

Paul's resurrection encounter was a post-enthronement spiritual disclosure years after Jesus had died. Matthew, Luke and John attest the spirit disclosure aspect of the early traditions, but mix that with later traditions describing bodily appearances—with both types (unlike Paul's encounter) understood as occurring prior to Jesus's enthronement.[4] Luke 24:36–37 does assert that when the Risen Lord first appeared to the eleven disciples they mistook Him for a spirit. But Luke 24:39–40 mentions that the Risen One said, "See my hands and my feet, that it is I myself; handle me, and see; for a spirit has not flesh and bones as you see I have." But the Luke 24:31 text had already said that the Risen Christ *who had been visible, "vanished out of sight."*

Luke 24:41–43 takes materialistic interpretation to the limit by depicting Jesus as asking "'Have you anything here to eat?' They gave him a piece of broiled fish and he took it and ate before them." In one of Luke's accounts the Risen Christ is said to have looked so much like a traveler that His presence went unnoticed (24:28–35).

Unlike the Gospels, the rest of the NT does not refer to a bodily resurrection of Jesus or an empty tomb. Resurrection as enthronement seems incompatible with both. *All traditions emphasize both continuity and discontinuity between Jesus of Nazareth and Jesus as raised from the dead.* According to Paul's attestation, he and the Jerusalem leaders expressed the linkage in terms of *spiritual encounters that thereby established continuity between Jesus of Nazareth and Jesus as the Risen Messiah.* The Gospels indicate the interrelatedness mainly through stories concerning supposed bodily aspects to Jesus's risen being. The Gospels occasionally also emphasize discontinuity, by saying such things as that the Risen Lord could pass through solid objects (John 20:19c, 26b), could vanish out of sight (Luke 24:31b), and was made known to them in the breaking of the bread (Luke 24:35).

---

2. Emphases on bodily resurrection appearances also likely reflect overreactions against docetic and gnostic denials of Jesus's earthly humanity. In this connection it has often been noticed that in the process of the development of the Easter tradition, the latest version in the apocryphal Gospel of Peter displays the most physical emphases.

3. That Mark believed in physical resurrection appearances could, however, be deduced from his empty tomb narrative.

4. For Christ's resurrection as enthronement see chap. 3, sec. 7.

Many years ago an interesting debate raged in the pages of *The Expository Times* between C. E. B. Cranfield and G. T. Eddy. In my opinion Eddy convincingly refuted Cranfield's argument concerning the bodily nature of Jesus's risen being. Cranfield recognized that according to the Gospels, Jesus's risen body was able to appear and vanish and thereby pass through closed doors. Yet Cranfield insisted that Jesus's risen body was "*the same body* as was crucified, but the same body wonderfully changed, transformed into a glorious body, no longer subject to the limitations of Jesus's historical life."[5] Eddy showed by penetrating questions that Cranfield could not substantiate his claim that the Risen Lord had "the same body" that Jesus of Nazareth had.

"Did Jesus eat and drink after his resurrection? If so, what became of the food? Was it metabolized, with the obvious sequel of evacuation? And if the body, though 'the same body as was crucified,' was yet so transformed as to be able to appear and disappear, and enter and leave a locked room, did the fish and the honeycomb undergo instant transformation along the same lines as soon as they entered his mouth? And what about his clothes? Did the risen Lord appear naked (that would have been a considerable shock to Jewish disciples)? If not, what was he wearing? If not the garments of his earthly life, nor the grave clothes: what then? And did their material share the power to appear and disappear, and pass through closed doors?"[6]

Questions such as these contribute to the conclusion that the early accounts found in Galatians 1:11–17, 1 Corinthians 15 and 9:1 take us nearer to the original experience than do the more materialistic aspects of those found in the Gospels. The NT as a whole rests on the fact that chosen witnesses encountered the Risen Lord and became convinced that God had raised Jesus to eternal life. The essential article of faith is that as risen from the dead, Christ manifested Himself to chosen witnesses. No affirmation of the bodily nature of Jesus's risen manifestations needs to be made.[7]

A problem with a physical or bodily resurrection of Jesus followed by enthronement at a later point concerns what would then have happened to Jesus's earthly body before being enthroned. If God's eternal realm is within a transcendent dimension beyond this universe, at the point of enthronement Jesus's earthly body would have been useless.[8]

What is generally *under debate* among Christians is not whether Jesus rose from the dead, nor primarily the meanings of His resurrection, but the more technical issue of the nature of Jesus's risen disclosures. This issue in turn has implications concerning Jesus's resurrection, whether the tomb became empty or remained full, and what constitutes Christ's risen being.

Those who pay attention to historical evidence should find Paul's account more convincing than those materialistic aspects of the narratives found in the Gospels. And those people should be able to resist intellectually dishonest harmonizing of incompatible perspectives.[9]

---

5. Eddy, "The Resurrection of Jesus Christ," 327, my emphasis.

6. Ibid., 328.

7. Ibid., 328–29.

8. An extra-biblical belief in vaporization seems to be required if Jesus's resurrection as enthronement is to be harmonized with the empty tomb tradition.

9. Though the earliest stratum of the Easter tradition as seen in Paul did not make Jesus's resurrection

3. Hope of Personal Identity in Fellowship with the Living God and Others

Paul drew a direct contrast between our present lowly bodies and the glorious mode we will receive in eternity (Phil 3:21). He thought that the new mode that God will provide will be similar to that of the Risen Lord (1 Thess 4:14; 1 Cor 15:35–55). "What is sown is perishable, what is raised is imperishable. It is sown in dishonor, it is raised in glory. It is sown in weakness, it is raised in power. *It is sown a physical body, it is raised a spiritual body*" (1 Cor 15:42b–44a NRSV). Paul must not have been entirely satisfied with the term "spiritual body," since in 2 *Corinthians 5:8 he not only does not speak of a new body, but of being away from the body.*

By the imperfect terminology of "spiritual body" Paul may have meant that by an act of sovereign power God can reconstitute or recreate us as manifesting "the dispositional characteristics and memory traces of the deceased physical organism," even when we are members of the transcendent world.[10] The body of flesh and blood no more emerges from the grave than a seed itself comes up out of the ground. Our personalities will be remade by God for a different form of existence, yet because of memory continuity we shall retain our sense of selfhood.

4. Agape Love Here and Beyond[11]

The essence of the eternal life to which 1 Corinthians 13 points is not only to be with Christ, but to share in divine love, and to truly love one another. "So faith, hope, love abide, these three; but the greatest of these is love" (vs. 13). Agape as divinely based self-giving love is no innate human aptitude, but is revealed in Christ and enabled by the Holy Spirit.

We are not inherently patient, but God can teach us to be. We often do not know what is good, but the living God can guide us. We are zealous about our own rights; God

---

depend upon an empty tomb, the Easter stories in the four Gospels come close to doing so. Casting doubt on the historicity of the Gospels' Easter stories is their differing character from the main body of the Gospels. Like the birth narratives, the Easter ones are mythical, with angels appearing as characters and addressing the chief actors, and an angel descending from heaven to roll away the stone that sealed the rock tomb. Also casting doubt concerning the historical accuracy of these traditions are the accounts' remarkable inconsistencies with one another. Mark describes no resurrection appearances, but predicts those in Galilee. Unlike Mark, Matthew describes resurrection appearances, but, consistent with Mark's prediction, affirms that Christ appeared to the eleven disciples in Galilee. In contrast to Mark and Matthew, Luke insists that all of the Easter events took place in or just outside of Jerusalem. John's account differs in many details from the above narratives, and the places of the Risen Lord's encounters differ considerably.

Even more conflicting evidence can be offered: "1. The number of women involved—two (Matt), three (Mark) or one (John)? 2. The timing—before dawn (Matt, John) or after dawn (Mark)? 3. Was the stone rolled back in the presence of the women (as Matthew may imply) or before they reached the tomb (Mark, Luke, John)? 4. Was there a communication on the first visit to the tomb (Matt, Mark, Luke) or not (John)? 5. How many angels—one (Matt, Mark), two (Luke), none (John)? 6. Did the women tell the other disciples (Matt, Luke, John) or not (Mark)? There are also distinctive features in Matthew (the guard at the tomb—Matt 27:62–66; 28:4) and in John (the involvement of Peter and the beloved disciple—John 20:2–10)" (Dunn, *Evidence of Jesus*, 63–64).

10. Hick, *Death and Eternal Life*, 279.

11. See chap. 26, secs. 9–10 for an additional discussion of Christian love.

can inspire us to be self-giving. Like the Corinthian Gnostics (1 Cor 8:2) we tend to puff ourselves up, but God calls us down from our thrones. We sometimes see only evil; God inspires us to see more. We often rejoice at wrong, but the agape-led rejoice at what is right. Paul insists that human moral behavior needs to be transformed through relationship with God that we may love as God intends. Thus those who share in God's love begin to transcend themselves.

5. Conclusion

With the following fitting words from Lampe we conclude these chapters on the nature and meaning of Jesus resurrection, historical issues related to Christ's risen appearances, and the nature of Christian hope.

> The resurrection . . . gives us sure hope of a life to come. There is nothing inherent in our own nature on which we can rely for our hope; nothing, . . . whether we call it a soul or anything else, which provides us with a built-in guarantee of survival. We believe that we shall live after death, not because of anything in ourselves, but because the God who raised Jesus is our Father, [whose love will continue even after we have died]. . . . The principle of our immortality, if we may call it that, is God's relationship to us which he has established by grace. It is this relationship which, we may believe, overcomes death. Of course, if my relationship to God continues, then I must continue, . . . not in this present bodily mode of existence, but living because the God on whom my life depends will maintain his grace toward me. I do not mean that my existence will depend on whether, or how firmly, I believe in God, but on the love of God through Christ for me. This does not imply that bodily existence is of only limited value or importance; the value of the material creation does not necessarily involve its eternity. For us, as the only mode of existence we know,[12] and as the mode which God has seen to be good, it is of [high] value and importance. Yet it [will] be transcended by the relationship of God with us in which he has made us his sons; and it is that sonship which assures us of life beyond death even though the mode of that life is entirely beyond our imagination.[13]

---

12. Yes and no. This is the material base from which we start, but even now we have experienced the Holy Spirit as real though non-material.

13. Lampe in Lampe and MacKinnon, *Resurrection*, 59–60.

Chapter 5

The Holy Spirit and Christian Vocation[1]

THE CHRISTIAN LIFE BEGINS with some experience of the Holy Spirit, often in connection with a sense of sinfulness, divine forgiveness and call to discipleship. This frequently happens before one has a well-articulated understanding of the meaning of faith in the Crucified and Risen Lord, and of the Father who is known in the Son by the Spirit.

The Holy Spirit was the mode of communication between Father and Son during Jesus's earthly life, was decisively poured forth following Jesus' resurrection, and is the bond between Christians and Christ today. The God known in the Son by the Spirit is the active source of every facet of Christian Faith.

By considering the Spirit at this early point I seek to emphasize the experiential dimension of Christian faith and to protect against confusing that faith with intellectual assent to doctrine, rather than heartfelt commitment to God's will and ways. However, if the Holy Spirit does not lead one to a Christ-centering of faith and life one has not experienced the true God.

1. Divinity of the Holy Spirit

The Spirit can bring us to God through Christ because the Spirit is divine.[2] And since the Spirit is divine, to lie against the Holy Spirit is to lie against God (Acts 5:3–4), and to blaspheme the Spirit is to blaspheme God (Matt 12:32; Mark 3:29; Luke 12:10).[3] Because the Spirit does the work of God, the Spirit's activity evidences divinity: As only God can do, the Holy Spirit convicts us of sin (John 16:8–11), places us within the sphere of God's influence, and begins to sanctify us (2 Thess 2:13; 1 Pet 1:2). Because the Spirit is of God, She can communicate the things of God (1 Cor 2:10–11). Thus the Spirit not only continues

---

1. This chapter's exposition concerning Holy Spirit relates to that aspect of discussions in many chapters. Sec. 10 directly relates to chap. 24, "The Christian as Witness."

2. 1 Cor 2:10–13; 6:11; 7:40; 2 Cor 3:3; Eph 4:30; see also John 4:24. "In First Corinthians 3:16–17 Paul reminds believers that they are *God's* temple and that His *Spirit* dwells within them. In chap. 6, he says that their bodies are temples of *the Holy Spirit* within them (vss. 19–20)" (Erickson, *Christian Theology*, 327, my emphasis).

3. Barth, *CD* 1/1:526.

the work of Jesus Christ (John 14–16), but regenerates and gives new life,[4] assists in praying (Rom 8:26), and enables a critical assessing of old covenant laws (2 Cor 3:4–18). The Spirit also grants charismatic gifts to Christians and guides us in the churchly exercise of such gifts (1 Cor 12:4–11).

The Holy Spirit is holy as is God alone and thus differs from the gods of our invention. As we live in relationship with this Holy One we experience God's judgment, know ourselves as sinners, and come to know a will and direction different from our own. God becomes our Master and we, His servants.

To become a Christian, to receive the Holy Spirit, to be born of God, is to begin the lifelong process of dying to ourselves and rising to new life in Christ. The Holy Spirit enables us to experience Christ as present in our lives and to trust in God's action of love in the past. In the following Pauline text the regularly printed words refer to present experience and the italicized ones indicate trust in God's manifestation in Christ: "I have been crucified with Christ; it is no longer I who live, but Christ who lives in me; and the life I now live in the flesh I live *by faith in the Son of God, who loved me and gave himself for me*" (Gal 2:20).

2. Jesus as Uniquely Led by the Spirit and Our Need to Be Born of the Spirit

As Christ's life was Spirit-led, so the Christ event was by the initiative of God as Spirit. According to Matthew and Luke's Gospels it was by the Spirit's initiative that the Son of God was born into human history (Matt 1:18c; Luke 1:35), though this point is unconvincingly linked with contradicting legends (Matt 1–2; Luke 1–3). These include denials that Jesus had a biological father (Matt 1:18–25; Luke 1:26–38) though Jesus's birth was traced through Joseph's lineage! (Matt 1:16; Luke 3:23a)

Because Jesus was uniquely chosen for the messianic task, because He was filled with God's Spirit, and because He responded faithfully He was not only able to speak on God's behalf (John 3:33–34), but was God's focused presence on earth. The measure of Jesus's Spirit-possession marks him out from people of the Spirit before or since (John 3:34–35).

The Spirit particularly inspired Jesus at His baptism (Mark 1:10) and drove Him into the desert to withstand temptation (Mark 1:12). The Spirit guided Jesus,[5] and empowered Him to make His self-offering (Heb 9:14b). And through the Spirit, God raised Jesus from death (Rom 1:4; 1 Tim 3:16).[6]

The Fourth Gospel, though an ahistorical source for knowledge concerning Jesus, emphasizes the need to be born of God, born from above, born of the Spirit (1:12–13; 3:3–6). First John adds that in response to God's saving action in Christ and by our exhibiting of brotherly love, "God abides in us and his love is made perfect in us" (1 John 4:12b).

---

4. 2 Cor 3:6; John 3:8; 6:63a; see also Ezek 37.
5. Luke 4:1b; 10:21; 12:10; John 3:34; Acts 10:38.
6. Berkhof, *Christian Faith*, 324.

3. Paul's Experiential Understanding of the Spirit and of the Spirit Basis of Christian Hope; Attestings by Wesley and Kierkegaard

Paul's conception and practice of Christianity was much influenced by his encounter with the exalted Christ on the road to Damascus (1 Cor 9:1; 15:8; Gal 1:13–16), which was the beginning of the personal relationship that dominated his life (Phil 3:7–10).

> It was his own *experience of grace* which made "grace" a central and distinctive feature of his gospel—grace as not merely a way of understanding God as generous and forgiving, but grace as the experience of that unmerited and free acceptance embracing him, transforming him, enriching him, and commissioning him.[7] Or again, Christianity was characterized for Paul by his own experience of being enabled to offer a worship that was real, direct, from the heart (Rom 2:28ff.; Gal 4:6; Phil 3:3), of a love and joy even in the midst of suffering (Rom 5:3–5; 1 Thess 1:5ff.), of liberty from a rule-book mentality of casuistry and fear (Rom 8:2, 15; 2 Cor 3:17), of immediacy of guidance in everyday conduct (Rom 7:6; 2 Cor 3:3; Gal 5:25). Such experience he could only attribute to the Spirit of God, and therein recognize that the new covenant had come into effect (the law written on the heart, 2 Cor 3:3); the harvest of the end-time had begun (Rom 8:23). It is such experience of the Spirit that he evidently regards as *quintessentially* Christian (Rom 8:9, 14); it is to the first such experience or beginning of such experiences (and not baptism as such) that Paul refers his readers to when he recalls them to the start of their lives as Christians.[8] In short, it is abundantly evident that Paul's own religious experience was as fundamental to his mission and message as was the religious experience of Jesus to his mission and message.[9]

According to Paul the Spirit sets up the already-not-yet tension in the believer's life. "The *Spirit is . . . the power of the not yet which has already begun to be realized in present experience*." The Spirit makes us sons or daughters of God in anticipation of fuller relationship at the eschaton (Rom 8:15, 23). Paul regards the Spirit "as the powerful manifestation of the future rule of God in and through the present life of faith (Rom 14:17; 1 Cor 4:20)." "If it is the not yet emphasis that separates Paul from the more gnostic ideas circulating in his churches, *it is the already emphasis that distinguishes him from most of contemporary Judaism*. . . . So too [much] apocalyptic hope was consumed by a yearning for the imminent intervention of God and had no gospel for the present. . . . [To the contrary, Paul's] hope for the future springs from his faith in the Christ event of the past, and from his experience of the Spirit in the present."[10]

"It [is] the Spirit whose existence and action makes possible and real . . . the existence of Christianity in the world. Up to this very day the Spirit calls into being the existence of every single Christian as a believing, loving, hoping, witness to the Word of God."[11] According to Paul one becomes a member of the Body of Christ by participating in the one Spirit (1 Cor 12:13). As circumcision and the written law were hallmarks of the old

---

7. For example, Rom 5:2, 17; 12:6; 1 Cor 15:10; 2 Cor 9:14; 12:9; Gal 2:9; Eph 3:7.
8. For example, Rom 5:5; 1 Cor 12:13; Gal 3:2–5.
9. Dunn, *Unity and Diversity*, 190–91.
10. Dunn, *Jesus and the Spirit*, 310, 310–11, 317.
11. Barth, *Evangelical Theology*, 55.

covenant, the receipt of the Holy Spirit is the essence of the new covenant (2 Cor 3; Phil 3:3).

A Spirit-guided life is inseparable from a Christ-centered/God-centered one. Thus Paul affirms both of the following, "If any [one] does not have the Spirit of *Christ* he is no Christian" (Rom 8:9b); "only those who are led by the Spirit of *God* are children of God" (Rom 8:14, my emphasis).

In addition to God's revelation in Christ and Christ's resurrection, the giving of the Spirit also guarantees that what is mortal will be "swallowed up by life" (2 Cor 5:4–5). The Spirit anticipates the end, when "we shall all be changed" (1 Cor 15:52), climaxing the transformation wrought by the Spirit by which already "we . . . are being changed into his likeness from one degree of glory to another" (2 Cor 3:18).

"The Spirit as [guarantor] is both the promise of the future inheritance and its first instalment. The same idea is conveyed when the Spirit is called the 'first fruits,' an image coming from a harvest (Rom 8:23). To live in the Spirit is thus partly to live in the present enjoyment of a future inheritance and also to have the assurance of its coming fullness. The church is the community of the future."[12]

Wesley and Kierkegaard were in line with the NT in insisting that people can directly experience the Holy Spirit and thus can receive the assurance of being children of God. As for Wesley's agreement: "The testimony of the Spirit is an inward impression on the soul, whereby the Spirit of God directly witnesses to my spirit that I am a child of God."[13] Similarly Kierkegaard thought that genuinely Christian faith offers new life in the fullest and deepest sense, as we here and now die to our sinful selves and continue to do so. Such a life is life indeed, for we can sincerely ask that the Holy Spirit may in all things direct and rule our hearts.[14]

4. New Testament's Attesting of the Outpouring of Holy Spirit and of Some of Its Effects

"The dominant idea [of late Judaism] was that the Spirit had no longer been at work since the appearance of the last prophets."[15] The full manifestation of the Spirit is the fruit of Jesus's resurrection and the outpouring of the Spirit of the Risen Christ. "Paul speaks of the Spirit's being given (Rom 5:5), of the receiving of the Spirit (Rom 8:15), and of the sending of the Spirit (Gal 4:6). We may add . . . the testimony of Acts: the Spirit is received (8:15, 17, 19; 10:47; 19:2, 6)." The Fourth Gospel "speaks of a time in which the Spirit 'had not been given' (7:39), for the eschatological event had not yet taken place! But the disciples were to receive the Spirit (7:39), and did receive it (20:22), . . . the Father [having given] the

---

12. Ziesler, *Pauline Christianity*, 67.
13. Wesley, *Forty-Four Sermons*, 115.
14. Croxall, *Kierkegaard Studies*, 212, 216.
15. Weber, *Foundations of Dogmatics*, 2:236–37.

'Spirit of truth'" (14:7).[16] The post-resurrection work of the Spirit in believers is especially emphasized by the Fourth Gospel and Paul.[17]

The Spirit has decisive effects in Christian lives, among other things *capacitating us for genuine Christian praying*. "Christians find that they can pray, despite all the objections to a dialogical meeting with God which our inbuilt skepticism and our secular culture can raise. We discover to our own surprise that we are free to address God with the certitude that our words will be heard. It is not so much that we are able to pray as that we are enabled to, even pressed to do so, and that we are led to an unexpectedly fresh sense of God in the course of our praying. Our experience teaches us that a power beyond our own is at work enabling us to assert the right to address God [as] . . . promised by Jesus Christ."[18]

As we know the character of God from the disclosure in Jesus (see particularly John 1:18; Col 1:15), the Spirit encourages those qualities in us, that looking to Jesus we may become more godlike (2 Cor 3:18; cf. 1 John 3:2).

5. God as Holy Spirit Is Personal and Has Attributes

As implied throughout this chapter, God as Holy Spirit is no impersonal force, but is God as spiritually present, a free agent having divine attributes.[19] She exemplifies divine intelligence and knowledge by teaching and leading disciples toward an understanding of the meaning of God's disclosure in Christ (John 14:26). The Spirit also evidences will-power, as when apportioning gifts of the Spirit (1 Cor 12:11). And the Holy Spirit has feelings and emotions, and thus can be sorrowful (Eph 4:30). Ananias and Sapphi'ra grieved the Holy Spirit by lying (Acts 5:1-4); Stephen accused his adversaries of resisting the Holy Spirit's will (Acts 7:51), and Paul said that the Holy Spirit could be quenched (1 Thess 5:19). The Spirit as divine can even be blasphemed (Matt 12:31; Mark 3:29). Such divine interactions assume that the Holy Spirit is personal and has attributes.

As a personal power the Spirit also engages in such moral actions and ministries as convicting of sinfulness, regenerating, illuminating, guiding, and commanding. An impersonal force could not convince people of their sinfulness and of divinely deserved judgment, and of undeserved forgiveness granted.

6. Holy Spirit as Revelation in Its Inwardly Communicative Aspect[20]

The Spirit empowers people to be reconciled through Jesus Christ. As wind blows forth, God as Spirit proceeds from Himself into people and makes them open, free, and capable to receive the Son.[21] To believe "that Christ is God's Son we . . . must start out by believ-

---

16. Ibid., 237.
17. See John 7:39; 14-16; 20:22; Rom 8:9; 1 Cor 15:45; 2 Cor 3:17; Gal 4:6; Phil 1:19.
18. Rosato, *The Lord as Spirit*, 90.
19. Biblical evidence for the deity of the Holy Spirit is discussed in chap. 11, sec. 7.
20. See chap. 24 for a related discussion.
21. Barth, *Credo*, 130.

ing in the work of God that is [manifest] in the fact that we believe!"[22] "No [person] can say that Jesus is Lord but by the Holy Spirit" (1 Cor 12:3). Luther testified that the Holy Spirit had called him through the Gospel, enlightened him by His gifts, and sanctified and preserved him in the true faith, as "He calls, enlightens and sanctifies the whole Christian church on earth and preserves it in union with Jesus Christ in the one true faith."[23]

7. The Paraclete Is Holy Spirit as Bearing Witness to God's Revelation in Jesus[24]

One way in which the Fourth Gospel refers to the Holy Spirit is by the use of the term "Paraclete." The Paraclete is the continuing presence of the Exalted Christ as Holy Spirit bearing witness to God's past revelation in Jesus and helping us to understand that.[25] The Paraclete is the Holy Spirit in hermeneutical mode, helping to bridge the understanding gap between then and now, enabling us to perceive Christ in more contemporaneous ways. "I tell you the truth: it is to your advantage that I go away, for if I do not go away, the Counselor will not come to you; but if I go, I will send him to you." "I have yet many things to say to you, but you cannot bear them now. When the Spirit of truth comes he will guide you into all truth; for he will not speak on his own authority, but whatever he hears he will speak, and he will declare to you the things that are to come. He will glorify me, for he will take what is mine and declare it to you'" (John 16:7, 12–14).

The Fourth Gospel highly regards the Spirit's activity of "teaching all things" (14:26) and "guiding into all truth" (16:13). Yet in view of the elaborate reinterpretive project that the Fourth Gospel is engaged in, it is unlikely that the author thinks that other Christians have no interpretive work to do. To the contrary, God will assist us in our efforts, increase our discernment, help us to recognize and correct our mistakes, and keep us from discouragement in the face of complexity. But we have interpretive labor to engage in.

The existence of biblical contradictions makes the interpretive task difficult, but God's Spirit of wisdom can help to equip fellow Christians to sort through the issues. A weakness of the Fourth Gospel Paraclete teaching is that it is either individualistic or can easily be so interpreted. Paul expressed more appreciation of the Spirit's work within the Body of Christ, whereby different Christians are led by a variety of spiritual gifts and are thereby able to minister to one another. For example, those who do not have particular interpretive gifts are encouraged to learn from those whom God has equipped for this task, and those with interpreting gifts should learn from those who can supplement and correct such

22. Ibid., 133.

23. Ibid., 132, quoting Luther.

24. "In the 'farewell discourses' of the Gospel of John (John 14–16) there occur five sayings that [deal with] the 'Paraclete' (14:16–17, 26; 15:26; 16:7–11, 12–15), though earlier in the gospel there is no reference to this figure and this figure is equated in 14:17 and 15:26 with the 'Spirit of Truth,' and in 14:26 with the 'Holy Spirit'" (Kummel, *Theology of the New Testament*, 314–15).

25. Though the Fourth Gospel uses the Paraclete term to refer to witnesses to Jesus Christ, testifying, teaching, and convicting (14:26; 15:26), First John uses the Paraclete word in a different, though related sense. According to 1 John the Paraclete engages in heavenly intercession (2:1), perhaps bringing the results of Christ's atoning work before the throne of God. But why would this latter task be needed, unless God is threesome and not triune?

teachers' deficiencies in other areas. Thus according to Paul the fullness of the Spirit's work can only be seen in communal dimension.

From what was said in this section's previous paragraphs we are in a good position to evaluate the *perspicuity* (clearness or lucidity) teaching of the Westminster Confession:[26] If ordinary Christians are guided by the Spirit, utilize their intelligence in reading Scripture, and learn from those with preaching and teaching and interpreting gifts, they should be able to understand those biblical teachings essential to salvation. However, as an expression of extreme orthodoxy the Westminster Confession did not recognize that the interpretive problem is not just between clear and unclear teachings, but sometimes between contradictory teachings—as for example between Paul and James concerning salvation by grace or works. The Confession thus denies and thereby ignores an essential interpretive challenge. Furthermore, as expressing extreme predestinarian and fatalistic ideas, the Confession implies that any who do not grasp the essential doctrines as summarized by the Confession are not destined to do so or to be saved. Which means that if we do not agree with them, too bad for us.

8. Some Aspects of Old Testament Understandings of Spirit of God

Because Hebrew is spoken concretely and has a scarcity of adjectives, the usual OT expression is "Spirit of God," rather than "Holy Spirit."[27] The supernatural working of God's Spirit in redemptive history was not in the OT period a widespread experience of Israelites.[28] The OT considered the Spirit of God to be particularly present in prophecy (Ezek 2:2; cf. 8:3; 11:1, 24).

The OT prophets experienced the sudden coming and going of the spirit. "It is true that scattered statements begin to speak of a permanent association with the spirit, but it is precisely the fact that this kind of thing is said of Moses and Elijah . . . that shows that in general the erratic incidence of the spirit continued to be the norm."[29] The old covenant hope was that at the dawn of the new age God would pour forth His Spirit more widely (Joel 2:28; Ezek 37:1-14).

Many later parts of the OT expected that the coming Messiah would fully experience the Spirit of God, stand in awe of God, and manifest true righteousness (Isa 11:2-5; see 42:1-4). The OT also thought that when the Spirit was experienced more widely, justice and righteousness, peace and devotion to the Lord would result (Isa 32:15-20; 43:3-5). "And it shall come to pass afterward, that I will pour out my Spirit on all flesh; your sons and your daughters shall prophecy, and your old men shall dream dreams, and your young

---

26. "All things in Scripture are not alike plain in themselves nor alike clear unto all; yet those things which are necessary to be known, believed, and observed, for salvation, are so clearly propounded and opened [considered?] in some place of Scripture or other that not only the learned, but the unlearned, in a due use of *the ordinary means*, may attain unto a sufficient understanding of them" ("The Westminster Confession," chaps. 1, 7, quoted in United Presbyterian Church, *Book of Confessions*, item 6.007, my emphasis). The Confession does not state what are "the ordinary means."

27. Erickson, *Christian Theology*, 866.

28. Berkhof, *Christian Faith*, 321.

29. Eichrodt, *Theology of the Old Testament*, 54.

men shall see visions. Even upon the menservants and maidservants in those days, I will pour out my Spirit."[30] NT statements about the Spirit should be read against the background of these later OT expectations. According to Paul, being guided by God's Spirit is a most distinctive characteristic of Christians.[31]

9. Barth's and Edwards's New Testament Interpretations of Spirit's Work

If it is granted that genuine Christian believing involves life-changing experience, Barth's following words are applicable: "A [person] *cannot* believe what is simply held *before* him. He can believe nothing that is not both *within* him and *before* him. He *cannot* believe what does not *reveal* itself to him, that has not the power to penetrate *to him*."[32] "In believing that Christ is God's Son we must . . . start out by believing in the work of God . . . [exhibited] in the *fact that we believe!*" "I believe that I cannot by my own reason and strength believe in Jesus Christ my Lord or come to Him" (Luther). In believing we must recognize that we are sinners, rebels against grace and incapable of the decision of faith. If it is nevertheless true that we [genuinely] believe, the miracle has taken place. To be personally affected by the journey from death to life that Christ accomplished on our behalf we must give God the glory, as amazed and thankful as before the cradle at Bethlehem and the cross of Golgotha."[33]

The Synoptic Gospels attest that Jesus was both led by the Spirit and was the bearer of the Spirit, thereby fulfilling messianic prophecies in these regards. "Jesus, Barth claims, had an absolutely unique relationship to the Holy Spirit. By being totally filled and governed by the Holy Spirit, Jesus . . . possessed the life-giving Spirit without measure."[34] Such affirmations are presupposed by the triunitarian faith that affirms that the Father is known in the Son by the Spirit. Such faith also affirms that experiential awareness of God runs in the reverse direction: from the Spirit to the Son and thereby to the Father.

Rosato again well describes Barth's perspective: "The Spirit turns people from enmity to God to peaceful coexistence with Him," "justifying and sanctifying them, and leading them toward the realization of their vocation as Christians." The Spirit can thereby enable us to recognize "the objective justification, sanctification and calling of all humankind in Jesus Christ," and the gathering of the community through faith (*CD* 4/1), the directing of it in love (*CD* 4/2) and the sending of it out in hope (*CD* 4/3).[35]

Consistent with NT teaching concerning the work of the Spirit, Jonathan Edwards insisted that deep knowledge of anything requires *affection*, so that if we are truly to know God, affection for Him must be evoked. "Where there is heat without light, there can be nothing divine or heavenly in that heat; [yet in] . . . a head stored with notions and

---

30. Joel 2:28–29; see Num 11:24–29; Jer 31:33; Ezek 37:5, 14.
31. 1 Cor 2:12; 3:16; 6:19; 2 Cor 1:22; 4:13; 5:5; Gal 3:2, 5; Rom 5:5, 8.
32. Barth, *Word of God/Word of Man*, 202.
33. Barth, *Credo*, 133, 131.
34. Rosato, *The Lord as Spirit*, 94.
35. Ibid., 112.

speculations, with a cold and unaffected heart, there can be nothing divine; that knowledge is no true spiritual knowledge of divine things. If the great things of religion are rightly understood, they will affect the heart."[36]

10. The Spirit's Leading concerning Christian Vocation

The coming of the Spirit gave the early disciples the power that Christ had promised and the ability to do what He had predicted: "You shall receive power when the Holy Spirit has come upon you and you shall be my witnesses in Jerusalem and in all Judea and Samaria and to the end of the earth" (Acts 1:8). In John 20:21 and Acts 1:8, the giving of the Spirit and the missionary movement are shown to interrelate, though mission outreach is only one aspect of Christian vocation.

The Holy Spirit calls us to very specific forms of faithfulness, many of which cannot be derived directly from the revelation in Christ. "God does not want everything from particular individuals; He always wants this and that." "The situation in which [a person] is summoned by the command of God, as opposed to that in which he already finds himself on the basis of divine creation and providence, may be astonishingly reversed in substance."

One's specific vocation "is for every person a special one, just as the divine calling is for everyone special." "Paul speaks in First Corinthians 3:5ff. of the relation between his own [vocation in contrast to] that of Apol′los. ['I planted, Apol′los watered,' v.6a], and in First Corinthians 7, with reference to the question whether or not to marry, he describes the decision as a matter of [one's particular calling] from God (v. 7)." The recognition of diverse Christian callings is implied by 1 Peter 4:10: "As each person has received the . . . one gift of grace, even so minister the same to one another, as good stewards of the *manifold* grace of God."[37]

With sensitivity concerning our own weaknesses, possibilities that exist for some may not exist for us; concerning our strengths, possibilities that exist for us may not exist for some. We are "invited to . . . become sources of astonishment not only to others but even to ourselves."[38]

According to Galatians 5:1, 13, only God the Creator and Lord who calls was the real frontier for determining Paul's vocation. So with us. We do not have final knowledge concerning ourselves, nor mastery over ourselves. Ever again we must let God show us who we are and what with God's help we are able or unable to do.[39]

The classic example of a divine challenging of fixed limits concerning human aptitudes is found in Exodus 4:10-13: "Moses said to the Lord, 'Oh, my Lord, I am not eloquent, either before or since thou hast spoken to thy servant; but I am slow of speech and tongue.' Then the Lord said to him, 'Who has made man's mouth? . . . Is it not I, the Lord? Now therefore go, and I will be with your mouth and teach you what you shall speak.'" Also notice the conversation between Jeremiah and God (Jer 1:6-8): "Then I said, 'Ah,

---

36. Edwards, *Representative Selections*, 223.
37. Barth, *CD* 3/4:595, 596, 600, 604, 603-4, my emphasis.
38. Ibid., 606.
39. Ibid., 606, 629.

Lord God! Behold, I do not know how to speak, for I am only a youth.' But the Lord said to me, 'Do not say, "I am only a youth"; for to all to whom I send you shall go, and whatever I command you, you shall speak. Be not afraid of them, for I am with you to deliver you, says the Lord.'"

As for divine callings "the older Pietists certainly had a rule: *'What we take ill, Will be God's will.'* Now this should not be stated as a general rule." Yet "a sphere of operation is certainly not chosen correctly if we do not ask whether or not it is inwardly commanded and decreed by God," "all creaturely factors being taken into consideration." If we pray that God will make us active hearers, we will always have enough awareness outwardly and inwardly to be on the right track "to the decision for this or that sphere of operation, . . . whether in conflict with what seems enticing and desirable or even . . . in relative harmony with it, but either way in obedience."

"A person can really learn to know his sphere of operation only as he occupies it and sets to work in it." "The necessity of outward and inward [re-examination] will now be manifested. It will now be shown whether or not . . . what he followed was the voice and calling of God." If it is believed to have been the voice of God, "without ceasing to be this sphere of operation, it [may] perhaps be amazingly broadened or amazingly constricted. . . . [One may need to] acquiesce to the fact that what seemed impossible yesterday has become possible today, and what seemed absolutely right yesterday is wrong today." One should "remain in one's calling so long and so far as the command of God summons to do so."[40]

"In obedience to one's calling, it is always possible to make a change, not [primarily] on the basis of one's own ideas and opinions or those of others, nor under the pressure of external circumstances or one's own rambling fancies, but in obedience to one's calling. . . . [It may be] right that I am summoned to choose again: to choose what God has perhaps chosen afresh and differently for me." Even within the same vocation "there may be changes in the human sphere of operation which are no less radical, though less striking,. For example every change of pastorate implies a tremendous break for the minister if he has taken his work seriously and is still prepared to do so. . . . Finally, sickness or age may bring with them quite unbidden problems of finding and occupying new spheres of operation." "*He was not left to himself when he entered on the way which led to this point and he is not left to himself now that he has reached it. He does not exist here without the God who was with him there, not even in the worst of cases.*"[41]

11. Attitudinal Implications

Christians should look to God and be neither sad existentialists nor jubilant nature worshipers. "The self-disclosure of God the Creator transcends . . . these two views of life. . . It speaks of a very different exaltation than that which the greatest exaltation of [creation] can deliver. But it speaks also of a very different misery than can be attested by the most vocal complaint about life. It is exhausted neither in the positive nor the negative verdict

---

40. Ibid., 635, 636, 637, 644, 645, my emphasis.
41. Ibid., 646, 646, 638, my emphasis.

of the creature. It pronounces an unconditional Yes and an unconditional No as the voice of being itself never does." "Since it is God Himself who assumes both aspects of existence, we are unambiguously summoned to take life seriously in its twofold determination, and unambiguously forbidden to evade . . . either sorrow or joy."[42] If you appreciate creation because you know the Creator revealed in Christ, fine. If you seek to move directly from the goodness of creation, arbitrarily ignoring the darker aspects of life, you end up creating a god on the basis of merely human projections.

---

42. Barth, *CD* 3/1:376–77, 377.

ADDITIONAL CHRISTOLOGY

Chapter 6

Mainly on the Implicit Self-Understandings of the Historical Jesus

CHRISTOLOGY PERTAINS TO THE meaning of God's presence in and through the life, death, and risen presence of Christ.

1. Nature of Sources

Even the Synoptic Gospels describe the pre-resurrection traditions concerning Jesus from the context of post-resurrection faith. "What the Gospels give us, inextricably fused together in a single picture, is the historic Jesus and the church's [Spirit-guided] reaction to and understanding of Him, as [those] developed over half a century and more. Seldom, if ever, can we distinguish *with certainty* and say: 'this is pure history' or 'that is pure . . . interpretation.'"[1] As best we can we should, however, seek to distinguish the earthly Jesus layers of tradition from the post-resurrection ones to perceive not only the likely continuity between the two, but also the likely discontinuity and sometimes even the incompatibility.[2]

"The picture of the earthly Jesus was never more than an aspect beside or in the preaching of the exalted Christ."[3] The Gospel writers reinterpreted the Jesus event because they believed that as risen from the dead the Messiah is still with us. *They thus freely proclaimed the Gospel as a current Word from the Living Lord, and not as mere stories about past events.*[4] The experiential knowledge of the Risen Lord that the community gained so colored the Gospel writers' selections, recollections, and interpretations of Jesus's earthly

---

1. Nineham, *Saint Mark*, 51, my emphasis. In contrast to the pretense of mere chronological records, all genuine historical writings interrelate facts with interpretations because events are remembered for particular reasons.

2. Systematic theology in general and this chapter in particular cannot go far discussing discontinuity and incompatibility since it is primarily concerned with theological meaning, and thus with detecting positive relationships between biblical traditions. For thorough studies concerning the Jesus of History authenticity and inauthenticity of various gospel traditions see Dunn, *Jesus Remembered*; Meier, *A Marginal Jew*, vols. 1 and 2.

3. Berkhof, *Christian Faith*, 273.

4. Weber, *Foundations of Dogmatics*, 2:32.

life that words are sometimes put into Jesus's mouth. None of these writers sought to provide "objective information," for they wrote that we "may believe that Jesus is the Christ, the Son of God, and that believing may have life in his name" (John 20:31).[5]

Since the church claims that it is precisely Jesus of Nazareth whom God raised from the dead, a high degree of continuity and consistency needs to be and can be shown to exist between the Epistles' affirmations concerning the meaning of God's unique disclosure in Jesus and the Synoptic content concerning Jesus's life and message. Otherwise the Son as the object of the NT church's proclamation would diverge so much from Jesus as He lived that NT interpretation would be a mythical creation of the church's imagination. We should, however, remember that with Jesus's resurrection a fuller stage of salvation history began, and that some of the discontinuity between before and after Jesus' resurrection is therefore understandable and essential.

2. Living Encounter with God through Christ by Means of Different New Testament Witnesses

While discussing various Jesus of history issues we must *avoid a Jesus of history ideology* that implies that only what came from Synoptic evidence concerning the example and teaching of the earthly Jesus is of value. Since God raised Jesus from death, our Lord cannot be imprisoned in the past. For He is alive and speaks amid the creative and critical conversation provided by the broad biblical witnesses, and amid today's churchly interpretations and proclamations concerning these. *Equally unacceptable is a Christ of faith ideology* that is indifferent concerning God's revelation through Jesus as He walked and taught on this earth.

3. Jesus as Sinless, but as Having Limited Knowledge

Though Paul attests that God sent His Son "in the *likeness* of sinful flesh" (Rom 8:3, my emphasis), that is obviously not the same as saying that Jesus was sinful. The author of the Epistle to the Hebrews is more precise, saying that Jesus was at all points tempted as we are, yet without sinning (4:15). A different question is whether Jesus had limited knowledge. He certainly did. For example, Mark 13:32 and Matthew 24:36 attest that Jesus said that He did not know when the consummation of history would occur. Jesus would not have been truly human if He had possessed unlimited knowledge. Yet Jesus was not a person just like us. Unlike us sinners, He was always dedicated to God's will and continually ministering to others. He did and said only what was aligned with God's will. And He was here because God willed to be savingly present in and through Him.

---

5. The Gospel writers' information concerning Jesus was sufficient to assure them that He is the One who opens the way to fellowship with God and therefore to salvation. Without attempting to summarize comprehensively, they portrayed His historical existence from the perspective of God's redemptive purpose (see John 20:30–31).

4. Implicit Christological Attesting

Were one to conclude that later NT Christology widely contradicts Jesus's example and teachings as exhibited in the Synoptic Gospels, one of these traditions would need to be rejected. For later NT Christology not only purports to interpret the meaning of Jesus's life, death and resurrection, but (like the Synoptics) attests that His resurrection validated *Him* and established *His* authority. It obviously could not do so if the conflicts between Jesus's life and preaching and the church's proclamation concerning Him were extreme. As will be shown in the next chapter, there is no prospect that widespread contradiction could ever be demonstrated.

Mere differences and tensions between the Synoptic Gospels and the NT's other writings do not raise major problems. For example, that Jesus primarily preached the kingdom and that the church preached faith in Jesus could demonstrate fundamental conflict only if in essential ways Jesus's proclamation of the kingdom contradicted the church's christological interpretations. This is not so, for Jesus perceived the eschatological shift of the ages as already beginning in and through Himself and His ministry, and after Jesus's resurrection the church proclaimed the Crucified and Risen Lord as the earthly dawning of the kingdom.

As one recognizes one's sin, and thus the need for the Savior, one is willing to affirm that Jesus is indeed what the NT church's theology *directly professed*. And which is also *implied* by Jesus: that He is God's Unique Agent of salvation.

5. Jesus as Kingship Manifestation and as Spirit Led

As for Jesus as the manifestation of God's kingship, the relative difference between the christological perspectives of the (post-resurrection) NT church and Jesus Himself (as evidenced in the Synoptic Gospels) is due to the proclamatory insights made available as a result of Jesus's death and resurrection and the outpouring of the Holy Spirit. These events clarified Jesus's messianic authority and saving significance.[6]

The most prominent theme of Jesus's preaching, the dawning of the kingship of God, points to Jesus's authority. From prison John the Baptist sent a messenger to inquire whether Jesus was the one who was to come, or whether they should wait for another (Matt 11:3/Luke 7:19). Jesus answered *by referring to what God was doing in and through Himself*. "Go and tell John what you hear and see: the blind receive their sight and the lame walk, lepers are cleansed, the deaf hear, the dead are raised up, and the poor have the good news preached to them. And blessed is he who takes no offense at me" (Matt 11:4–6/Luke 7:22–23). These Gospel authors likely exaggerated Jesus's healing results and even more likely invented Jesus's death-reversing capacities. Nevertheless, Jesus implied that Isaiah's predicted hopes for the messianic age and *the dawning of the God's reign*[7] were

---

6. Brunner, *Dogmatics*, 1:211.

7. The word "kingdom" fits well enough with Jesus's talk of "entering into the kingdom" (as in Matt 18:3; Mark 9:47), and of "sitting down" there (as in Matt 8:11; 20:21). But in many cases, unless the word translated as "kingdom" is accompanied by explanatory interpretations it fails to connote the dynamic, action-centered meaning usually denoted by "*basileia*." "Jesus likens the kingdom to seeds growing (Mark

being exhibited in His own activity.[8] Speaking to His disciples He said, "Blessed are the eyes that see what you see! For I tell you that many prophets and kings desired to see what you see, but did not see it, and hear what you hear, but did not hear it" (Luke. 10:23b–24).

"Jesus clearly implied that the final rule of God was *already* coming to expression in his own ministry. The rule of evil [at the time attributed to Satan] was already being broken (Matt 12:28; Mark 2:27)—something expected by his contemporaries only in the last days (Is. 24:21–22)." "There was healing and restoration and liberation taking place in and through his ministry . . . (Matt 11:5, referring to Isa 29:18; 35:5–6, and 61:1). Jesus' practice of table-fellowship . . . already mirrored the character of the festal banquet of the new age (e.g., Mark 2:18–19; Luke 14:12–24). . . . Jesus came not simply with a message of future hope; but rather, it was a message lived out before their eyes. What previously could only be hoped for was now beginning to happen."[9]

As Jesus loved the Father and perfectly subordinated His will to God's, He realized freedom in the face of His environment, and inspires His disciples to struggle to realize similar freedom. Jesus exhibited liberty "with respect to the temple and the cult, synagogue and commandments, priests and scribes, Sabbath and government, mother and brothers, food and clothing, property and money, popularity and the power of the state. In his life all these things became so secondary, temporary, and relative that those around him felt this attitude as an extreme threat to the established order. . . . It was the fruit of a strong carefreeness, which in turn was born from the absolute priority of the Father and of his gracious lordship. 'Seek first his [kingship] and his righteousness, and all these things shall be yours as well'" (Matt 6:33).[10]

Contrary to the Social Gospel interpretation of the meaning of the NT teaching concerning the kingdom of God, the latter does not teach that by our good deeds we can bring in God's kingdom, or that the human order will gradually evolve into that. The parables of the mustard seed and of the leaven (Matt 13:31–33 and par.) do not point to such gradual development, but contrast the minuteness and hiddenness of the kingship's beginning in Jesus's ministry with the enormity of its eventual results. Both the beginning and the completion are by God's miraculous initiative. One cannot hasten the kingdom's consummation either by pharisaic observance of commandments and penance or by the use of force. "The kingdom of God is as if a [person] should scatter seed upon the ground, and should sleep and rise night and day, and the seed should sprout and grow, *he knows not how*" (Mark 4:26–27, my emphasis).

Through Jesus's words and deeds people already confronted the future kingship (Matt 13:16). Jesus not only issued a call to repentance, but anticipated the kingdom's fullness and granted present participation in that future realm. Because Jesus was certain that in His own preaching and activity the future kingdom was dawning, He distinguished

---

4:26–29), or to leaven in a lump of dough (Luke 13:20), or to unexpected finds of immense value (Matt 13:44–46)." Thus "most New Testament scholars usually prefer to speak of God's 'rule' or 'reign'" (Dunn, *Jesus' Call to Discipleship*, 9–10).

8. Gartner, "The Person of Jesus and the Kingdom of God," 34.

9. Dunn, *Jesus's Call to Discipleship*, 11, 8, 11, 12.

10. Berkhof, *Christian Faith*, 296–97.

Himself from the Baptist as well as from the prophets.[11] As Spirit-led, Jesus manifested God's kingship.

6. Divine Forgiveness through Jesus

One of the ways Jesus embodied God's reign was by enacting divine forgiveness. In Jesus, God condescended to reach out to us sinners whose guilt has estranged us from God. "For the Son of Man came to seek out and to save the lost" (Luke 19:10). "Jesus's outreaching activity in God's name came to particular expression as He ate with tax collectors and sinners (Matt 11:19, and par.)."[12] When Jesus went into the tax collector Zacchaeus' house He thereby extended divine salvation to him (Luke 19:9). The parables of the lost sheep, the lost coin, and the prodigal son (Luke 15) interpret Jesus's consorting with the lost as involving nothing less than God's action in rescuing sinners. "In receiving sinners Jesus put himself in God's place, identifying his will with God's. Thus in Jesus's conduct we find a key to his self-understanding [as] God's eschatological representative."[13]

The Jewish authorities were correct in thinking that in the ultimate sense only God can forgive sins. It would be blasphemous for a mere mortal to claim such a right (Mark 2:6–7). Jesus, however, was God's Agent through whom God's heavenly kingship was breaking into history and through whom divine forgiveness was being enacted.[14] "The Son of man has authority on earth to forgive sins" (Mark 2:10).

Justification by grace is to be found not only in Paul's cross-centered interpretation of the meaning of the Christ event, but was prominently manifested in Jesus's pre-Calvary words and actions. Jesus told the story of the prodigal, who confessed, "Father, I have sinned against heaven and before you and am no longer worthy to be called your son"— who received his father's kind embrace (Luke 15:11–32). The proud and self-righteous are repugnant to the God who rejoices when sinners repent (Luke 15:1–10; 16:15; 18:9–14). Jesus rejected the counting up of merit and reward, since no one can earn their standing before God (Matt 20:1–15).[15] Coming under God's present and future kingship can only be received as a gift.

The Jesus of history basis for the hope of salvation is divine forgiveness and its grateful appropriation. "He told this parable to some who trusted in themselves that they were righteous and despised others: Two men went up into the temple to pray, one a Pharisee and the other a tax collector. The Pharisee stood and prayed thus *with himself*, 'God, I thank thee that I am not like other men, extortioners, unjust, adulterers, or even like this tax collector. I fast twice a week, I give tithes of all that I get.' But the tax collector, standing far off, would not even lift up his eyes to heaven, but beat his breast, saying, 'God, be merciful to me a sinner!' I tell you, this man went down to his house justified rather than

---

11. Pannenberg, *Jesus*, 217.
12. Ibid., 57. See Mark 2:15–17; Luke 7:39; 14:13, 21.
13. Kselman and Witherup, "Modern New Testament Criticism," 1141.
14. Nineham, *Saint Mark*, 90.
15. The gift nature of salvation and the human incapacity to earn our way is emphasized by Paul and will be discussed in more detail in chap. 18.

the other; for everyone who exalts himself will be humbled, but he who humbles himself will be exalted" (Luke 18:9–14).

7. Linguistic Manifestations of Jesus's Relationship with God

Only in Gethsemane is Jesus recorded to have addressed God as "Abba." "And he said, 'Abba, Father, all things are possible to thee; remove this cup from me; yet not what I will, but what you will'" (Mark 14:36). "Abba" is the Aramaic word that had been reserved for a loving father's close relationship with his children. The equivalent expression to "Abba" in English is "dad" or even "daddy." In Palestinian Judaism God was rarely referred to even as Father, and as far as we know was never called by the more intimate term "Abba." The Aramaic word "Abba" was likely suppressed by the Gospel writers with exception to Mark's reference in the Gethsemane text. However, that it was twice repeated by Paul, and as combined with "Father" (Rom 8:15c–17; Gal 4:6–7), indicates that "Abba" had likely acquired broad Christian usage as derived from Jesus.

Both "Abba" and "Abba, Father" say much about Jesus' sense of God's personal nearness, and of Jesus's confidence in God's leading. Furthermore, though Jesus is attributed as having used the expressions "my Father" and "your Father,"[16] there is no instance where He is recorded to have included Himself with His disciples by praying to God as "our Father." His general way of addressing God as "*my* Father" could have been so stated by the Gospel writers to emphasize His consciousness of His unique relationship with God. Or the church may have added this detail to reflect her own weakening of the "Abba" togetherness implication of Jesus with His disciples.

Jesus attested the nearness of the transcendent God. To a people sensitive concerning the distance between the Holy God and sinners, Jesus extended God's grace by granting disciples the right to call God "Father," or likely "Abba Father" or even just "Abba." This further authorizing seems likely because, though a non-Aramaic speaker, Paul used the "Abba" term. That term had to have been grounded in Jesus's own example when praying, and in Jesus's likely encouraging of disciples to use this term in addressing God in prayer. With such usage Paul as a gentile Christian demonstrated continuity with Jesus and with Palestinian Christians, though not with the later Gospel writers Matthew and Luke.

Paul wrote to the Galatian Christians "All who are led by the Spirit of God are [children] of God. . . . When we cry, 'Abba! Father!' it is the very Spirit bearing witness with our spirit that we are children of God" (Rom 8:14, 15c–16 NRSV). "Because you are children of God, God has sent the Spirit of his Son into your hearts, crying, 'Abba! Father!' So you are no longer a slave but a child [of God] and if a child then an heir" (Gal 4:6–7 NRSV).

Lest we trivialize our relationship with God, we should remember that God's intimate nearness in Jesus Christ does not diminish His majesty. Our Father is the Transcendent One who exists in Himself ("who art in heaven," Matt 6:9); He is also the demanding King (Matt 12:50) and Judge (Matt 10:33; 16:27).

---

16. Matt 7:21; 15:13; 18:35; 20:23; 26:29, 39.

8. "But I Say unto You"

Jesus's sense of unique authority is seen in the way in which He spoke and in His freedom in reinterpreting and even overturning traditions. Unlike the prophets He did not begin His various teachings with the characteristic formula of the prophets, "the word of the Lord came to me, saying" (Jer 1:11; Ezek 1:3). Though He continually sought to perceive God's will, He did not merely repeat words God told Him to say, but spoke on God's behalf. He emphasized His own words and actions more prominently than did most of the prophets concerning their words and actions. Though He likely read from those portions of the Hebrew pre-scriptural writings that by then were available, He, unlike the rabbis, did not make "it is written" appeals to pre-OT Scripture. As seen in Jesus's teachings collected by Matthew and Luke and placed as having been spoken from a mountain, [Jesus] referred to His own Spirit-grounded authority, and at several points contrasted His views with OT passages: "You have heard . . . But I say to you."[17] In the Matthew 5:21–48 portion of the "sermon on the mount" Jesus spoke directly on behalf of God, and transcended several laws found in today's OT.

Jesus's authority was widely recognized (Mark 1:27). "On the Sabbath he began to teach in the synagogue, and many who heard him *were astonished*. They said, 'Where did this man get all this? What is this wisdom that has been given to him?'" (Mark 6:2, my emphasis) The chief priests and scribes asked, "By what authority are you doing these things? Who gave you the authority to do them?" (Mark 11:28) Even if we take account of only His implicit claims, Jesus set Himself above past and present authorities in Judaism. "His well-spring of authority was not the law, the fathers, the traditions, or the rabbis, but his own certainty that he knew the will of God."[18]

Jesus regarded His own right to interpret and command as higher than even that of Moses (whose authority Jews believed was derived from and subordinate to the Torah). "When [Jesus] broke the laws of purification and of the Sabbath or when he rejected the traditional interpretations of marriage, fasting and prayer, oath and retaliation, or sin and righteousness, he exhibited an authority unsurpassed by anyone but God."[19]

---

17. Matt 5:21a–22a, 27a–28a, 31a–32a, 33a–34a, 38a–39, 43a–44a.
18. Dunn, *Unity and Diversity*, 186.
19. Gartner, "The Person of Jesus and the Kingdom of God," 36.

Chapter 7

Explicit Self-Understanding of the Historical Jesus

IT IS TOO SIMPLE merely to affirm that the one who proclaimed the kingdom of God became the one proclaimed, for Jesus in some respects also attested to God's disclosure through Himself.

1. New Quest for the Historical Jesus

Ernst Kasemann formally launched the New Quest with an article entitled "The Problem of the Historical Jesus."[1] In opposition to Bultmann's kerygmatic theology, that had nearly separated the NT church's proclamation concerning the Christ event from Jesus's life and message, Bultmann's pupil argued the following: (1) Only insofar as there is continuity between the One proclaimed by the early church and Jesus Himself does Christian Faith genuinely center upon God's action in *Jesus* and not become a non-historical myth. Thus Kasemann argued that historical inquiry concerning the continuity and discontinuity between these two attestations not only promotes NT understanding, but serves Christian Faith. For that faith should take close account of who *Jesus* was, what *He* taught and what *He* did.

(2) If the early church had been as disinterested in history as Bultmann thought, the Gospels would never have been written. Though the Gospel writers reinterpreted originally oral traditions and fragmentary written ones in the light of Jesus's death and resurrection, their portrayals of Jesus's life and teachings show that they assumed revelatory continuity between the exalted Christ in whom they believed and the earthly Jesus as also revealing God.[2]

(3) Who Jesus was and what He did and said are important for our understanding of God's manifestation in Him. It is inadequate merely to affirm (as Bultmann sometimes did) the "thatness" of revelation in Christ. Against evaporating Jesus into a timeless gnostic "redeemer" or a mythic symbol, Kasemann reaffirmed the scandal of particularity—God's

---

1. In Kasemann, *Essays on New Testament Themes*, 15–47. Nils Dahl wrote an equally significant article with the same title that same year, 1954. See Dahl, *Jesus the Christ*, 81–111.

2. Kselman and Witherup, "Modern New Testament Criticism," 1141.

revelation in a first-century Jewish person from Palestine who died on a cross.[3] In raising *Jesus*, God vindicated Him and proclaimed that in Him God had acted decisively for our salvation.

2. Some of the Criteria for Perceiving the Historical Jesus, with Additional Criteria Exemplified and Identified in the Following Sections

Utilizing the Gospel material itself, scholars have deduced *historicity assessment criteria* that can help to distinguish post-resurrection Gospel writers' additions from what *likely* came from Jesus and from what *more definitely* came from Him. We are hunting for places where Gospel writers would or would not have had reasons for making corrective alterations of their sources. Though systematic theology should learn from the use of relevant Jesus of history criteria, these *only indicate historical probabilities*. But that is no small achievement, since general historical study can only establish the same.

(A) The criterion of *embarrassment* argues for the likely historical authenticity of sayings or actions of Jesus that could have caused the Gospel writers to soften or suppress traditions, but did not do so. It argues for the probable inauthenticity of narratives to lessen the likelihood of deriving "wrong" ideas concerning events or earlier texts. The embarrassment criterion was *not* utilized to suppress the fact that Jesus was baptized or that He did not know when the consummation would occur. That such traditions were included in the Gospels shows that the Gospel writers had more interest in historical details than such form critics as Bultmann and Dibelius had assumed. But as we will see in this chapter, "corrective" alterations to avoid embarrassment did occur.

(B) A controversial standard that should be used only to ascertain the bare minimum of what is incontrovertibly historical is that of *discontinuity or dissimilarity*. This criterion assumes that if recorded words and deeds of Jesus differ considerably from the Judaism before Him or the Christianity after Him those are likely to be historical. This measure is useful in identifying unique characteristics of Jesus's teaching and life, for example, that He said something like "I say unto you," and that He associated with tax collectors and sinners. We, however, should not conclude that traditions about Jesus that agree with earlier Judaism or later Christianity are necessarily non-historical. That would result in a Jesus devoid of all continuity with the world in which He lived and that He influenced. Considerable continuity in both directions is to be expected, for the earthly Jesus was both a first-century Jew and a major influence upon later Christianity.[4] Since a total rupture from history before and after is improbable, this criterion is most useful in identifying Jesus's striking or unique characteristics and teachings. It can in some cases demonstrate strong evidence for or against historicity, but in many others cannot.

(C) "*The criterion of multiple attestation or multiple sources* focuses on material witnessed by a number of independent streams of early Christian tradition, often in variant forms (e.g., Jesus's prohibition of divorce in Mark, Q [a second source used by Matthew

---

3. Ibid., 1318.
4. Ibid., 1317–18.

and Luke], and 1 Cor 7; the institution of the Eucharist in Mark 14 and 1 Cor. 11)."[5] The point is that wider attestation increases the probability of those traditions being grounded in the historical Jesus. However the absence of multiple attestations does not disprove historicity; it is only one factor to be considered among others.

(D) "The criterion of the *rejection and execution* of Jesus does not tell us directly what is historical, but directs our attention to those deeds and words that would explain why Jesus met a violent end at the hands of Jewish and Roman authorities. A bland Jesus, a mere symbol-maker who spun riddles and who therefore did not radically threaten people's [ideas and traditions], especially the powers that be, could not be historical."[6] This standard may be useful in helping us critique innocuous stereotypes concerning who Jesus was, such as that He emphasized the "infinite value of the human personality." However, not every facet of the historical Jesus's life and teaching should be assumed to have been revolutionary. Even revolutionaries have non-revolutionary aspects in their lives and teachings. Tribal-challenging universalistic teachings, such as the requirement that we should love neighbors and even enemies and apply the "Golden Rule" may seem commonplace in Western culture. But this may be only because to a degree it is still influenced by Christian values. To the contrary, tribal values have been more common over the centuries and around the world.

(E) We can utilize the standard of *coherence or consistency* after a goodly amount of historical material has been identified by use of the previous criteria. Sayings and deeds of Jesus that are consistent with the base established by teachings having high historical probabilities of being grounded in Jesus's life and instruction gain additional historical probability. However, Jesus's precepts need not have been of only one type. Thus, for example, in many instances Jesus affirmed aspects of the wisdom and apocalyptic traditions,[7] and was widely influenced by the Judaism of His day, even though many of His teachings conflict with these sources.

3. Jesus's Use of Son of God Title

Jesus could have been the unique Son of God without utilizing this title. Yet granted the unique authority exhibited by many of Jesus's words and deeds, and granted Jesus's experience of God's fatherly nearness, it is not surprising that much current evidence points to the likelihood that He regarded Himself as the Son of God. This does *not* mean that Jesus was the source of all such purported self-references. We will consider only a few texts:

A *first* Son of God usage may not be grounded in the historical Jesus, *doubt in part being caused by close terminological and content similarities with the (late written) Fourth Gospel.* "All things have been delivered to me by my Father; and no one knows the Son except the Father, and no one knows the Father except the Son *and any one to whom the Son chooses to reveal him*" (Matt 11:27/Luke 10:22, my emphasis). Certainly according to the Synoptics, Jesus preached the Father's kingship, and in that way and many others was

---

5. Ibid., 1318.
6. Ibid., 1318.
7. Ibid., 1318.

mediatorial. But that Jesus might be against some people becoming His disciples seems far from the historical Jesus as otherwise attested in the Synoptic Gospels.

A *second* Son of God saying that, unlike the first, may contain authentic words of Jesus is the *Parable of the Evil Vineyard Tenants* (Matt 21:33-46; Mark 12:1-12; Luke 20:9-19; Gos. Thom. 65). *This parable ended simply with the death of the son, with no note of reversal, vindication, or resurrection.*[8] *Such a parable would be strange as an invention of the post-Easter church, but perfectly understandable in the mouth of Jesus as He clashed with His opponents for the last time in Jerusalem. The son in the parable stands very much in the line of the rejected and martyred prophets; hence the message coheres with Jesus's view of Himself as eschatological prophet.*[9]

As for a *third* Son of God text, it is unlikely that the church before Him or Mark himself would have *added* a "Son of God" appellation on Jesus's part to a tradition that attests His ignorance of when His second coming would occur (Mark 13:32). Because such an admission of ignorance is likely to be historically authentic—since the church would have had no motive for including such details (*criterion of embarrassment*)—so also is the accompanying affirmation of unique divine sonship.

Albrecht Ritschl believed that Jesus's sense of sonship involved a fearless commitment to His special vocation to mediate God's kingship. Jesus was able to remain loyal in this way because His trust in God enabled Him to gain freedom from the world. Though He faced massive suffering, rejection, and crucifixion, Jesus entrusted His life to God, and accepted death as the mark of His utter faithfulness to His vocation.[10]

4. Jesus the Mediator and Reconciler

"The disciples may have first begun to see in Jesus the divine power of reconciliation when they saw Him on His own authority forgiving the sins of a man, while those who were looking on protested that this was 'blasphemy' (Mark 2:1-12). Here there was a clear choice: *Either* this act was an act of blasphemy *or* Jesus was acting with personal divine authority" [see also Matt 9:6; Mark 2:5, 10-12]. The summation just given does not prove that Jesus was the mediator and reconciler. But it correlates with "the Parables of the Lost Sheep and of the Lost Son, or rather, of the Good Shepherd and the Forgiving Father [Luke 15:3-7]. These being commentaries on what actually happened in Jesus's forgiving action—God especially working 'in' and 'through' Him. Jesus is the Good Shepherd, who sought and saved the lost sheep. He did not merely say that God forgives, but in God's name He granted [divine] forgiveness; He did not merely *speak* of reconciliation, He effected it, with divine authority. His whole life involved the establishment of fellowship between God and [humankind]."[11]

---

8. See Jeremias, *Parables of Jesus*, 72-73.

9. Meier, "Jesus," 1324.

10. Ritschl, *Justification and Reconciliation*, 333, 442, 476, 484. That Ritschl did not discern the eschatological dimension of Jesus's thought should not blind us to the aspects that he did perceive and correctly understand.

11. Brunner, *Dogmatics*, 2:337, 336-37.

That Jesus willingly died on the cross is clearly evidenced and not contested, and thus the employment of historicity standards to prove such willingness is not required. The NT affirms and Christians believe that Christ's death on the cross, followed by His resurrection, are central to the implementing divine reconciliation, but such conclusions can be neither established nor disproven by scholarly criteria. Nevertheless, if Jesus were only a man, His death on the cross and His whole life would have no reconciling significance, and we would still be in our sins (1 Cor 15:17). The person who admits that he is a sinner who needs a Savior is open to recognizing the claim that Jesus is the Savior.[12]

5. Jesus's Expectation of Divine Vindication

Did Jesus foresee His own suffering, rejection and death, and believe that God would vindicate Him beyond such human renunciation by raising Him from the dead? A related question is whether Jesus understood His own rejection as paralleling that of many OT prophets. Or have such interpretations been added by the Gospel writers?

Being much influenced by OT prophetic traditions, Jesus likely regarded martyrdom in Jerusalem as an aspect of His vocation.[13] Knowing that His action in cleansing the temple would lead to condemnation by the Jewish authorities, He seems to have believed that God would vindicate Him beyond death and use His sacrificial self-giving to forward God's kingship.[14]

Not a biblical scholar to be blown about by scholarly fads, Nils Dahl writes: "It can be considered probable that Jesus not only foresaw his own death, but actually ascribed to it a vicarious significance and saw in it a necessary presupposition for the coming of the kingdom of God.... For the historian, such ideas of Jesus would come into consideration as one factor among others illuminating the course of Jesus's life. Then it would be understandable why Jesus did nothing to avoid the threatening danger, but through his purification of the temple seems to have provoked the intervention of the high priests."[15]

Last Supper accounts assert that Jesus expected that He would soon be rejected and die, and that *He regarded* His forthcoming death as a means toward realizing God's redemptive purpose. Unless such interpretations had some basis in Jesus's own consciousness, Last Supper meanings approximating those of the Synoptics and Paul are entirely churchly impositions of meanings.[16] Here, as at many other points, continuity (though not identity) of outlook is more likely than a complete split between the historical Jesus and the Christ of the church's post-resurrection Faith. If Jesus had for some period anticipated His own suffering and death, and was at His Last Supper again articulating those convictions,

---

12. Ibid., 336-37.

13. Mark 12:1-9 and pars. Matt 23:29-36/Luke 11:47-51; Luke 13:33. Matt 23:37/Luke 13:34.

14. Dunn, *Unity and Diversity*, 210. In line with the martyr theology then current (2 Macc 7:14, 23, 37-38), and the general belief in the vindication of the suffering righteous person (Wis 2-5), and with possible dependence on Isaiah 53 (vs. 12d, quoted in Luke 22:37b)—Jesus may have believed that His vicarious suffering and death would not only issue in His own resurrection, but would inaugurate the general resurrection (cf. 2 Macc. 7:11, 23; 14:46) (ibid., 211).

15. Dahl, *Crucified Messiah*, 75.

16. Berkhof, *Christian Faith*, 276.

the church's understanding of the Lord's Supper was an expansion of the meaning of Jesus's *Last* Supper, and not a creation out of nothing (*ex nihilo*).[17]

6. The Son of Man and Related Christ Title

The NT's use of the "Son of man" ascription refers to one who would pass through humiliation, suffering, and rejection, but who would eventually triumph and share in divine kingship. This ascription is every bit as "high" as the "Son of God" title and is attested in all four Gospels.[18] Within the NT there are few exceptions to Jesus's sole usage of this designation.[19] This title thus provides *little linguistic linkage* with the NT's churchly Christology, as is consistent with its grounding in the life of Jesus. Also favoring such grounding is that the reference to humiliation and then glorification parallels Jesus's preaching of the kingdom. Though in the present the kingdom and the Son of man are hidden in apparent weakness, both will finally be manifested victoriously. The church's post-resurrection Christology endorses *theological content* in close agreement with Jesus's "Son of man" usage. But that could mean only that the church learned from Jesus, regarding Him as God's ambassador, who though revealed in humility would return in glory.[20]

The NT uses the Son of man epithet in differing but overlapping ways. The humiliation aspect refers to the earthly suffering of Jesus in His ministry and to His predictions of His passion sufferings and dying. The glorification facet pertains to His resurrection, exaltation, and function as final judge. Son of man nuances may have contributed to Jesus's use rather than His employing of messiahship terminology that often carried militaristic and political connotations.[21]

Matthew 11:18-19 (par. Luke 7:34-35) likely attests a Jesus of history Son of man saying. "For John came neither eating nor drinking, and they say, 'He has a demon'; the Son of man came eating and drinking, and they say, 'Behold, a glutton and a drunkard, a friend of

---

17. In texts such as Mark 8:31 (and pars.), 9:31 (and pars.), and 10:33-34 (and pars.) the predictions of the exact events surrounding Jesus's rejection and then resurrection in three days may be churchly additions. Only the emphasized words in the following text from Mark 10:33-34 may go back to Jesus: "*Behold, we are going up to Jerusalem, and the Son of man will be delivered* to the chief priests and the scribes and they will condemn him to death, and deliver him to the Gentiles, and they will mock him, and spit upon him and scourge him and kill him, *and* after three days *he will rise*" (my emphasis). Rather than conclude that in the light of later developments the church created the whole of such passages, it seems more likely that she expanded Jesus's less detailed expectations.

Even if one thinks that no parts of the texts just cited came from the historical Jesus, we still confront several less detailed statements by Jesus concerning His anticipated suffering, rejection, and death: Mark 10:38-40 (and pars.); 14:8 (and pars.), 27 (and pars), and 35-42 (and pars.).

18. In the Fourth Gospel, see 1:51; 3:13-15; 12:23, 34; 13:31.

19. According to Acts 7:56, after his self-defense speech and full of the Holy Spirit, Stephen declared: "Behold I see the heavens opened and the Son of man standing at the right hand of God." For a non-titular ("*a* Son of man," not "*the* Son of man") usage, see Rev 1:13; 14:14.

20. The OT reference to the Son of man as found in Daniel 7 provides background for the NT's Son of man usage, but implies far from identical content. Daniel 7 refers to the coming of "one like the Son of man" (vs. 13a), who will establish an everlasting dominion (vs. 14) and defeat and subjugate those who oppressed the elect (vs. 27).

21. For other Son of man passages see Matt 17:22a; Mark 8:31-32, 38; Luke 12:8-9.

tax collectors and sinners.'" Is it likely that the church would have chosen to insert a "Son of man" appellation into a passage that refers to insults thrown at Jesus, and a text that does little to distinguish Jesus's status from that of John the Baptist? Is it not more likely that in the face of such false criticisms Jesus used terminology that identified Him "as the lowly and disreputable messenger of the powerful God."[22]

"Again the high priest asked him, 'Are you the Christ, the Son of the Blessed?' And Jesus said, 'I am; and you will see the Son of man sitting at the right hand of Power, and coming on the clouds of heaven'" (Mark 14:61b–62). Earlier he had said, "Whoever is ashamed of me and of my words in this adulterous and sinful generation, of him will the Son of man also be ashamed when he comes in the glory of his Father with the holy angels" (Mark 8:38). "And I tell you, everyone who acknowledges me before others, the Son of man will acknowledge before the angels of God, but whoever denies me before others will be denied before the angels of God" (Luke 12:8–9). In short, whoever confesses the lowly Son of man will be acknowledged by the victorious Son of man when He comes. In the texts just mentioned and a few others (Matt 10:32; 19:28; Mark 14:62) Jesus *may not seem* to have equated Himself with the coming Son of man, but it is speculative over-interpretation to suspect that Jesus expected one other than Himself as the future judge! Such a conjecture is based on an unnecessarily literal reading of Mark 14:61b–62 and three other texts. Luke 12:8–9 and Matthew 10:32–33 are *certainly parallels*, and Mark 8:38 is probably so. That Jesus expected one other than Himself thus depends on an overly literal interpretation of one or two original units of tradition (Matt. 19:28; Mark 14:62).[23] Matthew 19:28 is likely to be a community formulation, and therefore could not possibly refer to a Son of man regarded as other than the returning Christ, since the early church certainly understood the coming Son of man to be Jesus Christ.

Jesus did not see "Himself as the forerunner of anyone except God. Moreover, the scene of final judgment portrayed in these sayings collects all the significant actors involved in the apocalyptic drama: God, the angels, the confessors, the deniers, and the Son of man. Conspicuous by his absent is Jesus, the very criterion of judgment—*unless the [coming] Son of man is the vindicated and exalted Jesus.*"[24]

Why does the Son of man phrase occur almost exclusively on Jesus's lips? Perhaps because the church found other terminology (such as Son of God, Savior, and Lord) more useful in appealing to gentiles.[25] Since according to the NT only Jesus used this title to any great extent to refer to Himself, it likely goes back to Him.

As for the essential historical background concerning Jesus's final Son of man usage and messiahship confession: It is highly likely that there was Jewish complicity in Jesus's capture, for apart from Jewish encouragement the Romans would not likely have had adequate reason to regard Jesus as a threat to the political order. Though there may have been nothing as formal as a Sanhedrin trial, amid the humble circumstances of some kind of Jewish trial Jesus seems not only to have confessed to being the Son of man who would return, but to being the Messiah (Mark 14:61b–62). In that context the meaning of

22. Meier, "Jesus," 1325.
23. See Marshall, *Jesus the Saviour*, 83.
24. Meier, "Jesus," 1325, my emphasis.
25. The church may have largely abandoned Jesus's "kingdom of God" nomenclature for similar reasons.

messiahship would have been conditioned more by the situation than from previous word usage. It is highly probable that Jesus "publicly proclaimed his true, heavenly status and the glorious destiny awaiting him" in a moment of deep "humiliation and weakness, when he was completely at the mercy of his enemies. But also at the moment when he was denied and deserted by the last of his human supporters."[26]

7. Jesus's Consenting to Messiah Title

During most of Jesus's life He seems to have discouraged the use of the Messiah/Christ title, probably because of the political and military connotations many associated with it. "To be turned into the bearer of the national hopes of the Jewish nation was evidently viewed by Jesus as a temptation of Satan."[27] Only when it had become apparent that He would be a Crucified Messiah did He consent to its usage, likely because the meaning would be redefined by the context.

> His entry into Jerusalem and attack on the abuse of the temple may well have contained deliberate messianic overtones.... The main weight of the charge against Jesus at his trial [may have] rested on the obscure saying about the destruction and eschatological reconstruction of the temple, which must go back to Jesus in some form[28] and which would have constituted some sort of claim to messiahship... And Jesus's response to the specifically messianic charges of Caiaphas and Pilate are best taken in the sense, "If you want to put it that way" (Mark 14:62; 15:2), implying that it was hardly Jesus's own choice of expressions. According to our evidence... (Mark 8:29-33; 14:61ff.), *Jesus's primary concern at this point was to explain his role in terms of suffering and eschatological consummation rather than to dispute concepts of messiahship.*[29]

Jesus was put to death for the political equivalency of claiming to be the Messiah. Jesus's implied and asserted avowals of divine authority that had generated *religious* controversy in Judaism were at His trial before Pilate translated into the *political* charge that as the king of the Jews He posed a national threat to those in authority.[30] In that context, where it was obvious that He was not a political Messiah, He did not contest the affirmation.

---

26. Nineham, *Saint Mark*, 399.
27. See the Matthean (4:8-11) and Lukan (4:5-8) temptation narratives.
28. Mark 14:58/Matt 26:61; Mark 15:29/Matt 27:40; John 2:19; cf. Mark 13:2 and pars.; Acts 6:14; Gos. Thom. 71.
29. Dunn, *Unity and Diversity*, 42.
30. Matt 26:63b; Mark 14:61b; Luke 22:67a. Matt 27:11; Mark 15:2; Luke 23:2-3. Also see Matt 27:37; Mark 15:26; Luke 23:38; John 19:19.

Chapter 8

Post-Resurrection Faith in Christ of the New Testament Church

1. Spiritual Communion with Risen Christ and Father; Jesus Worshipped as Exalted Lord

PAUL SPOKE OF CALLING on the Lord Jesus Christ with the Father in prayer (1 Thess 3:11–13; 2 Thess 3:16) and even of praying directly to Christ (2 Cor 12:8–9; 2 Thess 3:5).[1] We cannot have spiritual communion with one who is less than God. Only because the early Christians understood the Risen Lord as one with God, could Paul say that the Christian life occurs "in Christ" or "in the Lord" [Jesus Christ].[2]

Worship of and prayer to Christ is signified by the often repeated phrase, "calling on the name of the Lord." In the NT we also find prayers directed "in the name of Christ" or "through Christ," each of which connote Christ's divine mediatorial role in our relationship with the Father.[3]

The most convincing evidence in the earliest NT churches that Jesus was worshipped is the Aramaic prayer of invocation "*Marana tha*" ("our Lord come") that Paul included in 1 Corinthians 16:22.[4] Only the earliest churches spoke Aramaic; thus only they could have been the source of such a phrase. Paul would have had no reason for including such foreign words in a letter to Greek speaking Christians, unless the words had liturgical associations going back to the earliest Palestinian church. Paul's use of such terminology would have helped to remind the church of her unity across space and over time.[5]

---

1. Weber, *Foundations of Dogmatics*, 2:76.

2. Rom 16:7–8, 11; 1 Cor 2:30; 7:39; 1 Thess 3:8.

3. John 14:13; 15:16; 16:24; Rom 1:8; 7:24; 2 Cor 1:20; Col 3:17. In the NT church the Risen Christ was believed to be present and (with the Father) was the object of adoration (Acts 13:2a). So much was Christ at the center of prayer and devotion that it is said that as Stephen was being stoned he prayed to the Lord Jesus that He would receive his soul (Acts 7:59).

4. Rev 22:20 states the same invocation, but without the Aramaic terminology: "Even so, come, Lord Jesus."

5. Martin, *Worship in the Early Church*, 31–32; Hunter, *Paul and His Predecessors*, 83–84.

Such an invocation certainly presupposes the presence of the One to whom prayer could be addressed, and whose consummation was awaited. "Not only is *Marana tha* the oldest Christian prayer of which we have record; it can only mean that [even] those who in the synagogue liturgy only lately had invoked the name of their covenant God as 'Lord' came to apply the same divine title to the Messiah. Long before the church had articulated the [trinitarian] Apostles' creed and the [triunitarian] Nicene one . . . it was confessing that Jesus is one with God, and is worthy of such divine and transcendent honors as most properly belong to the one, true, and living God, maker of heaven and earth. Christology was born in the atmosphere of worship."[6]

2. Jesus Christ as Savior and Lord

The word "Savior" is applied to Jesus in Luke 2:11; John 4:4; Acts 5:31; 13:23; and Philippians 3:20; eleven times in the Deutero-Pauline Ephesians and the Pastorals and seven times in the other epistles. The NT conceives of Jesus as the universal Savior come to save all humanity (John 4:42; 1 John 4:14; 1 Tim 2:4), and even to reclaim the universe (Phil 3:20; Col 1:19–20). For Paul and his churches Jesus was the Lord as the earthly One, the resurrected One, and the coming One. "For this purpose Christ died and rose again, that he might be Lord of the dead and of the living" (Rom 14:9).

The Christian *recognition* of Jesus's lordship began at Easter, when the Risen Lord began to penetrate closed hearts and to open blinded eyes. By raising Christ God showed that He validates and authenticates Christ as the Revealer and Reconciler, and as the Lord who has God's right to claim our lives. That Jesus's resurrection enabled His disciples *to know* of His lordship is indicated by the fact that though Luke (on the basis of post-resurrection insight) often uses the word "Lord" to refer to the pre-resurrection Jesus, *the characters* in his Gospel's pre-resurrection narratives never do.

"The first time in Luke that Jesus is called 'the Lord' by one of his contemporaries is immediately after His resurrection (Luke 24:34). Similarly in the Fourth Gospel. Despite the high Christology of John's presentation of the incarnate Logos (including the roll-call of titles in John 1 and the noting of Jesus's consciousness of pre-existence), *Kyrios* [Lord] is not used by Jesus's contemporaries until [the resurrection encounter described in] John 20:28. And the [writer] himself, unlike even Luke, shows a marked reserve in his own use of the title for Jesus prior to the resurrection."[7]

"In Paul the designation '*the Lord*' for Jesus Christ occurs frequently, and . . . the Christ hymn of the Philippian epistle describes as God's aim . . . that 'every tongue should confess that Jesus Christ is Lord, to the glory of God the Father' (2:11)."[8] In Paul's Hellenistic churches the affirmation of Jesus as Lord was the characteristic form of expression of the faith (Rom 10:9; 1 Cor 12:3). Paul wrote, "If you confess with your lips that Jesus is Lord and believe in your heart that God raised him from the dead, you will be saved" (Rom 10:9). "I want you to understand that no one speaking by the Spirit of God ever says 'Jesus

---

6. Martin, *Worship in the Early Church*, 32–33.
7. Dunn, *Unity and Diversity*, 51.
8. Kummel, *Theology of the New Testament*, 157.

SYSTEMATICS CRITICAL AND CONSTRUCTIVE 2

be cursed!' and no one can [sincerely] say 'Jesus is Lord' except by the Holy Spirit" (1 Cor 12:3). In particular, in worship people were to call on "the Lord Jesus Christ" (1 Cor 1:2) and remember the night on which He was betrayed (1 Cor 11:23).

Paul occasionally calls the pre-existent Christ "Lord": "You know the grace of our Lord Jesus Christ, that he, being rich, yet for your sake became poor" (2 Cor 8:9). That this usage is seldom employed by Paul shows that he "has projected the designation of Jesus as 'Lord' backward from the resurrected One onto the earthly Jesus and then onto the pre-existent One."[9]

God is not to be subject to us, but we to Him. Yet God upsets our ordinary conception of lordship. Jesus in manner and teaching was the Lord who became the servant of all. "And Jesus called them to him and said to them, 'You know that those who are supposed to rule over the Gentiles lord it over them, and their great men exercise authority over them. But it shall not be so among you; but whoever would be great among you must be your servant, and whoever would be first among you must be slave of all. For the Son of man also came not to be served but to serve, and to give his life as a ransom for many'" (Mark 10:42–45). God's lordship is exhibited most decisively not in earthquake, thunder, and fire, but in the self-giving service and sacrifice of a lowly carpenter and itinerant preacher who suffered a criminal's execution.

To believe that Jesus Christ is Lord is to know that as "truly God" He has the right to our undivided loyalty. Jesus Christ is to be our Master and we His obedient servants. Though in subtle and hidden ways Christ is at work in the world and in that sense is already the universal Lord, He wills that people explicitly honor His lordship.

Jesus would not be the Lord had not God raised Him from death. But that does not mean that Jesus only became Lord when God raised Him up. Since Paul believed that God came to earth in the Son, and so taught in Philippians 2:5–11, it is doubtful that in vss. 9–11 he meant to imply that Jesus only became Lord with His resurrection. The meanings of "Son of God" and "Lord" are too close to be sharply distinguished, as though Jesus could have been Son of God, but only became Lord with His resurrection.

In the OT the word "Lord" was used to refer to God. To apply this title to Jesus is to affirm that in Him we meet God.[10] Affirming Christ's lordship would be far easier if all required were such a profession, but truly to confess Christ's lordship involves becoming His faithfully servants (1 Cor 7:22). Paul uses very strong language. Not only does he say that disciples are to be slaves of Christ, but that apart from such service people are enslaved to lesser gods (Rom 6:16; 1 Cor 7:23). Without radical obedience to Christ, people worship creation rather than the Creator (Rom 1:22–25).

In the light of whom Jesus Christ was and is and what He expects of us, the NT recognizes the relativity of other loyalties. "For although there may be so-called gods in heaven or on earth—as indeed there are many 'gods' and many 'lords'—yet for us there is one God, the Father, from whom are all things and for whom we exist, and one Lord, Jesus

---

9. Ibid., 160.

10. Paul used OT texts that spoke of *Yahweh*, the Lord, as self-existent and eternal, and applied them to *Jesus* (e.g., Rom 10:9, 13; 1 Cor 2:16). "Most striking of all is the application of one of the sternest monotheistic passages of the OT (Isa 45:23) to the exalted Jesus in Phil 2:10ff., a hymn likely already in circulation before Paul took it up" (Ibid., 52).

Christ, through whom are all things and through whom we exist" (1 Cor 8:5–6). The early Christians regarded allegiance to the Lord Jesus as incompatible with allegiance to the various Hellenistic "lords." Christians were willing to die rather than confess that Caesar, rather than Jesus, is Lord. Would that we would be willing to confess the Lord Jesus Christ at such cost or even lesser cost.

What is most important in life is to *belong to this Lord*. "None of us lives to himself, and none of us dies to himself. If we live, we live to the Lord, and if we die, we die to the Lord; so then, whether we live or die, we are the Lord's. For to this end Christ died and lived again, that he might be Lord both of the dead and of the living" (Rom 14:7–9). *Strange and paradoxical as it is, our true standing and security lie in the fact that Christ has dethroned us from self-mastery and freed us from idols. Our true and only comfort in life and death is that He is our Savior and Lord.*

3. Son of God[11]

Jesus Christ is affirmed by the church as the unique Son of God in all sections of the NT witness, Paul, the Synoptics, the Fourth Gospel, Acts, and the other Epistles. All of these sources manifest the post-resurrection Son of God perspective, though the Synoptics also occasionally affirm that Jesus had such a self-understanding prior to His resurrection.

Paul's talk of the "sending" of the Son (Rom 8:3) indicates the Son's eternal pre-existence; what the latter means will be discussed in Triunity chapter 11, section 5. That God the Father *"was working salvation in what happened and will happen through Jesus Christ is what Paul wants to emphasize when he speaks of the Son of God"*[12]

With a variety of expressions the Fourth Gospel attests a unity of wills between the Incarnate Son and the Father, and insists that the Father who sent the Son was always with Him (8:16, 29; 16:32). Formulations from mysticism are used to help describe this unity: the mutual knowledge of Father and Son (10:14, 38) and the immanence of each in the other.[13] The Father loves the Son[14] and the Son abides in His love (15:10). Like the prophets, Jesus did not act on His own authority, but from God's guidance. Unlike the prophets,

---

11. See chap. 7, sec, 3 for Jesus's own use of the Son of God title and chap. 11, sec. 6 for more post-resurrection attesting concerning the meaning of the Son of God title. Terminology concerning the Son of God and the Incarnation greatly overlaps, and thus this and the next sec. could have been treated as one topic.

12. Dahl, *Jesus the Christ*, 122.

13. 10:38; 14:10–14, 20; 17:21–23.

14. 3:35; 5:20; 10:17; 15:9; 17:23–24, 26.

Jesus is said to have spoken and acted continually from oneness with God,[15] He and the Father being one (10:30).[16]

According to Paul and the Fourth Gospel, Jesus Christ was and is God's Son by nature, whereas we are children of God through forgiveness and adoption (Gal 4:4–7). "He who comes from above is above all; he who is of the earth belongs to the earth, and of the earth he speaks" (John 3:31; see also 3:13). "Just as we have borne the image of the man of dust, we shall also bear the image of the man of heaven" (1 Cor 15:49). Thus the purpose of God's coming is fulfilled in those who believe in Jesus the Son, and who, in and through the Son and by the power of the Spirit, already participate in eternal life (John 17:3). Such Christians share in God's divine love, which is the source of God's loving deed in Christ.[17] And as the Father "sent the Son" into the world, so the Son sends His disciples into the world (John 17:18).

In writing of the Son as the emissary from God, Paul described Christ's work as *God's* saving action, the result of God's initiative (Rom 8:32). Paul affirms "that Jesus is the eternal Son of God because the salvation he delivered to humankind has its origin in God. If the One who lived, suffered, and died for our salvation is not eternally from God, there is no real and certain salvation."[18]

4. The Incarnation

As mentioned in the footnote at the beginning of the previous section, the meaning of the Son of God references to Jesus greatly overlaps with incarnational ones. I will highlight the interrelated Son of God aspects of the incarnational texts discussed below, in this way showing the close relationships between these two ascriptions.

Though the term "incarnation" does not appear in the Bible, Paul refers to the idea of God coming among us when writing of "God sending His *own Son* in the likeness of sinful flesh" (Rom 8:3); and when attesting "the grace of our Lord Jesus Christ" who for our sake "became poor, that by His poverty we might become rich" (2 Cor 8:9ac). Paul urged having the mind among ourselves which we "have in Christ Jesus, who though he was in the form of God did not count equality with God a thing to be grasped, but emptied himself, taking

---

15. Bultmann, *Theology of the NT*, 2:49–50, 65, 62. The author of the Fourth Gospel writes as one far removed from the events he describes. The supposed following features of Jesus are not only unlikely to be grounded in the Jesus of history, but the portrait verges on Docetism. According to the Fourth Gospel Jesus had a memory of His pre-existent life with the Father (3:11, 32; 5:19, 30; 8:26, 28, 38, 40; 12:49; 15:15; 17:8). John also presents Jesus as the "divine man" in the Hellenistic sense: Jesus supposedly knew the thoughts of the people He met (Peter, 1:42; Nathanael, 1:47–51). Upon first encountering the Samaritan woman He already knew her past (4:17–19). Jesus astonishingly eluded harm, being miraculously snatched from His enemies' hands until His appointed hour (7:30, 44; 8:20, 59; 10:39), (ibid., 51, 61, 42–43).

16. Fuller, *Foundations of New Testament Christology*, 248. If interpreted literally, some NT texts go beyond the idea that God through the Son came forth into history. Such texts describe the incarnation as the voluntary act of will of the pre-existent Son Himself—from His own individual mode of being, whereby He surrendered His equality with God (Phil 2:3–11; 2 Cor 8:9), (ibid., 209). To think that the pre-existent Son was a separate decision-making agent is in my opinion tritheistic. For additional discussion of this problem see the Kenotic Christology discussions in chap. 10, sec. 8, and in chap. 11, sec. 2.

17. 1 John 4:16a; cf. John 17:26; 1 John 2:5; 3:17; 4:7–12.

18. Braaten, "The Person of Jesus Christ," 545.

the form of a servant, being born in the likeness of men" (Phil 2:5b–7). Such texts witness to the fact that in Jesus God came among us.

Also without utilizing the incarnation term, the Fourth Gospel provides the definition: the "Word became flesh," as in the sentence: "The Word became flesh and dwelt among us, full of grace and truth; we have beheld his glory, glory as the *only Son* from the Father" (John 1:14). An incarnation emphasis in the Fourth Gospel and 1 John, which overlaps with the Son of God designation, is that God has come in human form (John 1:1–5, 9–18; 1 John 1:1–3) that we might gain authentic life now and forever: "He came to his own home, and his own people received him not. But to all who received him, who believed in his name, he gave power to become children of God; who were born, not of blood nor the will of the flesh nor of the will of man, but of God. . . . No one has ever seen God; *the only Son*, who is in the bosom of the Father, he has made him known" (John 1:11–12, 18).

The emergence of the God-Person in history was not an inherent possibility, since we are undeserving of such. Nevertheless, in the exercise of God's free outreaching love He issued forth His Word: "In this the love of God was manifest among us, that God sent his *only Son* into the world, so that we might live through him. In this is love, not that we loved God, but that he loved us and *sent his Son* to be the expiation for our sins" (1 John 4:9–10, my emphases). God reconciled us in the incarnate one. "We love, because he first loved us" (1 John 4:19; see also Rom 8:37, 39).

According to Johannine thinking, the holy and infinite God is the antithesis of our sinful and finite humanity. It is thus not surprising that when God's glory shone forth in *the Son*, His identity was not apparent to natural perception (see John 3:4), since such discernment requires being "born anew" (John 3:7b). *The Son* can be fully recognized only after His glorification (John 14:28; 16:7), as the Holy Spirit brings disciples to deep understanding of what the Son has said and done.[19]

5. Fourth Gospel's Docetism

The "I am" affirmations of Jesus in the Fourth Gospel[20] would have shown some equivalent expression in the Synoptic tradition had these been part of what was known concerning the historical Jesus. John is likely depicting the historical Jesus with the already shining glory that would become His by virtue of His dying and rising.[21] Though the Synoptics also present Jesus in the light of Easter faith, they do not let that faith overwhelm knowledge of and interest in Jesus as He walked this earth.[22]

The Fourth Gospel is not an accurate source concerning the historical Jesus since it attests a Christ whose divinity transfigured His humanity. In that Gospel Jesus is seen as fully aware of His pre-existence and so attests (8:58; cf. 17:5), speaking continually of His own status, and ascribing titles and symbols of divinity to Himself. He knows and much

---

19. An interpreted paraphrase of 14:26; see also 15:26; 16:7, 13–14.
20. Such as in 6:35; 8:12; 10:7, 11; 11:25; 14:6; 15:1.
21. See particularly 1:14; 2:11; 11:4; 12:23; 13:31; 17:5.
22. Dunn, *Unity and Diversity*, 27.

attests that He is the bread from heaven, the resurrection and the life, and the light of the world. Though Jesus is regarded as having an ordinary human appearance, believers are regarded as able to perceive His glory.[23]

"In this gospel the divinity of Christ is dominant." "When the soldiers come to arrest him His statement 'I am he' is enough in itself to make them fall to the ground (18:6)." Here "Christ lays down His own life, and He Himself takes it up again (10:17f)." "Jesus is no longer seen as ignorant of 'the hour,' and dependent upon the Father to vindicate and raise him."[24]

6. Theological and Historical Analysis

For any contact to be established between the holy God and sinful humankind it was necessary for God to descend to our level, since of our own capacities we could never raise ourselves to God. "'The majesty of God is too high,' said Calvin, 'for . . . mortal men to attain to it.'"

"Never could we have been able to contemplate the glory of God face to face had it not been hidden under the veil of humanity."[25] "The union of the Logos [Word] with [Jesus's] human nature was understood by Barth to entail no divinization of the human. What is in view is a 'unity in differentiation,' 'a strictly dialectical union,' which *in no way* sets aside the qualitative distinction between divine nature and human nature."[26]

As can be seen from the following analysis, a problem with the Johannine understanding of the incarnation, and of the classical Lutheran christological traditions that decisively built from Johannine sources, is that these tended to deny the true humanity of Jesus. In contrast the Reformed perspective built more broadly from NT sources. Furthermore, a Reformed principle that emerged is that the finite is not capable of the infinite: "The eternal Son is present in history indirectly, never becoming directly identical with the veil of human flesh in which [God] conceals Himself (since divine attributes are not properly predicated of the human nature)."[27]

---

23. Mealand, "Christology of the Fourth Gospel," 452.

24. Mealand, "Christology of the Fourth Gospel," 452.

25. Wendel, *Calvin*, 215, 218, quoting Calvin, *Institutes*, 2:6, 4.

26. McCormack, *Barth's Critically Realistic Dialectical Theology*, 361, my emphasis.

27. McCormack, *Barth's Critically Realistic Dialectical Theology*, 366. Lutheran scholasticism affirmed a more philosophically constructed, two-nature (hypostatic) union of the Word incarnate with Jesus's human nature. This even entailed a communication of the divine attributes of omnipresence, omnipotence, and omniscience to the human nature of Jesus! Though this understanding may seem to square with docetic aspects of the Fourth Gospel, it is far from the synoptically attested personal relationship that Jesus had with the Father, which to a degree can also be seen in the Fourth Gospel. Lutheran doctrine went ever further in building from an abstract philosophy by assuming the ubiquity (omnipresence) of Christ's human nature, whatever that can possibly mean! To pile philosophical assumption on philosophical assumption, "if the Logos continued to fill heaven and earth subsequent to the hypostatic union, then the human nature of Christ must have done so, since the human nature of the Son is [supposed to be] present wherever the divine nature is present," (ibid., 363).

7. The Son as God's Agent of Creation

The NT regards God's Son as so much at one with God that it can speak of God's activity in creation by referring to the Son through whom the Father created the world (Col 1:16; Heb 1:2). "He was in the beginning with God; all things were made through him, and without him was not anything made that was made" (John 1:2–3; see also 1 Cor 8:6). To say that the Son was with the Father in creation means in part that what God intended in creation is what He realized through His reestablishment of the covenant in Jesus Christ. "All things were created *through him* and *for him*" (Col 1:16d, my emphases). The triune God's mind and purpose are at work in creation, in God's providential guidance, and in God's redemptive activity in Jesus.

When God came to us in the Son He ventured forth to reclaim His own possession (John 1:11), so if we reject the Son we deny the ground of our existence and abandon our reason for being. Since all people are creatures of this God, faith in Christ is laid upon all as a necessity of our very life and being, hence the conversion requirement and the mission mandate.

Paul writes in 1 Corinthians 8:6 that "for us there is one God, the Father, from whom are all things and for whom we exist, and one Lord, Jesus Christ, through whom are all things and through whom we exist." For us as for Paul, in terms of gaining knowledge of the Father from whom are all things we must encounter the Lord Jesus Christ through the power of the Holy Spirit, else belief in the creator is mere speculation. "The way of primitive Christian knowledge is also the way of every individual Christian, and therefore too the way marked out for dogmatic's Christology: from the historical foreground to the 'super-historical' background. Only thus does living personal Christian faith arise."[28]

Although Paul's undisputed letters show the beginnings of a cosmic Christology,[29] Colossians expresses a flowering of such ideas. Here we see that through Christ God is not only accurately disclosed, but that Christ is perceived as the mediator of creation.[30] Christ "is the image of the invisible God, the first-born of all creation; for in him all things were created, in heaven and on earth, visible and invisible, whether thrones or dominions or principalities or authorities—all things were created through him and for him. He is before all things, and in him all things hold together. He is the head of the body, the church; he is the beginning, the first-born from the dead, that in everything he might be pre-eminent. For in Him all the fullness of God was pleased to dwell, and through Him to reconcile to Himself all things, whether on earth or in heaven, making peace by the blood of his cross" (1:15–20).

The above passage proclaims that the pre-existent Christ was active in both creating and reconciling. "Yet our knowledge of Wisdom language must make us cautious; it is possible that what is meant is that the same full presence and activity of God evident in

---

28. Brunner, *Dogmatics*, 2:340–41.

29. First Cor 8:6; cf. 2:8; Phil 2:10; also see the attesting of Christ's victory over the cosmic powers in Rom 8:37–39.

30. Ziesler, *Pauline Christianity*, 123–24.

Christ's resurrection and reconciling work was also present at the creation, so that what is pre-existent is not Christ in person, but the power of God that came to be active in him."[31]

8. Was Son of God Conceived by and Born of a Virgin?[32]

If Jesus's baptism by John is as probable as any fact of ancient history, His virginal conception and virginal birth are equally improbable. First, oddly as these beliefs may seem to us, they are likely just ways of affirming that Jesus was and is the Son of God *by nature and from the moment of His conception*. The Pauline writings, the Fourth Gospel, and the remaining NT epistles make even more comprehensive christological avowals in other ways. Such writings understand the Jesus event as the outworking of God's eternal intention, present in God's mind before creation. The Son is God as coming forth to fulfill God's plan to enter into relationship with humankind.

These affirmations from Matthew and Luke in part say in their manner what the rest of the NT affirms in different ways—that the coming of Jesus Christ, the Son of God, our Savior and Lord, *is due to God's grace*. Matthew and Luke's virginal conception and virginal birth stories imply that though human beings have the capacity to beget children, *no human* has the ability to beget the Son of God. This happened only because God in His mysterious freedom chose to come among us in love. To imply that Joseph was excluded from participation in Mary's pregnancy is a clumsy way of affirming God's initiative in the Christ event.

Schleiermacher rightly argued that to believe that the Redeemer's birth was by divine initiative required no dismissal of Joseph's participation in Jesus's conception. Schleiermacher further insisted that God's unique presence in Jesus cannot be explained by Joseph not being involved in Jesus's conception.[33] Since in ancient times virginal conception legends were common in the cases of great people, such a claim concerning Jesus cannot establish His uniqueness. Of the two legends, Luke's is probably the older. Luke hints that his account is an aetiology—*a story told to account for an existing state of affairs*—namely, why Jesus is called the "Son of God" (1:35).

As Schleiermacher pointed out, the Lukan and Matthean virginal conception legends conflict with the genealogies *Luke and Matthew* record that trace Jesus's ancestry through Joseph in straightforward ways! (Matt 1; Luke 3:23–38) Similarly, Schleiermacher noticed not only that the Fourth Gospel says that Jesus was called the son of Joseph (6:42) but *Matthew and Luke* refer to Jesus as Joseph's son! (Matt 13:55; Luke 4:22).[34]

Paul was familiar with the idea of miraculous birth in connection with Isaac's birth to Sarah (Gal 4:23, 27). However in attesting that Jesus was born of Mary, Paul referred to

---

31. Ziesler, *Pauline Christianity*, 124.

32. The alleged *biological miracle* is commonly called a "virgin birth," but what is primarily under consideration is Jesus's supposed supernatural *conception*, though Mary is also said to have been a virgin when Jesus was born (see Matt 1:20, 23, 25; Luke 1:27, 34–35). Conception by the Holy Spirit implies that Mary became miraculously pregnant because God so willed.

33. Schleiermacher, *Christian Faith*, 405, 403.

34. Schleiermacher, *Christian Faith*, 403.

no biological miracle related to Jesus's conception or birth (Gal 4:4ab). Paul did attest that God's Son was "born of the seed of David according to the flesh" (Rom 1:3).

There is further evidence against the historicity of Jesus's virginal conception and birth. Aside from these two legends the only other information the NT offers concerning Jesus prior to the beginning of His public ministry is the story that as a twelve year old He stayed behind to talk to the elders (Luke 2:41–52). Why does the NT contain so little information concerning Jesus prior to His public ministry? Perhaps because by the time the Gospels were written there were few available traditions concerning Jesus's early years, or it could be because information of that type was not regarded as of proclamatory significance.

That Jesus was virginally conceived and born is not mentioned elsewhere in the NT. Furthermore, the details of the two birth narratives differ at most points.[35]

During Jesus's ministry we are told that His brothers did not believe in him (John 7:5). According to Matthew 12:46–50, Mark 3:31–35 and Luke 8:19–21 Jesus's family is said to have been so unresponsive to His preaching that they tried to end His public ministry by taking Him home. Would they have tried to do so if Jesus had been conceived and born virginally? In the context of trying to take Jesus home He affirmed that the true members of His family are His disciples.[36] A story unflattering to Jesus's family is likely to be historical, for the early church would have had no reason for inventing such a story.

Had an angel spoken to Mary prior to her marriage, telling her of the miraculous conception that would occur and explaining who her Son would be, surely those events would have made sufficient impression on her that she would not have opposed Jesus's public ministry.

The historical background for the virginal conception/birth traditions seems to have been the Greek mistranslation of a Hebrew prediction, which was then used by Matthew and Luke as a basis for explaining why Jesus came to be called the "Son of God." The Septuagint mistranslated Isaiah's prediction that a "young woman" would bear a son who would be the Messiah (7:14). The Hebrew text makes no reference to her being a "virgin."

We move now to the unfortunate historical church use of the tradition that Jesus was conceived and born virginally. The inclusion of the virginal conception and virginal birth legends in the Apostles' and Nicene Creeds was likely due to anti-adoptionist and anti-gnostic concerns[37] that today can be met in more convincing ways. As for *the anti-adoptionist concerns*,[38] this was certainly *a way* of attesting that Jesus did not become the Son of God at His baptism or resurrection. Opposing Adoptionism can be more convincingly countered by more credible christological beliefs.

---

35. Compare Matt 1:18–25 with Luke 1:26–35; 2:1–6.

36. "It is all the more startling, when we glance ahead to the history of the early church, to find Jesus's brother James mentioned in the early creedal formula listing witnesses to the resurrection (1 Cor 15:7) and in the leadership of the Jerusalem Church (Gal 1:19; 2:9, 12; Acts 15:13–21; 21:18)—with other family members following in his steps" (Meier, *A Marginal Jew*, 1:350).

37. Pannenberg, *Apostles' Creed*, 72; Pannenberg, *Jesus*, 141–42.

38. Adoptionism is the belief that Jesus was adopted into sonship at some point in His life, rather than the Christ event having been willed before Jesus was born.

The legend of Jesus's virgin birth/conception contradicts the Christology of the incarnation of the preexistent Son of God found in Paul and John. For, *according to the virgin birth/conception legend, Jesus first became God's Son through Mary's conception*. According to Paul "When the time had fully come, God sent forth his Son, born of woman, born under the law" (Gal 4:4)."

As for this belief's *anti-gnostic reason* for being included in the NT, it seems surprising to us that virginal conception/birth traditions counted as evidence of Jesus's true *humanity*, in opposition to those who denied that the redeemer had been born as a human. The gnostic Christians said that the Son of God only seemed to have had a body, only seemed to have been united with the man Jesus, and only seemed to have been born. They said this not because of historical evidence, but for philosophical reasons: They regarded matter as evil and thus believed that the unchanging God could not have been truly united with a changeable, suffering, and finite person. Contrary to such gnostic dualism that did not believe that God is the creator, the Apostles' and Nicene Creeds attest that the Son of God *was conceived and born* as a human.

The two ecumenical creeds could have made the anti-gnostic point merely by asserting that Jesus was born of Mary. To emphasize Jesus's humanity no biological miracle was needed. However, since in ancient times virginal conceptions were often attributed to prominent people,[39] it did not seem docetic to the writers of these creeds to attest legends concerning Jesus's virginal birth and conception. Unfortunately, the inclusion of these additional aspects in these often repeated creeds gave and gives these beliefs a prominence lacking in the NT. The idea that Jesus was born of a virgin seems today to detract from His true humanity. Since Jesus was genuinely human, would He not have been conceived and born in the human way, rather than in the historically doubtful way indicated by ancient myths and legends?

---

39. Greek mythology regarded Perseus and Hercules as born in this way, and the OT considered several prominent people as born in similarly unusual manners: Samson (Judg 13:3), Jeremiah (1:5), and the "servant of God" (Isa 49:5). Pannenberg, *Apostles' Creed*, 71–72.

Chapter 9

Interpretations and Misinterpretations concerning Who Jesus Christ Was and Is

1. New Testament's Attesting and Denial of Jesus's Humanity

IF WE DO NOT trust that the Christ of the Synoptic Gospels had a human mind, what perception could be trusted? When Jesus walked this earth neither friends nor enemies doubted that He was truly human. He not only grew in body, mind, and spirit (Luke 2:40, 52), but had genuine human needs, could be hungry, thirsty, and tired,[1] and had such human emotions as anger, sorrow, sympathy, and a sense of wonder.[2] He did not know everything (Matt 24:36; Mark 13:32) and thus prayed to God for guidance and asked questions of others.[3]

Jesus surely erred in attributing the available parts of the Pentateuch to Moses (Mark 12:26) and in asserting that the consummation would occur within the lifetime of His hearers. According to Mark 9:1 He said, "there are some standing here who will not taste death before they see the kingdom of God come with power."[4] Similarly Mark 13:30 reports Jesus as saying, "this generation will not pass away before all these things take place."[5] That these predictions were not fulfilled does not mean that Jesus erred morally or that He failed to trust His future into God's care. Unless we can draw a distinction between human error and moral wrongdoing our Christology will necessarily be docetic (Jesus regarded as less than fully human).

If God were the subject who just utilized Jesus's human body there would be no room left for what we surely find in the Gospel story: Jesus experiencing God through prayer and reflection. That Jesus regularly learned of God's will through prayed[6] evidenced that He did

---

1. Matt 4:2; Mark 4:38; John 4:6–7.
2. Mark 3:5; 6:6; 14:33–34; Luke 7:9; John 11:33.
3. Mark 9:21; 11:13; John 11:34.
4. See also Matt 16:28; Luke 9:27.
5. Cf. Matt 24:34; Luke 21:32.
6. Mark 1:35; Luke 9:28; John 11:41–42; Heb 5:7.

not inherently know God's will. He prayed especially when struggling to make important decisions, such as all night seeking God's will before choosing the twelve (Luke 6:12).[7]

"And they went to a place which was called Gethsemane; and he said to his disciples, 'Sit here, while I pray.' And he took with him Peter and James and John, and began to be greatly distressed and agitated. And he said to them, 'I am deeply grieved even to death, remain here, and keep awake.' And going a little further, he threw himself on the ground and prayed that, if it were possible the hour might pass from him. And he said, 'Abba, Father, for you all things are possible; remove this cup from me; yet, not what I will, but what you will'" (Mark 14:32–36 NRSV).

The author of Hebrews summarizes several aspects of Jesus's humanity. "In the days of his flesh, Jesus offered up prayers and supplications, with loud cries and tears, to him who was able to save him from death, and he was heard for his godly fear. Although he himself has suffered and been tempted, he is able to help those who are tempted" (5:7–8; 2:18; see Matt 4:1).

Jesus was and is the "pioneer and perfecter of our faith" (Heb 12:2). Yet because God destined Him to be the Redeemer and because (unlike us) He was perfectly faithful, His faith differs from ours. The Son mediates the Father to us, or, more precisely, we know the Father in the Son by the Spirit.

Unlike the Synoptics, the Fourth Gospel (a much later writing) exhibits a docetic denial that Jesus had a human personality. Though it attests that Jesus was a person of prayer, who diligently sought God's will, it undercuts that recognition by describing His daily life as based on a memory of His pre-existent experience.[8] Is not the latter point the equivalent of saying that Jesus had no human nature or personality, that God was the acting subject? The Fourth Gospel also believed that Jesus raised Himself from death (John 2:19b).

2. Philosophical Docetism's More Entrenched Denial of Jesus's Humanity

What came to be called Docetism began in the third century as a "Christian" attempt to understand God's disclosure in Christ. It derives its name from the Greek word for *"seeming"* and *"appearing."* Because of prior philosophical commitments and without careful reference to pre-NT evidence, Docetists thought that Jesus *only seemed to be human*. They so concluded because for philosophical reasons they believed that the Holy God would not have shared in an inherently evil material existence. Against this reasoning, the NT does not regard material existence as inherently evil and thus is able to affirm that God was disclosed in a truly human person, though one who alone was without sin. Docetism being under much dispute in the community addressed by 1 John, that writing criticized denials of Jesus's humanity. "By this you know the Spirit: every spirit which confesses that Jesus Christ has come *in the flesh* is of God, and every spirit which does not [so] confess Jesus is not of God" (4:2–3a, my emphasis; see also 1:1–3; 5:6–8).

---

7. Erickson, *Christian Theology*, 711.
8. John 3:11, 32; 5:19, 30; 8:26, 28, 38, 40; 12:49; 15:15; 17:8.

Docetism was heavily influenced by Neoplatonism, and like it believed that reality is of various kinds, with mind or spirit being of highest value and with matter or physical reality being of lowest worth. Such depreciation of physical existence conflicts with the Christian belief in the Creator God who takes pleasure in His creation. It also ignores the fact that mind and spirit have to do with thinking processes that takes place in peoples very physical heads.

As Neoplatonism had regarded God as absolutely transcendent and independent of the created world, Aristotle docetically added that God's only activity is His own self-contemplation. Here God was not only regarded as uninvolved with the world, but as unchangeable and devoid of feeling. The early "Christian" Docetists, as influenced by these thinkers, had philosophical motives for thinking that God could not and would not have been incarnate. For according to their thinking, had He been He would have diminished His godliness by interacting with humans.

Later Docetists tried to affirm Jesus's deity, but because they denied His humanity they had little basis for knowledge of His deity. So they ended up where they had begun, with the Neoplatonic and Aristotelian abstract and utterly transcendent being who is too self-preoccupied to interact with the world.

Neoplatonic and Aristotelian influenced Docetists were less subtle than the later *Apollinarians and Monophysites*, but these latter two ended up with similar theological results. Whereas Neoplatonic and Aristotelian-influenced Docetists totally denied the reality of Jesus's humanity, Apollinarians and Monophysites denied essential aspects of it. These Christians gave so little attention to the historical particularities of the Synoptic Gospels' portraits of Jesus that they could not conceive that Jesus grew in wisdom and in favor with God (Luke 2:40, 52).[9]

Of these two nearly synonymous later misinterpretations, Apollinarianism occurred first, and will alone be further discussed.[10] Such advocates did not think Jesus had human reasoning power, a human will, nor a human soul. They thought instead that Jesus had a *divine* mind and will and soul. Jesus was regarded as a direct theophany—God on display—rather than as known through the interpretive assistance of the Holy Spirit.

To maintain the unity of the Eternal Son with the man Jesus, Apollinarius interpreted John 1:14a ("the Word become flesh and dwelt among us") with absurd literalness, and believed that the Eternal Son assumed only the fleshly or physiological aspect of being human. Apollinarius granted that Jesus had a human body, and slept and ate and eliminated, but that was considered to be about the extent of his humanity.

Because Apollinarius thought the Logos controlled Jesus He was regarded as having no human thought process, feelings, or will, and experienced no inner conflicts, quite the opposite of what we see in the Synoptic Gospels. That the Logos was Jesus's mind may sound spiritual, but it means that *God did not make it all the way into human existence, and does not do so even today.*

Against such thinking, the church insisted that in all respects, sin excepted, Jesus *had a human mind and will.* Were Apollinarianism correct Jesus would have lacked the most

---

9. These Docetists built from Fourth Gospel Docetism.

10. Apollinarianism was rejected at the Council of Constantinople in 381, but Apollinarius and one of his followers had been previously condemned in Rome in 377.

characteristic aspect of human existence;[11] He would not have been biologically human. For the mind is as fully human as the other aspects of the body and it controls those other aspects.

Why did Apollinarians affirm these things? Because they believed that the incarnate Son's oneness with God and His sinlessness could be guaranteed only if the Eternal Logos were His mind and will. We, like the NT, can surely affirm Jesus's sinlessness without resorting to such intellectual acrobatics that conflict with many aspects of Jesus's earthly life, such as His seeking to discern God's will through prayer.

3. Apparent and Real Docetism Today

If a particular communicator presupposes and elsewhere utilizes Synoptic historical details, an assertion that sounds docetic or more specifically Apollinarian may not be so. One of Kierkegaard's most inspiring illustrations compares the incarnation with a king who, not wanting to overwhelm a peasant maiden by direct display of his splendor, disguised himself as a peasant. The King hoped thereby to win the free, loving response of the maiden.[12]

Illustrations usually illustrate only one point, and Kierkegaard used the story to show that our response must overcome the offense of God's hiddenness. Kierkegaard's writings did not generally detract from Jesus's humanity and certainly Kierkegaard would not have implied that Jesus did not need to pray to God and seek to obey Him. Kierkegaard's *Training in Christianity* pointed precisely to the Jesus of the Synoptic Gospels as the pattern for Christian discipleship.[13]

Not all of today's apparent Docetism is only apparent. In Northern Nigeria I sometimes encountered genuinely docetic thinking. Some of the students believed strongly that Jesus was God and were genuinely puzzled why Jesus needed to pray to the Father. "Can God pray to God?" These students also wondered how Jesus as God could have been tempted, and, contrary to Mark 13:32, did not think Jesus could have been ignorant concerning when the world would be consummated. Such Docetism was encouraged in Nigeria by a general lack of historical consciousness (as massively influenced by Fundamentalism's impact), so that people tended to read the Bible without recognizing its complexity and diversity. The lack of historical insight concerning the Bible also meant that many regarded the Fourth Gospel as being as valid as the Synoptics for gaining information concerning the historical Jesus.

---

11. Erickson, *Christian Theology*, 714–16.

12. Kierkegaard, *Philosophical Fragments*, 32–34.

13. However, in *Philosophical Fragments* Kierkegaard wrote, "If the contemporary generation had left nothing behind them but these words: 'We have believed that in such and such year the God appeared among us in the humble figure of a servant, that he lived and taught in our community, and finally died,' *it would be more than enough*" (130, my emphasis). If the NT canonizers had so thought they would not have included the Gospels and most else.

4. Denials of Jesus's Divinity

The first Christian group rejecting Jesus's divinity was the early Jewish Christians eventually called *Ebionites*,[14] who represented one type of Adoptionism. They did not regard Jesus as "truly divine," though they considered Him to be a highly moral and religious person, who at His baptism God called to fulfil the messianic purpose.[15] Jesus was thought by them to fulfil His special function only because in Him the power of God was present and active *to an unusual extent*. The Ebionites ignored or denied that the Jesus event was grounded in God's eternal resolve to come forth into history. They also rejected the widespread NT assertion that Jesus not only performed a qualitatively distinct function, but was qualitatively distinct.[16]

Like the Ebionites, Adoptionists did not believe in Jesus's divinity. They thought that because Jesus prayed to God and sought God's will He could not have been genuinely divine. They supposed that He could not have been the once-and-for-all Mediator between God and humankind—fulfilling the covenant on both sides—but was only a divinely approved human witness. If the Adoptionists are correct, God did not reveal *His very self in Jesus, was not incarnate, and Jesus was only an important witness to God*. If the Adoptionists are right, we cannot truly know God, and thus our salvation is uncertain.

5. The Nicene Creed's Challenging of Denials of Jesus's Humanity and Divinity

Here are historical details that led to the Nicene Affirmation of Faith. An Alexandrian Christian named Arius in the early fourth century tried but failed to make the relation between the Son and Father clear. He thought that the Son was and is a lesser divine being, created before everything else, greater than mere humans, but nevertheless created; in some respects "divine," but not really God.[17]

Somewhat like the previously mentioned Adoptionists, who denied Jesus's divinity and humanity, the *Arians* thought that God is so transcendent that He has not revealed His *very self*. They believed that as the firstborn of creation (Col 1:15) the Son was only partially divine, perhaps an angel or a created god. The Son on earth was not only thought to be less than divine, but was regarded as too exalted to be truly human. Arians thus regarded the Son as an intermediate being between God and humankind, neither truly divine nor truly human.

Like the Adoptionists, the Arians made the certainty of salvation impossible: Because God was not believed to have come into history we have no reason to think that we have been reconciled with God. Lest we suppose that such a teaching represents only an *ancient*

---

14. The Christians Paul criticized in his letter to the Galatians reflected such a Jewish Christian distortion of Christianity, since they believed in the saving significance of OT law. Whether they denied Jesus's divinity is uncertain, and thus it is not clear whether they were "Ebionites" in the sense here described.

15. Ebionites foreshadowed the liberal "degree Christology" prominent in the nineteenth and early twentieth century, which will be discussed in sec. 9.

16. Erickson, *Christian Theology*, 694.

17. Placher, *Jesus the Savior*, 31–32.

heresy, we should notice that the "christology" of the Jehovah's Witnesses is Arian to the core.[18]

From the Patristic period of the post-biblical church Fathers Athanasius, a monk who later became Bishop of Alexandria, led the opposition to Arius. Athanasius insisted that the Son lived and died for our salvation, and that if the Son were fundamentally different from the Father, we either owe our salvation to a creature or there are two Gods. To avoid such mistakes Athanasius insisted that Christians need to affirm two things: "that the Word or Son is 'begotten, not made,'[19] in other words, *comes from* God's own being ... and that this Word or Wisdom or Son of God is of the *very same being* ... with the one He called Father."

"When the Arian controversy first divided the church, Emperor Constantine was a recent convert to Christianity, hopeful that a rapidly growing church would help him unite his fragile empire. He soon found Christians bitterly split over the beliefs of Arius. So he gathered a council at Nicaea, and the 'Nicene Creed' they adopted ... condemned Arius, affirming that the 'Lord Jesus Christ, the Son of God' was 'God from God, Light from Light, true God from true God, begotten not created, of the same [being] as the Father.'"[20]

In opposition to Arianism, the Eternal Son may have always existed as a dialogical aspect of the godhead. And God's sonship decision to share Himself with a world and with a human creation was prior to the creation of worldly time and space. Thus the disclosure of God's loving resolve in Christ manifests the very essence of God.[21]

Paul, Pauline influenced writings, and the Fourth Gospel (unlike Arianism or Adoptionism) affirm that God created and redeemed through the agency of His Eternal Son, who was and is of one being with the Father and the Spirit. Christians certainly believe that God's presence with us in Christ demonstrates God's will to reach out to the world and to humankind in particular, and to share His life with us. Language of the pre-existent Son and Spirit may be ways of pointing to this divine intention behind creation. That the Son is also said to be the 'first born of all creation' (Col 1:15) most certainly implies that long before any human was created God willed to share His life with us through the Son.[22]

6. Separating the Two Natures

After the Councils of Nicaea (325) and Constantinople (381) had affirmed the genuineness and completeness of Jesus's divinity and humanity, the question of the relationship between the two natures arose as a christological problem. *Nestorianism* was the first Christian movement to address this issue. Though the Nestorian teaching is puzzling, it wished to emphasize the synoptically shown reality of Jesus's human nature, against Apollinarian/Monophysitic Christology.

---

18. See chap. 29, sec. 6.
19. Though born of Mary!
20. Placher, *Jesus the Savior*, 32, my emphasis.
21. For background on Arianism see Erickson, *Christian Theology*, 695–98.
22. In referring to the pre-incarnate Son as the agent of creation (Col 1:16; John 1:3; 1 Cor 8:6; Heb 1:2c) parts of the NT attest His eternal sharing in God's essence (Col 1:15a, 16c, 17; John 1:1; Heb 1:3). Does not pre-temporal sharing in divinity imply bi-theism? See the Triunity discussion in chap. 11.

Unfortunately Nestorius overreacted to Apollinarianism/Monophysitism. While granting that God had revealed Himself in Jesus, Nestorius so divided and separated (not just differentiated) between the divine and human in Christ, that the Son could not be the object of faith. Nestorius did not have faith *in Christ*, but only *in God through* Christ. Because Nestorius's Christology was merely functional, and did not pertain to Christ's being, it, like Arianism and Adoptionism, did not measure up to NT claims.

Failing to recognize *the unity or oneness between the human and divine natures in Jesus*, Nestorius in effect did not believe in *Jesus's divinity*. And with the human and divine linkage in doubt he could not consistently affirm that the Jesus event is the *God event*. Nestorius did not regard the Son as God incarnate, the name above all names, the object of prayer and worship, the Lord. Like Arianism and Adoptionism Nestorian christological restraint creates doubts concerning salvation: How can we be so sure that God reconciled the world in Jesus if Jesus is less that God come among us?

Nestorius's dissatisfaction concerning the union of being between the divine and human natures in Jesus was because he thought such a union eliminated the distinctiveness of each of the two natures,[23] thereby denying Jesus's true humanity. Thus he spoke of a *conjunction or joining together* of the two natures in Christ, *not of their union*, and compared the conjunction with the relationship between husband and wife in marriage. Jesus was thought to be only a supremely inspired person, the highest of saints, *a human side by side with God, not God in and through a human.*"[24] The difference from Adoptionism and Arianism is hard to detect!

Theodore, Bishop of Mopsuetia, the most famous representative of Nestorian Christianity, came so close and yet was so far from what the NT concludes concerning Jesus. According to Theodore, God indwelled Jesus *only* through a union of Jesus's human will with God's will, involving perfect moral and religious compatibility, but no uniting of Jesus's humanity with divinity. Such a moral union of wills is an essential aspect of NT Christology, but the NT avows much more and so should we. Like nineteenth and twentieth-century degree Christology,[25] Theodore understood the Son as differing only in degree from us, rather than being God's Word from Beyond. *Theodore correctly regarded Jesus as a window through whom we see God, but how can we be so sure we really see GOD through this window if the Son is less than divine?*

From commitment to Jesus as a perfect person Theodore tried to deduce faith in a transcendent God, which involves an unjustifiable leap from immanence to transcendence. Theodore's deduction manifests a mere religious preference and a highly arbitrary one. *For God is God and humans are humans—and on Nestorian terms Jesus was only human. Such Christology is mere Jesusology.* The Nestorian Jesus can only be a human example and teacher, not the unique Redeemer, the only Savior, and the Living Lord who through the Spirit energizes our moral wills. On such terms Jesus Christ must remain a figure from the past and cannot be the Risen Lord in whom Christians "live and move and have their being" (Acts 17:28a).[26]

23. Erickson, *Christian Theology*, 726–28, 730.
24. Bicknell, *Thirty-Nine Articles*, 57, my emphasis.
25. See sec. 9.
26. Nestorius was condemned at the Council of Ephesus in 431.

7. Patristic Christological Reasoning concerning Unity of Jesus in Time with God in Eternity; Athanasian and Chalcedonian Insights

"Faced with a document claiming the co-presence of the temporal and the eternal, the mainstream of philosophical tradition tried to present us with a choice: either time or eternity."[27] Against such bifurcating, the Athanasian thinking of the mid-fifth century that led to the Chalcedonian Settlement insisted that we must reason from what God has done for us in Christ, not from prior philosophical dogmas concerning what is possible and impossible for God to do.[28] *Chalcedon attests that what has happened must have been possible.*

If we assume that God could not be truly united with Jesus and Jesus with God we are founding our views on culturally based philosophical ideas concerning divine remoteness and changelessness, rather than on what the NT says God actually did. Reasoning from the given disclosure in Christ, the Chalcedon two-nature christological doctrine insists that God and humankind, eternity and time were united in Christ. Thus Chalcedon transcends Platonism's duality between the heavenly world of ideals and the shadow world of appearances.

Athanasius taught that Jesus of Nazareth "is not an unprecedented irruption or intervention of God upon the stage of history. . . . 'The Word of God comes to our realm, [yet] was not far from us before.' . . . The love of God which made the world is the same love as that which comes to it in person."[29]

Chalcedon affirmed that God was uniquely present *in* Jesus Christ, not just *through* Him. "God was *in* Christ reconciling the world to Himself" (2 Cor 5:19, my emphasis). Chalcedon regarded the Nestorian dividing of humanity and divinity in Jesus as oversimplifying and distorting, and as failing to grasp the uniqueness of the Christ event. Nevertheless, Chalcedon did not overreact by divinizing Jesus's humanity. It recognized that Jesus had to struggle to perceive God's will.

The two-nature Chalcedonian summation of NT Christology also challenged Apollinarian and Monophysitic Docetism with their belief that Jesus's humanity was in one way or another absorbed into His divinity. Those views implied that God had put Himself directly on display (theophany). To the contrary, Chalcedon reiterated what the NT had attested, that though *the man Jesus* had an unbroken *spiritual* relationship with God, the eyes of faith are required to perceive God's revelation in and through Jesus. Jesus was a real human being, not divinity on parade.

In opposition to the several misinterpretations concerning Jesus we have considered, the Council of Chalcedon (451) further clarified, insisted upon, and defended against attack what the NT concludes: that Jesus was truly human and yet truly divine. In saying that Jesus had both a divine and a human nature Chalcedon meant by "nature" the essence of what something is. *The Council affirmed that what makes God to be God was truly present in Jesus and what makes humans most truly human was fully actualized in him.*[30]

---

27. Gunton, *Yesterday & Today*, 207.
28. Gunton, *Yesterday & Today*, 94.
29. Gunton, *Yesterday & Today*, 133, quoting Athanasius, *On the Incarnation of the Word*, 62, my emphasis.
30. Braaten, "The Person of Jesus Christ," 550, 536.

The divine and human were united as differentiated, not confused. There was also no separation or division between them. Jesus not only had concord of will with God, but oneness of being with Him and with us. *The one and only God meets us in a genuinely human person.*

What Chalcedon said was formal and in no way solved the material christological problem of *how* Jesus could be truly human and truly divine and yet one person.[31] Chalcedon did not say everything that needs to be said concerning Christology. It did set outer boundaries beyond which Christian thought cannot stray if it wishes to remain faithful to the NT affirmation that reconciliation is certain because *God has come all the way into human history and is thus reconciliation's source.*

8. Reformed Theology's Additional Insight

Like Luther, *Calvin* affirmed the unity of the God-man, but more forcefully than Luther, attested the *distinction between the two natures*.[32] Calvin wrote what is hard to imagine Luther writing: "We ought *not* to understand the statement that 'the Word was made flesh' [John 1:14] in the sense that the Word was turned into the flesh or confusingly mingled with the flesh. . . . For we affirm [Christ's] divinity so joined and united with his humanity that each retains its distinctive nature unimpaired, and yet these two natures constitute one Christ." "The two natures [should] not be thought of as either fused or separated."[33]

Barth pointed out that Lutheran Christology believes in the communicating of all divine attributes to the Son incarnate. It not only affirms that the Father suffered in Jesus (which Reformed Christology also affirms), but that while on earth the Son remained the omnipotent, omnipresent, omniscient Lord of the world. To the contrary Reformed theology regards such additional divine attribute transfers as docetic. Reformed theology seeks to guard Jesus's true humanity and emphasizes *the act or event* whereby through the power of the Holy Spirit we appropriate grace.[34] The reason doctrine itself cannot come to terms with God's disclosure in Christ is because the Father is known in the Son by the Spirit— and by the Spirit on an ongoing basis.[35]

9. Modern "Degree Christology" in Contrast to Classical Christology

Modern Degree Christology is similar to Ebionitism, Adoptionism, Arianism and Nestorianism. It is an old type of heresy recurring in new form. Unlike the classical Christian position that Jesus was truly divine and truly human, thereby defining true divinity and

---

31. The next chapter shows that *kenotic* Christology and Jesus's own moral and religious experience shed light that helps indicate how Jesus could have been both truly human and truly divine The mystery remains, but is not an enigma.
32. Wendel, *Calvin*, 219.
33. Calvin, *Institutes*, 1:482, 486.
34. Barth, *Gottingen Dogmatics*, 159–60.
35. "Similarly, the Reformed tradition as interpreted by Barth contends that the sacraments have no inherent power to confer grace" (Migliore, "Karl Barth's First Lectures in Dogmatics," in Barth, *Gottingen Dogmatics*, xli).

true humanity, modern degree Christology has been unwilling to regard Jesus Christ as its point of departure. Such thinking has often been willing only to concede that Jesus is the highest instance of what Platonism already regards as good.[36]

Platonism over the centuries and around the world has assumed a commonality between natural humankind and God. More specifically, it has believed in a natural attraction to God that enables people to ascend from the earthly and temporal shadows toward the eternal forms.[37] *And in Augustinian perspective, this is seen as possible because hearts are regarded as restless until they rest in God.*

Because modern degree Christology has platonically divinized general humanity more consistently than Augustine did, it has regarded Jesus as only human, assuming that everyone has rational or intuitive continuity with God, and is thus capable of realizing their own salvation. Against such thinking, classical Christology is faithful to the NT in insisting that we are not to judge Jesus Christ by our pre-Christian criteria. He is rather to judge and radically transform us and our standards.

10. Conclusion

"That Jesus is fully human and fully divine points to the *mystery of the unity of his person*. According to classical christological doctrine the two natures of Christ are united in one person without confusion, change, division or separation." "As the Word of God and the man Jesus are totally oriented to each other in love, a unique unity of free divine grace and free human service occurs."[38]

We are sinful and finite and God is holy and eternal. Thus we cannot bridge the gulf between ourselves and God. If we are to understand Jesus Christ as God's unique representative and God's way of salvation we should take account of His life example. But we must make a leap of understanding if we are to believe what the NT and Chalcedon conclude concerning Him: that He was and is the true God and the true human. Such a transformation of viewpoint is possible as the Holy Spirit convinces us of our sinfulness and of our need for the Savior and Lord. Such can happen amid the church's proclamation and interpretation concerning Christ, or through such means as private encounter, reading Christian writings, talking with Christians, or in other ways.

---

36. Barth, *CD* 1/2:129. For a persuasive critique of degree Christology, see Kierkegaard, *Philosophical Fragments*.

37. See Gunton, *Yesterday & Today*, 52.

38. Migliore, *Faith Seeking Understanding*, 149, 150.

Appendix

Another Misinterpretation concerning Christ: Most New Testament Miracle Traditions

1. Kasemann's Critical Insights

"Historical research and the comparative study of religion led to the conclusion that the New Testament miracle stories (1) have been subject to a quite definite development, [namely] that in the course of the tradition they have been multiplied and heightened; (2) have countless analogies (from which they cannot be isolated) in classical antiquity; (3) are narrated according to a fixed form, so that it is possible to speak with accuracy of a technique of the miracle story."

"The technique of the miracle-story, even before and outside the Christian sphere of influence, includes such motifs as . . . the insistence on the long duration of the illness and the unsuccessful striving after healing, a transfusion of strength conveyed by physical contact, an action which demonstrates the success of the healing, and the precise marking of the end of the narrative—or the astonished cry of the witnesses which serves the same end. The adaptation of pagan motifs becomes particularly obvious when the woman with an issue of blood is healed through the mere grasping of the virtue-laden garment of Jesus [Mark 5:25–34; Luke 8:40–48], or when healing power is ascribed . . . to Peter's shadow [Acts 5:12–16] or Paul's handkerchief [Acts 19:11–12]." Such superstitious beliefs foreshadowed the Middle Ages cult of relics.

"Paul does not deny the possibilities of miracle and ecstasy. By his use of [spiritual gifts terminology] in 1 Cor 12ff. he indicates that he sets a certain value on these potentialities. But as these chapters show, he does it by putting them to work in the service of the Christ and of his community; in other words, he places them in the category of charisma. For this is what distinguishes charismata from heathen [superstition]: they are validated . . . by the edification of the community. . . . Even existing charismata can be misused, as in Corinth. According to 2 Cor 11:13 there can even be false apostles. The spirits must be tested."[1]

---

1. Kasemann, *Essays on New Testament Themes*, 49, 50, 66–67.

2. Luke's Attitude toward Miracles in His Gospel and in Acts of the Apostles

"Luke uses the phrase 'wonders and signs' uncritically. For Luke 'wonders and signs' appear to be something to boast of—this is why he uses the phrase so much.... His attitude [also] seems to be: the more eye-catching the miracle the greater the propaganda value.... Not only does Luke use the phrase far more frequently than other authors; but elsewhere 'signs and wonders' are almost always something to be suspicious of—the sort of spectacular [magic] that is more the stock in trade of charlatans and false prophets/apostles than of servants of God.[2] ... In contrast to the caution of the other New Testament writers, not to mention Jesus and some OT writings, Luke's uncritical parading of 'wonders and signs' ... seems to pander more to pagan superstitious veneration of omens and portents."[3]

"Luke did not see any great need to demonstrate the distinctiveness of the power active in early Christianity to heal and make whole. On the contrary he presented the early church as another, but more powerful wonder worker than its competitors. *He does not appear to recognize that there is a problem here—the problem of distinguishing the power of God from its counterfeits, the problem of weaning faith away from a diet of the miraculous.* The problem is recognized and tackled by the other leading New Testament authors.[4] But in presenting his account of the early church Luke hardly seems aware of it."[5]

"In Acts 19:11–20 Luke links miracles and magic closely to each other. His summary statement about the great miraculous powers of Paul includes magical elements (19:11f.). Magical traits can also be seen in the story of the miraculous 'executions' of Ananias and Sapphi'ra in Acts 5:1–11." "This story ... raises the possibility that there is a correlation between magical traits in Acts and another characteristic difference between the miracles of the Gospels and those of Acts. The Four Gospels are totally free of miracles that directly punish people. In contrast, in Acts Ananias and Sapphi'ra are both struck dead because they lied about the sale of a piece of property (Acts 5:1–2), Saul the future Apostle is temporarily struck dead for fighting against the gospel (9:8–9), Saul the Apostle strikes the magician (!) Bar-Jesus (Elymas) blind for the same sin (13:11), and the sons of Sceva suffer for their attempt to exorcise an evil spirit in the name of Jesus (19:13–18)."[6]

3. Fourth Gospel's Interpretation

In the Fourth Gospel miracles are primarily symbolic. "In John we have the strange circumstance that on the one hand the miracles are intensified to the highest and most marvellous degree, yet on the other they are made almost irrelevant by the interpretation which John himself adds to them." "What remains, or does not remain at all, if the miracles are held to be unhistorical? In John nothing is lost at all, for all the outward circumstances which he describes have the characteristic of meaning something different from what they literally

---

2. Mark 13:22/Matt 24:24; John 4:48; 2 Cor 12:12; 2 Thess 2:9; cf. Rev 13.
3. Dunn, *Jesus and the Spirit*, 167.
4. Matt 4:1–11/Luke 4:1–13; Mark 9:38–40; Matt 7:22–23; John 2:23–25; 4:48; 2 Cor 12:5–10.
5. Dunn, *Jesus and the Spirit*, 168.
6. Meier, *A Marginal Jew*, 2:565.

and at first sight imply. When God himself (in the Old Testament) and the man Jesus (in the New) are depicted as light, it is obvious that an image from the realm of the outward physical world is being used in order to express a fact in the human-historical sphere. 'To be in the light' is a possibility open to man; he can orientate himself in everyday life in this world in response to the proclamation of Jesus." "Jesus could not demonstrate his divine power of acting as the light of the world more graphically than by lightening the darkness of a blind man [John 9:6–7]. To be more precise a narrator who wants to depict Jesus's power could not do so more clearly or spectacularly than through such a story. Blindness has a symbolic meaning. It is the dark background against which the light of revelation shines out in splendour" [John 9:5].[7]

"As 'signs' the miracles of Jesus are ambiguous. Like Jesus's words, they are misunderstandable. Of course, they are remarkable occurrences, but that only makes them indicators that the activity of the Revealer is a disturbance of what is familiar to the world.... They are pictures, symbols. The wine miracle, an epiphany (John 2:1–12), symbolizes what occurs in all Jesus's work: the revelation of his 'glory'—not the glory of a miracle-worker, but that of him by whom the gift of 'grace and truth' is [accomplished]."

"Just because the miracles are 'signs' which require understanding, they also provide the possibility of *misunderstanding*. After the bread-miracle, which raises the question whether he is 'the prophet who has come into the world' (6:14), the crowd wants to make him king (6:15) because it expects material benefits from him (6:26). His brothers want to take him to Jerusalem to the Feast of Tabernacles so that he may make himself conspicuous there, saying 'No man works in secret if he seeks to be known openly. If you do these things, show yourself to the world' (7:4). They do not understand the way in which the Revelation works. They do not understand that from the world's standpoint the Revelation must always be a 'hidden thing' (cf. 'in secret' 7:4) and that it nevertheless occurs 'openly'—not, however, with demonstrative obtrusiveness ... [In the Fourth Gospel] what is true of the miracles is true of all that Jesus does: it is not understood. Even the disciples understand the cleansing of the temple no more than 'the Jews' do. Not until after the resurrection does its meaning dawn upon them (2:17); likewise with the entry into Jerusalem (12:16)."[8]

4. Conclusion

"No one becomes a Christian by believing in all the recorded miracles. And no one ceases to be a Christian because he does not believe in all the recorded miracles. But we may well assume that no one can be a Christian who does not believe in the one great miracle, which is Jesus Christ Himself."[9]

---

7. Keller, *Miracles in Dispute*, 137, 142, 140.
8. Bultmann, *Theology of the NT*, 2:44, 45.
9. Brunner, *Dogmatics*, 2:170.

Chapter 10

Soteriological Christology[1]

1. Interrelatedness of Person and Work

THE NT DOES NOT isolate Jesus's person from His work, nor His work from His person, but holds both closely together. The NT church "looked to His completed work, which was regarded as of absolute significance *as the work of this person*. And it looked to His person, which was regarded of absolute significance as *the Subject of this work*."[2] "The divinity of Jesus remains the *presupposition* for his saving significance for us and, conversely, the *saving significance* of his divinity is the reason why we take *interest* in the question of his divinity."[3] What Christians claim concerning Jesus as God's instrument of salvation generates the question of His identity. Yet Christology is not reducible to soteriology/saving significance because Christ is more than Savior.[4]

"The rise of the Christian movement and the production of its writings can only be accounted for because there were people who claimed and proclaimed that certain benefits follow for humanity, or even the whole cosmos, in consequence of the life, death, and resurrection of Jesus of Nazareth, and that these benefits would not exist otherwise. It is difficult to imagine that anyone would have become or remained a participant in the Christian movement, or in any of its communities, unless such a person saw a door opened into a new world as a consequence of the 'Christ event.'"[5]

"Neither the first article [of the Apostles' Creed] on God the creator nor the third article on the Holy Spirit and the church has any distinctively Christian content apart from its relationship to the second article. For Christian faith 'the Father Almighty, Maker

---

1. The study of Christ in the service of God's saving activity.

2. Barth, *CD* 4/2:193, emphases mine.

3. Pannenberg, *Jesus*, 38. In the gospels' telling of the story of Jesus—His ministry, message, passion, and resurrection—the work and the person of Jesus are so integrated that the NT supposes that it was because Jesus saves people from sin that His name was called Jesus (Matt 1:21) (Migliore, *Faith Seeking Understanding*, 143).

4. Hultgren, *Christ and His Benefits*, 207.

5. Hultgren, *Christ and His Benefits*, 8.

of Heaven and Earth' is identified as the Father of our Lord Jesus Christ, and 'the Holy Spirit' is primarily defined as the Spirit that empowered Jesus and continues his work in the world. Christology is not the whole of Christian doctrine, but it is the point from which all else is illumined."[6]

Seeing the person and work of Christ as *interrelated and interdependent* goes far toward overcoming the static/scholastic cast of much traditional Christology. Contrary to merely academic approaches, the NT shows the Son's divinity by telling the story of God's self-emptying act of humiliation in becoming incarnate *for our sake* and in the Son's going to the cross for the same reason.

2. Threefold Offices of Priest, King, and Prophet: Structural Design of Barth's Volumes on Reconciliation

What systematizing thinking describes as Christ's three "offices" *summarizes patterns of divine outreaching behavior through Christ on our behalf, which can elicit fitting discipleship responses from us.* The "threefold office" pattern also show the interconnectedness of Christ's person and work, helping to preserve the unity and totality of His witness. Each aspect of Christ's person and work and of our responses is important, and the threefold pattern helps to ensure that Christians emphasize all of these. Comprehensive and interconnected articulation of these offices is post-biblical. Yet the NT separately mentions each of these titles and affirms expected Christian responses.

Eusebius only alluded to these offices and medieval and early Reformation churches made only minor use of them, but Calvin and the Geneva Catechism developed a comprehensive understanding of these. As for Calvin's use of these three titles,[7] "nothing happens here 'for itself' but everything is 'for us.' Soteriology is nothing other than Christology properly understood and accepted."[8] Since Christ is our representative His activities are for us. By speaking of the priestly, kingly, and prophetic work of Christ as the outworking of who Jesus Christ was and is, Calvin showed Christology's saving significance. Through the same procedure, plus the structural design of his four volumes on Reconciliation, Barth accomplished the same purpose.

Like Calvin, Barth wanted to overcome the tendency in much of the older theology to develop Christology independently of concern for Christ's effects. Barth, however, also wanted to avoid the opposite (pragmatic) tendency common to Ritschlian and existentialist theology of separating Christ's work from His person—as though only His effects matter and as though He could save us even if He were not God's Unique Representative.[9]

---

6. Migliore, *Faith Seeking Understanding*, 139.

7. See Calvin, *Institutes*, 1:494–503.

8. Weber, *Foundations of Dogmatics*, 2:174. For the following I have been much instructed by this source, 173–77.

9. Much nineteenth and twentieth century Christology minimized NT claims concerning who Jesus Christ was and is. Such Christology, which includes Cullmann's salvation history perspective, was in line with Philip Melanchthon's famous statement: "To know Christ is to know His benefits." As though that in itself was enough. Such Christology was also encouraged by Luther's emphasis on Christ's saving activity *for us*, and his over-reaction against the scholastic ontological preoccupation with the nature of being, and

As seen in Barth's effort, the "threefold office" structure helps demonstrate and encourage needed christological and soteriological breadth. In contrast the first form of one-sidedness is when Christ *as priest* is the sole focus, which encourages Christians to revert to passive, quietistic, and egocentric religious individualism. Caring only about one's own present and future blessedness and doing little to serve Christ in the world. A second form of one-sidedness is when the *kingly office* (in its common understanding) is alone emphasized, Christianity being reduced to moralism and tending toward theocratic pretension. The church forgets that the hidden Christ reigns through Word and Spirit and that His kingdom is eternal. A third form of one-sidedness is when, as with the Enlightenment, the church thinks of Jesus as only a *prophet or teacher*. If this service is all God in Christ does for us, we sinners must pull ourselves free from bondage to selfishness and rely on our own moral strength for living the Christian life.

Christ as Priest. Barth shows that the true godliness of Christ was demonstrated through saving action. The Lord descended *to become a Servant* and the Judge *humbled Himself to stand in our place*. By so doing the Lord as *priest justifies us and counters the pride whereby we try to exalt ourselves as our own lords*.

The word *"priest" summarizes the Son's self-offering of perfect obedience on behalf of sinners*. The NT makes frequent reference to the priestly work of Christ, with the book of Hebrews preoccupied with this theme. "He had to be made like his brethren in every respect [sin excepted], so that he might become a merciful and faithful high priest in the service of God, to make expiation for the sins of the people" (Heb 2:17).[10] The "priest" concept is often implied even where the term is not stated: "When Christ had offered for all time a single sacrifice for sins, he sat down at the right hand of God. . . . For by a single offering he has perfected for all time those who are sanctified" (Heb 10:12, 14). "My little children, I am writing this to you so that you may not sin; but if anyone does sin, we have an advocate with the Father, Jesus Christ the righteous; and he is the expiation for our sins, and not for ours only but for the sins of the whole world" (1 John 2:1–2).

Christ as King. The Lord become Servant was truly faithful (thereby demonstrating true humanity) and, though rejected by humans, was raised by God to share in eternal lordship—the Servant became Lord. As the Exalted One, and in the exercise of His *kingly role*, the Risen Son *sanctifies us, raises us up morally and thereby counters our laziness and indiscipline*.

As *"king"* the God who disclosed Himself in the Son exercises authority over church and world. Though the NT speaks often of *God's* present and future kingly role, it only occasionally refers to *the Son's* kingly function, and this usually with reference to the eternal dimension.[11] The Fourth Gospel's heavily interpreted witness implies that Jesus pointed beyond His own time by saying "my kingship is not of this world; if my kingship were of this world, my servants would fight, that I might not be handed over to the Jews" (18:36). Ephesians 5:5 uses the kingdom of Christ phrase to refer to the eternal world, as does Colossians 1:13 and 2 Peter 1:11. However, the book of Revelation obliquely and confusingly

---

in this case of Christ's being.

10. See also Heb 3:1; 4:14, 15; 5:1, 5–6, 10; 6:20; 7:17, 26; 8:1.

11. The NT's reluctance may be due to fear that such terminology could be misinterpreted as implying worldly political ambitions.

attests that the Son in His earthly role was King, sometimes combining that affirmation with the concept of a self-sacrificing and humble Lamb. "They will make war on the Lamb, and the Lamb will conquer them, for he is Lord of lords and King of kings."[12] Just how the self-sacrificing Lamb conquers those who make war on Him is not clear, unless this is actually an eschatological reference.

Christ as Prophet. When the Lord became Servant and the Servant became Lord, God and humankind were representatively united. As the God-Person, Jesus Christ is *the true witness, whose prophetic work of teaching and of spiritual enlightenment counters our falsehood, our rejection of God's grace and claim. The Risen Christ in His prophetic "office" thereby enlists us for the vocation of being His witnesses.*

The *prophetic "office"* of Jesus Christ concerns His earthly and risen work as Revealer and Teacher. The NT seldom mentions this summarizing epithet, which is usually spoken by outsiders.[13] Terminological infrequency is in this case an inaccurate measure of theological significance, since according to the NT the teaching and revealing activity of the historical Jesus and Risen Christ is vital.

We now turn to Barth's dream-based and complex structural design for his masterful four volumes on reconciliation, which introduced a new patterning going beyond but not inconsistent with the threefold office differentiations. Barth's first reconciliation volume (*CD* 4/1) depicts the Lord's humbling of Himself to become a Servant, thereby countering human pride through justification/forgiveness, which as received through faith results in the gathering of the Christian community. Barth's second reconciliation volume (*CD* 4/2) attests the Servant as Lord countering human sloth and indiscipline, resulting in the sanctifying of disciples and the upbuilding of the church in love. His third reconciliation volumes (*CD* 4/3, *First Half* and *CD* 4/3, *Second Half*) represent the divine mediatorial challenging of human falsehood and lethargy by the Spirit's upbuilding of disciples and churches in Christian hope. And their sending into the world to witness to the hope that is possible through the Father known in the Son by the Spirit.

3. Savior

The scriptural use of the Savior ascription has similar meaning to the "Priest" title of the threefold office pattern. It also links the Son's person to His saving work. Since the Savior epithet is used to refer to both Son and Father, this title also manifests the unity between God's modes as Father and Son: God is Savior, Christ is Savior, God is Savior in and through Christ.

In the Son's labor as Savior, God works to deliver people primarily from sin (see Matt 1:21) and death (Phil 3:20). "*God . . . saved us* and called us with a holy calling, not in virtue of our works but in virtue of his own purpose and the grace which he gave us in Christ Jesus ages ago, and now has manifested through the appearing of our Savior Christ Jesus, who abolished death and brought life and immortality to light through the gospel" (2 Tim

---

12. Rev 17:14a; see also Matt 2:2; Acts 17:7; Rev 19:16.

13. Mark 8:28 and par.; Matt 21:11; Luke 7:16; 24:19; John 4:19; 7:52. This title's churchly use may have been long delayed because the NT rarely makes direct reference to it (Luke 13:33; Acts 3:22). Weber, *Foundations of Dogmatics*, 2:171.

1:9–10, my emphases; see also Titus 2:13). "We have indeed seen and testify that the Father has sent the Son as the Savior of the world."[14]

Often the Savior concept is most emphasized where the term is not used: "Christ also died for sins once for all, the righteous for the unrighteous that he might bring us to God" (1 Pet 3:18). "Behold the Lamb of God, who takes away the sin of the world!" (John 1:29)

4. Once and For All

According to the NT, God's act of reconciliation in Jesus Christ was unique and unrepeatable.[15] If Christian Faith is to be true to its particularistic grounding it cannot syncretistically mix with other religions. Because of the Christian belief that through a unique history God has shared His very self, God's revelation in Christ differs from "revelations" affirmed in other religions, a few of which will be briefly compared here. Only Christian Faith seriously claims that God became a human being. Islam speaks of a once-and-for-all "revelation," but Muslims believe that what was manifested was only information *from* God, *not concerning His essential nature*.[16] They do not claim that God Himself came to earth or that He revealed His own being. In Islam, as in Traditional Religion, God forever remains transcendently hidden. Hinduism believes in divine "theophanies," but these are thought to recur by the thousands. Because there is no historical evidence that such events have occurred, such "theophanies" are only mythological ways of expressing speculative *ideas*. The historical character of such "events" is as doubtful as their theological content is dubious.[17]

5. Non-Participatory "Proof" Is Impossible

The non-participatory spectator demand *par excellence* is that Christians "prove" that Jesus Christ is God's unique revelation. This is an odd requirement, since no one can "prove" to others that they themselves exist, nor that the world does. At most, if one assumes that one's own self-consciousness is real, one may through Descartian deduction "prove" one's existence *to one's own satisfaction*. But why would anyone want to do this, unless trained to doubt the obvious, since everyone recognizes their own existence by the self-consciousness by which they begin the activity of proving? To "prove" (conclusively deduce) anything one must begin from some premise that cannot be proven, such as that the external world is real or that one's own self-consciousness is genuine. One "proves" an assertion by linking it to and showing its connection with a higher reality, that one already assumes. Christians would have an inferior "revelation" if its actuality needed to be proven or could be.[18]

---

14. 1 John 4:14; see also vs. 42; see also Eph 5:23.

15. Rom 6:10; 1 Pet 3:18; Heb 7:27; 9:12, 26–28; 10:10; cf. Heb 10:12, 14.

16. Certainly the Qur'an's first Surah refers to God as "Most Gracious, Most Merciful," but where are such divine qualities evidenced in the Qur'an? "In the "name of Allah" is the first phrase and what the Qur'an attests is Allah's no-questions-to-be-asked legal dictates. These as supposedly given to and written down by the illiterate Muhammed. See chap. 29, sec. 5.

17. Brunner, *Theology of Crisis*, 39.

18. Brunner, *Theology of Crisis*, 38.

The superior principle used for the testing would, in effect, be more ultimate than the revelation.

In this regard Brunner restates a famous Kierkegaardian analogy: "What manner of faith is the faith that must be propped up by proof? It would be something like a suitor who, on the point of asking the lady of his choice for her heart and hand, was to employ a detective to spy out her character. *Faith is the venture by which one trusts the truth of [an ultimate and divinely constraining Christian affirmation] not because one is courageous and tries it out for once,*[19] *but because one cannot do otherwise under [such] constraint.*"[20] Reason is useful for systematizing Christian Faith and for comparing it with other faiths, but has no power to generate ultimate norms.

Kierkegaard argued that one cannot prove that Jesus was God's unique revelation by contemplating the historical consequences of His life. This because one cannot deduce from historical affects a cause that is *qualitatively* greater, in this case one that is transcendently divine. To claim to be able to do so is both poor logic and bad theology. That Christianity has influenced the world positively can only demonstrate that Jesus was a great and important person, not that He was God Incarnate.

Concerning Jesus Christ's uniqueness what the NT offers is not proof, but signs, pointers, and invitations to believe. It speaks of His authority in the light of His deeds, but not in terms of mere logical deduction or inference. Certainly His actions point to whom He was and is—but a leap of faith is required if one is to follow the pointers toward Christ as one's Savior and Lord. If faith could be proven in disinterested ways all reasonably intelligent people would be Christians merely by virtue of being reasonably intelligent, but would not thereby be truly committed.

6. Jesus's Perfect Faithfulness or Sinlessness

A number of NT texts affirm that Jesus was completely faithful to the Father's will, and thereby remained sinless. "For we have not a high priest who is unable to sympathize with our weaknesses, but one who in every respect has been tempted as we are, yet without sinning" (Heb 4:15). "He committed no sin; no guile was found on his lips" (1 Pet 2:22). "You know that he appeared to take away sins, and in him there is no sin" (1 John 3:5).[21]

Though the NT concludes that Jesus was sinless, the Synoptic descriptions of His endeavors and even struggles to do God's will, as in Gethsemane (Luke 22:44), do not describe mock efforts. Hebrews 5:7–9 summarizes this reality of Jesus's life: "In the days of his flesh, Jesus offered up prayers and supplications, with loud cries and tears, to him who was able to save him from death, and he was heard for his godly fear. Although he was a Son, he learned obedience through what he suffered; and being made perfect he became

---

19. Faith is not in this sense a "leap."

20. Brunner, *Theology of Crisis*, 38–39, my emphasis. I have substituted "an ultimate and divinely constraining norm" and "such" for "a word," and "constraint of a word," the meanings of which are is unclear to me.

21. See also John 8:46; 2 Cor 5:21; Heb 5:9; 7:26; 1 Pet 1:19; 3:18.

the source of eternal salvation to all who obey him." "Because he himself has suffered and been tempted, he is able to help those who are tempted."[22]

But the question remains, "'Is a person who does not sin truly human?' If we say no, we are maintaining that sin is of the essence of human nature.... God would then be the cause of sin, the creator of a nature which is considerably evil. Inasmuch as we hold that, on the contrary, sin is not part of the essence of human nature, instead of asking, 'Is Jesus as human as we are?' we might better ask, 'Are we as human as Jesus?' ... Our humanity is not a standard by which we are to measure his. His humanity, true and unadulterated, is the standard by which we are to be measured."[23]

There are questions concerning Jesus's sinlessness. For example, was He sinless as a small boy? One may so assert, but it is hard to know what such sinlessness might have meant. And what about the tragic life-choices many Christians find themselves faced with, where in some circumstances the morally best seems to consist of some lesser evil? Did Jesus face similarly tragic situations, and if so, could He even as an adult have remained sinless? But perhaps our lesser evil analyses of ambiguous moral situations and the resulting moral compromises we make are necessitated only by our sinful lack of moral clarity. If so, then unlike us, Jesus, the Sinless One, would have perceived the one and only faithful course of action, and would never have had to choose what was only a lesser evil.

Another difficult issue is whether Jesus was by nature incapable of sinning, or whether He could have succumbed to temptation but did not do so. Barth has often been criticized for not taking the "from below" christological aspect seriously enough, but on this issue he emphasizes Jesus's humanity. He argues that Jesus was not, by virtue of the structure of His humanity, incapable of sinning; He could have sinned but did not. This is what Barth means by saying that Jesus assumed "fallen humanity," humanity capable of sinning. One NT text clearly supports this claim: "For God has done what the law, weakened by the flesh could not do; sending his own Son in the likeness *of sinful flesh* and for sin, he condemned sin in the flesh" (Rom 8:3, my emphasis). That Jesus was *"in every respect"* tempted like us (Heb 4:15) also seems to imply that Jesus received a human nature capable of sinning. Jesus confronted temptation as though it were possible for Him to give way to sin. However were the Fourth Gospel correct in saying that Jesus lived His daily life on the basis of a memory of His heavenly pre-existent experience, it is hard to conceive how His temptations could have been very tempting. Yet much of the NT describes His temptations as very real.[24]

This issue has much to do with whether in considering Jesus's *human* nature we think in functional categories—so that His being reflects the actualizing of His relationship with God—or whether we think of His human nature as in and of itself incapable of sinning.

---

22. Heb 2:18; see also Heb 4:15.

23. Erickson, *Christian Theology*, 721; this statement reflects Barth's viewpoint.

24. Because Schleiermacher regarded the Fourth Gospel as a relatively accurate source for knowledge of the Jesus of history, he did not think Jesus was subject to inner conflict or temptation (*Christian Faith*, 382–84, 413–16). The Fourth Gospel's opinion that Jesus had a memory of His pre-existent life seems a near equivalent to an Apollinarian-Monophysitic absorbing of Jesus's humanity into His divinity, which would also support an ontological incapacity on Jesus's part to sin (see chap. 9, sec. 7; see also John 3:11, 32; 5:19, 30; 12:49; 15:15; 17:8).

If Jesus were unable to sin, He began with a different human nature than we have, and the Apollinarian and Monophysitic Docetists were not wrong.[25]

In the following words Barth describes his actualistic, dynamic, Spirit-oriented view concerning Jesus's sinlessness: "'Without sin' means that . . . He *did not [not could not] sin*."[26] Barth quotes an 1827 writing by the Scottish theologian Edward Irving: "The point at issue is simply this, whether Christ's flesh had the grace of sinlessness and incorruption *from its own nature or from the indwelling of the Holy Ghost;* I say the latter."[27] If from His own nature Jesus were sinless why did He pray to the Father for guidance? According to the Synoptics Jesus clearly did so, but in the Fourth Gospel such obedience-seeking praying is far from obvious.

Though Berkhof accepts a primarily functional understanding of Jesus's sinlessness, he yet wonders whether such a functional christological view can be entirely separated from the ontological sinlessness whereby sinning would have been impossible for Jesus. Not impossible because He had received a sinless human nature, but because we suppose that thereby God's purposes would have been hampered.[28] Berkhof attempts to resolve the conflict between functional and ontological thinking through practical words that distinguish Jesus's human psychology from God's purposes in the Christ event. But these words do little to solve the theoretical problem. I, however, cannot improve upon these, and at this point take comfort from the recognition that our knowledge of God is most certainly imperfect (1 Cor 13:12). In answer to the question whether Jesus could have sinned, Berkhof writes, "In retrospect, in the light of the resurrection, this question may be answered in the negative. But Jesus did not know that in advance and he felt the full impact of the opposing forces. *He had no idea of his sinlessness on which he, encouraged by it, could fall back*. 'We have not a high priest who is unable to sympathize with our weaknesses, but one who in every respect has been tempted as we are, yet without sinning' (Hebrews 4:15)."[29] As those embedded in history we must reason from what has happened, not from what might have happened. Even if Jesus could have sinned, Christian Faith has good NT reason for believing He did not.

As an atonement implication, Jesus's sinlessness manifests the exchange whereby God in His Son offers Himself in place of us sinners. "In this sinlessness He is according to Paul the 'second Adam' (1 Cor 15:45ff.), the One who by His obedience sets the many before God as righteous."[30]

---

25. See chap. 9, sec. 2.
26. Barth, *CD* 4/2:92.
27. Barth, *CD* 1/2:154. See chap. 9, sec. 7, second paragraph.
28. Berkhof, *Christian Faith*, 297.
29. Berkhof, *Christian Faith*, 297, my emphases.
30. Barth, *CD* 1/2:157.

7. Jesus's Experience of God's Leading: A Christological Clue

The NT witness concerning Jesus's experience of God's leading *can provide a clue for understanding the relationship between His divine and human natures*. Jesus's experience of God can help us to penetrate beneath Chalcedonian assertions, but not beyond them. We cannot hereby account for the incarnation, which was due to God's decision to share His love. But Jesus's religious/moral experience can shed light on the spiritual process by which the Incarnate Son related to His heavenly Father.

All four Gospels speak a good deal of Jesus's God-consciousness (Schleiermacher), His relationship of dependence upon and obedience to the Father. Jesus claimed *no independent* authority or goodness. Once when addressed as "good Teacher" Jesus replied that only God is good (Mark 10:17–18). This passage is not saying that Jesus was unfaithful, but that His goodness came through personal dependence on God.[31]

The NT describes Jesus as a person of prayer, who through this means lived from God and subordinated His will to God's (Matt 26:39). Thereby sensitized to God's leading, He ministered unto others (Mark 10:45) and stooped to serve (John 13:1–11). Jesus did not seek His own glory (John 8:49b–50). His one desire was to do the will of God and to finish the work the Father had given Him to do (John 4:34; 14:31; 17:4).[32]

Jesus realized perfect union with God. Unlike us Jesus's God-consciousness was (as Schleiermacher said) uninterrupted, manifesting the true and faithful relationship with God. Barth agreed with Schleiermacher in insisting that Jesus did not have the Holy Spirit only in virtue of "an occasional, transitory, and partial bestowal," "but lastingly and totally."[33]

The Son who lived and acted in and from God has been raised from the dead and wills to draw us into relationship with Himself, which is relationship with God. As He does so, we, like Him, can turn aside from self-generated religious strength and find freedom through captivity. Though (unlike the Son) we are sinners, we too can find freedom for God through prayerful subordination of our wills to God's, but we require the Savior's mediation. God through Christ can provide the direction we cannot give ourselves. Thus Paul wrote, "I have been crucified with Christ; it is no longer I who live, but Christ who lives in me; and the life I now live in the flesh I live by faith in the Son of God, who loved me and gave himself for me" (Gal 2:20).

In Jesus's human relationship with God we see that, like us, Jesus had religious experiences, though not the sense of sinfulness and repentance. Jesus as the true covenant partner, the truly faithful one, and the one eternally chosen to be the Savior was in a class of His own. He differs from us not in degree, but in kind. Yet He had a human religious life that finds some parallel in our own, helping us to penetrate beneath Chalcedonian assertions, but not beyond them.[34]

---

31. Baillie, *God Was in Christ*, 125–26.
32. Barth, *CD* 4/1:164.
33. Barth, *CD* 3/2:334.
34. For the related discussion of modern degree Christology, see chap. 9, sec. 9.

8. The Lord Become Servant and the Servant as Revealing the Lord: A Critical and Constructive Conversation concerning Kenotic Christology[35]

One of the classical kenotic (self-emptying) motifs is Philippians 2:5–11.[36] Philippians 2:6 sounds as though the Eternal Son was a separate being from God, for it says that *the Son* "did not count equality with God a thing to be grasped, but emptied himself, taking the form of a servant." According to form critical analysis the Philippians 2:5–11 passage was originally an early Christian hymn, and certainly not a precise doctrinal statement. The language of the pre-existent Son emptying Himself of His equal heavenly glory to come forth to save us from our sin seems very inspiring. But its binary poetical language concerning divine self-emptying seems to imply that two separate entities composed the Godhead, briefly interrupted by the Son coming forth from the Father, but then returning to His previous position. There is no mention of the Holy Spirit, and no notion of divine unity.

The other highly significant *kenosis* passage is 2 Corinthians 8:9: "For you know the grace of our Lord *Jesus*, that though he was rich, yet for [our] sake he became poor, so that by his poverty [we] might become rich" (my emphasis). Highly problematic is this affirmation of the pre-existence of "*Jesus*." Surely Jesus as a human being did not exist until He was born as a human being.

I regard the Son of God and the Holy Spirit as aspects of God, but not as with the Father separate entities in the Godhead, as the poetic language of kenosis depicts in terms of Father and Son. I agree with the belief in the Son's human life and death as Jesus of Nazareth (2 Cor 8:9; Phil 2:7–9; 1 John 4:2; etc.), in the redemption that was accomplished by Christ through His ministry of self-emptying love, and appreciate the moral appeal of divine self-giving as motivating Christians to live lives of humble love.

Rewording the kenosis passages to be reflective of the entire triune God: The creativity and sinlessness of the divine realm—from which God distinguished Himself from Himself by coming forth to redeem humankind—contrasts much with the realm of sin and death, which God through the Son and the Holy Spirit willed to enter. The source and ultimate explanation of this free saving act of renunciation was the grace of the entire Godhead. Of particular interest in the 2 Corinthian passage is that Paul used the outreach of God in Christ to encourage gentile Christians to help the needy in the Jerusalem church (2 Cor 8:10–15).

A critically rethought *kenotic* understanding of God's action in Jesus Christ can also help link belief to practice. "The deity of the true God revealed in the humility of Christ . . . can and must find its confirmation in our own humility" (see Phil 2:3–4).[37] In response to the Lord become Servant, we are to come down from our thrones, take up our crosses and follow our Crucified and Risen Lord. For the sake of Christ we can and should be content with "weaknesses, insults, hardships, persecutions, calamities"—for when we are weak (in the sense of highly dependent on God)—then we are strong (2 Cor 12:9–10).

---

35. The discussion of kenotic Christology is placed here because it links directly to sec. 1 of the Triunity chapter that follows.

36. See also John 16:28; 17:5.

37. Barth, *CD* 4/1:192.

DOCTRINE OF GOD

Chapter 11

God's Triune Being and Revelation

Primarily Biblical Foundations

1. Interrelating Differences between Christology and Triunity

IN SEARCHING FOR THE most accurate words to reflect biblical meaning, the word "Trinity" and "triad" are not the best terms to use to refer to God. These words emphasize only God's inner and revelational threeness, and not also His oneness. The more accurate words to convey the meaning Scripture intends are the noun "*Triunity*" and the adjective "*triune*," since the first half of each of these words denotes threeness, and the second half, oneness. Such word usage governs my statements, but not quotations.

The Christological question "'who is Christ?' cannot be answered apart from the question 'what is the nature of the God who is revealed in Christ?'—that is, the question of [Triunity]."[1] In Church history "though Christology and the doctrine of the [Triunity] *have always influenced each other*, it is no accident that in the fourth century there was first a controversy about the doctrine of [Triunity] and only thereafter about Christology. The doctrine of the [Triunity] is *concerned with the question of the unity of God in the context of a faith that in the same breath asserts not only the divinity of the Father, but also that of the Son and of the Holy Spirit*. In contrast, Christology pertains to the question of the relation between that which is divine and that which is human in the person of Jesus Christ."[2]

2. Kenotic Biblical and Theological Linkage to Triunity

The two essential kenosis texts (2 Cor 8:9; Phil 2:5–11)[3] quoted and critically reformulated in the just previous Christology chapter (sec. 8) are in their reformulated understanding assumed here for the sake of the light they shed on Triunity. If the previous critical analysis

---

1. Welch, *In This Name*, 241.

2. Lohse, *A Short History of Christian Doctrine*, 71, my emphases.

3. See also John 17:5; Heb 2:17–18; 4:15. Also see Gal 2:20 and Eph 5:2, which refer to God's giving up of the Son.

is accepted we should affirm that it was *God* (not the pre-existent Son as a separable entity) who in self-emptying love "accommodated" Himself to meet us in the human form familiar to us. With loving sympathy God "willed to live a real human life, to know our condition . . . from within by passing through a real human experience. . . . He willed to restrain [some of] His divine attributes so as to render this possible."[4]

Though God was incarnate in Jesus, *Jesus, unlike God, was not omnipresent.*[5] Unlike God as Holy Spirit, the incarnate Son could only be at one place at a time. Everyone will surely concede this since it is implied by the fact that Jesus was human. But this is a major concession, for it demonstrates that the Son incarnate did not retain all the attributes of divinity.

Another divine attribute whose reality was qualified in Christ concerns *power*, the expression of which was restrained by Christ's finite this-worldly reality, God's power assuming "the form of weakness and impotence and doing so as [power] triumphing in this form."[6] Even the Eternal Father only has superior power not omnipotence, being restricted by His love and His allowance of human freedom.[7] Like His power, *God's knowingness has also often been exaggerated.*[8]

Most Christians will agree that as a human being the Son's knowledge was limited in comparison with the Father's, not that even the Father foreknows the results of human events before they occur. Christians disagree as to how limited the Son's knowledge was, which in part depends on how historically accurate or inaccurate you think the Fourth Gospel is. Mark 13:32 attests that Jesus did not know exactly when the consummation would occur and apparently expected that to happen within the generation of those *then living.*[9]

That God came into the far country of human existence is the mystery of Christ's *deity.*[10] To affirm that Jesus Christ is Truly God is to believe that God humbled Himself that we may come to know Him. In love God came forth in Christ to stand with us and to minister unto us and to begin to draw us back to Himself.

"God is not proud. In His high majesty He is humble. It is in His high humility that He speaks and acts as the God who reconciles the world to himself."[11] God took the cause of His creatures upon Himself because He did not want to exist unto Himself, but desired to be "God with us" (Matt 1:23b).

Though while in human form God abandoned some of the eternal attributes inconsistent with being human,[12] even here on earth God was Himself.[13] Emptying Himself of the form of godliness on the behalf of us creatures was a fitting expression of God's being as

4. Bicknell, *Thirty-Nine Articles*, 67.
5. See chap. 13, sec. 13 for the Spirit as Omnipresent.
6. Barth, *CD* 4/1:187.
7. See chap. 13, sec. 11 concerning God's power as being superior, but not unlimited.
8. See chap. 13, sec. 10 for discussion on this topic.
9. Also see Matt 24:29; Mark 9:1; 13:24–27, 30.
10. Barth, *CD* 4/1:177.
11. Barth, *CD* 4/1:159.
12. See chap. 13, secs. 10–11.
13. Barth, *CD* 4/2:180, 185.

love. "God is God as equally in the hiddenness of the servant form as in the fullness of His transcendent glory.... The divine self-emptying is the highest affirmation of the lordship of God. It is the affirmation that the realm of sinful humanity is not foreign to God."[14]

Barth corrected Kierkegaard's illustration of the king who to win a peasant maiden's love disguised Himself as a commoner.[15] Though Kierkegaard recognized that the eyes of faith are required for perceiving God in hidden form, Barth insisted that for such people *God's act of humility reveals, rather than obscures knowledge of His nature.* "God does not . . . dishonor Himself when He goes into the far country, and conceals His glory. . . . His concealment, and therefore His condescension as such, is the image and reflection in which we see Him as He is."[16] The transcendent, holy, majestic God is this loving, this self-giving, and this humble. The paradox is deeper than Kierkegaard thought—for *the high God is the low God of cruciform love. Such humble love shows the very essence of the divine heart*. Worldly concepts of authority and power must be abandoned to perceive the God whose love was revealed on the cross.

As for church historical articulation of the kenotic theme, this belief found its way into Protestant piety through the influence of Zinzendorf and his impact on John and Charles Wesley. For example, in Charles Wesley's "Hark, the Herald Angels Sing," Christ's coming is characterized as involving the Son's emptying of His divine glory.

> "Hail the heaven-born Prince of Peace!
> Hail the Sun of Righteousness! . . .
> Mild he lays his glory by,
> Born that men no more may die."

The same contrast is present in another Charles Wesley hymn:

> "He left his Father's home above
> So free, so infinite his grace,
> Emptied himself of all but love,
> And bled for Adam's helpless race."[17]

In the nineteenth century Dorner and Thomasius took up the cause of Kenotic Christology and contributed to a revolution concerning the doctrine of God and Christology. Dawe summarizes Thomasius as teaching that "the highest expression of the divine nature is its power of self-determination," and this "is most fully expressed in the self-limitation that made the incarnation possible."[18]

In the twentieth century P. T. Forsyth attested that God's highest power is his ability "to accept the limitation of a human life and [yet] not become unlike himself. If this limitation could not be accepted, then there would indeed be a limit on God's power, namely, the

---

14. Dawe, *Form of a Servant*, 165, referring to Barth's view.
15. Kierkegaard, *Philosophical Fragments*, 32–34.
16. Barth, *CD* 4/1:188, my emphasis.
17. Quoted in Dawe, *Form of a Servant*, 84–85.
18. Dawe, *Form of a Servant*, 95.

necessity of avoiding limitation.... His ability to accept freely and fully the limitations of human life is ... evidence of his divinity."[19]

3. God Can Distinguish Himself from Himself; God Hidden and Revealed, Veiled and Unveiled

Triunitarian thinking *affirms what the NT assumes and implies*, that God can distinguish Himself from Himself and yet remain one. God did not cease being God in Himself when truly manifest on earth. In His revelatory unveiling He remained God in His other form. "Am I a God at hand, says the Lord, and not [also] a God afar off?" (Jer 23:23) When the Son prayed to the Father He did so because God is capable of such relationality. That God in Christ can distinguish Himself from Himself presumes the divine differentiating decision that founded His disclosure in the Son.

God "in unimpaired unity yet also in unimpaired differentiation is the revealer, the revelation, and the revealedness"; "the revealing God, the event of revelation and [the source of] its effects on [humankind]."[20] We come to know God by reversing His journey from eternity into time. We begin with the Holy Spirit, are led to the Son, and from the cross of Calvary perceive the very heart of God.

The doctrine of Triunity clarifies and articulates the biblical understanding of the nature of God and how we come to know God. The Presbyterian Church of Canada summarizes both aspects in a clever threesome that relates each of the three aspects of God's triune nature to soteriological effects, though I would add that all saving effects relate to the one triune God. "God is the Father *to whom we come*, the Son, *through whom we come*, and the Spirit *by whom we come*."[21] The post-NT church did not invent this doctrine, but used the language at its disposal (as similarly we must) to interpret what the NT teaches about God's self-communicating and the God known thereby.

4. The Father as Originator of Son's and Spirit's Work and as Creator

If theologians are interested in the Jesus of history issue to the point of integrating such findings into systematics, as I attempt to do, they will look at Christology, Triunity, and much else differently than those who have no such concern. In particular, that Jesus was simply God walking around on earth will not seem convincing. Yet Jesus was God's unique disclosure; God especially inspired Jesus and Jesus faithfully responded.

Because systematics necessarily wrestles with complex beliefs, it may give the impression that Triunity is extremely complicated. But many aspects of Triunity are not hard to understand, and mainly concern the revelational facet, and the insistence that God is in Himself as He is in His revelation. God is the Father because He willed to reveal Himself

---

19. Dawe, *Form of a Servant*, 36–37, quoting P. T. Forsyth, *God the Holy Father*, 33. Dawe says "the evidence," but this seems to me to be an overstatement.

20. Barth, *CD* 1/1:339, 343.

21. Presbyterian Church of Canada, *Living Faith*, Article 1.5, pages 5–6, my emphases.

in the Son, and Jesus is the Son because He is the revelation of the Father. And we know these things by the power of God's Spirit. *The Father is truly known in the Son by the Spirit.*

God's decision to create and to eventually have fellowship with humans underlies the eternal beginnings of Triunity.[22] Deciding for the covenant of grace preceded creation, and formed the reason why the universe's beginning occurred and the world began to evolve.

"We know now that older traditions of creation lie behind the two creation stories (P: Gen 1:1–2:4a; J: Gen 2:4b–25)" and that "Creation is the preamble of and pointer to salvation." "Barth introduced such changed perspective with his twofold thesis: 'Creation is the external basis of the covenant—the covenant is the internal basis of creation (*CD, 3/1*).'"[23] The world was created in anticipation of the results of the Son's coming and exaltation.

5. Fourth Gospel Threesome Language Is Not Triunitarian

Though a separate decision-making being, Jesus by God's design and by Jesus's faithful discipleship was the very presence of God. However the Fourth Gospel offers a good deal of dialogue between the Eternal Son and Father that sounds substantialistic, seeming to attest that within God's eternal being, Father and Son were and are separate beings. God as a small committee! This criticism seems to stand for much Fourth Gospel language.[24]

6. The Father Truly Known Only in the Son

With the exceptions noted in the previous footnote "the apprehension of the divinity of Christ in the New Testament . . . is precisely an apprehension of him as the revelation of God beyond. The divinity of Christ is therefore not a problem to be reconciled with an accepted monotheism, but an affirmation and explication of monotheism through God's revelation of himself."[25] Jesus "makes it quite clear that the unity which binds Him to God is one of dependence. He seeks only to obey God and conceives of His own work as an act of obedience to God (Matt 26:39; cf. Phil 2:8). [At one point He even] refuses to allow Himself to be called good, since this designation belongs only to the One God (Mark 10:18)"[26]

---

22. Barth, *CD* 2/1:263.

23. Berkhof, *Christian Faith*, 167, 168. See chap. 15 below, "God's Creation Purpose for Humans (Covenant and Creation)," for a fuller discussion of this paragraph's perspective.

24. That the Father sends the Son (6:29; 10:36; 11:42; 17:3, 8, 25) assumes the preexistence of the Son in the Godhead and sounds as though Father and Son have separate divine identity. Also the Son is not only seen as having personally pre-existed (1:1–11, 15, 30; 8:58; 17:5, 24), but on earth is described as having had a memory of His pre-existent personal life and of what the Father had said to Him (3:11, 32; 5:19, 30; 8:26, 28, 38, 40; 12:49; 15:15; 17:8).

25. Welch, *In This Name*, 231.

26. Mehl, "God, NT," 148.

7. By the Spirit

Knowledge of the Father through the Son is possible *only* by God's convincing, not by rational assent to christological or triunitarian doctrines. Neither the Son as the way to the Father, nor the Father Himself have meaning to us unless the Holy Spirit opens our eyes to behold God's glory hidden in the suffering and rejected man of Calvary. Were our knowledge of God *not* inspired by God as Holy Spirit, God would be a mere object of rational cognition, not the Living Subject.[27] To the contrary, through the Holy Spirit, Christ for us becomes Christ in us,[28] and thereby we learn of God. Our inner experience of forgiveness is an imperfect sharing in that forgiveness established once-and-for-all on Calvary. The Spirit opens our blinded eyes so we behold the Son and thereby experience our Father's love.

8. The Spirit of God and of Christ Truly Divine

Since the Spirit is truly divine, yet no separate God, belief in the Spirit (like belief in the Son) also implies that God can differentiate Himself from Himself and yet remain one. The NT speaks of the Holy Spirit not only as the Spirit of God, but also as the Spirit of *Christ*.[29] The Holy Spirit not only leads to Christ, but is the continuing presence of Christ. "God has sent *the Spirit of his Son* into our hearts, crying, 'Abba! Father!'" (Gal 4:6b, my emphasis)

9. Post-Resurrection Understanding that in Jesus God Has Come among Us[30]

Though God is truly known in Christ there is much about God we do not understand for we are both finite and sinful. Nevertheless, if we are to be faithful to the NT we must insist that He whom we see in Christ is really God. "The reality of God in His revelation is not to be bracketed with an 'only,' as though somewhere behind His revelation there stood another reality of God, but the reality of God which meets us in revelation is His reality in all the depths of eternity."[31]

The most important evidence concerning the belief in the deity of Jesus Christ is that He was raised from the dead and disclosed to chosen witnesses.[32] Some of the Pauline writings, the Fourth Gospel and Hebrews go further, regarding creation and providence as through the Son, though this requires a very substantialistic understanding of the Son prior to the Incarnation. "He is the image of the invisible God. . . . All things were created through him and for him. He is before all things, and in him all things hold together."[33] "He

---

27. Barth, *CD* 1/1:358, 346, 447–48, 468.

28. Gal 2:20; 4:19; Col 1:27.

29. Rom 8:9; 2 Cor 3:17; Phil 1:19.

30. See chap. 8, sec. 3 for additional post-resurrection Son of God usage, and chap. 7, sec. 3 for Jesus's possible employment of this title.

31. Barth, *CD* 1/1:548.

32. On the meaning of Jesus's resurrection, see chapters. 3–4.

33. Col 1:15a, 16c, 17; see also John 1:3; 1 Cor 8:6; Heb 1:2c.

reflects the glory of God and bears the very stamp of his nature, upholding the universe by his word of power" (Heb 1:3).

The Fourth Gospel's affirmation of *Jesus's* divinity is repetitiously explicit.[34] According to its narrative form of post-resurrection churchly reinterpretation, Thomas is said to have confessed his faith *in Jesus just risen* by saying "My Lord and my God" (John 20:28). Without rejecting Thomas's supposed sight-related faith, that Gospel also says, "Blessed are those who have not seen and yet believe" (20:29b).

Thomas's confession of the deity of the Risen Lord comes as the climax to the Fourth Gospel (20:28), but Christ's deity is there attested numerous times previously, though also likely as post-resurrection reinterpretations. The opening lines of that Gospel speak of the Word/Son as God's decision for creation and revelation. "In the beginning was the Word, and the Word was with God, and the Word was *God*. He was in the beginning with God; all things were made through him, and without him was not anything made that was made. . . . And the Word became flesh and dwelt among us, full of grace and truth; we have beheld his glory, glory as of the only Son from the Father. . . . No one has ever seen God; the only Son, who was in the bosom of the Father, he has made him known" (1:1–3, 14, 18).

The Fourth Gospel is more explicit about Jesus Christ's deity than are the others, but those to lesser extents also attest such post-resurrection reinterpretations. At its beginning Matthew's Gospel says that the One who will be born of Mary will be called "Emman'u-el (which means, God with us)" (Matt 1:23b). Similarly, Mark's Gospel commences with these words: "The beginning of the gospel of Jesus Christ, the Son of God" (Mark 1:1). All of the Gospels are Gospels because they proclaim the Good News that in Jesus Christ God has come among us for our salvation.

10. Father, Son, and Spirit

Another clear biblical evidence of our triune Faith is that in several places the NT speaks of the Son and the Spirit in the same context where it refers to God, attesting that Son and Spirit are also divine. "The grace of *the Lord Jesus Christ* and the love of *God* and the fellowship of the *Holy Spirit* be with you all" (2 Cor 13:14, my emphases). "Now there are varieties of gifts, but the same *Spirit*; and there are varieties of service, but the same *Lord*; and there are varieties of workings, but it is the same *God* who inspired them all in every one" (1 Cor 12:4, my emphases). Likewise the author of 1 Peter says that Christians are "chosen and destined by *God the Father* and sanctified by *the Spirit* for obedience to *Jesus Christ*" (1:2, my emphases). The conclusion of Matthew's Gospel commands that we "go therefore and make disciples of all nations, baptizing them in the name of the *Father* and of the *Son* and of the *Holy Spirit*."[35] Paul [spoke] of his own ministry in terms of "the grace given me by *God* to be a minister of *Christ Jesus* to the Gentiles in the priestly service of *God*, so that the offering of the Gentiles may be acceptable, sanctified by the *Holy Spirit*" (Rom 15:16, my emphases).

---

34. See also 1 John 5:20.
35. Matt 28:19, my emphases; see also Gal 1:1–2.

11. Necessity of Triunity Doctrine: God's Revelation of His Very Self

The NT affirms the divinity of God, of Christ, and of the Spirit who leads people to Christ and thus to God, and yet believes there is only one God. It thus implies a belief in God as triune and in the triune way of coming to know Him. If one thinks there is more than one God one avoids the Triunity problem, but at a high cost: The resultant polytheism implies the existence of self-directing and conflicting gods here below and perhaps above. The religious result is uncertainty concerning the nature of ultimate reality, divided moral allegiance, and doubt pertaining to salvation.

12. Triunitarian Recognition of Oneness of the Revealed God and Resultant De-divinizing of World

If *anti-triunitarian thought* affirms NT biblical revelation without recognizing the Son's and Spirit's equal nature with the Father, God could differ from His supposed revelation. Thus the oneness or unity of God would be called into question. Or if *anti-triunitarian thought* only affirms the oneness or unity of God, revelation as attesting the unique and particular actions of God in history and in our lives becomes doubtful. *All anti-triunitarian thought either ends up denying the oneness of God or God's revelation in Christ as known by the Spirit.*[36]

In NT times and today, truly to acknowledge the one true God involves de-divinizing the world, and leads to "the twilight of the gods." It is not surprising that the early Christians were accused of being atheists, this because they not only did not believe in the gods most people worshipped, but because they refused to look to such sources for moral guidance. A Christian monotheism that focuses upon the God disclosed in Jesus Christ is able to challenge such idolatry as was exhibited with the veneration of Adolf Hitler and Chairman Mao, and as similarly occurs today in many countries. From the Christian perspective "everything depends on God not only being recognized as the One who is unique, but . . . on the . . . trust, honor and service, which are His due, being given to Him as the only One to whom they can possibly apply."[37]

13. Highly Metaphorical Language Required for Referring to God's Inner Being; Time and Space within Eternal Dimension

As we move toward more closely examining the church's post-NT doctrine of Triunity, we should remember that language is inherently metaphorical. Though Christian beliefs should be determined by God's disclosure in Christ, the Bible had to utilize terms that in non-theological contexts carried somewhat differing meanings. The authors had to redefine and reemploy everyday usage. Since language is an imperfect instrument, and since word meanings continue to change, the church must ever anew examine its theological language to see if it communicates intended meaning.

---

36. Barth, *CD* 1/1:404.
37. Barth, *CD* 2/1:445.

Especially when seeking to describe God's inner being, our expressions will be highly imperfect. Though God has revealed essential aspects of His self, as for example His loving will, there is much about God's inner reality that we cannot conceive. Though God has disclosed Himself in time and now interacts with temporal beings, what does time mean for God in His eternal dimension and what will it mean for us? We don't know. And concerning God and our own eventual existence, what is the meaning of space in the eternal realm? In 1 Corinthians 15:40, 44–56 Paul stretches human language to the breaking point by writing of our future selves as "spiritual bodies." This phrase surely connotes separate entity existence in fellowship with God and others, but we can only imagine what else will be entailed in the dimension beyond this universe.

Primarily Post-Biblical Theological Contributions

14. God's Eternal Decision

The event whereby God became triune was apparently His decision to share His love. *Triunity is from eternity in that God's decision to create and to share was prior to His action in so doing.* "The entire triunitarian event is grounded in God's eternal determination to be a God of blessing . . . In his sovereign love God has made himself changeable. Together with us he is involved in a process, which also does something to him because as Father it enriches him with sons and daughters."[38]

God's decision to create and to share His life is consistent with His nature as love, but was not required by that. It was a free decision. In pondering the triunness of God's eternal being we should think of the pre-history in which God resolved to share Himself with those who would be other than Himself. The Son and the Holy Spirit may be said to have pre-existed as God's decision to reveal Himself by these means. Such eternal resolve may be "the mystery hidden for ages and generations" (Col 1:26; see also 1:15), and "the destining of the Son before the foundation of the world" (1 Pet 1:20).

15. Modes of Inner Relationship and Modes of Revelation

Tertullian did not advocate a "social" understanding of Triunity, one that asserts that there are three self-conscious personalities in the godhead. He believed that God is one, but is uniquely revealed in the Son and recognized by the power of the Spirit. To Tertullian a *persona* is a mode of divine being and of revelation, not an individual being with a rational nature. In speaking of God as existing in three "modes of one being" and in three "modes of revelation" we are not referring to three divine "I's,"[39] but to the one divine "I," who came to have threefold quality and is threefold in revelation. More specifically, the eternal Son may be God's willingness to come among us in history and the eternal Spirit may be God's determination to be uniquely present in Jesus's life, and more generally in the lives of others.

---

38. Berkhof, *Christian Faith*, 337.
39. Barth, *CD* 1/1:403.

Since God came forth for our salvation, the original and final will of God for His creation was in considerable part that He would be for humankind. When God reconciled us in Christ He remained faithful to His plan and purpose in creating us for fellowship with Himself and one another.

16. Distinctions and Interrelationships between Various Modes That Become Apparent in Revelation

Neither the Father nor the Spirit lived as a human being in history, though God came forth in the Son, and the Spirit sustained the Son in His work. (Jesus prayed to the Father through the Spirit.) Though God as Father and as Spirit suffered in the Son's sufferings, only the Son was crucified and died. The Son did not raise Himself;[40] the Father raised Him by the power of the Spirit. Because sanctification is primarily (though not exclusively) the work of the Spirit, neither Father nor Son were poured out at Pentecost. Yet the Spirit of the Risen Christ leads us to the Father.

17. Indivisibility of the Work of Father, Son, and Spirit

From the time of John of Damascus the church insisted that God's various modes interrelate, so that triplicity should never encroach upon divine unity.[41] To make this point the church showed the biblical basis of *"indivisibility"* and *"interpenetration"*: Scripture ascribes the Father's creational work also to the Son (John 1:1-4; Heb 1:2; Col 1:16) and to the Spirit (Gen 1:2), but this understanding does not square with much of the NT.[42] However, the NT convincingly attributes the instigating of the Son's reconciling and redemptive activity to the Father (e.g., 2 Cor 5:18-19) but less convincingly to the Spirit of God (cf., e.g., Eph 2:16, 18). Convincingly the NT also refers to the Father (e.g., 1 Thess 5:23), the Son (e.g., John 17:19; Eph 5:26; Heb 10:10), and the Spirit (2 Thess 2:13; 1 Pet 1:2) when speaking of God's reconciling work.[43]

18. Triunity and the Certainty of Salvation

In the fourth-century debates about Triunity Athanasius and the Latin West resolutely held out against any compromising concerning the principle that *God alone*, and no created being *can save from sin and death*. They so insisted because they believed that otherwise salvation and its certainty would be jeopardized.

---

40. At least not according to the Synoptics, but see John 10:18.

41. Weber, *Foundations of Dogmatics*, 1:390.

42. See sec. 5 above. I here requote a note from that section to once again raise the problem expressed there. That the Father sends the Son (6:29; 10:36; 11:42; 17:3, 8, 25) assumes the preexistence of the Son in the Godhead and sounds as though Father and Son have separate divine identity. Also the Son is not only seen as having personally pre-existed (1:1-11, 15, 30; 8:58; 17:5, 24), but on earth is described as having had a memory of His pre-existent personal life and of what the Father had said to Him (3:11, 32; 5:19, 30; 8:26, 28, 38, 40; 12:49; 15:15; 17:8).

43. Weber, *Foundations of Dogmatics*, 1:393.

As for the christological aspect of this theocentric affirmation, only if the Father's suffering love is reflected in Christ's nail pierced hands do we have reason for the assurance that in life and death we are in the hands of divine love. Had Christ been a mere prophet or religious genius we could not have sure and certain confidence that *God* has forgiven us. If Jesus were only human, we would have only a human word and not *the Word from God Himself*. We know that God is for us—rather than against us or indifferent—because God as Holy Spirit has convinced us that *He* really was in Christ reconciling the world *to Himself*. Had one less than God been present in Christ or had we, rather than the Holy Spirit, convinced ourselves of God's disclosure in Christ, our salvation would be insecure, because not divinely founded.

19. Avoiding One-Sided Theologies of Triune Modes

Triunitarian thinking seeks to help people to avoid focusing only on Father, or only on Son, or only on Spirit. (A) In contrast the religion of the Father assumes the possibility of the Christian worship of God apart from the coming of God in Christ and the presence of the Spirit. Against this, that God is Father means that He is first of all the Father of our Lord Jesus Christ, and through the Spirit's activity of drawing us to Christ has become our Father.[44] Furthermore, what the Father as Creator and Providential Lord is doing in general history cannot be known by natural reasoning, but only through Spirit-guided alertness informed by the Father's disclosure in the Son as known through the Spirit.

(B) Triunitarianism also seeks to avoid abstract christo-monism as, for example, results when we claim to obtain rationalistic or even biblically rationalistic "knowledge" of Christ in isolation from the Spirit's leading. or when our "relationship" with Christ does not lead to responsible service in our Father's world. "The religion of the Son fails to see that Christ is the center of the New Testament witness only as the revelation of One who has come forth in him, and that only in the Spirit do we through him have access to the Father."[45]

(C) Finally, triunitarian thought seeks to avoid a lop-sided emphasis on the Spirit that so focuses on religious feelings that it ignores the doctrinal and moral guidance disclosed in the Son. Sole emphasis on the Spirit also leads to inactive service in our Father's world. "The religion of the Spirit becomes only a deification of the human spirit, of who is possessed rather than the One who possesses, unless the Spirit is recognized as the Spirit of Christ and of God the Father of Christ." "The doctrine of the Trinity means that our affirmations about God as Father, Son and Spirit are inseparable and interdependent."[46]

20. Moral Implications

A particular understanding of the Christian moral life is consistent with a commitment to a triune conception of God. Those in the early Trinity debates who denied the doctrine

---

44. Welch, *In This Name*, 228.
45. Ibid., 228.
46. Ibid., 228–29, 240.

were optimistic about human nature and confident that we of ourselves, unaided by revelation, can discover and perform the good that is pleasing to God. The triunitarians were skeptical concerning such natural abilities, and insisted that we can gain moral clarity only by focusing on Christ and allowing Him to define the good. They also said that we sinners need the Holy Spirit to move us more deeply than historical focus alone can provide, and to empower us to do the good.

Anti-triunitarian cultural Christians believe that with a dash of Christianity and by following worldly trends, human philosophies, and the political and social conventions of the nations in which we live, we can lead lives pleasing to God. To the contrary, triunitarians affirmed that because we owe allegiance to the Transcendent Father revealed in the Son and known by the Spirit, our presence in the world must involve many critical aspects. This because Christ was not only "truly God," but was also the True Person, the ideal by whom God measures and judges our lives. Christ—not the cultures in which we live—is to be our standard. If we are faithful triunitarians our lives will become *more difficult*. Like our Lord, we will be *in*, but not *of* the world and will not fit in comfortably in the societies in which we live or in those churches that have been swept along by various cultural trends.

21. A Critique of Feminist Critique of Triunity

Concerning "female imagery of the Spirit we begin by noting that the word for Spirit is feminine in Hebrew (*ruach*), although it is neuter in Greek (*pneuma*) and masculine in Latin (*spiritus*). . . . Even so, the triune God is not "a divine company composed of two males and one female. That the triune God is also called Spirit teaches us to think and speak of God as uniquely personal, allowing gender-specific imagery, yet far transcending all such imagery."[47]

Scripture offers much support for feminist concerns for justice and equality. However I do not agree with those feminists who think that the Bible regards God as male,[48] and who think that therefore the references to God as Father[49] imply belief in God's maleness.[50] Scripture does not regard God as a sexual being, whether male or female. The male and female analogies the Bible uses to refer to God are merely that. Furthermore, the NT does not regard as of essential importance that God's incarnation occurred in a male. What

---

47. Migliore, *Faith Seeking Understanding*, 173–74, 174.

48. To an extent the OT avoided the use of images linked with motherhood because those were associated with the Baal fertility religion and temple prostitution. Today such analogies do not carry those connotations and thus need not be avoided.

49. Jesus based His understanding of divine fatherhood on His relationship with God, and was not unaware of the faults of earthly fathers and mothers, brothers and sisters. His mother and His brothers had been unsympathetic regarding His ministry, and in criticism of them He said that "whoever does the will of my Father in heaven [Matt] or God [Luke] is my brother, and sister, and mother" (Matt 12:46–50; Mark 3:31–35).

50. The father symbolizes God in the parable of the prodigal son (Luke 15:16–32), but in the parable of the lost coin a woman does so (Luke 15:8–10). Concerning creation the Spirit (feminine) is said to have brooded upon the face of the deep (Gen 1:2). We should strive to avoid sexism and cultural stereotyping. Judging should not be regarded as only a masculine activity, or comforting as only a feminine role. A fully human life as the "fruit of the Spirit" should not be stereotyped into supposed male and female activities (Gal 5:22–23) (Dawe, "The Divinity of the Holy Spirit," 27–28).

the NT and the later creeds emphasize is that God became a human who fully interacted within and greatly influenced human history. Christ's triune name "Son," while recognizing Jesus's maleness, stresses His humanity—not His maleness.[51]

22. Eschatology and Triunity

We read that "when all things are subjected to him [the Son], then the Son himself will be subjected to him who put all things under him, that God may be everything to everyone (1 Cor 15:28). Seemingly to the contrary, Ephesians 1:20–23 and Colossians 1:15–20 affirm that *Christ's* kingship is eternal, and Philippians 2:10 supposes that within the consummated kingdom "every knee shall bow, in heaven and on earth and under the earth, and every tongue confess that *Jesus Christ is Lord to the glory of God the Father*" (Phil 2:10). That Paul wrote 1 Corinthians and Philippians and highly inspired the authors of Colossian and Ephesian indicates that these lines of evidence are unlikely to be truly incompatible.

In reality the Son never had any other purpose than to be instrumental in reconciling humans to the Father. When God achieves what He sought in the mediator, no more mediation will be necessary. If (as most of the above passages attest) the Son continues to be honored in a somewhat separable sense from the Father, that may merely mean that all that God sought to accomplish in the Son will be recognized and honored. *God will bring His purposes manifested in the Son to fulfillment, and the Son will forever behold this wondrous result.*

Christ will forever share in the eternal victory that was achieved through His mediatorial activity on God's behalf. In the eternal realm Jesus as risen surely stands on the human and divine and sides, or put somewhat differently, *Jesus's humanity has become an aspect of the godhead.*

---

51. Wainwright, "The Doctrine of the Trinity," 118–20. Though the point of the incarnation is not that God became *male* flesh, it is a matter of historical fact that Jesus was a male. It is thus historically inaccurate to refer to Him with pronouns connoting the female gender.

Chapter 12

God's Revealed Transcendence

1. An Exposition and Critique of Natural Theology's Presumption That We Can Know God Apart from Revelation in Christ

OVER MANY CENTURIES NATURAL theology distorted the "Christian" doctrine of God. This occurred because many Christian thinkers believed that only the Son and Holy Spirit articles of the Apostles' and Nicene creeds require a revelational basis and a faith response.

Many Christian thinkers were content to regard God as the unmoved prime mover, the ground of everything, the true being,[1] the goal toward which everything tends, and the source of cosmic harmony. These same people also assumed that Judaism, Islam, the other world religions, and various religious philosophies attest the understanding of God to which Christians are committed.[2]

Medieval scholasticism used three speculative methods to deduce the attributes of God. Firstly, the *causality* method involved investigating the world and then imputing to God the qualities that would be necessary to bring about such observed effects; this based on the uncritical assumption that God is absolutely omnipotent. Employing this method, since sin and natural disasters exist God may not be regarded as a loving being. Secondly, the method of *eminence* took what natural reason presumed are positive human qualities and applied them in superlative form to God. On the basis of such speculation, natural reason concluded that God is absolutely omnipotent, in all respects free, all-knowing, and able to foresee what events will occur. Thirdly, the *negation* procedure removed from the idea of God all conceptions that natural reason regarded as reflecting human imperfection, and ascribed their opposites to God: We change and develop, can be understood, are finite, and have feelings. The deduction: God is *un*changing (*im*mutable), *in*comprehensible, *in*finite, and *im*passible (without feelings).

---

1. Patristic and later mediating theologians relied on the Greek philosophical use of "being" to understand God. Because that approach made it seem that what is definitive concerning God is His eternal self-existence, it viewed revelatory action as strange or extraneous to God (Dawe, *Form of a Servant*, 167–68).

2. Weber, *Foundations of Dogmatics*, 1:397.

GOD'S REVEALED TRANSCENDENCE

All three of these speculative methods are faulty. Firstly, since according to Christian Faith the world's Creator does not control all that occurs in the world, a god deduced from worldly effects (*causality procedure*) is a fiction of human imagination.

Secondly, since God is qualitatively distinct from humankind He is not natural reason's superlative projection of humankind at its best (*eminence method*). God does not differ from us only in degree, but in kind.

Thirdly, the *negation* procedure removed from the idea of God all conceptions that natural reason is supposed to regard as reflecting human imperfection, and ascribed their opposites to God. We change and develop, can be understood, are finite and have feelings. The deduction: God is *un*changing (*im*utable), incomprehensible, *in*finite, and *im*passible (incapable of having feelings). To the contrary God cannot be known by negating mere human qualities. God is of a different dimension from us, as, for example, sound differs from sight, and a three dimensional figure from a two dimensional one.[3]

The Belgic Confession (1561) combines the last two natural theology methods, with results that conflict considerably with what can be said on the basis of biblical revelation. Following the *eminence method* God is thought to be "infinite, almighty, perfectly wise and just, and the overflowing fountain of all good." To the contrary, though God has the power to accomplish His good purposes, God is neither all controlling (almighty) nor well defined by the label "infinite." He is indeed "perfectly wise and just, and the overflowing fountain of all good." Following the *negation method* this confession attests that God is "invisible," "incomprehensible," and "immutable." God certainly can work in invisible ways, as through the Holy Spirit, but we know nothing of God's visibility or invisibility within His eternal dimension. And the Bible contradicts the Belgic Confession philosophical claim that God is "incomprehensible and immutable," the former implying that we cannot know anything concerning Him, and the latter denying the divine mutability seen in the Bible. The philosophically determined qualities in this confession suggest little divine relationship with us, and thus the attraction of such a "god": He leaves us undisturbed!

Since human sinfulness distorts the natural perception of God, it is methodologically naive and misguided to suppose that the qualities of God's being can be known through creation or through philosophical speculation. Since God has revealed Himself in Christ, we are ungrateful if we look elsewhere for knowledge of God.

In contrast to natural theology methods, God shows His attributes in His self-revelation in Jesus Christ, so that what He does demonstrates who He is. "Our first and decisive transcription of the statement that God is, must be that God is who He is in the act of His revelation."[4] "What God is in revelation He is antecedently in Himself."[5] "In revelation we do not have a random slice from the circle of God's essence, but a section, a piece that reaches the very center."[6] From that disclosure we learn of God's love and His reconciling and redemptive will.

---

3. Erickson, *Christian Theology*, 316.
4. Barth, *CD* 2/1:262.
5. Barth, *CD* 1/1:466.
6. Berkhof, *Christian Faith*, 106.

2. Otherness and Nearness of Living God

There can be no personal relationship with the God revealed in Christ unless He is sharply distinguished from us, and His will from ours; otherwise we end up conversing with ourselves. In Christian faith, unlike mysticism, there can be no blurring of the distinction between the Holy God and us sinners, the creator and the created, the redeemer and the redeemed. God is our master and we—though His friends—are His disciples. Were God merely the hidden depths of our own being, He could not empower us to struggle against our selfishness. That Christians live "in Christ," and "in the Spirit" must not blind us to the ongoing qualitative difference between God and us.[7]

God's radical otherness from and yet nearness to His covenant people is recognized when the OT speaks of the *Holy One of Israel*. "For my thoughts are not your thoughts, neither are your ways my ways, says the Lord. For as the heavens are higher than the earth, so are my ways higher than your ways and my thoughts than your thoughts" (Isa 55:8-9). "For thus says the high and lofty One who inhabits eternity, whose name is Holy: 'I dwell in the high and holy place, and also with him who is of a contrite and humble spirit, to revive the spirit of the humble and to revive the heart of the contrite'" (Isa 57:15).

The Lord's Prayer emphasizes both God's nearness and otherness. The God who invites and enables us to pray is so near that His adopted children are to address Him as "Abba," Father, Daddy. Yet this God of intimate love is precisely the One who dwells in a world that transcends the created universe. God is near us and with us, and yet is above and beyond and different from us. He is eternal and we are temporal, He is holy and we are sinners; yet He came among us in Christ and remains with us as our guiding Spirit.

3. God as Personal, Self-Giving, with Genuine Agency Capacity

The Bible attests that God is personal and that an authentic relationship with Him must be personal. In speaking of God as spirit (John 4:24) and in using personal terms to refer to God (such as father, friend, and savior) Scripture guards against confusing God with an abstract idea, a force of nature, or structure of this world. God is a living reality, who acts independently and speaks freely, much in contrast with gods or idols that have no life (Jer 10:14; Acts 14:15).[8]

Scripture frequently likens God's love to that of a "father" and all too occasionally to that of a "mother" (e.g., Isa 49:15; 66:13). Though God's love far exceeds such comparisons, the Bible regards such human analogies as useful if informed and corrected by revelation. The self-giving love shown in Jesus can also be compared with that of a friend (John 15:13), but as love even for those who are enemies, it far exceeds the friendship analogy (Rom 5:7-11). The prophets like to compare God's love to that of a man for his wife, but because of the continual unfaithfulness of this wife, Israel, God's love also transcends this analogy (Jer 3; Ezek 16, 23; Hos 1-3).[9]

---

7. Barth, *CD* 1/1:528.
8. Barth, *Gottingen Dogmatics*, 401.
9. Berkhof, *Christian Faith*, 120.

God has true agency capacity, the ability to realize purposes through decision-making and action. Our decision-making capacities are more dependent on others and on the world. God's limitations are either manifestations of His nature or are self-imposed.[10] Unlike God, we sinners often treat others in dehumanizing and impersonal ways—as mere "its." Yet the personal and personalizing God can renew us, so that we live truly personal lives in dialogue with God and with others.[11]

God is the Free Agent whom we cannot manipulate for our own ends. Though no terminology perfectly fits, Scripture demonstrates that "he/she words" of personal agency are analogically adequate for referring to God, whereas "it words" are less apt. The Bible repeatedly shows that God has self-consciousness, subjecthood, and the capacity to enter into relationships. Though infinitely surpassing what we humans realize as personhood, God is certainly personal.

Instead of using action-centered personal words, many philosophers and philosophically influenced theologians prefer abstract terminology, and thus call God "Being Itself," the "Ground of Being," or the "Highest Being."[12] Or they use the language of moral abstraction, referring to God as the "Highest Good." These terms are no less analogical than are those used by Scripture, and are less helpful, since they imply that God is an impersonal abstraction, whom we come to know in intellectual ways largely divorced from moral and religious experience.

Unlike classical mysticism and much eastern religion, Christian Faith regards what is personal as higher than what is impersonal. Scriptural evidence that God is the Personal Agent is abundant.[13] The Bible attests that God has mind, will, and feelings, and is able to act and to express purpose.[14] God loves[15] and can be jealous (Exod 20:5; Deut 32:16) and grieved (Gen 6:6; Isa 63:10). God can get angry (John 3:36; Rev 14:10) and show pity and mercy (Isa 60:10; Jas 5:11).[16]

Because God is personal, relationship with Him involves warmth and understanding. "God is not a bureau or a department; he is not a machine or a computer. . . . He is a living, reciprocating being. . . . The idea that God is simply something to be used or something that [merely] solves our problems and meets our needs is not [reflective of the Christian] religion. Such attempts to harness him belong, rather, to the realm of magic or technology."[17]

10. See chap. 13.

11. Berkhof, *Christian Faith*, 131.

12. Though the Bible regards God as personal, many religions and some types of "Christian" thinking do not. Tillich, for example, regarded god as only the ground of and basis for what is personal. To the contrary, personality assumes separate agency capacity, which would be lacking in a god conceived as only the ground of being, being itself, or the structure of all that is. Consistently, Tillich abandoned prayer for meditation, the latter of which could be more harmoniously united with his "self-transcending naturalism."

13. I would not, however, refer to God as a "Person," since (even with the capitalization) such terminology seems to imply that human limitations apply to God.

14. Matt 6:8, 32; 7:21; John 6:39; 10:15; Acts 4:28; Rom 11:34; Eph 1:11; 1 John 5:14; 2 Sam 14:14; Jer 32:35.

15. Hos 11:1; Isa 43:4; John 15:9; 1 John 4:8, 10.

16. Bicknell, *Thirty-Nine Articles*, 25.

17. Erickson, *Christian Theology*, 270.

4. God's Living Word

"The word of God never becomes our property. The test of whether we have heard it aright is whether we are prepared always to hear it anew, to ask for it in every decision in life; whether we are prepared to let it intervene in the moments of decision; to let it convince us of our [unworthiness], but also of God's mercy, freeing us from all pride . . . (1 Cor 4:7), but also from any faint-heartedness (2 Cor 6:10). . . . God's word is not a general truth that can be stored in the treasure-house of human spiritual life. It remains the sovereign word, which we shall never master and which can only be believed as an ever-living miracle, spoken by God and constantly renewed."[18]

---

18. Bultmann, *Existence and Faith*, 169.

Chapter 13

Attributes of Our Loving and Free Interacting God

1. Christocentric Norm for Biblical Selectivity

BIBLICAL THINKING DEVELOPED OVER a long period before it reached the NT's insights concerning God. The proper way to investigate the attributes of God is to draw reasonable inferences from the scriptural references that measure up to God's disclosure in Christ, using the knowledge of God in Christ to critique earlier biblical understandings. (However we should remember that the NT is not everywhere an improvement over the Old.) Were we to affirm the first biblically attested qualities at each point in the following listing, rather than the second, we would use the Bible to affirm a god similar to that of traditional religion. Biblical thinking about God moved from belief in a localized god who was thought to reside on Sinai or in close association with the Arc of the covenant or the Jerusalem temple, to the God with whom believers have direct access through God's Spirit (John 4:24). From belief in a tribal god of war, who was thought to lead the battles against Israel's (and thereby His own) enemies, to the God who has no enemies and whose essence is love. From a belief in a territorial deity, whose concern was considered to be circumscribed by his own clan, to the recognition that God cares for and claims the entire world.[1]

Beginning with a god who was thought to have walked in a garden in the cool of the day and shown his back to Moses as a special favor, it ends with the God whom "no [person] has seen . . . at any time" (John 1:18), and in whom "we live and move and have our being" (Acts 17:28). Beginning with a god from whom at Sinai people shrank in fear, saying "Let not God speak with us, lest we die" (Exod 20:19b), and ending with the God with whom one can pray in a solitary place and whose indwelling Spirit is our unseen friend.[2]

---

1. Fosdick, *A Guide to Understanding the Bible*, 53–54.
2. Fosdick, *A Guide to Understanding the Bible*, 54.

2. He Who Loves in Freedom[3]

In God's eternal being—apart from and prior to creation and reconciliation—God was already love, but we know this only from manifestations of His love in Christ as known through the Spirit. God's decision to share Himself with us is in accord with His being as love and involves an overflowing of His love.

Though God is love, love is not God. That is, what God's being as love means must be learned from His act of love, not from merely human concepts. The same Johannine tradition that attests that God is love[4] insists that God's love is demonstrated by His sending of His Son into the world for our salvation, and in God's offering of His Son as an expiation [atonement] for our sins (1 John 4:10). "God so loved the world that he gave his only Son" (John 3:16a).[5]

As the free expression of God's essence as love, He in Christ extended the bridge from His side, and as Holy Spirit shines forth His light into our darkness. Though as sinners we are unworthy, God seeks and enables fellowship. The Shepherd comes forth to gather His lost sheep (Luke 15). The Son of Man comes to seek and to save the lost (Luke 19:10). God commends His love in that Christ dies for us (Rom 5:8), the "ungodly" (Rom 4:5). Similarly God as Holy Spirit wills to give life to the dead and calls into existence the things that do not exist (Rom 4:17).

Not only is love the essential characteristic of God, but should be the essential quality of Christian disciples. We are to love in response to God's love in Christ and through participation in God's Spirit. An absence of practical expressions of concern for others shows that one's experience of God is fraudulent and that God's love does not abide within a person (1 John 2:7–11; 3:11–18; 4:8).

3. God's Self-Existent and Moral Transcendence and Renewing Effect of Our Bowing to His Opposition to Our Opposition

God has necessary being (aseity) whereas we who are created and contingent have non-necessary being. God is transcendent in that He existed prior to His creation of and involvement with the world. He is no mere God at hand, but also God afar off (Jer 23:23). As for the moral facet of God's transcendence, unlike us God is all-righteous, unstained by evil.[6] Isaiah attests both God's separate self-existence and moral superiority (6:1–8).

We sinners tend to turn away from God toward self-mastering. In response God in His holy love "crosses our path to break our resistance" and leads us toward total commitment to Himself. God's *wrath* is the expression of His "injured love," whereby He seeks

---

3. "God's decisions . . . are not matters of internal compulsion. . . . Although God's decisions and actions are quite consistent with his nature, they are not constrained by his nature. . . . His love [did] not require that he create in order to have objects to love" (Erickson, *Christian Theology*, 352).

4. 1 John 4:8, 16; see also 1 Cor 13:11.

5. Because God in His self-giving love (*agape*) desires our faithful fellowship with Him, our grace-encouraged response fulfills God's desire (*eros*). When *eros* is understood in this restricted sense there is no absolute distinction between it and *agape*.

6. Traditional religion ("paganism") has regarded the gods as much involved in immoral behavior. To the contrary, the true God cannot be tempted by evil (Jas 1:13; see also Job 34:12).

to make us aware of our alienation and attempts to "induce us to surrender to His love."[7] To experience God's love involves knowing His correction and discipline.[8] To fall into the hands of the God of grace is an awe-full experience, that begins the process of sanctification (Heb 10:26–31).

"The revelation of God, just because it is a revelation of His love and grace, means the revelation of . . . *His opposition to the opposition in which [humans] exist over against Him*. . . . To believe in God means that we bow to His opposition to us—despairing of ourselves but not of Him—allowing His good will toward us to be our ground of confidence and hope."[9] God's opposition can have renewing effect because it expresses His saving will toward us, His *gracious* claiming of our lives.

Our initial experience of God's holiness may "not consist in the sense that love is approaching us, but in a feeling of being shattered." For "God is not engaged in choosing a sweetheart, but with elevating humanity to true goodness." Holy love "both *shatters and elevates*," and does so by drawing us to Himself. "This love can awaken life only if it has the ability to shake our self-confidence and transform it into God-confidence. The holiness that brings us down is simultaneously the forgiving love that lifts us up—God's own self-communication."[10]

God is "the high and lofty One who inhabits eternity, whose name is Holy" (Isa 57:15), whose thoughts are not our thoughts, nor His ways our ways. For as the heavens are higher than the earth, so are God's ways higher than our ways and His thoughts higher than our thoughts (Isa 55:8–9).

As we encounter the holy God and understand ourselves as judged by Him we realize our sinfulness (Isa 6:5; Luke 5:8).[11] Yet because we also experience forgiveness through Christ and empowerment by the Holy Spirit, we can share in and show forth God's holiness. God said to Israel, "I am the Lord who brought you out of Egypt, to be your God; you shall be holy, for I am holy" (Lev 11:45). God is perfect in holiness, and we who share in His holiness can and should become more morally like Him.[12]

God in His forgiveness accepts us, sinners though we be, but does not leave us as we were. He frees us to become responsible people who grow toward mature personhood (Eph 4:13), increasing in love for God and one another. To experience God's reconciliation is to allow God to begin to break down the dividing wall of hostility that separates us from Him and from others.[13]

---

7. Berkhof, *Christian Faith*, 123, 125.
8. Prov 3:12; Heb 12:6; Rev 3:19.
9. Barth, *CD* 2/1:362, my emphases.
10. Troeltsch, *Christian Faith*, 181, 182, my emphases.
11. Contrary to some of Luther's assertions (and of isolated readings of some of Paul's passages on the law), the consciousness of sin is not a mere function of the law, but of the Holy Spirit's judging, healing, and renewing activity, and [occasional use] of the law. The Holy Spirit convicts the world of sin (John 16:8–11) (Barth, *CD* 2/1:362–63).
12. Matt 5:48; see also 2 Cor 6:14–7:1; 1 Thess 3:13; 4:7; Eph 5:27.
13. 2 Cor 5:19; Eph 2:11–22.

4. God's Inherent Attributes (Love and Freedom) and Interrelating Ones

God's attributes are qualities of His being disclosed through revelation. "God is His attributes." "In each attribute we confess the fullness of God's being from a different perspective."[14] Since God is self-consistent, these characteristics interrelate and form a unity.

The NT certainly asserts that God is love (1 John 4:8b, 16b), but does so from knowledge of God's revelation of His love. Love and freedom as exhibiting divine self-direction appear to be the innate qualities of God, from which the relational ones have emerged. The reason we need to draw a distinction between God's *inherent qualities* (freedom and love) and those *whose concrete shape is conditioned by His relationship with us* is that we cannot conceive how the latter qualities could refer to God's being prior to creation and reconciliation. Relative to our sin the loving and free God demonstrates that He is merciful, forgiving, patient, and faithful. These other attributes have developed as He has interacted with the world and humankind. Even an attribute such as divine power is hard to conceive as existing in God prior to creation.

The Bible does not speak abstractly of enhancements of God's being, but lays the foundation for such thinking by repeatedly attributing qualities to God that as best we can understand could have had meaning only after creation and reconciliation. The God whom Jesus Christ called Father is the Father of mercies (Luke 6:36; Eph 2:4) and the "God of all comfort" (2 Cor 1:3). How could God be merciful and comforting apart from a creation with which He could embody His love in these ways?

5. God as Changeable in Some Respects (Partially Mutable) and Capable of Being Acted upon and of Having Feelings (Passible)[15]

The Platonic and Aristotelian concept of God denied all divine mutability/changeability. Plato and Aristotle assumed that change requires that things either get better or worse, each of which could be interpreted as implying prior divine imperfection. We can agree that if God can become morally better or worse He is imperfect. But that God is enriched by interaction with the world He has created does not imply that God is morally imperfect. Some types of change are neither from worse to better or better to worse. A caterpillar changes into a butterfly, but for the organism itself is one of these states better or worse than the other? A young person eventually develops into an adult, but is either state inherently better or worse than the other?

One who accepts Plato or Aristotle's divine immutability metaphysics will regard God as incapable of interacting with humankind, for such involvement would require that God in some respects changes. In opposition to such thinking, biblical thought attests that in particular regards God can and does change in interaction with the world. But the Bible

---

14. Berkhof, *Christian Faith*, 113.
15. See chap. 23, section on Christian Prayer.

does not suppose that such interaction and change implies movement from imperfection to perfection or from perfection to imperfection. God is love, always has been, and always will be. Yet because the God of love exercised His freedom by creating a world and interacting with the world and with us, the Bible affirms such beliefs as that God is merciful, patient, and forgiving. God changes in order to particularize love with reference to humankind.[16]

Because both Roman Catholic and Protestant scholasticism held largely Aristotelian doctrines of God, both tended to believe that not only is God *unchangeable*, but that He is *impassible*. As a particular aspect of unchangeability, impassibility means that God cannot be acted upon, cannot be moved emotionally, and cannot have feelings—all of which imply the capacity to change. To the contrary Scripture attests that God can be, has been, and is being acted upon, as when He responds to prayer. The Bible furthermore repeatedly implies that God has feelings and thus can be grieved and saddened, can rejoice, and can express judgment or mercy.

Insofar as classical theists like Aquinas and others built from Aristotelian deism their thinking conflicted with biblical affirmations concerning the interacting God. Such theists thought that if God could in any way be affected by the world, He would not be self-sufficient and self-determining. They failed to envision that God could freely impose limitations upon Himself by creating beings with degrees of freedom and with whom He willed to interact. A god who could not have done so would have been less powerful than one who could.

Aristotle thought that "God" is so timelessly remote from the world as to be unaware of what goes on here "below." "When the Aristotelian unchanging God was combined with the biblical God who knows the world, it became necessary, in order to achieve a self-consistent position, to deny all genuine contingency. If God knows everything that occurs in the world and knows this infallibly and unchangeably without any additions to the content of the divine knowledge, then the total truth about reality, including what is future for us temporal beings, must be completely [determined by God]."[17] In other words, our present is already the past for God, if indeed under such circumstances distinctions between past, present, and future have any meaning for God.

As with Thomism, classical theism overemphasized God's sovereignty *over* the world and minimized His involvement *within* it. It thought that God is untouched and unaffected by the world's pain and cannot in any respect suffer. Over the centuries the church in her *worship* and *preaching* has affirmed a different understanding of God. The God to whom she prays and whom she proclaims has feelings in general and compassion in particular—and lets us punch ourselves out on Him. He is the humble yet active God who condescended to come into history, and whose strength (as at the cross) was made perfect in weakness. Unfortunately the church's official theology has all too often reflected the opposite—Aristotle's silent staring God. Methodist theology proved an exception; all the way back to Wesley it stressed God's love rather than abstract omnipotence. Though many

---

16. See chap. 14, sec. 9 concerning God's lack of total foreknowledge.
17. Griffin, *God*, 44.

aspects of Methodist theology are subject to criticism,[18] it (unlike much Calvinism) has not failed by emphasizing God's power at the expense of His love.[19]

It is not surprising that United Methodist theology has in recent times been much influenced by process theology, which in some respects parallels the earlier philosophical personalism that has had much impact upon Methodist theology. Both process theology and philosophical personalism in some respects parallel Wesleyanism, though without the latter's evangelical aspects and biblical focus. Process theology's fundamental Whiteheadian thesis (which I find unobjectionable) is that reality is processive and interrelated. Unfortunately, Whitehead only retained a god of the gaps function and therefore existence for a purely immanent "god" sustainer of the body's complex neurological communication system.

I am obviously no fellow traveler with Whitehead at this point, and see no reason why (having thrown away all of his religious books) he saw the need for introducing god at this point. Why didn't he just describe the process and admit that he did not know how bodies came to have such an essential communication system?

6. Mutability as Flexible Faithfulness

God is and always has been and always will be love (1 John 4:7b–16b), but is enriched through relationship with His creation. When God created the universe, only at that point did He *become* the Creator and Sustainer, and this *affected* His being. And when humankind emerged after a long period of evolutionary development, He *changed* again. From then onward He lived in relationship with dialogue partners with increased capacities for freedom and initiative. Also God has been and is being *modified* by human rebellion. His own being was again *affected* when He entered into covenant with Israel, and even more when He came to earth in Christ. Jesus's death and resurrection and God's decision to pour forth His Spirit also *touched* God. In these ways and others God *changed*.

Though God is enhanced by His ongoing adventure in history, He is nevertheless the God of steadfast love (Exod 3:14) who fulfills consistent purposes. However God is so flexible and adaptable in His relationship with humankind that He can and sometimes does "repent" *in the sense of modifying His prior plans*, as attested, for example, in the (likely fictitious) book of Jonah. God, however, is not capricious or arbitrary, but remains faithful to His essential goal of bringing humans into relationship with Himself (Jonah 4; Joel 2:13).

Since God's modifying of His prior plans manifests God's faithfulness to His purposes, biblical writers can also assert that, unlike fickle humans, God does not abandon those. That the Bible says both that God repents and that He does not is not inconsistent. The

---

18. See chap. 21, secs. 2–3; chap. 22, secs. 15–17.

19. Within the context of the Greek philosophical denial that God has feelings, Eastern Christology also denied that God the Father suffered, and even that the Son in the divine aspect of His divine/human nature did so. Overreacting against Sabellius eastern Christology wrongly concluded that *patripassianism*, the belief that the Father suffered, is a heresy. To the contrary, that is an essential aspect of the Christian Gospel. Barth recognized that *patripassianism* preserves the Gospel truth that God the Father suffered in the Son's abasement (Barth, *CD* 4/2:357).

difference has to do with the dissimilar meanings the Bible attributes to the same word.[20] *God uses flexible methods but has a consistent goal.* Notice the combination of change and changelessness in Romans 9–11, where Paul speaks of God's changing relation with Israel, but concludes that *"the gift and the call of God are irrevocable."*

As more thoroughly discussed elsewhere,[21] reasoning from Philippians 2:7 nineteenth-century *kenotic* Christology rightly affirmed that God in His incarnate form laid aside His continuing heavenly power and His omniscience. Such self-emptying in the Son demonstrated that God is capable of changing. Dorner (later followed by Barth) located God's unchangeableness in His love, which required flexibility and adaptability in God's relationship with humankind. Analogously, good parents to a degree vary their parenting approaches to take into account their children's individual differences, as well as their stages of development. Yet such parents remain steadfast in their love for their children.

If we are to regard God's ongoing relationship with us as being as real for God as the Bible affirms, we need to understand that God is affected by the process of history.[22] Both constancy and development belong to the God revealed in Christ. God is eternal; He has always existed. Yet the cumulative historical process in which He has revealed Himself has involved Him in new experiences, which have affected Him.[23] "The struggle of God with his estranged image-bearers does something to him. He is enriched [by] reborn sons and daughters,"[24] there being joy in heaven over one sinner who repents (Luke 15:7).

7 Prayer and Divine Mutability

Christian Faith believes in the Living God who is affected by and responds to prayer, which assumes God's capacity to interact. For example, we are to bring our intercessions to God with confidence that He can intervene for us in ways that fulfill our true needs (Pss 50:15; 145:18–19). "The prayer of a righteous [person] has great power in its effects" (Jas 5:16b). "Ask, and it will be given you; seek, and you will find; knock, and [the door] will be opened to you. . . . If you then, who are evil, know how to give good gifts to your children, how much more will your Father who is in heaven give good things to those who ask him" (Matt 7:7, 11).

The Living God is not an irresistible fate before which people can only keep silent, passively awaiting and accepting the benefits or blows ordained. "There is, of course, a Christian patience and submission, as there is also a Christian waiting upon God. But it shows itself to be genuine by the fact that it is always accompanied by the haste . . . of the praying [person who] runs to God and beseeches Him, . . . rest[ing] on the knowledge that God takes our distress to heart and expects that we for our part will take His mercy to heart

---

20. See Num 23:19; 1 Sam 15:29; Ps 110:4; Zech 8:14; Mal 3:6 (Berkhof, *Christian Faith*, 141–42).

21. See chap. 10, sec. 8; chap. 11, sec. 2.

22. Static traditional societies regarded change as inferior to changelessness and thus as dangerous. With the modern understanding of the world as dynamic, a God who is a stranger to change seems a mere stranger. Modern Christians are thus receptive to the biblical conviction that general history should not only be meaningful for humans, but for God.

23. Berkhof, *Christian Faith*, 143–46.

24. Berkhof, *Christian Faith*, 146.

and really live by it. So that in our mutual turning to one another He may be our God and therefore a Helper in our distress, allowing Himself to be moved by our entreaties."

"The hearing of believing prayer is not to be reduced to the general truth that we are to live before God in humility as His servants and in gratitude as His children."[25] Though based on confidence in God's fatherly benevolence (Matt 6:9b), and though half of its clauses relate to seeking to obey God's will, the Lord's Prayer emphasizes petition (Matt 6:9–13). We pray as God's children (Matt 6:9b) and friends (John 15:14–15), who stand at His side and are invited to bring our requests, knowing that God will take them seriously.

8. The Loving, Righteous, and Truthful God Faithfully Honors His Promises and Requires That We Keep Our Promises

God does not command in whimsical, arbitrary, and immoral ways. God commands only what is consistent with His being as love[26] and that will have sanctifying effect upon those who obey. Because what the righteous God expects of others is consistent with His disclosed conduct (Jer 9:23–24), we are not only to imitate Christ,[27] but to imitate the God disclosed through Christ (Eph 5:1–2; 1 John 4:11).

God speaks truthfully and never lies (Titus 1:2). Because God is truthful He commands that His people be truthful in what they assert and in what they imply. Thus, for example, God told the Israelites to use the same set of weights for selling that they used for buying (Deut 25:13–15). Because God exhibits and requires candidness, Christians are to present the Gospel in honest and non-manipulative ways. We are to speak truthfully and to renounce disgraceful, cunning, and underhanded methods (2 Cor 4:2).[28]

Because of God's moral integrity He faithfully keeps His promises, as for example, holding fast to His will to save. What He has truly promised, He will fulfill.[29] Similarly God's people are to keep their promises, both those to God (Pss 61:5, 8; 66:13) and to others (Josh 9:16–21). When we give our word we are to remain faithful to the word we have given (Eccl 5:4–5).

9. God's Patient and Persistent Faithfulness

An aspect of God's faithfulness to His promises and of His grace and mercy is that He patiently preserves creation, and thereby gives us continuing opportunity to enter into

---

25. Barth, *CD* 2/1:511, 512.

26. Not everything Scripture attributes to God's commanding activity should be so regarded. Otherwise God's normative revelation in Jesus Christ will, for example, be compromised by tribalistic views of God found in some early parts of the OT.

27. John 13:15; 1 Cor 11:1; 1 Pet 2:21–23.

28. Erickson, *Christian Theology*, 290–91.

29. Num 23:19; 1 Cor 1:18–22; 2 Tim 2:13; 1 Pet 4:19. The Bible is not a direct transcript of God's promises, as though every supposed biblical promise from God had its origin in Him. We must use the christocentric norm to judge concerning such issues.

relationship with Him and to grow in our discipleship. In spite of massive human unfaithfulness over many centuries, God does not retract His covenant.[30]

God's patience is not the enforced patience of one who impotently watches the course of events, but of one who patiently waits for us to sincerely respond, that our destiny may be fulfilled. God is persistent.[31] A series of OT texts attests how long-sufferingly persistent God is.[32] Some of these stories do not describe historically factual narratives, but are parable-like sagas told to depict characteristics of the God whom Israel had come to know through her history. The historical core behind such sagas was Israel's repeated experience that though she had often proven unfaithful, God had ever again remained faithful.

A more dastardly crime is hardly imaginable than murdering one's brother, but God is concerned even for the likes of Cain. As the legend narrates, Cain's mark was a protective sign of God's guardianship over him in the land east of Eden (Gen 4:1–17). According to some legal systems people like Cain deserve death, but God grants even wretched sinners time for amendment of life,[33] as should we.

The Noah tale (Gen 6–9) indicates how persevering God is with unfaithful humankind. Though God has good reason for abandoning His noble experiment, He has not. Instead the rainbow in the sky reminds us of His promise to remain faithful (Gen 9:12–17). Until the time chosen by God, He will sustain His creation.[34] This is not because humankind deserves such, for many people have been wicked from youth (Gen 8:21); it is because God perseveres. God's covenant with Abraham at Sinai and in Jesus Christ built from and depended upon God's prior covenant with humankind to which the Noah saga points.

The legend concerning Jonah not only tells of God's mutability and flexible faithfulness (see sec. 6), but of God's merciful patience in contrast with merciless human indifference. As the story goes, because Jonah lacked love and mercy he desperately tried to escape from God's call to mission. Though it is said that the people of Nineveh were so dense they could not distinguish their left from their right hands, God even cares about such people. Jonah, however, had no extra-tribal concern. Nevertheless the patient and faithful God of mercy was steadfast and is said to have left Jonah no option but to do as God had first commanded: Go to Nineveh and preach repentance. Jonah is depicted as reluctantly doing so, and the response is said to have been so overwhelming that even the animals repented! (Jonah 3:7–8) According to the story, in reaction to Nineveh's positive response, God changed His mind and no longer wished to judge Nineveh, but to save her (3:10). And yet the disobedient and then reluctant Jonah, whom God had continued to preserve, was resentful when God exhibited similar patience toward Nineveh. Never having wanted to reach out, Jonah was so annoyed at Nineveh's repentance that he asked that God strike him dead, which, of course, the forbearing God would not do (4:3, 8b–11). And so the legend ends with the unresolved contrast between unmerciful Jonah and the God who is "gracious" and "merciful," "slow to anger and abounding in steadfast love" (4:2c).

---

30. See chap. 15, "God's Creation Purpose for Humans (Creation and Covenant)," especially secs. 6–7.
31. Exod 34:6; Ps 86:15; Rom 2:4; 9:22; 1 Pet 3:20; 2 Pet 3:15.
32. Exod 34:6; Joel 2:13; Jonah 4:2; Neh 9:17; Pss 86:15; 103:8; 145:8.
33. Barth, *CD* 2/1:407, 410, 412.
34. We could, of course, destroy ourselves.

Moving from tales to the historical reality that underlay these: Israel perceived an essential element of God's love in His capacity to forgive and once again call people to repentance. God's patient persistence "made possible a new beginning for the people after every disaster and judgment." Of course God's patience was never intended as "cheap grace." God's judgment was to be received and a new beginning made. Nevertheless, divine perseverance was and is real. "[Thus] in the established formula with which ancient Israel summed up the divine attributes (Exod 34:6; Pss 86:15; 103:8; 145:8) patience has a fixed place alongside grace, mercy, and righteousness."[35]

As the book of Judges emphasizes, Israel was guilty of an ever-recurring cycle of apostasy, resulting in God's wrath as expressed in her being handed over to the results of her misdeeds. This was followed by God's invitations to return to Him and by fresh manifestations of God's help and deliverance.[36]

In the NT, as in the Old, God's persistence in providing time and space is seen as helping to bring people to repentance. One thinks, for example, of the loving and patient father in the parable of the prodigal son, the father symbolizing God (Luke 15:11–32). Second Peter suggests that Christ's future revelation has been delayed because of God's forbearance and His desire that all repent (2 Pet 3:9). Though in Christ the new age has dawned, only a segment of the world has yet responded positively to Christ, and many of those may not have genuinely done so.

10. Divine Suffering through God-World Self-Limitation;[37] Nothing Takes God by Complete Surprise; God's Knows That His Ultimate Salvific Goals Will Be Achieved

"Divine self-limitation is an integral aspect of the God-world relationship. This free act of self-limitation, [was] taken entirely at the divine initiative for the sake of relationship. . . . God has so entered into the world that God cannot but be affected by its life, including its spiritual [and lack of spiritual] life. Because of this condescending, God fully relates to sinful creatures . . . and . . . *cannot but suffer, and in manifold ways*."[38]

God is infinitely wise[39] and understands all possible choices we face. Nothing that happens takes Him by complete surprise (Heb 4:13). God not only sees us through and through, but wills to disclose to us our every deception, so as to lead us in the way of holiness. Therefore with the Psalmist one can and should pray, "Search me, O God, and know my heart! Try me and know my thoughts! And see if there be any wicked way in me, and lead me in the way everlasting" (139:23–24).

---

35. Pannenberg, *ST*, 1:439. "As a function of God's world governance, patience is close to the wisdom by which God founded the world (Job 28:25ff.; cf. Prov 3:19–20; Wis 8:4) and which is also at work in the sending of the prophets (Luke 11:49), and according to Paul also in [the sending of] the Kyrios [Lord] and of his crucifixion (1 Cor 2:7–8)." "In [Christ] the merciful love of God reaches its goal . . . of the reconciliation of the world. In the fine saying of Barth . . . Jesus Christ is the 'meaning of God's patience' (cf. *CD*, 2/1, 432)" (Pannenberg, *ST*, 1:440, 441).

36. Pannenberg, *ST*, 1:413–14.

37. See chap. 14, sec. 4 for further exploration of this theme.

38. Fretheim, *Suffering of God*, 58, my emphases.

39. Matt 10:29–30. See also Ps 104:24; Rom 11:33.

"God knows that God's ultimate salvific goals for the people and world will be achieved one way or another and that God's purposes in moving toward those goals will be constant. But there are innumerable paths for people to take along the way; these are known to God as probabilities or possibilities."[40]

11. God's Superior but Not All-Controlling Power

Less Directly Biblical and Church Historical Evidence. If creation is really creation and not an emanation or outflowing of God, it must be filled with contingencies, actions and events that God does not control. If God dominated everything, human causation would be an illusion. Of course one can say that God has absolute control, and also say that secondary agents also have genuine freedom. Zwingli and Calvin affirmed both statements, presuming that they are compatible. What they did not do is explain how they could be; thus what they said on this topic does not seem convincing. If creation is real, all organisms have degrees of freedom. The God of power, creativity and love works for good in part by interacting and even struggling with agents having varying degrees of freedom.

In eternity we will surely come to realize the intensity of God's opposition to forces that have opposed Him. And we will face a final judgment, not a revelation that everything was as God intended.

Job was a great improvement over the retribution theory of much of the OT. He quite rightly did not believe that virtue is rewarded with prosperity and vice punished with poverty. Job offered no prosperity gospel. But he did believe in absolute omnipotence. Though his encounter with God gave him comfort, he, like much of the OT, imagined that God causes all events, and in Job's case caused his boils and his other suffering, but not as punishment. Though Job finally came to know God personally, God remained an enigma, as He may if conceived as absolutely omnipotent.[41]

In the late OT and Intertestamental period came increasing recognition of the freedom of secondary agents. Thus the NT's insistence that the kingdom of God battles against a hostile kingdom. God is not fate, but our Loving Father who freely interacts with, but does not dominate creation. God is even the Waiting Father of the final paragraph of the parable of the prodigal son, who does not omnipotently prevent his sons or daughters from leaving, nor want them to do so, but who waits patiently for our return (Luke 15:11–32).

Though God can accomplish good even amid events marred by sin, we must not blame our sinfulness on God. I agree with the old conundrum that *if* God is absolutely omnipotent and if evil exists, He is not loving. I, however, do not believe that He is absolutely omnipotent, and therefore I do not think that this conundrum ensnares the true God. Rather than understand divine power as in conflict with divine love, let us rethink divine power in the light of the humble and interacting God revealed in Christ.

Let us understand the world as it is, rather than reinterpret in ways that deny its harshness. We come from Oregon, which is located on the "ring of fire," areas of land that

---

40. Fretheim, *Suffering of God*, 47.

41. One other NT critique of Job: Contrary to Job's insistence on his virtue (29:14–27; 32:1; 33:9), no one is without sin, except our Lord Jesus Christ, and His suffering most certainly was not due to His sinfulness.

border the Pacific Ocean. The US Northwest has many beautiful mountains, but now and then one of the volcanic ones blows its top, as did Mount St. Helens some years ago. This caused death and destruction. Science now understands much concerning plate tectonics, that deep beneath earth and ocean the continents rest on plates that slowly move. When the pressure builds up it results in volcanic eruptions and/or earthquakes. Though people can be in the wrong place at the wrong time, our Father surely does not directly will the untold suffering and death that these can cause.

The flu epidemic of 1918 is thought to have killed forty to fifty million worldwide, 2.5 percent of the world's population at the time. We know that viruses can spread from wild animals to humans, and as currently under the COVID-19 epidemic, many millions may die before the vaccines are distributed widely enough to stop the spread. Meanwhile responsible people will wear masks and keep their distances. Because nature can be cruel in various ways, living in particular places or with specific exposures has risks related to those factors. Climate change is causing death and destruction, but abuse of God's good earth is not God's will; our creative and loving God is struggling within the world, working to bring good amid suffering and evil. And He calls us to do the same. Jesus healed the sick and cared for the suffering; He did not tell the sick and suffering that they should accept their condition because the omnipotent God willed their sickness.

I know a person who has a serious disease. Did God cause this by directly controlling all events, giving him such a genetic disposition and seeing that he encountered other factors that contributed to the onset of the disease? If God so willed, is He a loving God worthy of worship and service? Would He not instead be Allah, Fate, the name for everything that happens?

God is neither weak nor inactive in our lives nor in the world, but neither does God's activity negate the power and freedom of other agents. "*In everything God works for good, but not everything that occurs is caused by God*" (Romans 8:28a RSV). Though not omnipotent, God is supremely powerful and is involved in an adventure with this dangerous and threatening world, and seeks to orient it toward a higher good. God invites us as His disciples to share in this adventure by cooperating with His revealed purposes, rather than conforming to whatever seems to be happening.

More Directly Biblical and Church Historical Evidence. When dealing with God's patience we will see that God allows humans considerable freedom and initiative and does not force His way.[42] We see His vulnerable relationship with Israel in God's laments.[43] God's respect for His covenant partners' freedom is also evidenced in several parables that compare God with owners who went on journeys and did not exercise direct control.[44]

God's power is His capacity to accomplish His loving purposes as revealed in Jesus Christ. The Apostles' and Nicene Creeds thus qualify God's sovereignty by grounding it in God's fatherliness ("*Father* Almighty")[45] and by understanding divine power in relation to other realities (such as that Jesus was crucified). The creeds would have been wiser and

---

42. See sec. 9.

43. Mic 6:1–5; Mal 1–3.

44. Matt 24:45–51; 25:14–30; Mark 12:1–11.

45. "The conception of 'Almighty' receives its light from the conception of 'Father' and not vice versa" (Barth, *Credo*, 19).

more faithful to the NT had they avoided the word "almighty," since that word implies absolute power. Because God is love, He is not free to do anything and everything, to be an arbitrary tyrant and thereby negate His own nature.[46]

Being supremely powerful *in His love* God has decided to make room for humankind's power. [God] *"decided to lose power to gain fellowship.* [Being graciously unwilling to be powerful] without us and against us. And so He has involved Himself in a history with us in which for the sake of the genuineness of the covenant partnership, He hides His superior power and manifests it in [apparent] defenselessness, to give us the room we need to become ourselves."[47]

Much Christian theology in recent years has rightly emphasized divine goodness and refused to attribute evil to God. God is not directly responsible for everything that occurs, such as Hitler's or Stalin's or Idi Amin's atrocities. Recent thinking is closer to the relative dualism of the NT than to the OT's more monistic orientation. God has the power to create a universe in which He does not have absolute control. Though *God does not will everything that happens, He wills something in everything that occurs.*

"Islam proclaims the fatalistic doctrine that everything that occurs is the inscrutable will of Allah." To the contrary, Christian faith "refuses to attribute to God [what] the Gospel attributes to Satan." "Faith looks upon existence as a *dramatic struggle* and sees the inner meaning of existence emerging out of [God's] struggle . . . with hostile forces. . . . If God's will were comprehended in everything that happens there would be no need of 'revelation.' The very fact that faith points to a divine revelation indicates that it does not accept everything that happens as reflecting God's will." Nevertheless, "divine love is capable of making itself effective in every situation. No situation can arise that would overpower God"[48] or would be able to bring the power of divine love to naught.

To a generation of Protestant theologians a syncretistic belief in God's providence, with no specifically biblical and Christian substance, inevitably "proved to be inadequate . . . in face of the Lisbon earthquake (1755), let alone the external and internal catastrophes of the nineteenth and twentieth centuries. The hour had to come . . . when belief in history and its immanent demons could replace faith in God's providence, and the word 'providence' could become a favorite one on the lips of Adolf Hitler."[49]

Without identifying God's will with an ideology concerning history, one who has faith in God's providence will perceive "God's will and purpose [amid] very definite events, relationships, connections and changes in history. [We can] note in this history disposings and directions, hints and signs, set limits and opened possibilities, threats and judgments, gracious preservations and assistances. . . . [We can] perceive . . . the call of the hour, and act accordingly."[50]

---

46. The NT calls God almighty primarily with reference to eschatological contexts—when God will be all in all. (Not surprisingly, with only one exception, NT texts referring to almightiness are from the book of Revelation.)

47. Berkhof, *Christian Faith*, 139, my emphases.

48. Aulen, *Faith of the Christian Church*, 170–71, 171.

49. Barth, *CD* 3/3:33.

50. Ibid., 23.

In faith in God's providence what is needed is the relationship to history of which we have an exemplary form in the OT prophets. What makes them prophets is not that they can rightly perceive and publicly appraise past and present and future history, but that the hand of the Lord seizes them (cf. Isa 8:11), that He says something to them which in relation to the thoughts of their contemporaries and even their own is always new and strange and unexpected and even unwanted, a "burden" laid upon them (Hab 1:1), a fire kindled and burning in them (Jer 20:9), even a super-abounding joy filling them (Jer 15:16).... The Lord God does nothing "but that he reveals his secret to his servants the prophets" (Amos 3:7). Hence it is not from history or from their own view of history, but into history, apart from and even against their own view, that a very definite light is given to the prophets in the form of concretely directed and fashioned perceptions.... Basically and structurally this prophetic relationship to history is also that of the belief in providence. It consists in the fact that the [person] who is apprehended and freed by the Word of God is not without light and therefore [can see] light in the obscurity of world occurrence.

It is to be noted again that this is not the light in which all things are [known by] God.... It is ... as much light as God thinks necessary and salutary for the believer in his time and place, and [that God] will therefore give him."

Knowledge of God's providence sometimes arises as a person listens openly and attentively to what God is saying through the biblical witness. "He will not be ashamed if it can be shown that he once thought or spoke otherwise. The [person] who believes in the providence of God is distinguished from [one] who does not, but rests instead upon his own prudence, by the fact that he is not too proud to be a continual learner."[51]

12. God's Permissive Will

God did not create or intend evil, opposes it, and yet interacts with it. A biblical example of God's permissive will in and through human disobedience is the establishment of the monarchy in Israel. Though according to the OT God did not approve of this development, because it would introduce confusion between such representatives and God, He allowed the monarchy to develop and accomplished some of His purposes in and through it. The essential element in the permissive will understanding is that because God wills something amid everything that occurs, the person of faith should seek to discern God's will with reference what is happening, but not by deifying what is happening!

God did not betray Jesus, but accomplished good in and through permitting Judas's betrayal, an unjust trial, and Jesus's crucifixion. Though sinful and evil people rejected

---

51. Ibid., 24, 25. What other responses should follow upon knowledge of divine providence: "Gratitude of mind for the favorable outcome of things, patience in adversity, and also incredible freedom from worry about the future" (Calvin, *Institutes*, 1:210).

"Question: What fruit doth it yield to know the creation and providence of God?

Answer: That we should be patient in adversity and thankful in prosperity, and that for the future we should have confidence in our faithful God and Father that no creature will separate us from His love" (*Heidelberg Catechism*, Question 28 and partial answer, in United Presbyterian Church, *Book of Confessions*).

God's Son, nevertheless—right in the midst of that—God worked creatively to accomplish salvation. "Whatever evil is, God is its Lord."[52]

> God is like a . . . judo expert who redirects the evil efforts of sinful [people]. A dramatic case of this is the story of Joseph. Most of His brothers wanted to kill him. This desire was neither caused nor approved by God. Yet he permitted them to take some steps toward this goal. Reuben urged the other brothers not to kill Joseph, but merely to throw him into a pit, thinking to free him later (Gen 37:21–22). . . . Midianite traders came by and the brothers (unbeknownst to Reuben) sold Joseph as a slave. . . . God allowed and used the evil intentions and actions of the brothers for ultimate good. The Lord was with Joseph (Gen 39:2). Despite the scheming and lying of Potiphar's wife and the lack of faithfulness by the chief butler, Joseph became successful and through his efforts large numbers of people, including his father's family, were spared from starvation. Joseph was wise enough to recognize the hand of God in all this. He declared to his brothers: "So it was not you who sent me here, but God; and he has made me a father to Pharaoh, and lord of all his house and ruler over all the land of Egypt" (Gen 45:8). After the death of Jacob he reiterated to them: "As for you, you meant evil against me; but God meant it for good, to bring it about that many people should be kept alive, as they are today (Gen 50:20)."[53]

Here the clear distinction is made between the particular intentions that guide a finite action and the divine intention that uses or lies behind such actions. So Joseph could and did forgive, responding to the "Infinite in his reactions to the finite."[54]

Though moral decision-makers must weigh probable consequences, the results of our deeds cannot be fully anticipated or controlled, and should be entrusted to the Lord. "God . . . acts as the Lord even of the effects of creaturely activity." "It remains the word that I uttered, but . . . it acquires its own history quite independently of anything that I contributed to it. I have no further power over the fact to which I gave rise." The effect is at the disposal of God and subordinated to His wider purpose. "It is, therefore, in good hands."[55]

"A certain pietistic exposition of Providence, in the sense of direct 'guidance' which [supposedly] removes all difficulties, and constantly turns everything to good has done a great deal to discredit the idea of Providence . . . [To the contrary] the Good Shepherd permits His sheep to go through the Dark Valley (Ps 23:4). The just [person] must suffer much (Ps 34:19). Indeed is there not a secret proportion between the measure of Christ's presence and a share in His sufferings? (2 Cor 4:8–11) . . . Things do not happen as they do in little pious tracts; they do *not* 'always turn out for the best.' God does not take sides with His own in the sense of the secular idea of good fortune or happiness." "But this does not mean that there are no . . . signs of divine help and guidance. A purely ascetic and heroic conception of Divine Providence is just as untrue as an exaggerating [well-being notion] of the experience of faith or of the divine promise."[56]

---

52. Barth, *CD* 4/1:408.
53. Erickson, *Christian Theology*, 400.
54. Niebuhr, *Responsible Self*, 169.
55. Barth, *CD* 3/3:152, 153, 154.
56. Brunner, *Dogmatics*, 2:158, 159.

Concluding Sectional Remarks. One helpful "little pious tract" affirms that nothing can happen that can *finally* defeat God.[57] We may then argue, "'Very well then . . . if God can use evil as well as good, let Him get on with it. Nothing we do matters.' But here is the old argument that Paul fought with such strength in his Epistle to the Romans. When people said, 'Shall we continue in sin, that grace may abound?' he said, 'God forbid. How shall we who died to sin any longer live therein?'" (Rom 6:1)[58]

At the point where we much need special guidance from God His will may be discerned, and we may perceive the way forward. Our problem is often that we do not want to discern God's will, but want God to sanction our wills.[59] "The guiding principle—I will do His will as far as I can see it—is one that answers a great many of our conflicts and, therefore, brings us peace and strength."[60]

13. God as Omnipresent Spirit

Though having been incarnate, God does not possess a this-worldly physical nature or have this-worldly visibility. *"God is spirit, and those who worship him must worship him in spirit and in truth"* (John 4:24).[61] Because God is omnipresent, His activity is not limited to particular spatial locations (see Acts 17:24). Even when incarnate in Jesus, God was not only there. Thus we can be confident that wherever we go God will be present to assist us in fulfilling the tasks to which He calls us (Matt 28:19–20; Acts 1:8) and in helping us deal with whatever problems we may confront. We can always count on God's presence, even if it involves judgment.

"All questions as to whether God is in a flower or in a stone, [or in the bread and wine,] and the like, are immaterial to faith. [Apparently no pun was intended.] The 'omnipresence' Christian faith affirms is entirely different. It implies nothing less than the ability of divine love to maintain itself everywhere unhindered by limitations of space. There is no place closed to the sovereign power of divine love. God can reach us wherever we are, and it is useless for a [person] to attempt to flee from his power. 'If I ascend to heaven, thou art there! If I make my bed in Sheol, thou art there!'" (Ps 139:8)[62] God is present with judgment and grace, guidance and help, even when we least expect Him.[63]

---

57. Weatherhead, *Will of God*, 28.
58. Weatherhead, *Will of God*, 29.
59. Weatherhead, *Will of God*, 38.
60. Weatherhead, Will of God, 44.
61. Mormons believe that Father, Son and Holy Spirit are three distinct beings (tritheism), and that Jesus and the Father have perfected physical bodies, as will we, whereas the Holy Spirit is a spirit without a physical body. Except for the non-physical Holy Spirit, these teaching conflict with scripturally-based belief in God's transcendence, as well as with Paul's related teaching concerning the *"spiritual* bodies" we will have in eternity (1 Cor 15:42–50). See chap. 29, sec. 7.
62. Aulen, *Faith of the Christian Church*, 128.
63. Berkhof, *Christian Faith*, 113. The Bible only gradually evolved toward the subtle viewpoint just summarized. Early parts either think of God as normally residing at a distance beyond the earth, or insofar as present in this world, as confined to particular places. The book of Genesis supposes that God had to come down from the mountain to be able to see the Tower of Babel (11:5) and to recognize what was going on in Sodom and Gomorrah (18:21). First Samuel considers God's presence as restricted to the territory of

14. God's Beauty

In Christ we see that God is *infinitely beautiful*. Not that in this respect God exemplifies natural standards, for Christians behold the splendor of God in the Christ who had nowhere to lay His head and who died in shocking circumstances. Even so, as by God's Spirit we continue to look there and learn what God through Christ wishes to teach, we perceive that the God known in this way is infinitely alluring or attractive and is the ground and norm of all beauty.

Beauty is not a distinguishable attribute of God, as is grace or mercy, but *summarizes the impact or impression His interrelated and unified qualities make upon us*. The God we behold in His revealed attributes is attractive, magnificent, worthy of love. Thus in response to God's self-giving in Christ and by the enabling of God's Spirit, we become genuinely grateful for God's grace, not just glad that God turns away His punishment. Insofar as we become God's children and friends (John 15:15), we desire to do His will.[64] His love evokes our love; "we love, because He first loved us" (1 John 4:19). We thus accept God's invitation to participate in Him (2 Pet 1:4) and to glorify Him. Neither now nor for all eternity have we sinners any prospect of being divinized or becoming gods.[65] Nevertheless we need not remain ugly, but can share in the beauty of God that shone forth in Christ.

Israel (26:19). Ezekiel's elaborate symbolism is an effort to picture God as present in Babylon, rather than merely in Jerusalem (1:4) (Bicknell, *Thirty-Nine Articles*, 28).

64. Camfield, "The Doctrine of God," 69.
65. Contrary to Mormonism's traditional religion ("pagan") viewpoint.

Chapter 14

God's Creative and Transformative Suffering and Interaction with the World

1. Calvary as a Consistent Development

TRULY TO LOVE ANOTHER person involves sharing in their suffering. Similarly God's love causes Him to suffer intensely because of some of His experiences with the world. God is nevertheless able to accomplish His purposes even in and through weakness and apparent defeat. The God of self-emptying love not only came to earth but went to the uttermost limit of Calvary. Extreme self-giving is characteristic of God, and His long-suffering love has supported humankind both before and after Christ.

The OT leaves no doubt that God suffered because of His faithfulness to Israel. That Israel so frequently grieved and disappointed God and even rejected His love caused Him anguish: "How can I give you up, O Ephraim! How can I hand you over, O Israel! . . . My heart recoils within me, my compassion grows warm and tender. I will not execute my fierce anger, I will not again *destroy* Ephraim; for I am God and not man, the Holy One in your midst, and I will not come to destroy" (Hos 11:8a, 9, my emphasis; see also Jer 31:20).

2. God Can Give Us over to Historical Results of Our Misdeeds

God in His judgment can surrender us to the results of our immoral behavior,[1] thereby hoping to bring us to our senses and woo us back to Himself. Such paradoxical outworking of God's redemptive purpose pains Him deeply. Human disobedience also causes God to be present in different ways than originally intended, but even under such circumstances God is not absent. "He is present in his judgments when he allows his unfaithful covenant partner to walk his self-chosen path all the way to the bitter end. But when [a person] has

---

1. See Rom 1:24–32.

reached that end and stands there with empty hands, he [may] discover that God is there waiting for him as his redeemer."[2]

3. Divine Power through Empathetic Suffering

God is the great fellow sufferer who stands with us in our anguish. However, a sympathetic and empathetic God can rescue us only if He is strong and effective amid apparent weakness. Like a counselor who is overwhelmed by a counselee's problems, a god who is finally weak and inept cannot help. Even so, God's power is not that of "an absolute monarch multiplied to infinity"; "the cross testifies to a God whose love is made perfect in weakness."[3] Contrary to the simplistic assumption that God's sovereignty is without restriction, God does not move people around like pieces on a chess board. If God is cruciform and is the universal sufferer, atheistic protests against an all-powerful but cruel potentate lose their point.

4. The God Who Suffers, Feels, and Interacts

Classical theists (like Aquinas) believed that were God capable of suffering He would not be immutable, unchangeable. Therefore they said that God can neither suffer nor change. Modern process theologians reject classical theists' premise by affirming that God does suffer and thus He must in some respects be capable of changing, general affirmations which I do not dispute. Process theology rightly recognizes that God is active within world process, but unfortunately regard Him as only slightly more than the process.[4]

If God experiences suffering love there must be some gap between what God anticipates and what occurs. "It must be possible for the world *to bring something new to God each morning*."[5] In real relationships participants are affected, and the Bible attests that God is much affected by relationship with human beings.

We grow as persons as we take risks and to degrees move toward newness. In creating us who are non-divine, finite, and capable of sinning, and in calling us into covenant partnership, God took risks and ventured on a pilgrimage of love. However, since God's power is vastly superior to ours, God faces no prospect of being ultimately defeated. Nevertheless, a Creator who interacts with His creation, a God who responds to and answers prayers, is much affected by the world. He does not thereby become less divine—but more richly fulfills His own loving being.

---

2. Berkhof, *Christian Faith*, 138.
3. Fiddes, *Creative Suffering of God*, 32.
4. Process theology's main error is its panentheism, as seen in Hartshorne, who regarded the world as God's outer aspect. Whitehead, though having influenced process theology, was neither a process philosopher, a theologian, or a Christian, but influenced what came to be called process theology. This influence was perhaps in part because of his god-of-the-gaps theory concerning neurological communication systems, which he attributed to divine capacitating of a purely imminent sort. Why he didn't just say that this is the way things are is puzzling, since he believed in no "god" beyond that process.
5. Fiddes, *Creative Suffering of God*, 55, my emphasis.

5. The Vulnerable yet Active Sufferer

God did not create human beings nor the rest of freely interacting creation because He wanted to suffer. But in giving degrees of autonomy, He gave us not only enough latitude to hurt ourselves and others, but to hurt Him. Though endowing us with the freedom that makes sinning possible, God did not will that we sin. God feels pain because of His children's rebellion.

If God knew no vulnerability in His "suffering," if that were something He wished to experience, He would not really suffer, but would merely be engaged in some self-fulfilling activity. Because of our foolishness and sin (neither of which are willed by God) we often bring suffering upon ourselves, others and God, though not all human suffering is due to foolishness and sin. The all-wise and all-righteous God suffers in large part because we repeatedly turn away from Him. We break His heart and He is vulnerable to such effects. As Scripture repeatedly shows, He can be hurt!

Is God then at the mercy of His world and us? Does this world and we ourselves determine God? Not really. God chose to be affected by the world and by us. In creating the world and in allowing it to develop *He imposed limitations upon Himself*. Also, God does not passively endure under constraint, but actively responds to the suffering entailed by His freely chosen relationship with the world.

6. Old Testament Witness concerning Divine Suffering

An early text that speaks of God's suffering with reference to Israel uses the language of grieving: "How often they rebelled against him in the wilderness and grieved him in the desert! They tested him again and again, and provoked the Holy One of Israel" (Ps 78:40–41; see also Jer 3:20). "'The speech that opens the book of Isaiah [1:2–3] . . . deals . . . with the sorrow of God [by describing the fate of some parent]. The prophet pleads with us to understand the plight of a father whom his children have abandoned.' It is important to note, in addition, that the focus is not on Israel's disobedience to an external legal code, but on the broken state of a relationship between parent and child. Jesus's parable of the prodigal son cannot help but be recalled here."[6]

God's sad memory concerning Israel is expressed in poignant form in Hosea 11:1–4, 8.

> "When Israel was a child, I loved him,
>   and out of Egypt I called my son.
> The more I called them,
>   the more they went from me;
> they kept sacrificing to the Baals,
>   and burning incense to idols.
> Yet it was I who taught Ephraim to walk,
>   I took them up in my arms;
> but they did not know that I healed them.

---

6. Fretheim, *Suffering of God*, 114, quoting Abraham J. Heschel, *Prophets*, 80.

> I led them with cords of compassion,
>> with the bands of love,
> and I became to them as one
>> who eases [their] yoke . . . ,
>> and I bent down to them and fed them."
> "How can I give you up, O Ephraim!
>> How can I hand you over, O Israel!"

"The image here, obviously, is not that of some heavenly General Patton having difficulty tolerating acts of insubordination. Rather, it is the image of the long-suffering parent and, given the roles in child-rearing in Israel, it is probably more the image of mother than father. God is pictured as one in great anguish over what her children have done, but her love is such that she cannot let go. Any parent with a prodigal [wastefully extravagant or unruly] child should know something of what God must feel."[7] That God bears the suffering while struggling to heal the relationship shows how committed God is to His redemptive goals. God's patience again and again goes beyond justice.

7. Divine Suffering and Future Glorification

In the latter parts of the OT and in the NT, glory is seen as having to do with eschatological fulfillment. Israel hoped for the day when all people would share in God's glory,[8] and the NT looks forward to Christ's final revelation and the consummation of history. According to Paul, the Risen Christ has already shown forth God's eschatological glory (Rom 6:4), but humankind's full participation is yet incomplete.

"If we are indeed to trace the path of God from suffering to glory . . . we must try to understand [divine] suffering as *unfulfilled desire* and essential glory *as satisfied* desire."[9]

God wills to bring humankind and all creation to eschatological fulfillment,[10] and such perfecting will also lead to His own glorification.[11] Thus the future that God envisions for His creation and His own future interrelate. Meanwhile *God in part moves toward glorification through the path of suffering as do we*. The Bible attests that God suffers because He is pursuing a goal He has yet to fully accomplish.

8. The Related Issue of God's Knowingness

Hartshorne has argued that God is perfectly related to the reality available to be known; but in response to new events continues to surpass His present knowledge.[12] If God knew everything ahead of time He would not be the God of suffering love, but Allah, the unknown and unconcerned potentate believed to predetermine all that occurs (see below).

---

7. Ibid., 119–20.
8. Num 14:21; Isa 40:5; Zech 14:20.
9. Fiddes, *Creative Suffering of God*, 85, emphases mine.
10. Rom 8:23; 2 Cor 5:5; Phil 3:21; Col 1:27.
11. Rev 1:6; 7:10; 19:1; cf. Rom 11:36.
12. Fiddes, *Creative Suffering of God*, 93.

He would be but another name for fate, not the source of human freedom from the principalities and powers.

God has perfect knowledge of all that is knowable, but the general teaching of the Bible is that *God does not know possibilities as actualities.*[13] God can envision every possible choice and every possible consequence of choices, but God only knows occurrences as they happen.[14] Otherwise events would not be genuinely contingent. Because we have freedom, even God cannot infallibly foreknow and infallibly predict events. Only by understanding God in this way do we take seriously what the Bible assumes and implies by its recognition of the world's createdness and by historical narratives that depict God freely interacting with humans who also have freedom.

Not only does God not eternally predetermine the actions of others, but does not generally predetermine *His actions*, and is thus able to freely respond. This in contrast with much traditional doctrine concerning God's knowingness, that taught not only that God is aware of everything that has happened, but foreknows all that will happen. And this because He determines everything! Belief in divine predetermination was apparently based on the feeling that it would be demeaning for God to need to learn things, and impious for us to think in this way concerning Him.

But if God knows all that will happen before it occurs, we have no freedom to do otherwise than He has determined.[15] Absolute divine foreknowledge seems to assume divine omni-causality . Among other things, such reasoning implies that God is responsible for human sin.

In many respects, especially concerning conversion and divine ongoing guidance, God does directly lead, though in diverse ways. But no Christian can honestly claim that every decision we make is even directly guided by God. To a considerable but unspecifiable extent we are free decision-makers and God does not know with complete certainty what we will decide. Even so, because God knows us thoroughly He has a good idea what we may choose to do in the near and distant future. And He is always present to guide us more directly.

9. God's Healing Ministry with Reference to Our Temporality

God has a wise and creative, innovative and interactive relationship with time. Thus God can heal our fragmented and broken lives and help us to integrate past, present, and future.

As a secular philosopher addressing secular people Heidegger pointed to the nature of such people's predicament as the inability to unify the experience of past, present, and

---

13. God told some OT prophets to issue warnings of the results that would occur unless people repented. For example, Exod 32:14; Num 23:19; Jer 26:19. Here contingency was involved, since a people's repentance could affect the divine response. The OT also attests prophecies that God will cause such and such to happen, and that it is too late for repentance to have mitigating effect.

14. Fiddes, *Creative Suffering of God*, 92. Fiddes is here indebted to Hartshorne.

15. The Bible speaks of God changing His mind, as, for example, attested in the legendary book of Jonah, where God is said to have "repented" of His intended judgment against Nineveh (3:10). See chap. 13, sec. 5.

future.¹⁶ Such people cannot integrate *their present with their past*, either because they nostalgically mourn the loss of their past, or because their failure to confess their guilt prevents any healing of their past's crippling effects. And such people sometimes cannot integrate *their present with their hopes for the future* because of escapist enslavement to *wish-fulfilling dreams* that interfere with realistic attitudes toward the future. The other future-related source of such people's present immobility comes from paralyzing *fears concerning the eschatological future*.

Insofar as we cannot unify past, present, and future we are broken and fragmented people. The Living God can overcome our brokenness and fragmentation by empowering the unification of our past with our present, and our present with our future.¹⁷ God does so by forgiving our sin and sins, by encouraging present faithfulness, and by leading us into a responsible future free from bondage to the crippling effects of our guilt.

Divine empowerment can embolden us to *live responsibly in the present*, rather than *fantasizing concerning the future or living in dread*. Divine forgiveness can enable us to see that the prospects that await us are not what could have resulted from our deserving—and thus *we can live in hope rather than in fear*.

---

16. Fiddes, *Creative Suffering of God*, 103, citing Heidegger, *Being and Time*, 236–37, 279–80.
17. Fiddes, *Creative Suffering of God*, 103–4.

GOD THE CREATOR
AND GOVERNOR

Chapter 15

God's Creational Purposes for Humans (Covenant and Creation)

1. Why Does the World Exist?[1]

TO A LARGE EXTENT the world was created and continued to evolve that humankind could eventually arise, be sustained, come to share in God's love and love God and one another. The world was also created and evolved that we might not only appreciate our lives on this planet, but further our well-being and that of other life-forms by treating our planetary home responsibly. Our very existence on earth necessitates that we meet the requirements needed for sustaining life on this planet.

2. That God Created through the Word/Son Points to Interrelationship of God's Will in Creating and in Reconciling

Saying that created reality came into being through the speaking activity of God[2] attests that we are to respond to God's Word and encounter the Lord.[3] The NT presupposes and utilizes such OT linkage, but with christological affirmations as central. "In the beginning was the Word, and the Word was with God and the Word was God. He was in the beginning with God, and all things were made through him, and without Him was not anything made" (John 1:1–3). "And the Word became flesh and dwelt among us, full of grace and truth; and we have beheld his glory, glory as of the only Son of the Father" (John 1:14). Similarly 1 Corinthians 8:6 quotes from an early Christian affirmation of faith concerning "God, the Father, from whom are all things and for whom we exist, and one Lord, Jesus Christ, through whom are all things and through whom we exist."

Faith in God the Creator is founded on Spirit-inspired trust in God's reconciling and revealing activity. "For in [the Son] all things were created, in heaven and on earth, visible

---

1. This chapter presumes the related triunitarian discussions of chap. 11.
2. See Gen 1:3, 6, 9, 14, 20, 24, 26; Pss 33:6; 148:5; Isa 48:13b.
3. Berkhof, *Christian Faith*, 153.

and invisible, whether thrones or dominions or principalities or authorities, all things were created through him and for him" (Col 1:16; cf. Heb 1:2)—that is, for the sake of realizing God's purpose as revealed in Him. Language concerning the preexistent Son signifies God's decision for covenant fellowship, the Son and the Spirit being the means whereby God accomplished that purpose.

God does not have a split personality. What God intended in creation is what He established when He came in Christ. Fellowship with the God known in Jesus Christ is thus the inner meaning of human life itself.

3. The Father's Decision for Triunity Shows Linkage between Creation and Covenant and Expresses God's Nature as Love

It is meaningful to emphasize God the Father as the creator of heaven and earth because there exists a correspondence and likeness between the Father as the originator of God's modes of being as Son and Spirit, and the Father as the creator of the world; and these two originative aspects interrelate. God's resolve to come forth in the Son and to be known through the Spirit lie behind His will to create.[4]

God's decision to create was consistent with His nature as love, but was not necessitated by that. Here we have a free decision of God. It was not conditioned by anything outside of God, nor by anything in God's own nature that required Him to enter into fellowship with beings other than Himself. The relationship that God established with humankind in Christ through the Spirit was a graceful choice.[5]

4. In Jesus Christ God Remained Faithful to His Creational Purpose for Humans

"Mussner writes correctly about the connection of creation and salvation in Col 1: 'The purpose, which is expressed in this linking of the two aspects, is the conviction of faith that redemption means that creation is led back to its original goal, and that this is done through the same One "through whom" it was also created and is upheld in its existence'"[6] More specifically in terms human reconciliation, "If the final thing is true, that in [Christ] God has become [human] for us, then we cannot escape the first thing, that it [was] the original will of God active already in and with creation that He should be God for us."[7]

---

4. Barth, *CD* 3/1:48. God's will for fellowship seems to have been prior to and independent of human rebellion, though the particular history that occurred in the Son was shaped by and responsive to human sinfulness.

5. Camfield, "The Doctrine of God," 72, agreeing with Barth's view.

6. Berkhof, *Christian Faith*, 166–67, quoting Muessner, *MS* 2, 460–61.

7. Barth, *CD* 4/1:38. Prior to Barth, Albrecht Ritschl had affirmed that if the true destiny of the human race involves spiritual fellowship with God, this end cannot be unrelated to God's goal for creation. Thus God created and governs the world largely so that He can bring people into participation in His kingship or reign (Ritschl, *Justification and Reconciliation*, 272, 283).

"God created [us] to lift [us] in His Son into fellowship with Himself. This is the positive meaning of human existence."[8]

5. Understanding "Sagas"

I am using the term saga as "an intuitive and poetic picture of a [supposed] pre-historical reality."[9] God's decision to create was prior to the existence of the sequences that science can trace, even prior to the existence of energy. Whereas science traces cause and effect relations within this universe's order, sagas point to events prior to the universe's existence.[10]

In speaking of God's will and decision to create, we must not try to turn the Bible's imaginative portrayals into scientific descriptions. Rather, faith should consider sagas' interpretations to ponder God's willingness to create and to enter into relations with creation, and to contemplate the connection of creation with covenant. We thus now exegetically probe two OT narratives to think about their theological significance.

6. Genesis 1:1—2:4a, Priestly Account: Creation as External Basis of Covenant

The Genesis 1:1—2:4a account manifests a teleological view of creation, pointing toward the goal of human relationship with God.

Some Generalizations. Firstly, with its repeated statements about creation's goodness, which more precisely means its *purposiveness*, this account affirms the instrumental value of creation in the service of relationship with God. "'It was very good' means concretely that [creation] was adapted to the purpose which God had in view; adapted to be the external basis of His covenant of grace."[11]

Secondly, this account leads toward the description of human creation as the final form of creation, its pinnacle. Only humans were created in the image of God, which according to this passage implies a special destiny for humans, responsible deputyship over the rest of creation. According to this text, with human creation, creation received its culminating meaning. God found the primary object of His love and was so satisfied that He is said to have ceased from His work of creating.[12] These texts may thus indirectly point toward human relationship with God as an ultimate goal of creation.

Until uniquely human existence emerged the relationship with God of which the Bible speaks was not possible. An additional complexity is that even humans continue to

---

8. Barth, *CD* 3/1:376.

9. Ibid., 81. Unlike the continuation of the quotation I obviously do not regard sagas as limited to being "within the confines of space and time."

10. Even a "big bang" is from prior condensed energy and thus occurs within creation. Similarly, condensed energy is already from within creation.

11. Barth, *CD* 3/1:213. "The statement that the world was created good (*tob*), even very good (*tob mesod*, Gen 1) [has often been] wrongly taken as evidence of perfection; *tob*, however, does not mean 'perfect,' but, 'suitable for its purpose,' as providing a framework for communication between God and [humankind]" (Berkhof, *Christian Faith*, 171).

12. Barth, *CD* 3/1:217.

evolve. Since humans, however, will always need divine forgiveness and guidance from God, continuing evolution poses no obstacle to what is here being said.

Thirdly, asserting that God rested on the seventh day is likely told as a way of hallowing and blessing the Sabbath (Gen 2:2–3). Sabbath observance was one of the ways in which the people of Israel were encouraged to live from the relationship with God, which is the purpose of human creation. The Christian equivalent Sunday worship helps disciples to live the Christian life as ever accountable to God.

Further Interpretive Details. The Genesis 1:1—2:4a creation saga is described shortly before the beginning of the salvation history in which God's relationship with humankind is said to have begun. God's own resting on the Sabbath is a way of saying that God was and is satisfied with His creation. It also prepares the reader for the covenant history that—according to the OT, but not according to evolutionary insight—immediately followed creation, in which God's purpose for human creation began to be realized.

"The first biblical creation story... describes creation... externally as the work of powerful... and perfectly supervised preparation, comparable to the building of a temple, the arrangement and construction of which is determined both in detail and as a whole by the liturgy which it is to serve."[13] Not only is creation oriented toward realizing the covenant, but that goal was in God's mind from the beginning.

As hinted at some places in Scripture, God may take pleasure in the non-human creation, not just regard that in terms of how it serves His purpose for human beings. "We should realize that the nonhuman creation everywhere, and especially in the infinite space of the interstellar world where there are no humans, has its own for us inaccessible relatedness to God. This must keep us humble. God [is also said to have] made the Leviathan [whale], apart from us, 'to amuse himself with' (Ps 104:26)."[14]

7. Genesis 2:4b–25, Yahwist Account: Covenant as Internal Basis of Creation

The Genesis 2:4b–25 narrative so focuses on human creation that it evidences little interest in extra-human creation. Unlike the earlier discussed text, this one does not describe the great connective structure of the universe that enables the covenant purpose to be realized, but writes primarily of the covenantal meaning of creation.[15] It single-mindedly affirms that God created because He wills to enter into fellowship with humankind.

In this account God is already addressed as the "Lord God," the name He later revealed to Israel. This terminology, the human-centering of the account, and the obedience said to be required show that the narrative is much molded by the history that enabled Israel to come to know God.[16]

---

13. Barth, *CD* 3/1:98. More broadly put, nonhuman earthly reality is the basis for human life, though not only for us. The relationship of humans to nature has many aspects. "Nature is our mother, our companion, our servant, and is also that which threatens as well as feeds us" (Berkhof, *Christian Faith*, 165). As a high level part of nature, we, unlike the lowest levels of organisms, will die.

14. Berkhof, *Christian Faith*, 165.

15. Barth, *CD* 3/1:233, 232.

16. Barth, *CD* 3/1:234.

This Eden creation story is best understood as a poetic depiction of existence as intended by God, not as describing our first human ancestors. When life is lived as God expects, people look to God for guidance and do not seek to know good and evil in and of themselves, the latter as reflected in the story of the fall (Gen 3:1–7). The focus of the Eden creation story foreshadows the need for relationship with Christ and points toward the eschatological fulfillment whereby God will fully realize His purposes for His human creation.[17]

---

17. See 1 Cor 15:20–26.

Chapter 16

The Evolution of Species and an Emergent Evolution Perspective

CHRISTIANS SHOULD NOT FEEL obligated to reject evolution and should welcome evolutionary insights that do not imply atheistic assumptions.

1. Evaluating Darwin's Understanding of Evolution as Due to Random Variations, Overpopulation, and Natural Selection;[1] Evolutionary Insights beyond Darwin

Darwinian natural selection has only to do with the survival of organisms best suited to their environments, and does not deal with evolution from inorganic to organic, which likely also occurred. "Darwin compared the origin of present-day species[2] to the process of selective breeding for domestic animals, such as cattle, to favor certain traits,"[3] but as a natural process without a breeder making the selection. However the development of more complex species from less complex ones implies a degree of goal-directedness that Darwin implicitly rejected!

Darwin understood evolution as including three elements, some of which I will compare and contrast with the recent insights of the evolutionary biologists, Jablonka and Lamb. (1) Darwin thought that within species "organisms vary, and these variations are inherited (at least in part) by their offspring."[4] He surmised that most of these variations are due to biological inheritance combinations from parents, though he had no understanding of the role genes play in this process. Surprisingly, he also recognized that some variations are caused by random mutations.[5] Extensively supplementing Darwin, Jablonka and Lamb offer strong evidence that socially acquired traits or habits are sometimes passed on biologically. Also, and especially when organisms are under great stress, mutations

---

1. Darwin, *Origin of Species*, 250, 251, 271.
2. Species are organisms that can reproduce.
3. Allen, *Christian Belief in a Postmodern World*, 58.
4. Gould, *Ever Since Darwin*, 11.
5. Darwin, *Origin of Species*, 263.

multiply, and when one or more help the organism to survive, those traits can be inherited biologically.[6]

(2) Organisms often produce more offspring than can possibly survive. A point Darwin learned from Malthus, whose thinking solidified Darwin's ideas at their inception.[7] However, with the advent of contraception, having more children than can survive has today become less true.

(3) "On average offspring that vary most strongly in directions favored by the natural environment will survive and propagate. Favorable variations will therefore accumulate in populations by natural selection."[8] Darwin (as against Lamarck) generally (but not consistently) held the view that *socially acquired traits or habits cannot be passed on biologically*. But he consistently claimed that such behavior can influence the behavior of immediate offspring, whose tendencies can be further *passed on socially*.[9] And he regarded such social inheritance as vital to human development.

Jablonka and Lamb, having greatly expanded Darwinian ideas concerning biological inheritance (see second paragraph), also offer strong evidence that acquired *habits* can be passed on *otherwise and socially*. A strong example of "otherwise" inheritance are human babies developing particular food preferences based on what their breastfeeding mothers were eating! As for behavior changes passed on socially: One example concerns English tits as influenced by a brave bird that started stealing milk from bottles delivered to porches. Then the other birds went on to steal milk from the bottles still in the open bed of the vehicle! Another example of socially transmitted change is one brave Israeli black rat introducing the behavior of living in trees, followed by other Israeli black rats long continuing to do so after the brave rat had died. An additional socially transmitted inheritance pattern was seen in Japanese macaque monkeys. Those studying them used potatoes to entice them into moving from the forest to the seashore. But the monkeys then taught themselves to wash the humanly supplied potatoes in a nearby stream, thereby removing dirt. Then they learned to bite potatoes and put them in the salty ocean water, thereby improving their taste. These changes were encouraged by one brave female monkey (Imo), but once these new habits were exhibited, they were socially passed on to future generations.[10]

2. Additional Evolutionary Thinking beyond Darwin

Darwin's understanding of evolution involved no endorsing of an ideology of selfish individualism or extreme individual competition. He only insisted that behavior that is favorable to the survival of particular species tends to be pursued by such members. One thinks, for example, of carnivores that cooperate in hunting, as did our humanoid ancestors.

[Many] animals do quite a number of things that can be called *altruistic* in the full and natural sense, because they are actually *aimed* at serving others. Many creatures take

---

6. Jablonka and Lamb, *Evolution in Four Dimensions*, 113–54.
7. Barbour, *Religion in the Age of Science*, 154.
8. Gould, *Ever Since Darwin*, 11; see Darwin, *Origin of Species*, 251.
9. Gould, *Ever Since Darwin*, 12.
10. Jablonka and Lamb, *Evolution in Four Dimensions*, 155–79.

great trouble over rearing their young, and also defend them vigorously, sometimes getting killed in the process. Many also defend and rescue young that are not their own; some will adopt orphans. Some (for example, dolphins, whales and elephants) also help and rescue adults of their species in difficulties, and some, such as wild dogs, will also feed sick and injured adults. Many baby sit [temporarily take care of others' young], and some (such as wild dogs) will bring food to the baby sitter. Beyond these things, however, there is a very wide and heterogeneous set of further activities that [also] appear to [benefit] others and not the agent: for instance, mobbing predators, giving warning cries, taking risks in finding new homes or food sources, and even leaving the nest when you are injured, with the result that your fellow worker-ants are not inconvenienced by your dead body.[11]

Selection works by favoring behavior useful to group survival, which often does not involve fighting.[12] "A species may prevail because it is better at finding food or turns to a food that is more plentiful,[13] or because it grows protective coloration, or indeed because it becomes less quarrelsome and more cooperative. Very often the best means . . . is to move aside—finding a slightly different habitat, food, or mode of escape—inventing for oneself a new ecological niche." Contests between species seldom entail direct combat. Often aggressive animals "come to the feeding place and find it [empty]." Others "find their eggs gone or they unwittingly nurture a cuckoo."

Violent behavior within and between species must be carefully circumscribed if species are to survive. "Animals must avoid fighting that leads to serious injury; they have no doctor. Thus even a very hungry lion will abandon its kill to hyenas when the odds are against it, and vice versa. This is even truer of competitiveness within a species. While it has its uses, [in terms of group survival] it can easily turn out very badly. The rival-fights of deer, for which they have evolved their antlers, are useful because they select powerful fathers for the young. But as the system develops, and the few strongest stags begin to monopolize the mating, things go less well. . . . Where [aggressiveness] is [too] strong, it is hard for a species to get out of such a cul-de-sac. Strong fighting stags simply will not allow others to mate."[14]

3. Whitehead's Contribution[15]

Against Darwin, Gould, and Midgley, but in agreement with Whitehead, *some amount of teleology or purposiveness is implied in evolution*,[16] especially when one considers the

---

11. Midgley, *Beast and Man*, 131. Such altruistic behavior generally involves only "love" of "friends," but one reads of dolphins near Australia encircling humans to protect them from shark attacks. However, the dolphins may regard humans as their "friends."

12. There are major exceptions, such as lions, leopards, apes, crocodiles, and tigers,

13. Colobus monkeys have the evolutionary advantage of being able to eat leaves that to other monkeys are poisonous.

14. Midgley, *Beast and Man*, 132, 133.

15. For additional discussion of Whitehead, see chap. 13, sec. 5; chap. 14, sec. 5; and Ray, *Systematics Critical and Constructive 1*.

16. See the next section.

transition from inorganic to organic,[17] and the increased capacities of humans in contrast with our pre-human ancestors. "In *The Function of Reason* Whitehead argues that the struggle for existence and adaptation to environment cannot explain 'the fact that organic species have been produced from inorganic distributions of matter, and the fact that in the lapse of time organic species of higher and higher types have evolved.'"[18] Whitehead quite rightly insisted that only a force of creativity in the universe could account for such developments. Unfortunately Whitehead's "god" was only the immanent force of creativity in the universe.

Granted the evolution of the organic from the inorganic, and of humans from simpler life-forms, mere species survival success is not the whole story. Yet with Darwin and biologists, rather than philosophers of progress, one must still insist that the longest surviving species have not evolved toward the higher types of existence. Many successfully surviving organisms have not struggled to "live better" (Whitehead), but only to live.

4. Human Continuity and Discontinuity with the Rest of Creation: An "Emergent Evolution" Perspective

In tracing more complex forms of existence back to simpler ones, fluid and imprecise evolutionary transitions have often been emphasized. But even these are transitions to other forms of existence—as "Emergent Evolutionism" insists. "Everything forms a unity, but . . . everything also has its own place and character: Spirit is not really matter, [and] a plant is not an animal, though there are transitional life-forms between these two, the sea anemone, for example. . . . A widespread misunderstanding with respect to the popularized idea of evolution often leads to the worldview which has been called the 'nothing but': Man is actually 'nothing but' a higher animal, thinking nothing but [an electrical] movement [within] brain cells, animal life nothing but a form of more mobile plant life, life nothing but a more complex form of the inanimate, and this globe nothing but a revolving speck of dust. With these kinds of reductions one jumps lightly over the question as to the nature of the differences and how it is possible that a particular form of existence can break through its own limits."[19]

Emergent Evolutionism is able to account not only for the continuity of humankind with the rest of creation, but also for the discontinuity—recognizing the emergence of new levels, and comprehending the resulting existence of diverse life forms within the world. It sees our universe as a multiverse and reaches the opposite conclusions to the "nothing but" mentality. "*Emergent evolution means . . . that in the evolutionary process new qualities, new modes of action, and qualitatively new entities arise when physical structures become more complex and integrated.*" It also insists that to a considerable extent "we know what

---

17. Because Darwin did not ponder the transition from the inorganic to the organic, he may have foreshadowed the era of narrow scientific specialization.

18. Thomas, *Religious Philosophies of the West*, 384.

19. Berkhof, *Christian Faith*, 162.

anything is by what it does, and [many of] the things that people do are radically different from the things that [other animals do]."[20]

The evolutionary quest to live better should be affirmed by Christians. But God-intended human uniqueness—as those who can live in conscious relationship with God—should be even more seriously affirmed. And the attesting of human uniqueness is just as possible for those who grant the legitimate insights of evolution as for those who do not.[21]

If we recognize human discontinuity as well as continuity with other animals we will avoid errors associated with one-dimensional types of evolutionary interpretations. Firstly, that humans came into existence by ascending from lower creatures, and that the present reality of creaturely life was not present from the beginning, does not mean that the biblical belief that God has willed to bring humans into fellowship with Himself is jeopardized. If the emergence of uniquely human existence is granted, creation via ascent does not conflict with essential biblical affirmations. Secondly, that humans emerged from somewhat rational and communicative animals does not mean we are nothing more than those animals. This fallacy assumes that beginnings are all-determinative. If such logic were consistently applied, modern science would be nothing but primitive magic, since that was sciences' ancestor. Against such reasoning Aristotle argued that things should be considered in the light of their fulfillments, rather than merely from their starting points. Though we are influenced by our zoological ancestry, we should be regarded in terms of what we are now. Thirdly, and related to the previous points recognizing both continuity and discontinuity with other primates—though we are primates according to our biological structure—we differ in kind from other primates.

Humans have thinking and communicating capacities that exceed those of other animals and other primates. Though our bodily form links us with our primate ancestors, our larger brains cause us to use our bodies differently. Many higher animals emit sounds that constitute rudimentary speech well understood by others of their kind. But our verbal communicating is far more complex. Though early tribes had no written languages and even today many people have not learned to read or write, humans are alone able to learn to do these things, and thereby more accurately preserve knowledge. Through the long period of childhood dependence parents and teachers are able to nurture the young and help educate them. But if parents and others do not teach, children will be ill-equipped, because mental development depends much on learning.

Humans have further advantages and also disadvantages compared with other primates and other kinds of animals, and the pluses and minuses are sometimes two sides of the same coin. Our erect posture, inability to hang on with our feet, and to run with four legs distinguishes us from our primate ancestors. Consequently we are not good at moving around in trees or jumping from limb to limb, but our hands are free when we walk or run, which has advantages. Our use of our hands differs in part from other primates' use of theirs because of the different purposes that control our hands and their hands,

---

20. Trueblood, *General Philosophy*, 172, quoting G. T. W. Patrick, *Introduction to Philosophy*, 112.

21. The church's original conflict with science centered more over the application of scientific methods to the study of Scripture than to its application to natural science. Those Christians who are today hostile to scientific understandings of creation also oppose the scientific study of the Bible and utilize a fundamentalistic hermeneutic to close their minds to both and to much more.

which are determined by our minds and their minds. Our eyesight is not as keen as that of some animals (birds in particular); our sense of smell is exceeded by most animals; and our ability to distinguish sounds is less refined than that of many animals. Though our mouth and throat structure help us to effectively communicate verbally—one of our great advantages—this structure causes us to easily choke while eating. Our bodies' lack of [thick] hairy covering makes us less adapted for survival in cool climates, but because of our rational capacities we have devised ways of keeping warm.[22]

Contrary to Aristotle's ideas we are not the only animals capable of reasoning and of solving problems, as will be shown in the next chapter. In the seventeenth century John Locke noted that some other animals have rational abilities and twentieth-century science has proved his point. Mind arises as soon as *conscious* choice is utilized in response to one's environment, and thus appears before the emergence of uniquely human existence.

Though we are not the only animals with reasoning capacities, we have far greater faculties for learning than do other animals, and are capable of learning what is genuinely new. Because other animals are more extensively influenced by instinct, their memory capacity is generally less and their curiosity temporary and shallow. Yet elephants, whales and dolphins have better memory than most non-human animals, as do some birds, dogs and other primates. But only humans can conceive of learning as a limitless activity involving much creativity, and enabling individuals to think beyond usual human ranges.[23] That many humans do not actualize these capacities does not disprove that humans are capable of such. The tribal cohesiveness of traditional life discouraged and still discourages innovation, and yet even primitive people had and still have such capacities, sometimes exhibited by leaders or extraordinary members of the tribe.

Because humans are less dependent on instincts, we are considerably indeterminate and incomplete. Thus we must experiment. What distinguishes beavers' building of dams from human construction of houses is that (controlled primarily by instinct) beavers build as their ancestors had, whereas humans are capable of experimenting endlessly with new designs. Though even ants and bees exhibit remarkable behavior, their techniques are so controlled by instinct as to allow little innovation. Human thought and action can be more flexible than that of other living creatures because we are influenced decisively by social conditioning, a long period of nurture/training, and our own reflection.[24]

"One great difference between [humans] and all other animals is that for [animals] evolution must always be a blind force, of which they are quite unconscious, whereas [humans] have, in some measure at least, the possibility of consciously controlling evolution according to our wishes."[25] This is much more so with the discovery of the human genome, the resulting gene-splicing possibilities, and the use of therapeutic cloning to eliminate tendencies toward particular diseases. Being more indeterminate and more capable of self-determination, Pascal indicated that we can rise higher or sink lower than other animals.[26]

22. Trueblood, *General Philosophy*, 158.
23. Trueblood, *General Philosophy*, 157, 158, 163–64.
24. Trueblood, *General Philosophy*, 162–63.
25. Trueblood, *General Philosophy*, 163, quoting J. B. S. Haldane and J. Huxley, *Animal Biology*, 335.
26. Trueblood, *General Philosophy*, 161. The ecological challenge illustrates the capacity of humans to influence evolutionary developments for good or for ill.

Humans as having greater capacities for self-consciousness than other animals leads to greater self-direction. Sometimes differences in degrees are so extensive as to result in differences in kind. Though high levels of self-consciousness do not bring us into fellowship with God, they do mean that when God reveals Himself He encounters reflective and communicative beings, capable of understanding His revelation in history and with whom He can enter into personal relationship.

To an extent our greater degree of regular consciousness distinguishes us from other animals. Like navigators in contrast with the other sailors, we can learn about and reflect upon our geographical location. (Birds, however, also have a strong sense of location, but are guided more by sighting or radar capacities than by reflection.) Every non-human animal lives in a circumscribed place, but humans can so extend their horizons that they regard themselves as living in the universe.[27] The consciousness of our location in space and in time is part of our self-awareness.

"The experience [of self-consciousness] is one which everyone shares but which we seldom analyze. *The experience, in its simplest form, is that in which an individual makes his own state of mind, or his own feelings the objects of his attention.* There is a crucial difference between the experience of a creature who wants, and the experience of a creature who [can think critically about] his wanting. It is one thing to have the experience of pain; *it is quite another if the pain is felt in the contemplation of one's own character.*[28] It is one thing to criticize a method of achieving satisfaction; it is wholly another to criticize the character of the satisfaction permitted. Man became man, not when he became clever, but when he asked himself whether he was justified in performing the clever act." "*Man is not often wise and is not really good, but he is disturbed by needs which other known creatures do not share.*"[29]

Because we can think *about ourselves* we can critically examine our motives, decisions, and actions, though our sinfulness causes us to resist being called radically into question. For the latter self-awareness we need empowerment by divine grace.

An animal can experiences the dying of other creatures (some of whom he may have killed and eaten). And though he has an instinct to protect himself from the pain of being wounded and eaten by other animals, it is highly unlikely that he can in an anticipatory way experience the concept of being dead, let alone of living beyond death. Because humans can think abstractly—in this case beyond the here and now—we can conceive of our own deaths. "Our knowledge of death is part of our knowledge of life."

Humans differ fundamentally from the other animals that cannot 'regret the past nor have hopes for the [distant] future. Humans . . . have spiritual powers, creative energies, forward-looking hopes. If these be left undeveloped and unsatisfied, nothing else that [we] acquire can be felt as sustainingly worthwhile."[30]

---

27. Trueblood, *General Philosophy*, 167, 170.

28. However, see chap. 17, secs. 2–3, 5, concerning the cow example.

29. Trueblood, *General Philosophy*, 166–67, 169, my emphases. These sentences do not mean that we have a natural awareness of sin, i.e., of having broken relationship with God. We may, however, have a natural awareness of guilt, in the sense of realizing that we have not fulfilled our ideals.

30. Trueblood, *General Philosophy*, 170, quoting Susan Stebbing, *A Modern Introduction to Logic*, 25.

Chapter 17

Humans as Hereditarily Influenced by Other Members of the Animal Kingdom

CHRISTIANS ARE HUMANS AND humans should welcome awareness of our similarities and differences from other members of the animal kingdom. In the previous chapter some similarities and differences that we have with our animal ancestors have from an evolutionary perspective been noted. Here from a more directly case study behavioral standpoint affinities with and differences from various other animals have been noted. Here we deal with the discipline of *ethology*, the study of the behavior of the other animals.

1. Innate Tendencies Can Sometimes Reveal Evolutionary Background: An Example concerning Staring

"In most social creatures a direct stare constitutes an open threat. Normal social approaches to those one does not know well always proceed somewhat indirectly, with various forms of greeting to show one's friendly intentions. . . . Eye contact in particular is at first limited to brief glances, often broken off and renewed. To stare steadily while you approach someone, or to stand still staring after he has seen you, is as direct a threat as can be made. Why this should be so is an interesting field for inquiry. It may well have something to do with the fact that predators naturally stare fixedly at a prospective prey before jumping on it. And they are of course regarding it as a [mere] object, not as a possible friend—which is just the effect a direct stare conveys to a human being."[1] "I have seen a cheerful baby eight months old burst into tears and remain inconsolable for some time on being stared fixedly at by [unfamiliar] aunts."[2]

---

1. Midgley, *Beast and Man*, 11. "So strong and so general is this tendency that a number of species have been able to exploit it by developing eyelike spots on their bodies, with which they frighten off their enemies" even while sleeping (ibid., 11). As, for example, with some bats and many species of butterflies.

2. Trueblood, *General Philosophy*, 12. "Dogs can be 'stared down.' . . . All this actually shows is that, if you exhibit hostility to someone smaller than yourself he will dislike it and probably go away. Dogs do not stare at each other except in the challenge to a fight, when the stare appears, along with the obligatory slow, steady approach, the growl, and the bristling hair, as a natural expression of hostility. And the primates seem to avoid the direct stare strongly" (Trueblood, *General Philosophy*, 12).

2. Other Characteristics Social Animals Have in Common

"All specifically human faculties . . . could have evolved only in a being who, before the very dawn of conceptual thinking, lived in well-organized communities. Our pre-human ancestor was indubitably as true a friend to his friends as a chimpanzee or even a dog, as tender and solicitous to the young of his community and as self-sacrificing in defense, eons before he developed conceptual thought, and became aware of the consequences of his actions."[3]

"Several groups of animals, *not* closely related, have independently [developed] fairly advanced forms of social life. They are, that is, not 'anonymous herds' whose members stay together but take no notice of one another. They *do* things together, help and look after one another to some extent, and have individual friendships. Examples are (at their own level) many birds (such as geese and jackdaws), such carnivores as wolves and wild dogs, elephants [who are so social that they grieve the death of comrades], many primates, and probably whales and dolphins." "Right across this range, social life shows certain common structural features. The first of these, noted by Lorenz, can be crudely summed up by saying that it *rests on peacemaking*—that the positive social bond consists of friendly gestures that arise from the need to counter an existing possibility of aggression. Species incapable of mutual attack [find less] occasion to become friends."[4]

Not only is love [as affection] a product of family care, but social animal parenting may explain why normal human adulthood requires the retention of some qualities of childhood. This is because parents still need to communicate with children, and even with grandchildren. Eric Berne was right in thinking that in each normal human adult the child still survives, and not in a passing role, but as a lasting aspect of character. "'Actually,' Berne writes, 'the Child is in many ways the most valuable part of the personality, and can contribute to the individual's life exactly what an actual child can contribute to family life: charm, pleasure, creativity,'"[5] spontaneity, and playfulness.[6]

3. From Social Animal Ancestors We Have Inherited Capacities for Interpreting and Communicating

Humans are not the only animals capable of communicating. "Dogs and horses, hawks and elephants also 'make themselves understood by those who are normally with them,' whether members of their own species or human beings. 'Making oneself understood' is an immensely wider field than 'talking.' It supplies the . . . only possible context within which human talking makes sense." A threatened animal shows its submission in ways that communicate clearly, "not by doing just anything its mood might dictate, but by a regular signal, such as bowing or (in dogs and wolves) lying on the back." The animal shows that it will not respond aggressively to the threatening animal. Similarly, in certain situations people respond with instinctive actions that also communicate clearly. "When [people all over the world] are slightly embarrassed [they] mask their faces either slightly or completely.

---

3. Trueblood, *General Philosophy*, 274–75, quoting from Conrad Lorenz, *On Aggression*, 246.
4. Midgley, *Beast and Man*, 335–36, 336.
5. Trueblood, *General Philosophy*, 342, quoting from Eric Berne, *Games People Play*, 25–26.
6. Aging can diminish the sense of playfulness, unless one makes an effort to avoid such dullness.

This is certainly a ritualized hiding movement . . . [Eibel-Eibesfeldt] observed a small boy who had been born blind hiding his face with his hands in embarrassment,"[7] evidence for the hereditary basis of such non-verbal communicating. The human capacity to interpret expressions builds from animal communication capacities. "In a normal infant, the power to read expressive movements simply unfolds, not needing conditioning any more than does the power to walk and run in the manner suitable to one's species."[8]

Though humans have innate capacities to interpret the meaning of non-verbal expressions and gestures, we can grow in this regard, as well as in the ability to interpret verbal communication. We interpret spoken communication by understanding it within the context of the non-spoken communication that is occurring.

> Most human language, even for the most literate of us, is spoken, not written. And when it is spoken, the words themselves are only the peak of a pyramid, of which tone of voice, gestures, facial and bodily expression, pace, timing, silences, and the relation of the whole to what is going on at the time form the major part. To see what I mean by *major*, anyone can try the experiment of saying his words in a tone and with gestures that do not suit them. This is not easy to do. It is difficult in just the same way as making two consecutive remarks that do not make sense together or saying the words in the wrong order. Our habitual sense of order and meaning protests against it. But if it is done, one thing is certain—the hearer cannot just accept the words at their face value. A conflict is set up, and the words are not going to win it. The tone, gesture, and so on will be taken as probably *more* informative than the words. . . . The relation between the words and the way they are spoken . . . are parts of the same meaning-system. We use them as complementary tools for the same job.[9]

Speech makes sense to those who from their animal ancestors have learned other ways of communicating, and who speak from that hereditary rootage. Similarly, that some chimpanzees have been taught to communicate with sign language is possible only because chimpanzees's prior communicating was but one step removed from more formal processes of communicating.

When comparing the basic elements of human social life with those of any other species we notice that *humans share some qualities with a variety of species*, not just with primates. "[Non-human] primates do not have big cooperative enterprises, nor therefore the loyalty, fidelity, and developed skills that go with them. Nor do they have fixed homes and families. But the hunting carnivores do. And neither apes nor wolves have anything like the human length of life, nor therefore the same chance of accumulating wisdom and of deepening relationships. But elephants do. And no mammal really shares the strong visual interest that is so important both to our social life and to our art, nor perhaps needs to work as hard as we do to rear our young. But birds do. This is why it is vacuous to talk of 'differences between man and animal' without saying *which* animal."[10]

---

7. Midgley, *Beast and Man*, 234, 312, quoting Irenäus Eibel-Eibesfeldt, *Love and Hate*, 49.

8. Midgley, *Beast and Man*, 311.

9. Midgley, *Beast and Man*, 240–41.

10. Midgley, *Beast and Man*, 335. Midgley's point is surely that we have similarities with these non-ape non-ancestors. On the same page she refers to pair bonding among wolves, numerous birds, mites, painted shrimp, gibbons and lemurs. Only the gibbons and lemurs are primates and could have been anywhere close to our ancestor line.

4. Struggle for Quality of Life and Related Need to Balance Conflicting Tendencies

Midgley wrote that "we want incompatible things, and we want them badly. We are fairly aggressive, yet we want company and depend on long-term enterprises. . . . We are restlessly curious and meddling, yet long for permanence. . . . We cannot live without a culture, but it never quite satisfies us. . . . What is special about people is their power of understanding what is going on, and using that understanding to regulate it. Imagination and conceptual thought intensify all the conflicts by multiplying the options, by letting us form all manner of incompatible schemes and allowing us to know what we are missing, and also by greatly increasing our powers of self-deception."[11] Yet the power of self-understanding and the knowledge it brings helps us to sort out the conflicts.

5. Comparison of Intellectual Abilities and Behavior Patterns between Non-Human and Human Animals

Turning to *scientific ethological studies*, a remarkable finding is that monkeys have pre-mathematical reasoning capacities. They are able to understand the abstract concept of *numeracy (of number as differentiated from particular items being enumerated)* and to sequence from lower to higher.

Quoting C. Randy Gallistel, Rick Weiss writes that these capacities do not mean that monkeys can be taught math, but that they are capable of learning what must be known before math can be learned. "Monkeys . . . can grasp the relatively sophisticated concepts of 'twoness,' 'threeness' and so on, and can comprehend how these concepts relate to each other about as well as a human 3-year-old can."[12]

Sarah Brosnan and Frans de Waal of Emory University engaged in a study of female brown capuchin monkeys that concluded that such animals (also) have *finely developed senses of grievance and individual rights*. The animals they studied became so outraged at being treated inequitably that they would not accept the reward that previously they had been happy to accept, and protested concerning the unjust treatment.[13]

A series of studies of *a border collie* in Germany named Rico showed that he had a stunningly large vocabulary and by a process of elimination *could figure out "that a sound he had never heard before must be the name of a toy he had never seen before."* "While many species can be trained to recognize the names of objects, what made Rico unique is that he recognized so many words, could puzzle out the names of new objects on the first try, and was surprisingly good at remembering what he learned weeks later."

"In the first experiment [at the Max Planck Institute for Evolutionary Anthropology in Leipzig, Germany] the researchers put 10 of Rico's toys in one room and Rico and his owner in another. The investigators then instructed the owner to order Rico to fetch two randomly selected items [whose names Rico knew]. As Rico ran into the other room

---

11. Midgley, *Beast and Man*, 282–23.
12. Weiss, "Monkeys Have Pre-Mathematical Reasoning Capacities."
13. Brosnan and de Waal, "Female Brown Capuchin Monkeys," 83.

and began searching for the items, he could not have picked up any hints from his owner because he was out of sight. In 40 tests, Rico got it right 37 times."

"The researchers then repeated the test, except this time they put seven of his toys in the other room along with one he had never seen before. His owner then called out the unfamiliar name of the new toy. Rico correctly retrieved the new item in 7 out of 10 tries. 'This tells us he can do simple logic,' Fischer said . . . It's like he's saying to himself, 'I know the names of the others so this new word cannot refer to my familiar toys. It must refer to this new thing.' Or it goes the other way around and he's thinking, 'I've never seen this one before so this must be it.' *He's actually thinking.*"

"'Of course, for a child, a word very rapidly means much more than it does for a dog. They will quickly know it's a color word or an activity word. Their representation will be much richer than it is for a dog,' Fischer said. 'But in terms of this task, he is as smart as [three year old] kids are.'"[14]

Some animals have rich emotional lives, as exhibited in their grieving capacities. Not only do elephants grieve, but so also do cows and bulls. Ken Larsen of Canada wrote that "the most memorable incident I witnessed . . . was the killing, by the cow herd itself, of one of its own members. The victim was an ill-tempered beast. One pleasant summer evening the herd members were taking it in turns to charge the unfortunate animal. They (all mature females) had obviously knocked her to the ground several times. It was with great difficulty that I separated her from the herd. . . . She was crying copious tears. Although not obviously injured, she died the next morning"[15]

Summarizing a number of studies, scientists have found that members of the crow family, corvids (which include crows, magpies, ravens, jays and jackdaws), are able to learn from their own experience and adjust their actions accordingly. They can also weigh the motives of other birds and even project their own experiences and memories onto the others.

"These findings are important because there has long been a debate about whether animals can demonstrate planning and conscious thought. The research also has implications for the 'theory of mind'—the ability to read another individual's intentions and desires. This ability develops in [normal] humans between the ages of two and three. The new findings suggest that jays can also project [insights from] their own experiences and memories onto others."[16] Like the jays, ravens have recently shown that they understand that others have minds, and ravens thereby are capable of both *empathizing* and *deceiving*.[17]

6. Moral Responsibility to Other Animals

"It does matter how we treat animals—since cruelty is vicious in its own right, and not just because it might lead to ill-treating people. . . . Conflicts of interest must be recognized both within the human species and outside it. We have to take sides, and are entitled to

---

14. "Reasoning Capacity of Smart German Shepherd," my emphasis.
15. Harker, "A Cow's Grieving Capacity."
16. "Members of the Crow Family," 83.
17. "Jays and Ravens," 77.

put our own species first. All species do this. No creature can in fact subsist without killing some others, if only by competing with them for food. The point is not that we can hope to avoid injuring either animals or people. It is that we ought to recognize that such an injury matters, and try to avoid it where no adequate reason justifies it. Suffering inflicted on experimental animals, for instance, is not just a null term that can be dropped right out of the moral equation. It has a weight, and that weight ought to be proportional to the demonstrable value of the research. Not just anything justifies absolutely everything. Some scientists may be brutal, but that does not make brutality scientific."[18]

---

18. Midgley, *Beast and Man*, 217, 223.

RECONCILIATION
BY GOD THROUGH CHRIST

Chapter 18

God Reconciled Humankind to Himself and Thereby Demonstrated His Love[1]

Biblical Basis

1. God's Merciful Outreach to Sinners through Jesus's Life and Teaching

"THE PRACTICE OF ASSOCIATING with the religiously 'lost' or marginalized put Jesus in a constant state of ritual impurity as far as the stringently law-observant were concerned. Jesus's insistence on offering admission to the kingdom to . . . Jews who were considered to have departed from the covenant, without demanding that they employ the usual mechanism of Jewish repentance and sacrifice was probably a major reason why zealously pious Jews opposed this nonconformist preacher. Jesus's message was one of joy that the eschatological banquet was at hand, a banquet anticipated in the meals he shared with sinners. In keeping with this festive mood, he did not practice voluntary fasting; nor did he enjoin it on his disciples (Mark 2:18–20 par).[2] . . . His non-ascetic ways not only distinguished him from the Baptist but also exposed him to ridicule from the more conventionally devout. In their eyes he was . . . a 'glutton and drunkard' (Matt 11:19 par)."[3]

---

1. The NT exhibits fluid and varying ways of describing God's saving work in Jesus Christ. This and the next chapter use the words "reconcile" and "reconciliation" to refer to the entire atoning work of God in Christ. But in sec. 7 of this chapter, NT passages are quoted in which reconciliation terminology is particularly employed. However, even there such terminology is mixed with other word usage.

2. Mark 1:13 says that Jesus was in the wilderness for forty days and makes no reference to fasting or being hungry. As for ahistorical legends: Matthew 4:2 says that "he fasted forty days and forty nights, and *afterwards* was hungry" (my emphasis). Luke 4:1–2 attests the same.

3. Meier, "Jesus," 1320.

2. Jesus's Dying on a Cross

"In the early days of Christianity the cross was obviously shocking and scandalous. The Romans reserved crucifixion for the most despised of criminals, generally escaped slaves, traitors, and political rebels. Death on a cross was not only painful, but shameful. Roman citizens, no matter how terrible their crimes, would at least not be crucified. In the Jewish context, too, a cross meant shame and scandal. In Israel the dead bodies of the worst criminals were sometimes hung on trees, (see, for instance, Josh 8:29; 10:26–27), as signs that they were cursed by God (Deut 21:23). To pious Jews, as Paul attests (Gal 3:13), Jesus was thought to have fallen under just such a curse by hanging on a cross."

"Until the third or fourth century, therefore, Christian art never portrayed Jesus on the cross and rarely even used the cross itself as a symbol. Yet the NT itself never dodges or downplays the hard reality of the cross. All four Gospels lead up to the crucifixion as a central dramatic climax. 'When I came to you, brothers and sisters,' Paul wrote, 'I did not come proclaiming the mystery of God to you in lofty words of wisdom. For I decided to know nothing among you except Jesus Christ and him crucified'" (1 Cor 2:1–2).[4]

"'Jesus' death,' Elizabeth Johnson has written, 'included all that [*could make*] death terrifying: state torture, physical anguish, brutal injustice, hatred by enemies, the mockery of their victorious voices, collapse of his life's work, . . . and betrayal by close friends.'"[5]

3. Jesus's Rejection and Crucifixion Did Not Take Him by Surprise

Though the Son strove to fulfill His divine vocation to manifest God's love, in His passion and dying He voluntarily assumed the consequences of His faithful life of obedience. Jesus was prepared to pay the price required to bring God's kingdom near. Because He remained loyal to God it is not surprising that in this sinful world He perished.

It seems probable that Jesus long foresaw the likelihood of rejection. "In Mark, which has sixteen chapters, the first announcement of suffering [and rejection] occurs already in 8:31 (the second in 9:31, the third in 10:33f.); but Jesus's suffering casts its shadow ahead as early as 3:6.[6] For that reason Martin Kähler called Mark a 'passion history with an elaborate introduction.'"[7]

Not only did Jesus embody God's kingship, but invited people to enter it and be willing to "drink the cup" to the bitter end (Matt 20:22b). Whether or not Jesus long foresaw His betrayal, by the time He went up to Jerusalem He was surely aware of the likelihood of rejection and possibly death. Yet as late as Gethsemane—though praying that God's will would be done—He was still in doubt as to whether or not His death was imminent (Matt 26:42).

---

4. Placher and Willis-Watkins, *Belonging to God*, 70–71.

5. Placher, *Jesus the Savior*, 128, quoting Elizabeth Johnson, *She Who Is*, 158.

6. "The Pharisees went out, and immediately held counsel with the Hero'dians against him, [as to] how to destroy him."

7. Berkhof, *Christian Faith*, 300. Kähler actually referred in this way to all of the Gospels, a doubtful contention.

4. Jesus's Crucifixion as World's Judgment

Those who took the initiative in rejecting Jesus felt that in the name of the God of their covenantal understanding they had to eliminate Him. For He had exhibited much freedom in interpreting the law and had welcomed people who had not kept the law. That the Son of God was rejected and crucified demonstrates that humankind cannot tolerate the true God and thus seeks to eliminate Him when He comes too close.[8] It was not criminals who crucified Jesus or the lawless or the non-religious, but those of high moral and religious conviction. Let us not single out these people, for to an extent all people have participated in the opposition to God demonstrated by the condemnation of Jesus. We should not think optimistically about humankind nor expect that salvation will come from ourselves.[9]

5. Jesus's Death on the Cross as Lowest Point of Divine Concealment; the Father's Raising of the Faithful Son as Validating Son's Faithfulness; Covenant Thereby Being Representatively Fulfilled from Human and Divine Sides

God came forth to demonstrate and to enact His love and thereby to redeem us. God did not just come near, but genuinely shared our humanity in Jesus.

From a merely human perspective Jesus's death signified that in and of Himself at that point He had no future. After His crucifixion and prior to His resurrection He had become a figure from the past and thus (like all others who have died) accessible only through memory. Jesus's death stamped Him as truly human. "An angel or an idea or the 'essence of Christianity' obviously cannot be buried. But Jesus Christ was buried."[10]

Nothing more truly indicates the extent of God's condescension and humiliation—and the hiddenness of revelation—than that Jesus died rejected by humankind. The lowest point of divine concealment was precisely the human condemnation of Jesus, His crucifixion as a common criminal, His death and burial. In the light of His resurrection, the eyes of faith perceive through these actions that God in His suffering love so identified with humans as to allow Himself to be shoved out of the world He created and which He came to redeem.

With Jesus's rejection and death the covenant would seem to have collapsed, but was actually fulfilled. The Son remained faithful to the Father and clung to Him to the end. The Father remained faithful to the Son and by raising Him from death upheld Him beyond His end. Thus the covenant was representatively fulfilled from the human and divine sides.[11]

---

8. Berkhof, *Christian Faith*, 193.

9. Berkhof, *Christian Faith*, 193. People may say that they are "notoriously religious," but so also were the Jews who crucified Jesus.

10. Barth, *Credo*, 85.

11. Barth, Credo, 87.

6. "Christ for Us" Citations and Christ's Representative History on Our Behalf

"Many times Paul uses a traditional formula, probably of liturgical origin, for his specific purpose. We think here above all of the formula 'Christ died for our sins,' which is found in one of its many forms in the oldest confessional tradition in 1 Corinthians 15:3-9.... Its variants speak of the death of Jesus sometimes as a gift of God and evidence of the love of God (Rom 4:25; 8:32) and sometimes as the self-giving love of Christ (Gal 1:4; 2:20; 2 Cor 5:14ff).... The apostle develops an important nuance in the formula when he speaks of [Christ] dying for the godless and sinners (Rom 5:6ff), for the brethren (Rom 14:15), and for all [people] (2 Cor 5:14). The 'for us' always forms the central motif. *It includes both the meaning, 'for our sakes,' 'to our advantage,' and the meaning 'in our place,' 'as our representative.'* This interchange of meaning illuminates the depth and breadth of the formula. It confirms the fact that we are incapable of working out salvation for ourselves. Salvation comes to us always without our assistance, as a gift, according to Romans 3:24, and before we fulfilled the will of God, as Romans 5:6ff. passionately emphasizes."[12]

Beneath the NT's reasoning concerning reconciliation or atonement is the idea of *representation*, which is no merely ancient notion. For example, in modern times a school's sports team is regarded as representing the school, so that its victories or defeats are regarded as the school's. More seriously, an armed force's military victory or defeat is that of the nation on whose behalf the war was fought.

The early Christians and the Jews before them also believed in representation. They thought that one person could so completely stand for others that what happened to that person, a king or prophet, for example, happened on their behalf and for their sake. The idea goes even further. Even granting great differentiation, a person's experience *can become foundational for other people's experience*. The NT affirms that Jesus Christ died and rose for the sin of the world, but also attests that because this is so and because humankind shares in this victory, people analogously can and should die to sin and rise to new life in Christ (Rom 6:1-14).

Jesus Christ is the Representative Person because God regards His life, death, and resurrection as standing for us. God has not only chosen to come forth in Christ, but to see us in the light of Christ rather than in terms of what we deserve. We are clothed in the righteousness of Christ. Jesus's history is more truly our history than the immediate events of our own lives. For whether or not we respond positively, God regards us in the light of Jesus's history.[13] The Christian Gospel is not the message of a mere possibility, but of an accomplishment, a reality that exists apart from and prior to our faith. Our participation in Christian faith thus involves a realization of reality.

---

12. Kasemann, "The Pauline Theology of the Cross," 158, my emphasis.
13. Barth, *CD* 4/1:548, 249.

7. New Testament's Specific "Reconciliation" Understanding and Its Linkage with Justification and Right-Wising[14]

Paul uses reconciliation terminology only twice, both in conjunction with references to justification or its equivalent: "God shows his love for us in that while we were sinners, Christ died for us. Since, therefore, we are now *justified* by his blood, much more shall we be saved by him from the wrath of God. For if while we were enemies we were *reconciled* to God by the death of his son, much more, now that we are *reconciled*, shall we be saved by his life" (Rom 5:8–10, my emphases). "If anyone is in Christ, he is a new creation; the old has passed away; behold, the new has come. All this is from God, who through Christ *reconciled* us to himself and gave us the ministry of reconciliation; that is, God was in Christ reconciling the world to himself, *not counting their trespasses against them*, and entrusting to us the message of reconciliation. So we are ambassadors of Christ, God making his appeal through us. We beseech you on behalf of Christ, be reconciled to God" (2 Cor 5:17–20, my emphases).

Likely written by a student of Paul's, Colossians 1:15–22 relates reconciliation to *God's overcoming of human hostility and the establishing of peace through His action in Christ*. This passage furthermore regards such reconciliation as applying to all creation ("all things," vs. 20a), as involving *a reclaiming of creation* (vs. 18, my emphasis), and as constituting Christ's preeminence as head of the church (vs. 18a). In addition, all things are said not only to be created through Christ but for Him (vs. 16c). In Him all things hold together (vs. 17b) and He will be preeminent in everything (vs. 18c).

Even less likely to have been written by Paul, Ephesians attests that reconciliation means that God in Christ has provided free access to Himself. Thereby God has *established peace*, and ended hostility between humankind and Himself (Eph 2:11–18).

New Testament "reconciliation" imagery pictures the overcoming of humankind's battle against God. Eschatologically the enmity will be finished and to a degree is even now being overcome because God through His action in Christ has set His wrath aside and provided access to Himself (Eph 2:18). "All this is from God, who through Christ reconciled us to himself" (2 Cor 2:18a).[15] "The supremacy of God is crucial to Paul, for [divine] reconciliation functions not as a reciprocal activity in the sense that two friends who had become estranged agree to sit down and talk out their differences. Reconciliation is not to be equated with 'making up.' It is rather a way to describe God's saving of a lost and disoriented world, which is in no position to negotiate a truce."[16]

Coming into relationship with God through Christ is the goal of creation. In Christ God wishes to unite all things, those on earth and those in heaven (Eph 1:10; cf. Col 1:16).[17]

---

14. See chap. 19, sec. 7 for a discussion of Paul's "righteousness of God" terminology, which can be more clearly expressed as God's *"right-wising"* action. The latter word usage also has the advantage of more clearly expressing the English language linkage with God's *"justifying."*

15. The NT regards God as the subject of the verb "to reconcile." Though Ephesians 2:13–17 regards the work of *God* as taking place through the Risen Christ, the Risen Christ is a dimension of the triune God.

16. Cousar, *Theology of the Cross*, 182.

17. See chap. 27.

8. Divine Love as Source of Reconciliation

People have lived from themselves rather than with trusting dependence upon and obedience to God. Though as the guilty party humankind cannot establish relationship with God, God enables this through Christ by the power of the Holy Spirit. God, not humankind, reconciles; and humankind, not God, is reconciled. Reconciliation occurs as God through Christ forgives sin as the barrier between ourselves and God, and as God as Holy Spirit convinces us of His forgiveness and empowers us to become more faithful.

Whereas in Traditional Religion *people* do various things to placate or appease the gods to try to win favorable terms from them, Christian Faith affirms that God has taken the initiative. "*All this is from God*, who through Christ reconciled us to himself" (2 Cor 5:18, my emphasis). "It was the good pleasure of the Father . . . through [Christ] to reconcile all things unto himself" (Col 1:19–20; cf. Eph 2:4–6).

Historical Theories concerning Divine Reconciliation

9. Dissatisfaction with Anselm's Satisfaction Theory of Divine Reconciliation[18]

Anselm's satisfaction theory of the atonement assumed that pre-Calvary divine forgiveness was impossible, because God was not thought to be willing to forgive until appeased by the supererogatory (duty surpassing) suffering of Jesus [in His human dimension] on the cross.[19]

This theory represents the atonement as involving the merciful Son's appeasing of the honor of a Father reluctant to forgive. This being achieved by the Son *in His human dimension* enduring representative suffering on our behalf, and thereby providing to our credit a work of supererogation (doing more than duty requires).

Anselm said that the incarnation and atonement were necessary because sin offended the moral dignity of the implanter of the natural law. Lest the natural law come to be held in disrepute, Anselm believed that God required that compensation be paid to Him. Since as a sinless human Jesus did not need to make amends for His own deficiency, His suffering on the cross went beyond what God required. Thus God's honor and His naturally implanted moral order could be preserved, and God could forgive *without violating these supposed higher values*.

Against Anselm's thinking, "within the New Testament there is no thought that God seeks to have justice done for offenses against him, [so] that Christ must step in to appease God's wrath on behalf of humanity, and that Christ's sacrifice, as being perfect, satisfies divine justice. . . . Even in those places at which sacrificial and cultic terminology is used, it is clear that *God* offered Christ for the sake of human redemption. There is an *indissoluble solidarity between God and Christ*."[20]

---

18. Anselm lived from 1033–1109 and was the Archbishop of Canterbury.
19. Ritschl, *Justification and Reconciliation*, 543.
20. Hultgren, *Christ and His Benefits*, 198, my emphases.

Anselm separated the incarnate Son's humanity from His divinity. According to Anselm's dichotomous understanding, God required satisfaction and Jesus as the sinless human provided it by His suffering. "The direction is separational, with Christ suffering as man what God's justice demanded."[21] Jesus loves us this we know, but with this theory we are left to wonder whether the transcendent God really does.

As for Anselm's related triunitarian mistake, his atonement thinking isolated and divided the "*personas*" (modes of being and of revelation) of the triune God. The merciful Son was regarded as the source of reconciliation, not the Father. To the contrary, the NT represents the transcendent God as the source of reconciliation: "*God shows his love for us in that while we were sinners Christ [lived and] died for us*" (Rom 5:8, my emphasis). We love because in and through Christ, *God first loved us* (1 John 4:19). The Son came, lived and died *not* so that God would begin to love humankind, but because *from all eternity God has done so*. "The love of God the Father precedes our reconciliation in Christ; or rather it is because He first loved that He afterwards reconciled us to Himself."[22] *The Father's love is the cause, not the result of our reconciliation.*

With Anselm God's honor seems higher than His love, as though God were honor rather than love. To the contrary, reconciliation occurred because God in His love willed it and enabled it to happen. Analogously, Christian parents' love should be the unconditional and reliable source of all else in the relationship with the children.

10. Evaluation of Representative Punishment Theory; Distinction between Expiation and Propitiation

Luther and Calvin changed Anselm's satisfaction theory (that the Son by His suffering appeased the Father's honor) into the teaching that the Son by His suffering endured the punishment we deserve and thereby enabled the Father to forgive us,[23] both theories being unbiblical.

An OT representative punishment text that *with its past tense reference could not have been pointing forward to Christ* is Isaiah 53:4–6. "Surely he has born our griefs and carried our sorrows; yet we esteemed him stricken, *smitten by God and afflicted*. But he was wounded for our transgressions, he was bruised for our iniquities; upon him was the chastisement that made us whole, and with his stripes we are healed. All we like sheep have gone astray; we have turned everyone to his own way; and the Lord has laid on him the iniquity of us all" (my emphasis). Certainly prophetic witnessing has its costs, then, with Jesus, and now, but this past tense OT reference does not contribute to a theory of God's atoning action through Jesus. And though prophetic witnessing has its costs, should we agree that God inflicts such punishments on His prophets?

The 1 Peter 2:24–25 text that has been thought to validate *representative punishment* atonement comes nowhere close to doing so, though at first reading it might seem to. This

---

21. Gunton, *Actuality of the Atonement*, 180.

22. Calhoun, *Lectures*, 398, quoting from Calvin with no source indication. For Calvin only some were regarded as the objects of God's love.

23. The Christology implied by Anselm, Luther, and Calvin's reconciliation theories at these points seem to be Nestorian (involving the separating of the divine and human natures).

text does not say that God representationally punished Jesus so as to be able to forgive us, which is based on an over-interpretation of verse 24c (see below). The broader text points to the divine love in response to which we can begin the lifelong process of dying to sin and rising to costly discipleship: "He himself *bore our sins* in his body on the tree, that we might die to sin and live to righteousness" (vs. 24ab). Then the disputed verse: "*By his wounds [we] have been healed*" (vs. 24c). This occurs by Jesus's disclosure of divine love, not by God's representative punishment of Jesus. "For [we] were straying like sheep, but have now returned to the Shepherd and Guardian of [our] souls" (my emphases) (vs. 25).

As for *the distinction between expiation and propitiation*, unlike the implications of propitiation, expiation does not entail God changing from being angry and wrathful into being loving, but assumes that *God* in His love set the possibility of wrath aside (1 Thess 5:9; cf. Rom 1:18). If one considered only the linguistic possibilities, one could in Romans 3:25, 1 John 2:2 and 4:10 translate as "propitiate," rather than "expiate." So translating the Romans 3:25 would imply Christ's appeasing of God's anger. However, the context of the Romans text argues against such a linguistic choice, for it says that *God put forward* the Son. Similarly, the wider Johannine context of 1 John 2:2 and 4:10 makes it clear that "expiation," not "propitiation," is intended. First John 4:14 affirms that *the Father* sent the Son to be the Savior. *Rather than demanding to be appeased, the Father is the source of reconciliation.*

The wider theology of Paul and of the Johannine school indicate that God is the source of the Christ event and of atonement through Him: "God was in Christ reconciling the world to himself, not counting their trespasses against them" (2 Cor 5:19ab). "For God so loved the world that he gave his only Son" (John 3:16a).

11. Peter Abelard in Contrast to Anselm and Socinus

Abelard's understanding of atonement or reconciliation was formulated in reaction to Anselm's perspective. In contrast to Anselm, Abelard did not believe that the Father was reluctant to forgive. Even before becoming incarnate in Christ, God loved humankind and had the burden of humankind on His heart. And thus God came to us in Christ.

Abelard believed that the Son came to earth to reconcile us to God by showing forth God's love, which can evoke our loving response. The Son came to seek and to save the lost (Luke 19:10) and to bear witness to the truth (John 18:37). Abelard understood Jesus's death as but one of the ways—albeit the most important—in which God in Christ demonstrated His love. Though the Son did not come to earth to be rejected and crucified, these occurred as consequences of having remained faithful to His calling to manifest God's love in this sinful world.

Abelard's understanding of how we gain at-one-ment with God has often been confused with the Socinian (Unitarian) view, but was considerably different. The *Socinians* did not believe in Jesus's divinity, and thus *regarded Jesus's life and death as only exhibiting true human love for God*. Unlike Abelard they did not believe that Jesus demonstrated God's love for us who as sinners cannot save ourselves. Socinians had an optimistic understanding of human nature. Failing to recognize that Jesus lived from dependence on God's leading, they regarded Jesus's example as useful only in manifesting the kind of behavior we must exhibit if we are to earn our way, as they thought Jesus did. This humanistic viewpoint regarded Jesus as an autonomous moral agent, not as dependent upon and obedient to the Father.

Unlike Socinian works-righteousness, Abelard emphasized the divine basis of the Son's work, and regarded His life, death and resurrection as demonstrating the love whereby God forgives sinners. Like the Socinians, Abelard emphasized the moral response to the Christ event, but regarded God's loving forgiveness in Christ as not only the source of our salvation, but the motivation for living the Christian life. Unlike the Socinians' atonement theory, Abelard's is not a mere "moral influence" type.

Abelard believed that God can so transform people by His revealed love that hearts of stone can be thawed and replaced by hearts of flesh (Ezek 36:26). That Christ gave Himself for people and suffered for them can evoke responses of gratitude and love for God, and the desire to serve others as did Christ. Though Abelard *did not tell us how love can be poured forth from a past event*, this can happen as the Spirit leads us to the Son and thereby to the Father. In response to the Father known through the Son and by the guidance of the Spirit, we "love because he first loved us" (1 John 4:19).

"Abelard affirms that God has freely chosen to display his love . . . , but why in a death?" "I believe that it is to find an answer to this pressing question that Abelard returns to the range of traditional images and theories of atonement that he previously found to be unsatisfactory. Expositors of Abelard often express surprise that, having propounded his own theory of redeeming love, Abelard still resorts to images of sacrifice, expiation, purchase and the defeat of Satan that he had previously weighed and found wanting."

Evaluation. "In portraying the crucified Christ as a sacrifice . . . [Abelard] shows consistency by refraining from mentioning any notion of appeasing God. Christ sacrifices himself, as both priest and victim . . . in an act of love 'for us.'" "There is, of course, a straightforward answer to the question as to why the love of God is demonstrated finally in the death of Christ: it is because God Himself undergoes the bitter depths of human experience on the cross. God, we may say, shows his love by enduring to the uttermost the estrangement of His own creation. This is the depth of God's identification with us. But Abelard, like others of his time, is not able to give this answer. He is working with the presupposition that the divine nature cannot suffer or change in any way, so that it is only the *human nature* of Jesus which suffers on the cross."[24]

12. Ritschl's Abelardian Contribution

Albrecht Ritschl teaches that God wishes to make us adult children of God who honor God's kingship. Because sin separates us from God and from realizing His purposes for our lives, only divine forgiveness can reunite us with God and enable us to best contribute to God's purposes. Ritschl insists that God's love is the ground or basis of forgiveness, but that Jesus in His divinely authorized vocation is the means whereby we come to know of divine forgiveness. Unlike the Enlightenment theologians he does not take God's loving forgiveness for granted, but trusts in it because Jesus has convincingly shown forth God's love.

---

24. Fiddes, *Past Event and Present Salvation*, 155, 156, 156, 157.

Ritschl conceded that divine forgiveness is also demonstrated in the OT, but thought that such manifestations are "indefinite and imperfect" compared with that granted in Christ (an assessment shared by the book of Hebrews).[25]

Ritschl thought the church was justified in emphasizing the primacy of Jesus's death in revealing God's forgiveness, since Jesus's words at the Last Supper pointed to the sacrificial reality of His forthcoming death. But like Abelard, Ritschl also insisted that the atoning importance of Jesus's death should not be understood in such a way as to negate the Gospels' conviction that Jesus extended divine forgiveness in His pre-Calvary life and action.[26]

13. Faith Involves Recognizing Objective Atoning Value of What God Has Done for Us in Christ

As the NT perceived, reconciliation *occurred outside of our existence and prior to our experience*.[27] In criticism of Bultmann, Dahl writes, "The saving act of God in Christ is visible only to faith; but this is not to say that only preaching and faith make the Christ-event the saving act of God. It is God's saving act apart from our faith and before our preaching. This is what Paul expresses when he depicts the death of Christ as expiatory sacrifice, substitution, cosmic event, and so forth. It is also expressed when, in opposition to the Gnostics at Corinth, he adduces evidence for the historicity of the resurrection."[28]

In raising Jesus from the dead God validated the saving efficacy of Jesus's life and death, and Jesus's resurrection was prior to our participation in the power of the Risen Christ. Similarly, reconciliation is objective in that *Christ did not live and die only for Christians, but for all people.* Thus Paul spoke of Jesus Christ as reconciling *the world* unto Himself (2 Cor 5:19).[29] "For the love of Christ controls us, because we are convinced that one has died for all; therefore [representationally and anticipatorily] *all have died*" (2 Cor 5:14, my emphasis).

A purpose of the Spirit's action in our lives is to draw us to Christ and to open our minds to what God has done in Christ, that we may thereby live as God's grateful children. As a free-standing mystical substitute for faith in Christ, religious experience loses its uniquely Christian dimension. Galatians 2:20 holds the balance between past revelation in Christ and present participation in Christ: "I have been crucified with Christ; it is no longer I who live, but Christ who lives in me; and the life that I now live in the flesh I live by faith in the Son of God who loved me and gave himself for me."

---

25. Ritschl, *Justification and Reconciliation*, 320, 540, 538, 541. Like Harnack, Ritschl was less than faithful to the NT in being indifferent to Christ's ontological status as God's unique agent of redemption. Nevertheless, Ritschl was true to the Synoptic Gospels in regarding Jesus's forgiving activity as due to His consciousness of standing in close relationship with God. And Ritschl was faithful in emphasizing Jesus's vocation of calling those who had responded to the divine forgiveness of sin to become adult children of God (Ritschl, *Justification and Reconciliation*, 542).

26. Since the Synoptic Gospels attest that the earthly Jesus extended divine forgiveness with His words and actions (e.g., Luke 19:9), the book of Hebrews cannot be correct when it says that without the shedding of blood there is no divine forgiveness (9:22).

27. See chap. 19, secs. 4 and 7; chap. 20, sec. 6.

28. Dahl, *Jesus the Christ*, 208.

29. Weber, *Foundations of Dogmatics*, 2:187.

Chapter 19

Justification and the Righteousness of God[1]

1. Challenging Boastfully Supposing We Can Gain Salvation through Works

A SPECIFICALLY HUMAN STRIVING that generates pride and is common to all people is seeking recognition of one's achievement. Because we are divinely justified apart from our accomplishments, boasting concerning ourselves has no place (Rom 3:27–28). *No human being is to boast in the presence of God* (1 Cor 1:29), and we always are in that presence. "Paul's conversion to belief in Christ entailed precisely the abandoning of all self-glorying. It was not the product of [prior] contrition and repentance for a life gone wrong, but was the surrender, the sacrifice of everything of which he had been proud."[2] Paul's conversion consisted of "obedient submission to the judgment of God, made known in the cross of Christ, upon all human accomplishment and boasting."[3] Upon encountering the Risen Christ, Paul learned to regard the irreproachable law-righteousness of his Jewish past as loss for the sake of Christ (Phil 3:7–9; see section 10 below). "Far be it from me to glory except in the cross of our Lord Jesus Christ" (Gal 6:14a).

> In his very attempt to obtain righteousness from God through his works, the original sin of man is latent. . . . He imagines he can live [by] his own strength and earn his acceptance with God. This is simply the Jewish form of a tendency inherent in all [people]. The Greek form of it is boasting of one's wisdom. The hankering after something to boast about is the root of [much, but not] all other evils. It is sin, rebellion against God, [failure to] live by the grace of God. "What have you that you did not receive? If then you received it, why do you boast as if it were not a gift?" (1 Cor 7:4b) This is just what man must own up to. He must make an absolute surrender to the grace of God. That is what is meant by "believing." And that is

---

1. Divine justification/right-wising as related to reconciliation is dealt with briefly in chap. 18, sec. 7.
2. Bultmann, *Essays Philosophical and Theological*, 174.
3. Bultmann, *Theology of the New Testament*, 1:188.

the stumbling-block for natural man, with his hankering after recognition. That is what makes the gospel message for him a scandal and foolishness (1 Cor 1:23). It is a scandal because it is the message of the Cross. For by causing Christ crucified to be proclaimed as Lord, God crushes human pride. That is why Paul refuses to boast any more "save in he cross of our Lord Jesus Christ, by whom the world is crucified to me, and I to the world" (Gal 6:14).[4]

"Being ignorant of the righteousness that comes from God, and seeking to establish their own, [the Jews] did not submit to God's righteousness" (Rom 10:3). Similarly, "in the face of the Greeks and Gnostics who [were] proud of their wisdom [Paul asked]: 'what do you have that you did not receive?' And he called out to them in Jeremiah's words, 'he that glories, let him glory in the Lord' (1 Cor 1:31; 2 Cor 10:17)."[5]

2. Jesus Proclaimed and Embodied Justification as Divine Forgiveness

The experience of divine acquittal is common to the Gospels as well as to Paul, but in the Gospels is only once reflected in the terminology of "justification." Such phraseology concerning justification is seen in Jesus's teaching that the tax-collector who recognized His sinfulness was justified, acquitted, and forgiven, and thereby set in right relationship with God (Luke 18:9–14). In contrast, the Pharisee who gloried in his own religious and moral attainments was unable to appropriate divine forgiveness, to experience justification as pardon (Luke 18:9–14).[6]

3. Paul and Pauline Writers Attest Divine Forgiveness, Sometimes with Linkage to Justification

Belief in divine forgiveness in Christ was crucial to Paul, though he seldom used only that terminology. Paul preferred to use the language of justification even when referring to divine forgiveness. He may have favored such alternative terminology because appropriated justification implies not only pardon, but moral empowerment. Yet in one place Paul employed only forgiveness terminology. In Romans 4:7 and quoting from Psalm 32 he wrote, "Blessed are those whose iniquities are forgiven, and whose sins are covered; blessed is the [person] against whom the Lord will not reckon his sin." Divine forgiveness terminology is utilized in Colossians and Ephesians, but there being little possibility that Paul wrote the former, and no likelihood that he wrote the latter. Broadening beyond mere forgiveness, the Colossians passage links forgiveness with moral renewal: "He has delivered us from the dominion of darkness and transferred us to the kingdom of his beloved Son, in whom we have redemption, the forgiveness of sins" (1:14). As for Ephesians's divine forgiveness

---

4. Bultmann, *Primitive Christianity*, 183.

5. Bultmann, *Essays Philosophical and Theological*, 47.

6. Paul's teaching on justification as acquittal differed from Jesus's by centering upon the completed action of God in Christ, specifically upon the crucifixion and resurrection.

attestation, "In [Christ] we have redemption through his blood, the forgiveness of our trespasses, according to the riches of his grace which he lavished upon us" (1:7).

Even as we share in God's presence and power, and live at the overlap of the two ages we must continue to confess our daily need for divine forgiveness. Never in this life do we sinners outgrow our need for God's forgiveness.

4. Substitutionary Understandings of Atonement in General and of Justification in Particular[7]

Paul evidenced a substitutionary atonement perspective, affirming that Christ "died for all, therefore all have died" (2 Cor 5:14b). Paul not only repeatedly spoke of "Christ for us" but affirmed that God sees us in Him whom God has made our wisdom, righteousness, sanctification, and redemption (1 Cor 1:30).[8] Paul was not saying that God saves us by punishing Christ rather than us, as in Calvin's penal satisfaction theory. But Paul did affirm that God regards us as clothed in Christ's righteousness, rather than in our own sinfulness.[9] Through a costly *exchange* our sin has been assumed by the sinless one, and *His righteousness has become ours*. This seems to be the meaning of the cryptic passage that "For our sake [God] made him to be sin who knew no sin, so that in him *we might become the righteousness of God*" (2 Cor 5:21, my emphasis).

"We must be careful not to describe . . . the coming of Jesus Christ in place of us sinners, this exchange between the divine and our false human position, as an exchange only in appearance . . . If anything is in bitter earnest it is that God Himself in His eternal purity and holiness has in the sinless man Jesus Christ taken up our evil case in such a way that He . . . has made it His own. He did not, in fact, spare His only Son but delivered Him up for us all (Rom 8:32)."[10]

Concerning eschatological acquittal through substitution picture a courtroom: After the Divine Judge has scrutinized our lives and pronounced us guilty, He steps down and comes to stand in our place. Consequently we need no longer fear the penal effects of divine judgment, but can gratefully go forth to serve.

What is said with the legal image concerning justification is in many respects the same as is affirmed with the other images of atonement. In all of these our desperate situation as sinful people is implied and the unreserved love of God in Christ is attested.

---

7. See the chap. 18, sec. 7.

8. Weber, *Foundations of Dogmatics*, 2:290.

9. A substitutionary understanding of atonement may be implied by the Pauline-influenced 1 Peter. "Christ also died for sins once for all, the righteous for the unrighteous, that he might bring us to God" (3:18a).

10. Barth, *CD* 4/1:237.

5. Justification as God's Faithfulness to His Purpose in Human Creation

In the free exercise of His love God created human beings for loving relationship with Himself and humankind. In spite of massive human sinfulness, God remains faithful to His loving purpose. He vindicates[11] and upholds His original resolve, and thereby manifests His faithfulness. These convictions form a major aspect of Paul's thinking concerning "justification" and of his (linguistically and theologically) related concept "the righteousness of God."

In the background of Paul's Romans 1:17 language about the righteousness of God and justification is the OT and Jewish belief that God is righteous in that He acts to sustain His people Israel and remains loyal to His promises to them.[12] Paul broadened and extended such thinking: He understood God's righteousness as demonstrated by God's saving action on the cross and by Jesus resurrection. And regarded such righteousness as involving God's faithfulness to Jews, gentiles and humankind.[13] God in Christ offered Himself in our place and for our sake—and thereby maintained His faithfulness to His human creation (2 Cor 5:21).

In justifying humankind "God . . . justifies Himself," remaining faithful to His purpose. Humankind's unfaithfulness cannot destroy God's faithfulness (Rom 3:3). Paul's proclamation involved no balancing of Yes and No, for in Christ all the promises of God find their fulfillment (2 Cor 1:18–20). Let God be true, though the whole world be false (Rom 3:4). "The wrong of [humankind] cannot in any way alter the right of God. . . . He is unchanged in His right, the right of the One who is . . . the Creator and the Lord of the covenant. Whatever [people] may do in the folly of [their] pride . . . cannot disrupt this self-determination of God."[14]

6. Justification as Received through Faith Leading toward Obedience

The good news of God's grace is known only through faith. Paul attests that he is "not ashamed of the gospel: it is the power of God for salvation to everyone who has faith, to the Jew first and also to the Greek. For in it God's righteousness [God's right-wising activity] is revealed through faith and for faith; as it is written, 'He who through faith is righteous shall live'" (Rom 1:16–17).

One aspect of faith involves believers being brought under God's dominion and thereby empowered for obedience. Believers coming under the sway of God's gracious leading (Rom 6:15), submitting to God's righteousness (Rom 6:13, 18–19; 10:3), and bearing fruit toward sanctification (Rom 6:22).

---

11. It is clear that the word "justify" can mean "vindicate." For example, the lawyer in Luke 10:29 wished to "justify" himself, i.e., to vindicate his position.
12. Ziesler, *Paul's Letter to the Romans*, 70.
13. Pannenberg, *ST*, 1:434.
14. Barth, *CD* 4/1:534.

7. Righteousness of God/Justification as Double-Sided Concept

Though Paul uses the full "justification *by faith*" phrase frequently in his letters, as indicated in this note,[15] he speaks of justification several times without the "by faith" addition. The latter passages from Romans are the following: "Since all have sinned and fall short of the glory of God, they are justified by his grace as a gift through the redemption which is in Christ Jesus" (3:24–25); Christ "was put to death for our trespasses and raised for our justification" (4:25); "Since, therefore, we are now justified by his blood, much more shall we be saved by him from the wrath of God" (5:9); "As one man's trespass led to condemnation for all persons, so one man's act of righteousness leads to justification resulting in life for all persons" (5:18); and "it is God who justifies" (8:33).[16]

It is obvious that the language of justification is used by Paul in two ways. "(1) He can speak of the justification of *humanity* through Christ's 'act of righteousness' (Rom 5:18), which is known only through the gospel." This usage is "*theocentric and cosmic* in scope, and does not deal with the appropriational aspect." "(2) He can [also] speak of the 'realized' justification of believers through faith. . . . [Whereas] the first [usage] is rooted in the righteousness of God . . . manifested in the coming of the Messiah or messianic age, . . . [and is apocalyptically oriented], justification in the second sense is *anthropocentric . . . and personal*, [focusing on appropriation] . . . The believer lays claim to the . . . . grace of God, freely given, apart from works of the law."[17] As justified by God the believer no longer faces any condemnation (Rom 8:1), is a new creation (2 Cor 5:17) and belongs to the age to come.

8. Justification as Received through Faith, Not Works

Paul certainly thought that faith should encourage obedience to God (Rom 1:5). But "*works" in Paul's usage are the proud achievements of people fulfilled by their own strength.* In contrast, the obedience that is commended by Paul involves humble dependence on the gift of God's presence and leading. Paralleling Paul's understanding, one notes that the Pharisee in Luke 18:9–14 "misused the law in order to glorify himself in the presence of God, to stand in God's presence in his own strength, and . . . to establish a claim on God. Such a [person] does not fulfill God's demand [for] . . . pure self-surrendering obedience, but sees in his obedience an achievement of which he may be proud."[18] Not so with the tax collector who "standing far off would not even lift up his eyes to heaven but beat his breast saying, 'God, be merciful to me a sinner!' I tell you, this man went down to his house justified rather than the other; for everyone who exalts himself will be humbled, but he who humbles himself will be exalted" (vss. 13–14).

Not only do we not gain our standing before God on the basis of our works. We also are not made righteous with God *by our faith*, but by God's action in Jesus Christ received

---

15. Rom 3:26–30; 5:1; 10:4; Gal 2:16; 3:8, 24; Phil 3:9.
16. Hultgren, *Paul's Gospel and Mission*, 83.
17. Hultgren, *Paul's Gospel and Mission*, 96–97.
18. Bultmann, *Essays Philosophical/Theological*, 170–71.

through faith. Through our trusting relationship with Christ we appropriate the saving reality of what God has done for us, and this faith is also the foundation for the Christian moral life. However, our faith in Christ does not change God from being against us to being for us, but changes us from being closed to God's influence to being His disciples.

We must be saved by grace through faith (Eph 2:8a) and not by works, and this in part because we have already failed morally.[19] But this is also because we need to live in relationship with God and with God guiding us.

Jesus emphasized that though Christians must become genuine disciples, no quantity of good works can enable us to earn our salvation. Even had we done all that God commands we would only have done our duty (Luke 17:10). But if our "relationship" with God does not morally empower, we have not truly experienced relationship with God (Matt 7:16–30). Article twelve of the Thirty-Nine Articles of Religion of the Church of England puts the matter well: "Good works, which are the fruits of faith and follow after justification, cannot put away our sins and endure the severity of God's judgment, yet they are pleasing and acceptable to God in Christ, and spring *necessarily*[20] of a true and lively faith; insomuch that by them a lively faith may be as evidently known as a tree is discerned by its fruit."[21]

Hebrews 12:14 writes of "the holiness without which no one will see the Lord."[22] Though we experience justification and rebirth by grace, this text teaches that in all cases God will require a degree of moral sanctification in order to attain eternal salvation. Such a quantitative way of thinking not only means that final salvation is by both grace and works, but that the thief on the cross to whom Jesus is said to have promised eternal life (Luke 23:34) could not have been saved. For he would have had no remaining years with which to show forth the sincerity of his faith by doing good works.[23] The Hebrews teaching would not only rule out the possibility of last minute conversions, but would entirely foreclose the universal salvation issue.

The book of Hebrews has another problematic teaching that for centuries caused the church to exclude the book from the emerging NT canon. It teaches that if after first repenting one falls into apostasy there can be no second repentance (6:4–6). This teaching caused many early Christians to delay being baptized until shortly before their deaths. It

---

19. Rom 1:18–3:20; cf. Gal 3:10.

20. Wesley excluded this word when he condensed these for American Methodist use and may have done so because he was more Pelagian/Arminian/synergistic concerning the relationship between works and faith. See chap. 21, secs. 1–3.

21. See Bicknell, *Thirty-Nine Articles*, 207, my emphasis.

22. Roman Catholics, John Wesley, many United Methodists, Holiness Christians, Seventh-Day Adventists, and Jehovah's Witnesses have taken Hebrews 12:14 at face value, affirming that final salvation is by a combination of grace and works.

Contrary to Paul's experience and teaching, Wesley's prevenient [preceding] grace teaching even insists that good works are needed for bringing oneself to the experience of justification. Contradicting this teaching, Wesley and the earliest Methodists spent much time preaching to condemned criminals on their way to be hung. Concerning the prevenient grace teaching see chap. 21, secs. 2–3.

23. Even if one doubts the historicity of the saying as grounded in the crucifixion context, the general point still stands: There can be life-renewing conversions even when there is no time left to morally exemplify one's new orientation.

misunderstood repentance, thinking it can only occur once, whereas, as Luther insisted, it is surely an ongoing experience.

Luther and Calvin did not wish to minimize the importance of good works, and Calvin emphasized that God commands us to be faithful disciples. Contrary to what Luther sometimes affirmed, good works often do not *spontaneously and abundantly* flow from the new relationship with God. But both Luther and Calvin rightfully objected to the Catholic and Medieval synergistic way of conceiving the relationship with God, whereby the experience of God's grace is understood as at the behest of unregenerated human will-power. They could no longer think in such terms because they regarded human sinfulness as so extensive as to incapacitate such human abilities, and also because they had experienced freely bestowed grace.

Much the Reformation person at this point, Albrecht Ritschl argued against the popular tendency in the churches to regard good works as a concurrent or supplemental cause of salvation.[24] Ritschl also singled out his philosophical hero Kant for censure in this same regard. "The conjunction of justification and good works is seen in Kant, who says that our hope of salvation is based on two causes: forgiveness by the Divine Judge, and walking in a new and dutiful [way]. In such a case forgiveness is emptied of a good deal of its meaning. Forgiveness just gives us a new [self-saving] start."[25]

We should understand the relationship of works to faith in qualified ways that neither make final salvation dependent on some combination of works and faith, nor negate the possibility of universal salvation. Yet a genuine Christian must use the remaining years after becoming a Christian in genuine service. Of course we will all face a final judgment and knowing that we move toward that final judgment encourages moral integrity. Though God will judge the actions and activities of our lives, *no one will be justified* or *saved by their works*. Were eternal life based even partly on works, the Good News of salvation by grace in Christ would mean no more than that we are given a second chance to earn salvation—an attainment impossible for sinners to achieve.[26]

9. Confidence in Justification by Grace Provides Sense of Security, Invulnerability, and Peace with God

Jesus Christ calls us forth to serve Him in the world, yet provides a point of security. "Justification imparts to us an . . . invulnerability, which at the same time is a source from which we derive strength to fight against sin and to endure and to serve."[27] "What then shall we say to this? If God is for us, who is against us? He who did not spare his own Son but gave him up for us all, will he not also give us all things with him? Who shall bring any charge against God's elect? *It is God who justifies; who is to condemn?* . . . Who shall separate us from the love of Christ? Shall tribulation, or distress, or persecution, or famine, or nakedness, or peril, or sword? No, in all these things we are more than conquerors through him

---

24. Some argued that such a teaching was necessary to combat antinomianism.
25. Ritschl, *Justification and Reconciliation*, 494.
26. See chap. 27 on eschatology.
27. Berkhof, *Christian Faith*, 433.

who loved us. For I am sure that neither death, nor life, nor angels, nor principalities, nor things present, nor things to come, nor powers, nor height, nor depth, nor anything else in all creation, will be able to separate us from the love of God in Christ Jesus our Lord" (Rom 8:31-34a, 35, 37-39, my emphasis).

Romans 5:1 links the appropriation of justification through faith to gaining peace with God through our Lord Jesus Christ. Clarifying the notion of peace with God, Ziesler writes that "for Paul this may well include a subjective feeling of having peace with God, but the focus is on the objective reality which would give grounds for the feeling."[28]

10. Some Theologically Based Social Implications of Divine Justifying/Rightwising

Paul quotes Genesis 15:6 "Abraham believed God, and it was reckoned to him as righteousness" (Gal 3:6). Paul also combines Genesis 15:6 with his restatement of Psalms 32:1-2: "Blessed are those whose iniquities are forgiven, whose sins are covered. Blessed is the [person] against whom the Lord will not reckon his sin" (Rom 4:7).

Paul associates Genesis 15:6 with the promise that *Abraham would be the father of a multitude of nations* (Gen 17:1-7, my emphasis), *and that in him all the nations of the earth would be blessed* (Gen 12:1-3, my emphasis). Vital to Paul's argument is that God promised and Abraham believed *before Abraham's circumcision*. Therefore the Jewish law requiring male circumcision and much else cannot be required for receiving the promise that God made to Abraham. Instead it is through the proclamation of Christ and the giving of the Holy Spirit that Gentiles come to share in the promise God made to Abraham (See Gal 3:14; 4:6-7; Rom 8:15-17).[29]

Paul's statement that "there is neither Jew nor Greek, neither slave nor free, male nor female; for you are all one in Christ Jesus"[30] was made amid a discussion of *justification's social consequences*. Advocating the Christian Jewish perspective, Peter and Barnabas recommended withdrawing from table fellowship with Gentile Christians unless they were willing to practice the whole of the Mosaic Law. Having come from a Jewish background, but as a Christian ministering to Gentile Christians, Paul thought that such a requirement constituted a rejecting of justification by grace through faith.

Though the doctrine of justification is theological and soteriological (pertaining to salvation), the framework that Paul uses to locate the doctrine is to a considerable extent social and historical. Even more the doctrine of justification is closely connected to Paul's personal experience:[31] "We are the true circumcision, who worship God in spirit, and glory in Christ Jesus, and put no confidence in the flesh. . . . If any other man thinks he has reason for confidence in the flesh, I have more: circumcised on the eighth day, of the people of Israel, of the tribe of Benjamin, a Hebrew born of Hebrews; as to the law a Pharisee, as to zeal a persecutor of the church, as to righteousness under the law blameless. But whatever

---

28. Ziesler, *Paul's Letter to the Romans*, 136.
29. Dahl, *Studies in Paul*, 107-8.
30. Gal 3:28; cf. Rom 3:29-30; 10:12-13; Gal 5:6; 6:15.
31. Dahl, *Studies in Paul*, 109, 110-11.

gain I had, I counted as loss for the sake of Christ. Indeed I count everything as loss because of the surpassing worth of knowing Christ Jesus my Lord. For his sake I have suffered the loss of all things, and I count them as refuse, in order that I may gain Christ and be found in him, not having a righteousness of my own, based on the law, but that which is through faith in Christ, the righteousness that comes from God that depends on faith; that I may know him and the power of his resurrection, and may share his sufferings, becoming like him in his death, that if possible I may attain the resurrection from the dead" (Phil 3:3–11).

In defense of the right-wising that comes from God through Christ that depends on faith, Paul in Galatians argues against the requirement that male Gentile believers in Christ needed to be circumcised, and that such converts should at least obey some of the ceremonial commandments and ordinances of the Mosaic Law.[32] To the contrary, *Gentile converts need not and should not first become Jews, nor need Jews who become Christian give up everything Jewish.* Paul uncompromisingly asserts the universality of the gospel while insisting that all Christian should to an extent remain members of the ethnic groups from which they came.[33] Nevertheless, he insists that justification is not through the law. "For I through the law died to the law, that I might live to God. I have been crucified with Christ; it is no longer I who live, but Christ who lives in me; and the life I now live in the flesh I live by faith in the Son of God, who loved me and gave himself for me. I do not nullify the grace of God; for if justification were through the law, then Christ died to no purpose" (Gal 2:19–21).

Paul's description in Philippians makes it clear that his experience in Judaism differed much from Luther's sense of having failed to live up to Christian standards. To the contrary, "Paul's life as a Pharisee was, by the Law's standards, 'blameless'; his zeal for the Law made him a persecutor of the church." Upon encountering the Risen Christ, Paul shunned the prior self-righteousness in which he had once hoped. "He accepted a status equivalent to that of pagan sinners, in order to obtain a righteousness which was not his own but a gift from God."[34]

"What Paul stated systematically, Jesus had already lived, in his attitudes and his activities.... As Jesus's work destroyed the significance of the distinction between sinners and the righteous in Israel, so Paul's fidelity to the truth of the gospel forbid discriminating within the church between Jews and Gentiles."

"The urgent task is to rediscover the social relevance and implications of the doctrine of justification.... To what extent does the current practice of the church deny *de facto* the doctrine of justification, because it excludes certain groups of people from free access to God's grace in his church?"[35] If the churches in the United States or elsewhere had been better able to resolve the racial issues and separations in their congregations, they would have made it easier for the society to find political solutions to the same. And what of sexual orientations? Granted the requirement of marital fidelity, need Christian marriage

---

32. Paul did not deny that Christians should honor the ten commandments.

33. Dahl, *Studies in Paul*, 108–9.

34. Dahl, *Studies in Paul*, 111. Luther came to genuine Christian faith because he looked to Christ and away *from his moral failings*. In contrast, Paul as a Pharisee had no pre-conversion sense of moral failing, but upon encountering the Risen Christ no longer took confidence in his prior legal uprightness.

35. Dahl, *Studies in Paul*, 119, 115.

only be between male and female? Many denominations are quite rightly willing to sanction such other types of marriages.

Has the message of the doctrine of justification had a major impact on the social structures of the churches? "Do I go too far to suggest that middle class social standards and stereotyped forms of conversion experiences and of religious expressions have become the ceremonial and ritual law of our time? . . . Everything depends on what Christ's ministers preach from their pulpits and on how the faithful response."[36]

---

36. Dahl, *Studies in Paul*, 120.

Chapter 20

Sacrifice, Redemption

1. Atonement as Sacrifice

GOD CAME FORTH IN Christ, stood in our place, and thereby proved to be our Savior. To make this point the NT sometimes utilizes language derived from cultic sacrifice. Jesus Christ is said to be the Priest who with His incarnation, life and death representatively offered Himself as the perfect sacrifice for our sin (1 John 2:2; 4:10; Heb 10:12). Unlike other priests who present sacrifices, this one is Himself the sacrifice offered.[1] "Since then we have a great high priest who has passed through the heavens, Jesus, the Son of God, let us hold fast our confession. For we have not a high priest who is unable to sympathize with our weaknesses, but one who in every respect has been tempted as we are, yet without sinning. Let us then with confidence draw near to the throne of grace, that we may receive mercy and find grace to help in time of need" (Heb 4:14–16).

In their representative capacities other priests, including OT ones, needed and still need to do for themselves what they do for others, making atonement for themselves, for their households, and for the congregation of Israel (Lev 16:6; Heb 9:7b). In contrast the Son of God acts exclusively on the behalf of the people. For this reason He is the true, essential and original Priest, the "great high priest" (Heb 4:14).[2]

2. Jesus's Sacrifice Began with His Incarnation and Included His Entire Life—Not Merely His Death

The Johannine writings regard the Son's death as the accomplishment of the "work" that began with His incarnation. "*Jesus's death . . . is conceived as of one piece with the whole life-work of Jesus, being its completion.*" John the Baptist is said to have indicated that the pre-Calvary Jesus was already "the Lamb of God who takes away the sin of the world" (1:29). "First John 3:5 parallels: 'he *appeared* [not just died] to take away sins.'" The figure of

---

1. Heb 9:14, 23, 26; cf. Eph 5:2; Heb 7:27; 10:14. Barth, *CD* 4/1:275, 277, 281.
2. Barth, *CD* 4/1:275.

the Lamb ... compels us to think of sacrifice. But nothing compels us to conclude that the evangelist sees this sacrifice only in Jesus death rather than in his whole ministry."[3]

3. Additional New Testament Evidence for Atonement as Sacrifice

Paul also regards Jesus's work of reconciliation as involving self-offering or sacrifice. Paul refers to Jesus Christ as the "paschal lamb" who "has been sacrificed" (1 Cor 5:7). Similarly the author of Ephesians affirms that "Christ loved us and gave himself up for us, a fragrant offering and sacrifice to God" (5:2). First Peter calls Jesus Christ the Lamb without spot or blemish, referring specifically to His death as a self-offering (1:19). "In the hymns of the Apocalypse, chiefly Revelation 5:12ff (where the 'Lamb' is mentioned regularly), it can be seen that the praise of Jesus, the sacrificed Lamb, is already totally integrated into the singing of the Community."[4]

4. Jesus's Sacrificial Self-Offering as Abolishing Cultic Sacrifices

Though the book of Hebrews (and much of the rest of the NT) uses cultic imagery to refer to Jesus's death, it does not describe a cultic event; Jesus was not sacrificed on an altar in a temple, but on a cross in a marketplace. Hebrews speaks of Jesus's sacrifice as inaugurating the new covenant (prophesied by Jeremiah)[5] that invalidates and abolishes the cultic sacrifices that were regarded as important to the old covenant. Such invalidating and abolishing is because He has achieved what those could only approximate as a shadow (Heb 10:1).[6] The Son by His self-offering has shown forth and enacted divine forgiveness, and the Risen Lord as Holy Spirit has poured forth the Holy Spirit. In these ways the new covenant has supplanted the old.[7]

"The centering of the new meaning of the word *sacrifice* on ... Jesus brings it about that there is now only one sacrifice that really matters. The author of Hebrews, the New Testament writer most responsible for the development of this theme, stresses the once-and-for-all nature of the sacrifice (7:27). . . . The metaphorical sacrifice has done what no repeated animal sacrifice can do, 'purify our consciences from dead works to serve the living God'" (Heb 9:14).[8]

---

3. Bultmann, *Theology of the New Testament*, 2:52, 55, 53–54, my emphases.
4. Weber, *Foundations of Dogmatics*, 2:191.
5. Jer 31:31–34; Heb 8:6; 9:15; 12:24.
6. Weber, *Foundations of Dogmatics*, 2:189.
7. Morris, *Cross in the New Testament*, 249.
8. Gunton, *Actuality of the Atonement*, 123–24. Hebrews thinks that the sacrifices of the old covenant never took away sin, but provided only a yearly remembrance of sin (10:3).

5. Christ Redeems and Delivers Us from Bondage to Sinfulness, from Condemning Power of the Law, and from Sense of Futility and Meaninglessness in Face of Fate

Jesus Christ our Redeemer was rejected, humiliated, and crucified. That He went this far in offering Himself for our deliverance demonstrates that we were "bought with a price."[9] When the NT uses redemption/deliverance terminology to refer to atonement the image in the background is that of prisoners or slaves unable to buy their freedom, and who thus require outside intervention to be rescued. Like all NT discussions of atonement, this terminology implies that only God can free us from bondage to sinfulness by forgiving our sin and leading us in the way of righteousness.[10] Here is an aspect of atonement understanding that relates directly to the activity of the Holy Spirit.[11]

Paul also speaks of redemption as deliverance from the indicting or condemning power of the law (Gal 3:13). Redeemed by God's action of grace in Christ, Christians are freed from the law in that they know that the law's demands should not be directly equated with God's will, that the law cannot procure salvation, and that the law has no power to condemn us eternally. Jesus was rejected by those following the letter of the OT law, and in that sense died as cursed by that law—but not by God.

Galatians 3:13 attests that the innocent Christ's taking upon himself the curse of the law has nullified the indicting power of the law. "According to Paul, Christ has ransomed us from the curse of the law by His death under the curse, in order that the Gentiles who have little regard for OT legal traditions might share in the blessing of Abraham (Gal 3:14; cf. Rom 11:11ff.)."[12] Colossians understands Christ's death as relativizing OT law (2:14), as does Ephesians (2:15a). And like Paul, Ephesians links Christ's death and resurrection and the relativizing of the OT law with the launching of the mission to the Gentiles.

According to the NT Jesus Christ not only redeems us from bondage to sin, guilt, and the condemning power of the law, but from the sense of futility and meaninglessness that comes upon those who feel helpless in the face of fate. Paul regards people together with the whole creation as in bondage to futility. "'The creation,' he says, 'was subjected to vanity' (Rom 8:20), and again 'we know that the whole creation has been groaning in travail until now' (Rom 8:22). His thought is that, apart from Christ . . . meaninglessness runs right through creation."[13]

6. Objective-Subjective, Reality-Realization, Victory-Awareness of Victory

That atonement or reconciliation summons our Spirit-led acceptance (2 Cor 5:20b) does not mean that it achieves its validity only through our acceptance, as though God in Christ

---

9. 1 Cor 6:20a; see also 1 Cor 7:23; Titus 2:14; 1 Pet 1:18.
10. Ziesler, *Paul's Letter to the Romans*, 68.
11. See Rom 1:18—3:9; 5:12-21; 6:1-23; 8:1-11. Eph 1:7; Col 1:14.
12. Pannenberg, *Jesus*, 250.
13. Morris, *Cross in the New Testament*, 206.

only issued an invitation. Through the incarnation, life, death and resurrection of Jesus Christ God forgave sin and reconciled the world unto Himself. One can refuse to accept this, but cannot thereby undo these events. The Gospel is the message of an actuality, not a mere possibility. "God was in Christ reconciling the world unto himself" (2 Cor 5:19a). Though reconciliation has already occurred, the Holy Spirit calls us to conform to reality, to be the children of God that we are in Christ, rather than continue in falsehood.

In these regards Barth polemicized against Bultmann's thinking, insisting that the Christian Gospel is no mere invitation to have an existential experience of Christ, which alone is of saving value: "I do not see why [the cross] only acquires [significance for every age] by being taken up into the kerygma and evoking the obedience of faith. On the contrary, it seems to me that the New Testament describes the cross of Christ as an event with an inherent significance of its own. It is just because it has this inherent significance that it can become significant in the kerygma and for the faith of its recipients. . . . The New Testament asserts that in faith the believer attaches himself to something . . . which took place for him on God's initiative in the [life], death [and resurrection] of Jesus Christ."[14]

A famous illustration concerning the atonement victory that has been won retains its usefulness: After the Japanese surrender, which ended World War 2 in the Pacific, Japanese soldiers in the Philippines continued to fight. They acted in tragic ignorance and their actions had unfortunate consequences for themselves and others. But they did not have the power to invalidate the truce. Analogously, the Son of God came, lived, died and rose. These events have occurred and their meaning is valid prior to and independently of human acceptance. Yet it makes much difference whether one recognizes Christ's victory; otherwise one lives in darkness and behaves accordingly. Even so, human blindness and continuing sinfulness cannot annul the Son's atoning life, death and resurrection. Sinners cannot negate the eschatological consequences of Christ's radiant victory, nor can they thwart or neutralize the practical daily consequences for those whose eyes are opened to behold this reality.

7. Summary of Some Permanent Elements in Understanding Christian Reconciliation

Here are summarized some of Carl E. Braaten's points concerning how salvation is attained, which are useful in depicting these three chapters on reconciliation. I here and there use bracketed additions to show clarifications, slight alterations or supplementations.

1. "*Only God can save*. Human beings cannot save themselves, no matter how hard they try. Every synergistic doctrine [that makes present illumination and eternal salvation finally dependent on human will-power] is a heresy, even though the majority of Christian denominations are guilty of overt or covert synergism."

2. "*God's . . . saving bridge to the world is Jesus Christ*" [as known through the power of God's Spirit], though Jesus Christ was foreshadowed in the Old Testament." "[Christ]

---

14. Barth, "Rudolf Bultmann," 98–99.

alone is the saving mediator between God and the world." God could have revealed Himself differently—but Christians must reason from the givenness of revelation."

3. "*The whole life of Christ from incarnation through resurrection must be taken into account.* The . . . cross cannot bear the whole brunt of salvation, even though the atonement centers on the cross of Jesus."

4. "*The atonement is a once-for-all act which is inherently and antecedently valid prior to any [appropriational] response on the part of believers.* Faith does not produce the meaning of the salvation event; it can only receive it in radical gratitude [leading to greater moral faithfulness]."

5. "*The human condition [involves] sin as guiltiness before the living God that can be rectified only by divine forgiveness.* Christocentric salvation has revealed that the human condition in its radical extremity consists of more than human finitude, social injustice, or existential anxiety."

6. "*God's way of salvation is by identification with sinful humanity.* . . . Luther . . . spoke of the 'happy exchange,' in which God in Christ exchanges place with sinners, so that sinners might share *gratis* the righteousness of God (cf. 2 Cor 5:21)."

7. "*In Christ God [reconciled] the whole human race, not one individual at a time* [though the Holy Spirit reaches out to individuals one by one]. The whole of humankind is a family; we are all in Adam's boat[15] and can be saved only by God's action in the New Adam.

---

15. Braaten, "The Christian Doctrine of Salvation," 126–27.

APPROPRIATING CHRISTIAN FAITH

Chapter 21

Grace to Appropriate Atonement and to Persevere in Christian Faith

1. Understanding Creational versus Appropriational Grace: A Prelude

BOTH THOSE WHO UNDERSTAND appropriation as due to creational "grace" and those who believe that appropriation occurs as God as Holy Spirit takes up fresh relationships with particular individuals have claimed they were affirming that the human response to God is due to grace—not to human effort on its own. Whether the creational/prevenient/preceding grace tradition can be sustained is questionable, since natural human capacitating is not what the NT means by grace.

Believers in prevenient/preceding grace not only believe that the Creator gifted human nature with the innate capacity to respond to God, but that even now this capacity is intact. John Wesley claimed to believe that people are inclined to evil, but he also thought that *all people possess* "God-given 'grace to balance the corruption of human nature.'"[1] Does this not mean that people are not all that sinful—as many within later nineteenth and early twentieth-century liberal theology descendants of Wesley insisted—and as many later descendants still do. Election tradition believers understand human nature as more radically sinful, supposing that humans have sinned away their God-relatedness. Thus natural humankind's existing capacities are not considered capable of moving people toward God.

The historical debate between Wesley and the orthodox Calvinists of his day about prevenient grace versus election concerned more than the issue of how people come to faith in Christ. It also related to whether one believes that God wishes to save all humankind or only a small segment. There is much NT support for believing that God wishes to save all humankind, as we will see in chapter 27, section on Universal Salvation and Eschatological Peril Teachings. Also in agreement with Wesley it seems impossible to reconcile the belief that God is love and in Christ acts with love, with orthodox Calvinism's conviction that God does not desire to save everyone. However, that God created humankind for

---

1. "The Doctrine of Original Sin," *Works, IX*, 268, quoted in Outler, *John Wesley*.

fellowship with Himself and thus wills to save everyone does not necessarily mean what Wesley thought: That the Creator implanted *within fallen human nature* the capacity to respond positively to God, and therefore people are not all that sinful.

Because there is a good deal of NT evidence for the belief in universal salvation, Wesley's objection that election defies divine love is to an extent met.[2] Thus I do not agree with Wesley that the only alternative to double predestination is the belief in naturally implanted and still intact "grace," that capacitates all people to bring themselves into relationship with God. This belief conflicts with massive amounts of NT evidence. The enigma that remains concerns why the God who wills to bring all to salvation does not here and now call everyone.[3]

2. Prevenient Grace Teaching

Prevenient grace[4] is regarded as "a measure of free-will supernaturally [?] restored to every [person]" by which people can choose for or against God.[5] Believers in prevenient grace regard decision for Christ as a function of common human nature, and as being not so different from other decisional capacities, rather than based on a new manifestation of the Spirit (cf. John 3:1–8).

Many teachings attributed to Jesus seem to presume a natural capacity to respond to God. The burden of decision is seen as so much one's own responsibility that one is threatened with punishment if one fails to decide.[6] Jesus, of course, spoke prior to His own resurrection and the outpouring of the Spirit, and those events encouraged the belief that decision for Christ becomes possible in response to the direct leading of the Spirit.

Additional New Testament evidence for the prevenient grace teaching that human nature has been and still is graced seems implied twice by the author of Acts, a late NT writing whose historical accuracy is much doubted. At Lystra Paul and Barnabas are said to have announced to an excited multitude, "In past generations [God] allowed all the nations to walk in their own ways; yet he did not leave himself without witness" (Acts 14:16–17). Indirectly implying something like prevenient grace, in the Cornelius narrative Peter is supposed to have said, "Truly I perceive that God shows no partiality, but in every nation anyone who fears him and does what is right is acceptable to him" (Acts 10:34–35). This second passage affirms that those who have not heard the Gospel can gain salvation by their good works. Because I interpret Luke's account of Paul's Areopagus speech (Acts

---

2. See the second section of chap. 27, "Universal Salvation and Eschatological Peril Teachings."

3. Unlike Calvin, Luther rejected double-predestination—some to "heaven" and some to hell—because he would make no statement about God's activity apart from faith. And he thought that faith must speak of God's grace, and of divine wrath and judgment only insofar as those serve the purposes of grace. Though he defended single predestination (to heaven) he admitted that it is an impenetrable mystery why God does not bring all people to faith.

As for terminological clarification, "predestination" terminology tends to locate the capacity to respond to God in a pre-temporal decision, whereas the language of "election" tends to detect it within divine activity in history.

4. Anabaptists utilize the concept, but not the term.

5. Wesley, "Predestination Calmly Considered," *Works*, X, 229–30, quoted in Outler, *John Wesley*.

6. Matt 18:8; 25:1–12; Luke 12:8–9; 16:1–8a.

17:22–34) with emphasis on the concluding verses (29–32a)—which accuse the Athenians of idolatry and call them to repent—that text is not understood as a defense of natural theology or of prevenient grace.

Wesley often associated prevenient grace with natural conscience. In Wesley's understanding what is often called *natural conscience* is *preventing grace*.[7] He thought this inward monitor enables all people to distinguish between good and evil.[8] Wesley also understood prevenient grace as reflected in natural conscience's enabling of people to work their way toward the experience of justification.[9] Wesley credited all people with having capacities for self-transcendence that put them *in moral (but not genuinely relational)* contact with the God revealed in Christ. In the light of today's knowledge of the great diversity of moral standards as exhibited in various cultures, Wesley's confidence in the self-transcending capacity of natural moral conscience seems naive.

Wesley's insistence that prevenient grace is a "supernatural" gift of God seems a merely verbal claim. If all humankind has always been blessed with such grace, the moral capacities believed to be enabled by grace are surely as natural as other God-given natural endowments.

Wesley thinking differs from that of Augustine, Luther, and Calvin, and in some respects is similar to Roman Catholicism and later Liberal Theology[10] in regarding the God within as an aspect of humans' creaturely nature. With Wesley, Liberal Theology and Catholicism God's Holy Spirit becomes indistinguishable from the natural human spirit. If prior to experiencing justification one's "relationship" with God is merely the expression of one's human nature, there is no real "relation" with God at such points.

The prevenient grace understanding of the first stage of "communion" with God involves a works-righteousness that places the burden of gaining salvation on human shoulders. If everyone's human nature has been so graced that everyone is here and now able to respond to God, salvation depends decisively on whether by will-power and good deeds people move themselves toward saving faith. Thus contrary to Paul's insistence,[11] every Christian has much of which to boast, namely, that they have brought themselves to saving faith.[12]

The prevenient grace teaching conflicts with the NT's massive recognition of the corrupting effects of sin that incapacitates natural humankinds' knowledge of God, as well as with the NT's widespread insistence that faith is due to the fresh outpouring of the Holy

---

7. Smith, "Some Notes on Wesley's Doctrine of Prevenient Grace," 68–80.
8. Smith, "Some Notes on Wesley's Doctrine of Prevenient Grace," 68–80.
9. A notion vehemently denied by Luther.
10. As with Ritschl, Schleiermacher, and the Social Gospel.
11. Rom 4:2; 1 Cor 4:7; see also Eph 2:8–9; Phil 3:3.
12. Because Wesley thought that by doing good deeds and utilizing the means of grace people can move themselves toward the appropriation of salvation, he eliminated Article XIII from the Anglican Thirty-nine Articles when commending a condensed version to American Methodists. That article rejected the saving value of works prior to justifying faith. The paraphrased rejected article: Works done before the grace of Christ and the inspiration of His Spirit are not pleasing to God. They do not spring from faith in Jesus Christ, do not enable people to receive grace, and, contrary to the teaching of the Medieval scholastics, do not deserve the grace of congruity (God's synergistic cooperation in faith's genesis). He also omitted Article XVII that teaches single predestination.

Spirit. *If a grace-implanted natural capacity is under our control and part of our human nature, we in and of ourselves are responsible for bringing ourselves to God.* Is not the prevenient grace teaching essentially reducible to the modern middle-class assumption—that God helps those who help themselves.

3. Historical Development of Prevenient Grace Teaching; Pietism

The prevenient/enabling grace teaching stems originally from Augustine, who inconsistently combined it with his affirmation of predestination and his belief that faith is a new supernatural gift from above. Only Augustine's prevenient/enabling grace teachings on this subject were retained by Medieval Catholicism. In terms of Trent's affirmation concerning prevenient grace, the appropriation of Christian Faith is said to begin with the stimulating and assisting grace that makes it possible for *all people* to believe. "Humankind under the influence of prevenient grace and by applying free will was regarded as [capable of] moving toward the appropriation of justification."[13]

Anabaptism (which began as early as 1522) did not and does not have an explicit prevenient grace teaching. But like Wesley, Anabaptists believe in divine-human synergism, the cooperation of the human will in coming to faith in God. They recognize that the human will is impaired, yet think that human nature is sufficiently free to capacitate all recipients of Christian proclamation for decision for Christ.[14] In effect they believe in the natural co-existence of a duality in human nature and (in this respect like Kant and Liberal Theology) teach that humans can lift themselves Godward by exerting will-power and trying harder.

In opposition to the Anabaptists and Erasmus, Luther and Calvin were pessimistic concerning human nature and the human capacity to move toward Christian Faith. Luther and Calvin (like Paul and the Johannine tradition in particular) affirmed natural humankind's bondage of the will to sin. Whereas medieval Christianity had linked divine grace with mere human assent and cooperation, Luther and Calvin began with the recognition of one's utter sinfulness and held that we sinners are justified solely by the grace of God shown forth in Christ.[15]

Jacob Arminius (1557–1609, Dutch pastor and briefly theological lecturer) was the first Protestant to explicitly affirm the Catholic prevenient grace teaching, and thereby much influenced Wesley. Arminius thought not only that all people are inspired by prevenient grace, but that *without additional divine help* all can repent and believe. He thought that God does not compel belief, and thus (contrary to Augustine) did not regard faith as irresistible.[16] "The Remonstrants [Arminians] emphasized faith as an act of [humankind],

---

13. Weber, *Foundations of Dogmatics*, 2:299.

14. See Hillerbrand, "Anabaptism and the Reformation," 410. Early Anabaptist leaders were Grebel and Manz and originated in Switzerland and Germany. The earliest such Church was the Swiss Brethren, and current such churches are the Amish, Hutterites, Mennonites, Bruderhof, and the Church of the Brethren.

15. Hillerbrand, "Anabaptism and the Reformation," 406.

16. Erickson, *Christian Theology*, 914.

based on grace . . . *[given in creation] which [humankind] can resist, abandon, or ignore*,"[17] or to which one can respond positively. Wesley's later teaching precisely![18]

Pietism was an eighteenth-century movement that much influenced Wesley. Its leaders were Moravians such as Zinzendorf, Bohler, Frank, Halle, and Spener. Barth summarized the objections that Valentin Ernst Loscher (1673–1749) had to pietism, and those I mention apply to the convictions of John Wesley, the first four seeming to overlap with Wesley's borrowings from the Anabaptists. (1) Pietism tends to confuse nature with grace by conceiving the essential aspect of human nature as damaged only slightly. (2) Pietism confuses the righteousness of faith with that of works. Along this line Wesley taught that good works move people toward experiencing justification, and that extraordinary individuals can be saved by works. (3) Pietism understands justification as primarily a process that takes place within human experience, rather than first of all through Jesus Christ. Though Wesley believed that God had acted in Christ for human salvation, he thought that what God achieved in Christ had only invitational significance. According to Wesley's teaching everything hinges on the free human response. (4) Pietism tends to understand repentance as limited to the beginning stage of the Christian life, with sanctification as the Christian life itself. (5) As for the non-Anabaptist aspect of Wesley's Pietism, he taught that absolute perfection in this life is possible. This teaching encourages pride for those who think they have attained this and despair for those who realize that they have not or cannot.[19] Though Wesley never claimed to have achieved perfection, though quizzing others as to whether they had achieved it, his considerably confused teaching about perfection seems well within the range of what Loscher was criticizing.

4. Supernatural Grace as Evoking Faith: Primarily Biblical Evidence

Many Christians are not accustomed to thinking of faith as being as much of a gift as the Gospel to which it responds. Yet the biblical emphasis on the gift nature of faith is not esoteric and finds formal parallels in everyday experience. When someone smiles at us, our smile is evoked. Though our responding smile is very much our own, we do not generate it; the gift of the other person's smile evokes ours. A more profound illustration comes from decision-making with reference to "choosing" a spouse. If one finds that one genuinely loves another person, one is much involved. Yet one's feelings and commitment are evoked and are not autonomous decisions. Certainly one should be rationally aware of the strengths and possible weaknesses of one's prospective spouse, but no mere arithmetic should be used to reach the decision that this is the person with whom to spend one's life. Such illustrations show that the idea that Christian faith is evoked by fresh grace cannot be dismissed as irrational, on the assumption that human decisions never occur as responses to analogous gifts or enablings.

---

17. Berkhof, *Christian Faith*, 444–45, referring to *The Five Articles of the Remonstrants of 1610*, Articles 4–5.

18. Though John Wesley in later years called himself an Arminian, his "Arminian" views came more directly from the Church of England, which had long been influenced by both Erasmus and Arminius.

19. Barth, *Protestant Theology in the Nineteenth Century*, 140–41.

That faith is evoked by supernatural grace assumes that people in themselves are in no position to make genuine decisions for Christ. God's reaching out to people does not encounter those already predisposed or prepared for it, but to a considerable extent encounters the 'godless' (Rom 4:5; 5:6). "*God's Yes, which is present for us in Jesus Christ, does not find the responding Yes present in us but rather [God] evokes it from us.*"[20]

The insistence that coming to faith is due to God's initiative is affirmed many times in the NT. For example, Paul says that "God *chose* what is foolish in the world to shame the wise, God *chose* what is weak in the world to shame the strong, God *chose* what is low and despised in the world, even the things that are not, to bring to nothing the things that are, *so that no human being might boast in the presence of God*" (1 Cor 1:27–29, my emphases). If we by the exertion of willpower can bring ourselves into saving faith we have much of which to boast. If, however, even our response of faith is grace-inspired afresh, we cannot credit our faith to ourselves (see 1 Cor 4:7).

Along related lines Paul affirmed that though he planted and Apollos watered *God gave the growth* (1 Cor 3:6–7). Since God guides and utilizes our testimony within His time-frame and within the mystery of His power, we are encouraged to do our best in witnessing and to entrust the results to God's care. Were we to understand the repercussions of Christian witnessing as our responsibility, on the assumption that the decision for Christ is within everyone's capacity, we might conclude that if people do not respond positively we have been unfaithful. Then to avoid such responses and maximize our effects we would be prone to use compromising and manipulative methods. Such has been seen among "church growth" advocates of "the homogeneous unit principle," catering to people's tendencies to prefer being with people of their own kind, i.e. tribe!

The NT expresses God's unmerited favor not only in the Christ event, but in the response that God elicits. "For by grace you have been saved through faith; and this is not our own doing, it is the gift of God—not because of works, lest [anyone] should boast."[21] "It is vital to Paul's teaching on salvation that a person should not be in a position to claim credit in the least degree for one's new-found relationship with God. . . . [Humankind] must receive as a beggar receives alms; only then can we receive in full measure the gifts which we so badly need."[22]

Much of the NT teaches that people have no natural capacity to bring themselves to God. Natural humankind is often regarded as dead through trespasses and sins and by nature children of wrath (Eph 2:1–3), spiritually blind and insensitive to God (Rom 1:22–23). Matthew 13:14–15 quotes Isaiah 6:9–10 to the effect that non-Christians hear

---

20. Weber, *Foundations of Dogmatics*, 2:446, my emphasis. Highly unlikely to be grounded in the historical Jesus is the Synoptic Gospels' election related explanation as to why Jesus often spoke in parables: "To you it has been given to know the secrets of the kingdom of heaven, but to them it has not been given" (Matt 13:11 and pars.). Equally unlikely as grounded in the Jesus of history is Matthew 11:25–27, concerning God's hiding from some and revealing to others. More likely based in the Jesus of history, but less Christocentric is the phrase "He who has ears to hear, let him hear" (Matt 11:15; 13:9; 13:43; Mark 4:9; 4:23; 8:18; Luke 8:8; 14:35).

21. Eph 2:8–9; see also Rom 4:2; Phil 3:3. "For we know, brethren beloved by God, that he has chosen you; for our gospel came to you not only in word, but also in power and in the Holy Spirit and with full conviction" (1 Thess 1:4–5a).

22. Houlden, *Paul's Letters from Prison*, 284.

but do not understand, see but do not perceive because they of themselves are spiritually incapable of doing otherwise. "Even if our gospel is veiled, it is veiled only to those who are perishing.[23] In their case the god of this world has blinded the minds of the unbelievers, to keep them from seeing the light of the gospel of the glory of Christ, who is the likeness of God" (2 Cor 4:3–4).

The Johannine tradition affirms that "the wind blows where it wills, and you hear the sound of it, but you do not know whence it comes or whither it goes; so it is with everyone who is born of the Spirit" (John 3:8). Those who believe in the Son of God are not born of human will-power but of God (John 1:12–13). "You did not choose me, but I chose you" (John 15:16a). According to such teaching no one can come to Christ unless the Father who sent Christ draws him (John 6:44a; see also vs. 65).

Matthew's interpretation of Jesus's understanding of the meaning of our call to discipleship also implies that faith in Christ is elicited by a direct gift of God. "At that time Jesus declared, 'I thank thee, Father, Lord of heaven and earth, that thou hast hidden these things from the wise and understanding and revealed them to babes; yea, Father, for such was thy gracious will. All things have been delivered to me by my Father; and no one knows the Son except the Father, and no one knows the Father except the Son and any one to whom the Son chooses to reveal him'" (Matt 11:25–27).

Paul speaks of himself as "called to be an apostle" (Rom 1:1; 1 Cor 1:1). "He who had set me apart before I was born . . . called me through his grace, [and] revealed his Son to me" (Gal 1:15). Paul's call caused him to affirm that his ministry came from God alone, so that by the grace of God he was what he was (1 Cor 15:9–10). "For we know, brethren beloved by God, that he has chosen you; for our gospel came to you not only in word, but also in power and in the Holy Spirit with full conviction" (1 Thess 1:4–5a). For Paul the election-based hope of Christian participation in the glory of the risen Son of God (Rom 8:28–30) is so certain that in verse 30 he can already say: "Those whom he justified he also glorified," the last term being an odd reference to one still living. "Paul wishes . . . to give expression to the joyous certainty of faith that God in Christ will lead those who are called to a sure deliverance."[24]

What can the synergist—one who supposes that human cooperation is required for regeneration—say to someone who has utilized the means of grace and has sought to do good works, and wants to believe in Christ, and yet does not yet seem able to do so? Those Christians who think that faith is a genuine gift can at least understand and sympathize with people struggling to appropriate Christian faith, rather than insisting that such struggling is because Christians have not witnessed properly or because seekers have not exerted enough will-power.

---

23. Unlike this passage I am not willing to link the gift nature of faith with an eternal dividing between the saved and the damned.

24. Kummel, *Theology of the New Testament*, 234. Surprisingly Paul also alludes to the possibility of falling from grace. "He who thinks he is standing should take heed, lest he fall" (1 Cor 10:12).

5. Supernatural Grace as Evoking Faith: Augustine, Luther, Chalmers, Edwards, Barth, Brunner

Augustine thought that human free will is so seriously compromised by sin that natural humankind is incapable of *genuinely desiring to be God-centered*. He believed that the grace of God is both necessary and sufficient to transform human wills, thereby evoking desires to center lives in God through Christ and to trust in Him.[25]

Luther emphasized our renewal by God as *ex nihilo* (out of nothing), having learned this from 2 Macc 7:28 and Rom 4:17c: God is the One "who gives life to the dead" (Rom 4:17c) and calls into Christian existence those who in themselves were unworthy sinners with no potential for genuine discipleship and for sharing in eternal life.[26] God's gracious call works by irresistible personal attraction, by granting *"the expulsive power of a new affection"* (Chalmers) evoking faith in Christ and love for others.[27]

Along Augustinian lines, Jonathan Edwards taught that all people's self-determination is limited by the fact that *the strongest motives determine the will, and that such dominant motives are in turn controlled by what seems the apparent good*.[28] The deep issue concerning Christian freedom and the freedom to respond to Christ is not whether people are self-determining, but whether the governing self is free from bondage to self-centeredness. Self-interest dominates natural humankind (Augustine's "city of man") and perverts love for others.[29] People may differ concerning how enlightened their self-interest is, but according to Edwards *no one—unless moved by supernatural grace—can escape from the circle of selfishness*. Edwards understood decision for Christ as evoked by the gift of the Spirit.

Augustine, Luther, Chalmers, and Edwards at this point are much in line with Paul. "The notion of a recreation of the will, a redirection of the life, so that whereas [previously] the gravitation of his soul was pulling him downward, now the gravitation in his soul pulls him toward God—this resetting of [one's] whole life is clearly in accord with St. Paul's conception of what happens when God intervenes and makes [one] righteous."[30]

Barth thought that the gift of faith evokes the recognition of our need, and enables us to become open to receiving the Gospel and God's ministration. That we believe means that by the *fresh* working of the Holy Spirit we come to know ourselves as bankrupt sinners, proud people humbled—enabled to receive God's judgment and grace concerning ourselves. The gift of the Spirit causes us to despair of ourselves and come to know ourselves in Christ.[31]

"The whole conception of [humankind] as a Hercules at the crossroads able to choose between faith and sin, and therefore unbelief, is a pure illusion. . . . This Hercules has

---

25. McGrath, *Justification by Faith*, 37.

26. See Althaus, *Theology of Martin Luther*, 119.

27. Calhoun, *Lectures*, 360, my emphasis.

28. Edwards, *Representative Selections*, 267, 292; Faust and Johnson, "Introduction," xlviii, in Edwards, *Representative Selections*.

29. Edwards, *Representative Selections*, 279, 281. 293-95, 300-302; Faust and Johnson, "Introduction," xlix, in Edwards, *Representative Selections*.

30. Calhoun, *Lectures*, 224.

31. Barth, *CD* 4/1:628, 619-20.

always already chosen unbelief."[32] We are not ourselves strong when we believe, but the One in whom we believe has gained affective and effective power over us. Of our own reason and strength we can neither believe in Christ nor come to him (Luther). When we come to faith, God does for us what we can never do for ourselves. This, however, does not mean that before the light dawned we were merely passive.

We can never *earn* grace, and further, we cannot believe the word of grace save as the Holy Spirit opens our hearts to do so. But in all this the transaction between God and us is personal and takes place within the sphere of responsibility. Though sinners we are subjects and not objects, and the receiving of grace is a personal act, and not the mere effect of a cause. And even as recipients of grace we remain responsible subjects.[33]

6. Grace to Persevere in Christian Faith

"The more the believer, prompted by his security in God, ventures the life of new obedience, the more he needs, as he struggles along, the certainty that God's faithfulness . . . will carry him through."[34] The NT regularly attests that because Christians can be sure of God's faithfulness, they can be confident that God will enable them to persevere in the Faith. Paul concludes the train of thought of the first half of his Epistle to the Romans by affirming his conviction that by God's grace believers will persevere and overcome (8:28–39). Our wavering faithfulness is countered by God's unwavering faithfulness. God's faithfulness is not dependent on ours; instead ours depends on His.[35] "He who began a good work in you will bring it to completion at the day of Jesus Christ" (Phil 1:6; see also Rom 14:4). "Great Is Thy Faithfulness."

One way our Lord preserves the saints is by helping disciples cope with temptations: "No temptation has overtaken you that is not common to [humankind]. God is faithful, and he will not let you be tempted beyond your strength, but with the temptation will also provide the way of escape, that you may be able to endure it" (1 Cor 10:13).

In addition to Paul, the author of 2 Timothy also believed in the perseverance of the saints: "I am not ashamed, for I know whom I have believed and I am sure that he is able to guard until that Day what has been entrusted to me" (1:12). The Johannine tradition regarded the assured faith involved in the appropriation of grace and the assured hope concerning abiding in grace as closely interrelated realities. Both depending on God's leading Christ's sheep to hear His voice and follow Him. And since the Father has given them to Christ, no one can snatch them from the Father's hand (John 10:27–29).[36]

---

32. Barth, *CD* 4/1:746.

33. Brunner, *Dogmatics*, 1:316. "It was especially the Reformers' interest in the *'sola gratia,'* the desire to get rid of all traces of synergism, which led them to understand man as a mere *object* of grace, and thus faith simply as the working of divine grace. The right element in this idea is that . . . faith is neither a merit nor an achievement. But this theological idea [*'sola gratia,'*] led to the psychological notion of passivity. Instead of that which is 'purely receptive' arose the idea of 'purely effected'" (Brunner, *Dogmatics*, 1:315).

34. Berkhof, *Christian Faith*, 476.

35. Berkhof, *Christian Faith*, 476.

36. John 6:37; see also 1 John 2:19.

That God will empower disciples to fulfill their calling is an emphatic assurance when given in the face of the persecution predicted to occur in the fulfillment of their vocation. Jesus warned his disciples that they would be persecuted and promised that the Spirit would give them the words they needed to say (Matt 10:19-20; Mark 13:11; Luke 21:14-15). They should fear nothing, for even death will not defeat their mission (Matt 10:16-33). According to Acts's considerably later perspective, Paul was warned to expect persecution; but was assured that as a chosen vessel through whom the Gospel was to be carried to the nations he would succeed (Acts 9:15-16; 26:17-19).[37]

7. Belief in Election Correlates with Divine Perseverance of the Saints, whereas Belief in Prevenient Grace Correlates with Recognition that Genuine Christians Can Totally Fall from Faith

According to those who believe in election "the grace that God accords to His elect in Jesus Christ is irreversible, and is accompanied by gifts that enable [disciples] to struggle effectively against sin and to make progress on the path to holiness." "Calvin affirms... that from the moment that God chooses and calls [disciples] and accords to them the grace to begin their new life, he will assure them of [the capacity too pursue][38] the struggle throughout their earthly careers. Indeed, 'the Spirit of God, being consistent with himself, nourishes and confirms in us the love of obedience that was instilled into us from the beginning.'"[39]

To the contrary, the prevenient grace belief that faith is based on the human exertion of a God-given natural capacity is consistent with the idea that authentic Christians can "backslide" from genuine faith to no faith at all. There is some biblical articulation of such backsliding, though not of its prevenient grace background. According to the Fourth Gospel even those in Him like branches in the vine can fail to abide in Him, and like dead branches can be cut off (15:6). Similarly Paul reminded the Corinthians of the failure of

---

37. McKenzie, *Vital Concepts of the Bible*, 110-11. Augustine was the first post-biblical thinker to deal specifically with perseverance, and what he said linked directly with his election-based understanding of eschatological hope. He thought that though at earlier stages of their lives the elect could lapse, they could not finally fall from Christian Faith.

With the Protestant Reformation the perseverance topic again surfaced, though more in the Reformed than in the Lutheran communities. The Arminian Calvinists feared that belief in perseverance would make people careless and indifferent. Because the Pietistic wing of Lutheranism put its main emphasis on the assurance implicit in the appropriation of justification, it not only underemphasized sanctification, but felt less need for assurances accorded by belief in perseverance (Berkhof, *Christian Faith*, 477-78).

Early Pietists and Methodists generally knew the security that an experiential assurance of salvation provides, so they felt little need to affirm a doctrine of perseverance. However, Wesley's goal-oriented perfection teaching may be an imperfect Arminian alternative to a goal-oriented perseverance teaching. See chap. 22, sec. 17.

The less experiential orthodox wing of Calvinism sought to comfort the fearful with assurances concerning perseverance, but might not have needed to do so if it had as much experiential emphasis as the Lutheran Pietists and Methodists.

38. Wendel says "of the possibility of pursuing," but such a mere possibility is inconsistent with the next sentence and with Calvin's teaching that the elect will never finally turn aside.

39. Wendel, *Calvin*, 245; see Calvin, *Institutes*, 2:3, 10; 2:3, 11.

Moses and His flock to enter the land of promise (1 Cor 10:5, 8–10). Therefore Paul generalizes: "Let anyone who thinks that he stands take heed lest he fall" (1 Cor 10:12).[40]

At the time of the Arminian Calvinist versus Orthodox Calvinist dispute, and later with Wesley's conflict with Orthodox Calvinists, all sides rejected the possibility of universal salvation. Since there is considerable NT evidence for the latter,[41] the perseverance-backsliding issue may be understood as primarily having to do with whether genuine Christians' relationships with Christ will necessarily endure to the end. Not with whether they ultimately may be saved. The stakes in the debate can thus be considerably lowered.[42]

The abundant NT evidence that it is possible to abandon the Faith cannot be consistently combined with the even stronger NT view that God in His faithfulness will ensure the perseverance of the saints. Here Berkhof's wise reminder is very relevant: "*Systematic reflection poses great intellectual problems.*"[43] It, of course, does not create the problems, but its comparative analyses enable people to see conflicts they otherwise might not notice.[44] The perseverance idea and the backsliding one are in themselves coherent, but some NT authors do not perceive the inconsistency between the two and thus affirm both.

In view of the logical incompatibility between these two sets of beliefs, and recognizing that a belief in universal salvation would qualify what was originally seen to be at stake

---

40. See also Gal 1:6; 3:2–3; 5:4. Additional Biblical Evidence that Genuine Believers Can Fall from Faith: Jesus is recorded as having warned His disciples about the danger of being led astray (Matt 24:3–14). After describing various events that He thought would take place before His second coming, He added that "many false prophets will arise and lead many astray. And because wickedness is multiplied, most [people's] love will grow cold. But *he who endures to the end will be saved*" (vss. 11–13, my emphasis). Would Jesus have issued such a warning to his disciples if He had not thought it possible for them to fall away? Or would the Gospel writer have so attested on Jesus's behalf if He had not thought it possible to fall away?

When speaking of his own diligent efforts to remain faithful so as not to fall, Paul wrote: "I pommel my body and subdue it, lest after preaching to others I myself should be disqualified" (1 Cor 9:27). Colossians suggests that there is a conditional character to salvation: "And you, who once were estranged and hostile in mind, doing evil deeds, he has now reconciled in his body of flesh by his death, in order to present you holy and blameless and irreproachable before him, provided that you continue in the faith, stable and steadfast, not shifting from the hope of the gospel which you heard" (1:21–23a). "The writer of Hebrews was especially vehement, calling his readers' attention on several occasions to the dangers of falling away and the importance of being on guard. One notable example is Hebrews 2:1: 'Therefore we must pay the closer attention to what we have heard, lest we drift away from it.' A slightly different injunction is found in 3:12–14: 'Take care, brethren, lest there be in any of you an evil, unbelieving heart, leading you to fall away from the living God. But exhort one another every day, as long as it is called "today," that none of you may be hardened by the deceitfulness of sin. For we share in Christ, if only we hold our first confidence firm to the end.' It is difficult . . . to understand why such warnings were given if [it was not thought that believers could] fall away" (Erickson, *Christian Theology*, 989–90. See also Heb 6:4–6; 10:26–27).

Second Peter 2:20–21 certainly assumes that lapsing is a real possibility. "For if, after they have escaped the defilements of the world through the knowledge of our Lord and Savior Jesus Christ, they are again entangled in them and overpowered, the last state has become worse for them than the first. For it would have been better for them never to have known the way of righteousness than after knowing it to turn back from the holy commandment delivered to them."

41. See chap. 27, section on "Universal Salvation and Eschatological Peril Teachings."

42. Orthodox Calvinists admitted that genuine Christians are often less than fully obedient, but doubted that those truly called could backslide completely away from faith. They thought that those who appeared to do so had never been truly called.

43. Berkhof, *Christian Faith*, 476, my emphasis.

44. And cynical readers may be muttering: "Thanks a lot!"

in both, a practical reformulation of each may be required. To do so we could take some elements from one, some from the other, each affirmation *being made in such qualified ways* that the two could become more compatible. The perseverance teaching could then be seen as encouraging Christians not to give up the discipleship struggle, since the faithful God will continue the good work of leading that He had begun. The practical reformulation of the backsliding teaching could warn us against moral unfaithfulness, and implore us to remain genuine disciples. Nevertheless, since God's faithfulness is great, so also is God's capacity to shake our foundations, judging us and leading us back to God's path.

8. Conclusion

Differences concerning the belief in election versus that of prevenient grace translate into differences as to whether decision for Christ is enabled by supernatural grace or by creational capacities still inherent in sinners. Most biblical evidence supports the belief in election. Yet those who believe in election must insist that those empowered by grace can and must strive to lead lives pleasing to God, encourage one another toward ever more decisive commitment, and do so because the God of love has won the allegiance of their hearts. Those election-believing "Christians" who do not struggle to be faithful are taking refuge in correct belief, without having received the gift of genuine relationship with the Father known in the Son by the Spirit. My sympathy for the biblically dominant notion that faith is a direct gift from above is not without recognition that there is scriptural evidence to the contrary.

My defense of the election-related perseverance teaching has also been apparent. However, I have tried to avoid sweeping biblical evidence under the carpet, or slanting the exposition. Pre-critical opinions, such as those of Orthodox Calvinists and Wesley, are not honest concerning biblical diversity on these topics. Nor are current apologists who attend to only one side of the biblical evidence. Since the tradition that backsliding is possible is biblically strong, though the perseverance teaching is stronger, in section seven I tried to restate these matters in more practical ways to avoid the logical contradictions between these scriptural views. This was done to retain the practical implications of the backsliding recognition even as the dominant perseverance teaching was retained.

I invite the reader to consider whether my expositions are accurate and whether my claims and practical restatement are convincing. I hope you will do so without returning to pre-critical, denominationally prejudicial tendencies to honor only one side of the biblical evidence.

Chapter 22

Appropriational Themes Related to Becoming and Being a Christian

1. Biblical Terminological Variations for Becoming Christians

THE NT USES A variety of overlapping terms to describe the beginnings of the response to and experiential appropriation of divine reconciliation—and these same expressions describe aspects of the ongoing process of the Christian life. Through such similar events as rebirth, dying and rising with Christ, and repentance-conversion God enables us to share in the results of His atoning work in Christ. As part of the same activities God also empowers and enjoins us to begin to become holy or sanctified,[1] and calls us to the life

---

1. Different denominations emphasize different terms to describe Christian moral renewal. Roman Catholics speak of sanctification, as do Reformed Christians, Anglicans, Methodists, and Anabaptists. In addition to sanctification, those influenced by Pietism, such as Brethren and Methodists, often employ regeneration and conversion terminology, which from the beginning and throughout entails moral renewal. Lutherans prefer to use only the language of justification even when referring to moral transformation. Eastern Orthodox customarily speak of "deification" with reference to all aspects of response to God.

Along lines that might seem similar to Eastern Orthodoxy, Colossians 3:9 refers to putting off the "old nature with its practices" and putting on "the new nature." But such terminology may only designate attaining to the *likeness* of God for which God created humanity in His image (Col 3:10). Eastern Orthodoxy takes its terminology from 2 Peter 1:4c, which refers to becoming "partakers of the divine nature." To many the terminology of 2 Peter and of Eastern Orthodoxy seem to imply the capacity to gain moral and religious status in ourselves, and may even imply mystical confusion between God and transformed Christians. Against such understandings "the frontier is never removed or crossed between God, Jesus Christ and the Holy Spirit on the one side and [humankind], including Christians, on the other. That Christians are sanctified by the God of peace (1 Thess 5:23), that we strive to be faithful to God as known in Jesus Christ (Rom 6:11), has nothing whatever to do with deification, but everything with relationship with God and humble submission to God's will. Though Paul says of himself in Galatians 2:20 that he no longer lives, but Christ lives in him, he at once [qualifies that statement and points away from Himself by saying]: 'The life that I now live in the flesh, I live by faith in the Son of God, who loves me, and gave himself for me'" (Barth, *CD* 4/2:377).

of service and witnessing on Christ's behalf.[2] And the appropriation of atonement is not confined to the initial phase.

Even mature Christians must continue to live from God's judgment and forgiveness, continue to confess their sinfulness and seek to be more faithful. Recognizing the sharp contrast between God's ways and ours, and remaining open to God's judgment, correction, and guidance encourages moral holiness and more faithful witnessing to Christ.

2. Rebirth/Regeneration

Underlying rebirth or regeneration, dying and rising with Christ, repentance-conversion, and sanctification is the biblical conviction that human beings are out of relationship with God and therefore need to be radically transformed. The need for and promise of a grace-induced centering of human life in God are the themes of the prophecy of Jeremiah 31. "Behold, the days are coming, says the Lord, when I will make a new covenant with the house of Israel and the house of Judah, not like the covenant which I made with their fathers when I took them by the hand to bring them out of the land of Egypt, my covenant which they broke, though I was their husband, says the Lord. But this is the covenant which I will make with the house of Israel after those days, says the Lord: I will put my law within them, and I will write it upon their hearts; and I will be their God, and they shall be my people. And no longer shall each [person] teach his neighbor and each his brother [or sister], saying, 'Know the Lord,' for they shall all know me, from the least of them to the greatest, says the Lord; for I will forgive their iniquity, and I will remember their sin no more" (vss. 31–34).

A new action on God's part is required, a fresh outpouring of the Holy Spirit that enables people to experience God's forgiveness and empowerment. Thus Ezekiel anticipated the day when God would take away His people's hearts of stone, give new hearts and spirits (36:26), and they would live from God's grace and submit to His kingship. Such regenerated and reborn people are no longer who they were, but are new people as set in new relationship with God.[3]

According to Johannine traditions, the Risen Christ grants and enables new life as a miracle from above. "To all who received him, who believed in his name, he gave power to become children of God; who were born, not of blood nor of the will of the flesh, nor of the will of man, but of God" (John 1:12–13). "Truly, truly, I say to you, unless one is born anew, he cannot see the kingdom of God" (John 3:3). "That which is born of the flesh is flesh,[4] and that which is born of the Spirit is Spirit. Do not marvel that I said to you, 'You must be born anew.' The wind blows where it will, and you hear the sound of it, but you do not know whence it comes or whither it goes; so it is with everyone who is born of the Spirit" (John 3:6–9).

---

2. The latter of which will be dealt with in chap. 24.

3. Barth, *CD* 4/2:561–63. There are nevertheless degrees of continuity, such as memory of our pre-Christian lives, values and ideas, which must be remembered in order to be effectively challenged.

4. "Flesh" refers to "our sinful, alienated-from-God existence versus that which is worked in us by the renewing power of the Spirit" (Berkhof, *Christian Faith*, 470).

The rebirth idea is implied by the belief that Jesus came to enable us to experience eternal life in the present (John 10:10b, 28). "[Whoever] is born of God overcomes the world; and this is the victory that overcomes the world, our [Spirit-generated] faith" (1 John 5:4). Similarly, according to 1 Peter 1:3–5, by the great mercy of the God and Father of our Lord Jesus Christ people can be born anew to a living hope through participation in Christ's risen reality. Titus 3:4–7 puts the same point in an only slightly different way by using the language of regeneration and renewal: "When the goodness and loving kindness of God our Savior appeared, he saved us, not because of deeds done by us in righteousness, but in virtue of his own mercy, by the washing of regeneration and renewal in the Holy Spirit, which he poured out upon us richly through Jesus Christ our Savior, so that we might be justified by his grace and become heirs in hope of eternal life."

Old nature/new nature terminology (Col 3:5, 9), 2 Peter's deification language (1:4), and some of the other NT word usage cited in this section on the surface may sound non-dialogical or non-relational, but this is not likely intended by these passages. What is surely meant is not different from the putting on of *Christ* (Gal 3:27).

The NT does not advocate the mere mystical probing of our natural selves, on the assumption that we are not very sinful, and need no transcendent Word from beyond! Inner self-examination is a fine part of Christian piety, but as a seeking of and not as a substitution for divine guidance from the transcendent God revealed in Christ as known by the Spirit.

"'Regeneration,' like all . . . related concepts, is to be understood eschatologically [as making] the salvation-occurrence present."[5] "*The regenerate person is, so to speak, ahead of himself; he lives on the basis of what is coming toward him.*"[6] "If the doctrine of regeneration found a ready entrance into the Christian teaching, it was because [it was] adequate to express the sense of newness which [people] experienced in Christ: the sense that the old life had ended and a new life had begun—new, not merely in direction and intention, but in essence; the sense that the supernatural, the heavenly, the divine, had broken in."[7]

3. Dying and Rising with Christ

To be reborn and to begin to share in the risen reality of Christ is possible only as the Holy Spirit enables us to begin to die to sinfulness. For only one who is dying to sinfulness can follow Christ. "Do you not know that all of us who have been baptized [by the Spirit] into Christ Jesus were baptized into his death? We were buried therefore with him by [Spirit] baptism into death, so that as Christ was raised from the dead by the glory of the Father, we too might walk in newness of life." "We know that our old self was crucified with him so that the sinful [self] might be destroyed, and we might no longer be enslaved to sin" (Rom 6:3–4, 6; see also Gal 2:20; 5:24; 6:14). Contrary to the impression that an isolated reading of Romans 6:6 and Galatians 2:20 might suggest, this process does not happen

---

5. Bultmann, *Theology of the New Testament*, 1:312.

6. Weber, *Foundations of Dogmatics*, 2:357, my emphasis.

7. Beare, *First Epistle of Peter*, 38. Closely related conceptually to the regeneration belief is that people become Christians by receiving the Spirit (John 20:20–23; Acts 1:5; 11:16; 1 Cor 12:13). See the next section and chap. 5.

all at once, but should continue throughout the Christian life.[8] "Crucifixion is a slow and painful process. Our old sin-loving self was, so to speak, nailed to the Cross when we first believed in Christ and accepted Him as our Savior. But it is not yet dead and will take a long time to die."[9]

Paul writes that "it is no longer I who live, but Christ who lives in me" (Gal 2:20b). "For the love of Christ controls us, because we are convinced that one has died for all; therefore all have died. And he died for all, that those who live might no longer live for themselves but for him who for their sake died and was raised. . . . Therefore, if anyone is in Christ he is a new creation; the old has passed away, behold, the new has come" (2 Cor 5:14–15, 17).

According to Paul as we begin to die with Christ we come under the Risen Christ's moral leading,[10] another way of referring to the process of sanctification.[11] "For [Paul] the sign of the cross expresses the fact that Christians must still hope for the completion of their salvation. Christ's own victory has already occurred with His resurrection, but for others participation in His resurrection has not yet taken place. The apostle applies the term [new] 'life' to the present existence of the faithful, but reserves 'resurrection' either for Christ's own resurrection or for others' *future* resurrection."

"In [Paul's] language of redemption, verbs associating us 'with' Christ play a prominent role. We 'suffer' with Christ, are 'crucified' with him, 'die' with him and are 'buried' with him. But the parallelism breaks down at the point of resurrection. Paul is [unlikely to have maintained] that 'we now rise or have already risen with Christ,' but only that 'we believe that we *shall* live with him' (Rom 6:8)."[12]

In contrast to Paul's usage, Ephesians and Colossians speak of Christians as having here and now died *and risen* with Christ (Eph 2:5–6; Col 2:12; 3:1). I have no objection to the latter usage, as long as it is not confused with our final resurrection, and in the next section I employ that terminology in the sectional heading. According to these sources it is through the gift of the Spirit that we begin both to die and rise to newness of life.

4. Indicative and Imperative: Ongoing Process of Receiving Holy Spirit and Continuing to Die to Sin and to Rise to New Life in Christ

From the gift of Christ's presence and power (indicative) comes the incentive (and in part the capacity) to conform to Christ (imperative). Having died to sin (Rom 6:2, 6, 8) we are to persist in doing so (Rom 6:11–13). We whom God has called from darkness into His light (1 Pet 2:9) must continue to "cast off the works of darkness and put on the armor of light" (Rom 13:12; see 1 Thess 5:4–11). Having been freed from slavery to sin (Rom 6:17),

---

8. See the next sec.
9. Bicknell, *Thirty-Nine Articles*, 211.
10. Rom 6:1–11; see also Phil 3:10–11.
11. See secs. 9–12.
12. O'Collins, *Resurrection of Jesus*, 123. Judging according to content and style it is unlikely that Paul wrote Colossians, and a virtual certainty that he did not write Ephesians.

we remain free only as we persist in yielding ourselves to God (Rom 6:19–22; see Eph 4:22–24).

The Christian exists through an ongoing process of becoming. This is because though the gift of God's Spirit establishes the basis of a relationship between us and God, the Spirit does not eliminate our tendency to live in lonely isolation from God. A new relationship has begun, but must be taken up afresh. Ever again we must *become who we are in Christ*. "If we live by the Spirit, let us also walk by the Spirit" (Gal 5:25; see also Col 3:3–5). Having put on Christ, we are to so continue (Gal 3:27; Rom 13:14). Though under the Risen Christ's leading, we must daily "seek the things that are above, where Christ is, seated at the right hand of God" (Col 3:1). The power of God's eternal kingdom has broken into history with Jesus's resurrection from the dead. Though through faith in Christ Christians share in God's kingship the influence of our selfishness is still very real.

To become a Christian is to be set amid a raging battle between God and the forces of evil within and without. In Christ the battle against sin has been won—therefore battle against it. You have died to sin—therefore die daily. You have received the Spirit—therefore receive it anew. Because the gift is given—the demand is made. You now have a firm standing in Christ, but "take heed, lest you fall" (1 Cor 10:12). Though God has given His Spirit, Paul ends all his letters with ethical exhortations. The NT says as much about ethical obligations as about religious mysteries. Though granted deliverance from bondage to this evil age (Gal 1:4), we must still be exhorted: "Do not be conformed to this world but be transformed by the renewal of your mind, that you may prove what is the will of God, what is good and acceptable and perfect" (Rom 12:2).

It is all very easy: Surrender to the gift of God's Spirit, look up to heaven, open your hands to God. It is all extremely difficult: Count the cost; be prepared for lifelong struggle; don't begin unless you are committed to continuing (Luke 14:27–32). Christianity is not for dabblers.

As an example of how we must become who we are in Christ, consider how *the Holy Spirit teaches us to love*. The Holy Spirit as the Spirit of God is also the Spirit of love (1 Cor 13). "God's love has been poured into our hearts through the Holy Spirit which has been given to us" (Rom 5:5). God through the Spirit empowers us to love, but what Christian doesn't need to become more loving? Hypocrisy? No. It's that our calling is high and we sinners have far yet to go (Phil 3:12–14). We are on the road returning to our Father's house. We know ourselves forgiven in Christ; we have the assurance of our Father's love; but we have many miles ahead (see Luke 15:11–32). Hard Christian work continues to be required and much discipline. Prayer, corporate worship, biblical and theological study, and specific deeds of love are still needed.

Gift and demand; demand and gift. But the demand is possible only because of the continuing gift of God's presence and power. We act not from our own strength but through participation in the divine salvation that has appeared. Thus in all seriousness Paul, moral exhorter *par excellence*, asks, "What do you have that you have not received?" (1 Cor 4:7) We are not required to earn our salvation, which for us sinners is impossible, but to hold fast to God as disclosed Christ. It is only because God is really at work in us, both to will and to do, that we can work toward our salvation with fear and trembling (Phil 2:12b–13).

5. Repentance

"In Hebrew thought repentance entailed not simply feeling sorry or changing one's mind. It involved a turning round, a radical alteration of the course and direction of one's life, its basic motivations, attitudes, and objectives. This is why the best [synonym] for the word 'repent' as used by Jesus would be 'convert,' understood in its literal sense, *'turn around,' and head in a quite new direction.*"[13]

John the Baptist preached "Repent, for the kingdom of heaven is at hand" (Matt 3:2). Repentance also featured prominently in Jesus's preaching, but in connection with the dawning of God's kingship in His person and deeds. "The time is fulfilled, the kingdom of God is at hand; repent and believe in the gospel" (Mark 1:15). Repentance was also an aspect of the early church's proclamation.[14] As the demands of discipleship flow from the gift of Christ's call, the imperative from the indicative, so the attitude and behavior alteration summarized by the word "repent" is a response to God's grace and to the presence and power of the Holy Spirit.

Repentance is much more than mere regret. Regret may only deplore the consequences and only for that reason the deed that caused them.[15] We may just be sorry we got caught. In true repentance there is regret over sin and the disavowing of it even if one has suffered no unfortunate personal effects because of it.[16] Repentance involves being genuinely sorry we broke God's heart. When we repent we take full responsibility for our sin and do not come to God with excuses.

Repentance does not involve mere self-examination, but subjecting ourselves to God's judgment. If we are engaged only in self-examination, as a rule we will find some ground left under our feet, even if we only discover our better self by which we pass judgment on our lesser self. In authentic repentance we realize that our repentance falls far short of the guilt to which it relates. And yet genuine repentance does not leave us in despair, because the Living God who awakens and induces repentance is the one who forgives our sin, sustains us, and puts us back on our feet. The difference between ongoing despair and repentance is the difference between Judas and Peter after their denials of Jesus. Judas, unlike Peter, never came to trust in the God whose love in Christ he had betrayed.[17]

Blessed is he who recognizes God's holiness/grace and thus his own sinfulness.

> "Blessed are the poor in spirit" (Matt 5:3). The poor in spirit look away from their own righteousness to the God who fills their outstretched empty hands. They know their desperate need, and realize they are beggars before God. To such belongs the kingdom of God. "For thus says the high and lofty One who inhabits eternity,

---

13. Dunn, *Jesus' Call to Discipleship*, 20; see Isa 55:7; Jer 3:12, 14, 22; Hos 6:1. The only biblical use of the word "convert" is found in Acts 15:3.

14. For example, Acts 2:38; Rom 2:4; 2 Cor 7:10.

15. Berkhof, *Christian Faith*, 428.

16. Erickson, *Christian Theology*, 937–38. This is a viewpoint quite different from that of African Traditional Religion and its close parallel in the modern "Prosperity Gospel." Today there is much Prosperity Gospel talk about "being saved," but little emphasis on contrition, repentance, and moral transformation. Often the primary concern is with using God to gain current prosperity and the assurance of going to heaven.

17. Berkhof, *Christian Faith*, 428–29, 429.

whose name is Holy: 'I dwell in the high and holy place, and also with him who is of a contrite and humble spirit, to revive the spirit of the humble, and to revive the heart of the contrite'" (Isa 57:15).

"The Christian life is not only entered by the gate of repentance, but is characterized by repentance through its whole extent."[18] To repent is by God's grace to become painfully conscious of our sinfulness and our incapacity to save ourselves, and to receive God's pardon and power that enables us to begin to recenter our lives in and through Christ.[19] Repenting refers to a double-sided concept—recognition of sin and conversion.

"Without repentance all the notes of the Christian faith are off-key or fall silent. Then the gospel is changed from a marvelous message of [judgment and] liberation into a more or less self-evident ideology of cheap grace."[20] Of course God loves us, since we are so lovable. "I'm ok, you're ok." It is not enough simply to believe in Jesus and accept the offer of grace; there must be a real alteration of the inner and outer person. If belief in God's grace were all that is necessary, who would not wish to become a Christian? "But Jesus said, 'If any[one] would come after me, let him deny himself and take up his cross daily and follow me'" (Luke 9:23). If there is no conscious repentance, there is no real awareness of having been saved from the power of sin. [Thus] there may be a corresponding lack of depth and commitment. . . . Any attempt to increase the number of disciples by making discipleship as easy as possible ends up diluting the quality of discipleship instead.[21]

Repentance can be and often is evoked by awareness of God's grace, as is depicted in the story of the conversion of the chief tax collector, Zacchaeus (Luke 19:1–10). To that tax-collector it seemed quite inconceivable that Jesus would want to visit him, despised as he was and avoided by everyone. Yet Jesus stayed in his home and ate with him. This kindness provoked Zacchaeus to confess his moral wrongdoing, promise to give half of his goods to the poor, and to restore fourfold to those he had defrauded (v. 8). Repentant recognition of guilt is also seen in the parable of the prodigal son (Luke 15:18; see also vss. 11–32) and in the story of a tax collector (Luke 18:9–14), who beat his chest in despair (Luke 18:13b), and who is said to have pleaded using the opening words of Psalm 51, "God, be merciful to me a sinner" (Luke 18:13c).

Repentance entails a *turning away from sin and the recentering of life in God*, with such effects as a rich person desisting from the quest for riches (Mark 10:17–31), a proud person becoming humble (Matt 6:1–18), and an unjust person making good (Luke 16:1–13). From henceforward, discipleship would come before other concerns (Matt 7:24–27).[22]

---

18. Clark, *Outline of Christian Theology*, 402.

19. "The Reformation was born out of controversy about repentance. The practice of selling indulgences . . . had aided attrition [feeling sorry out of fear of punishment] and abetted a superficial [moralism]. Luther attacked the hawker of indulgences Johann Tetzel. [Luther's] ninety-five theses . . . opened with: 'Our Lord and Master Jesus Christ, by saying "repent," intended that the whole life of believers should [involve] repentance.'" With what human dynamics "a particular person becomes repentant depends on many factors. *Something which with one person is a psychological fact [should] not be imposed upon others as a psychological law*" (Berkhof, *Christian Faith*, 431–32, my emphasis).

20. Berkhof, *Christian Faith*, 429.

21. Erickson, *Christian Theology*, 938.

22. Jeremias, *New Testament Theology*, 156–57, 152–53, 153.

6. Paul's Conversion-Repentance and That of Others[23]

Before discussing Paul's conversion we need to question the sharp distinction some biblical scholars have made between Paul's account and the Synoptic description of conversion-repentant responses to Jesus's outreach. Of course Paul was encountering the Risen Lord and the others were responding to Jesus's teaching and merciful behavior as God's representative. And that is a big difference. Paul as a Pharisee had been doing what he had thought was right—persecuting members of the Jesus sect. So Jesus's resurrection disclosure to him was prior to his repenting of what he had been doing. But that encounter led to a lifelong reexamination and alteration of his previous life course. And though Paul's conversion is different from ours in being the last apostolic calling, it otherwise has much in common with our conversion experiences. Like ours, Paul's encounter was direct from above, a function of the free outpouring of the Spirit as the presence of the Risen Lord.

It is clear from Paul's letters that his conversion was not preceded by a prior sense of contrition/repentance akin to Luther's Law-Gospel schema, in "which after long suffering under an afflicted conscience and inner resistance he finally succeeded in confessing his guilt before God and thereby [was] inwardly set . . . free."[24] According to Luther's sequencing of Law and then Gospel, one must first become aware of one's sinfulness before being able to receive grace. To the contrary, before Paul's conversion he had been self-righteous and proud. His encounter with the Risen Christ *did not free him from a burden he had long known, but [enabled him to sacrifice] a proud past* (Phil 3:6ff.)."[25] Nevertheless at that point and thereafter his life was redirected, *which must surely have involved a deep sense of contrition concerning his previous life, which much conflicted with his life from then on.*

One can repent only as one has a sense of God's presence and leading. For to repent is to recognize one's alienation from the living God, not merely to become aware of moral failure. To repent is to become so shockingly cognizant of the brokenness of one's relationship with God that one realizes that God is just in His judgment against oneself.[26] Repentance involves experiential knowledge of God leading to self-knowledge of a critical sort—the awareness of guilt *before God*.

Initial conversion to Christ involves a real event in one's life history, a conscious turning to Christ, though conversion need not be instantaneous or singular. But that Christians must grow in grace and receive the Spirit afresh does not mean that we do not need to be initially converted. Nevertheless, initial conversion is only a beginning. All of those whom the Living Christ has called need to be illuminated and awakened ever again. "What makes a [person] a Christian is that the One who has wakened him once is not content with this, but as the faithful One He is (1 Thess 5:24) wakens him again and again. . . . What makes him a Christian is that he has a Lord who to his salvation will not leave him in peace but

---

23. The word "convert" is only used in Rom 16:5 and the word "conversion" only in Acts 15:3, but the idea of converting to faith in Christ is common throughout the NT and largely overlaps with repenting.

24. Bultmann, *Existence and Faith*, 114.

25. Ibid., 115, my emphasis. This view of Paul's pre-conversion self-understanding is thus compatible with Philippians 3:3–7, especially vss. 5–6, which refers to his *pre-conversion self-understanding*, and even more specifically to vs. 6b: "As to righteousness under the law blameless." Perhaps so "under the law," but . . .

26. Berkhof, *Christian Faith*, 428.

constantly summons him to wake up again."[27] Led by God's ongoing grace, conversion involves an ongoing warfare, quarrel and falling-out with ourselves. It consists in the fact that we are seriously at odds with ourselves.[28]

Conversion/repentance as a centering of life in Christ makes impact upon the whole person. "Repentance is a root and branch affair, a cleansing of inside and outside, affecting those who repent from the depths of their personalities right through the whole of their lives. . . . The commitment Jesus calls for must transcend all others. . . . Half measures are not enough."[29] Jesus is attested as having said that "he who loves father or mother more than me is not worthy of me; and he who loves son or daughter more than me is not worthy of me" (Matt 10:37; strangely overstated in Luke 14:26–27).

The scope and structure of conversion/repentance can be further specified. (A) Because conversion affects the total life of the Christian, such renewal concerns both the relation to God and to humankind.[30] As we realize that God is for us, we can and must be for God and for others. "We love because he first loved us" (1 John 4:19). By empowering us to love Him God enables and requires that we love one another (Mark 12:31) and even our enemies (Matt 5:44; Luke 6:27, 35) as we love ourselves.[31]

Genuine conversion affects our attitudes, thereby capacitating us and disposing us toward faithful outward behavior.[32] By insisting that we are to love God with heart and soul and mind and strength (Mark 12:30) Jesus emphasized the inner aspect of repentance.

"Not surprisingly Jesus saw clearly . . . (as had John the Baptist, according to Luke 3:10–14) . . . that the crunch would come for many on the matter of *material possessions*. So it was in the case of the rich young man. . . . 'Jesus looking upon him loved him, and said to him, "You lack one thing; go, sell what you have, and give to the poor,[33] and you will have treasure in heaven; and come, follow me." 'At that saying his countenance fell, and he went away sorrowful; for he had great possessions' (Mark 10:21–22). In contrast, Zacchaeus . . . realized quickly what he must do. 'Behold, Lord half of my goods I give to the poor, and if I have defrauded anyone of anything, I restore fourfold' (Luke. 19:8). It was in reference to such repentance that Jesus said, 'Today salvation has come to this house'" (Luke 19:9).[34]

One would, however, misunderstand conversion if one thought all God requires is outward action. Paul recognized that one could utilize one's goods to feed the poor, and even offer one's very self in service to others, and have not love (1 Cor 13:3). Genuine love is based upon relationship with the God of love who transforms our inner selves, and thereby our outward behaviors.

---

27. Barth, *CD* 4/3 *Second Half*, 512.
28. Barth, *CD* 4/2:570.
29. Dunn, *Jesus' Call to Discipleship*, 22–23.
30. Barth, *CD* 4/2:563.
31. Matt 19:19; 22:39; Rom 13:8–9; Gal 5:14.
32. Dispositions link inner attitudes to outward behaviors.
33. This text should not be understood as a general call to the monastery, but warns of the importance of responsible financial stewardship.
34. Dunn, *Jesus' Call to Discipleship*, 22.

(B) Though conversion may begin with a striking experience, "it is neither exhausted in a once-for-all act, nor is it accomplished in a mere series of such acts.[35] Otherwise how could it be an affair of the whole person?" "Conversion extends over the whole . . . life-movement of a person."[36]

Evangelicalism has often placed most emphasis on once-and-for-all conversion experiences, narrowly interpreted as highly emotional and "instantaneous." Early in his career as an evangelist Wesley advocated such a "Moravian" understanding. But his sense of complete trust in God did not come through his early Aldersgate experience, but came later in connection with his field preaching involvement. Though Wesley's understanding of the psychological processes involved in Christian religious experience was highly programmatic and even legalistic; his stress upon growth in sanctification separated him from those who spoke lopsidedly of once-and-for-all conversions. Not surprisingly many of Wesley's sermons explained the structure of the Christian moral life and did not concern only initial decision. He preached much from the Sermon on the Mount.

7. Challenging Pentecostals' Two-Stage Understanding of Becoming a Christian

Pentecostalists mistakenly believe that people first receive Christ and later receive the Spirit. However according to Paul experiencing the presence of the Risen Christ and experiencing the presence of the Spirit are two ways of referring to the same event. This is especially clear in Romans 8:10 which takes up and repeats verse 8:9b, with "Christ" substituted for "the Spirit of Christ." And similarly verse 11 repeats the two preceding verses' thought, but in terms of the Spirit of God. These verses describe the same fact and experience.[37] It is by the Spirit of the Risen Christ as the Spirit of God that one becomes a Christian.[38]

8. Relationship between Sanctification and the Ongoing Need for Pardon

Christians are freed from slavery to the power of sin (Rom 6:2, 18). Having thereby become God's servants "the return we get is sanctification and its end, eternal life" (Rom 6:22). "For the law of the Spirit of life in Christ Jesus has set [us] free from the law of sin and death" (Rom 8:2). Though these things are so, unless Christians' ongoing need for

---

35. See sec. 3 above, in which the exegetical basis of this theological claim is demonstrated with reference to dying and rising with Christ, and sec. 4 concerning continuing to receive the Spirit.

36. Barth, *CD* 4/2:566.

37. Dunn, *Baptism in the Holy Spirit*, 148. "Paul knows of only one reception of the Spirit, not two. The concepts of anointing, sealing, outpouring, promise, gift, etc. all refer to that one coming of the Spirit and the coming of the Spirit is the very heart and essence of conversion-initiation. Even [Pentecostals'] own terminology of 'baptism in the Spirit' is used by Paul to describe nothing other than God's means of incorporating the convert into Christ" (ibid., 170–71).

38. Dunn, *Baptism in the Holy Spirit*, 95–96. See "Mark 1:8; Acts 11:16ff; Rom 8:9f; 1 Cor 12:13; 2 Cor 3:6; Gal 3:3; Titus 3:6f.; John 3:3–8; 20:22; 1 John 3:9; Heb 6:4" (Dunn, *Baptism in the Holy Spirit*, 226).

pardon continues to be recognized and emphasized moral activity may encourage self-righteousness.[39] Christians could imagine that atonement only means that God gives us a second chance to save ourselves by self-generated good works. (This is a common teaching of the Seventh-Day Adventists and can be found in some of Wesley's writings.) To the contrary, however holy we become, we remain sinners, and our good works are ambiguous.

"Only he who knows himself accepted by God is . . . open to the renewing work of God. Only he who no longer needs to justify himself has become free to . . . lose his life for the sake of God and [humankind]."[40] One's good works need no longer be done for acquisitive or selfish purposes, but out of love for God and others in response to God's freely given love in Christ.[41] Living from God's loving forgiveness we can become instruments for the extension of love to others.[42]

As Paul's nuanced understanding of "justification" indicates,[43] the experience of mere pardon is also not enough, for God wishes to empower us for faithful witnessing. "What is the forgiveness of sins . . . if it is not directly [accompanied by some] liberation from the committal of sin? . . . What is faith without obedience?" We must not allow sanctification to be swallowed up in pardon, with an exclusive emphasis on the cross and a doctrine of mere forensic (declaratory) justification, which has all too often happened in Lutheranism. "In this [one-sided emphasis] the necessity of good works may be maintained only lethargically and spasmodically, with little place for anything more than rather indefinite talk about a life of forgiveness, or comforted despair, or Christian freedom. . . . If we do not understand [grace] as sanctifying grace . . . we begin to look for the indispensable norm of the Christian way of life elsewhere than in the Gospel [which we regard as] only the consoling word of [pardon], and are forced to seek and grasp a law formed either by considerations drawn from . . . natural law or by historical convenience. But this means . . . tacitly or openly we are subjected to other lords in a kingdom on the left[44] as well as to the Lord Jesus Christ whose competence extends only, as we think, to the forgiveness of sins."[45]

Though for us *sinners* pardon is *foundationally* superior to sanctification, sanctification as the goal of pardon for sinners *called to be saints is teleologically* superior to pardon.[46] Both are superior, but in these different ways. Pardon is foundationally superior because we sinners require divine forgiveness before we can start anew. Sanctification is teleologically superior because the goal of divine activity is to gain faithful disciples.

"To be in God's power-sphere, in His Spirit, is not just a new subjection, for Christians obey not as slaves but as sons [and daughters] who can call God 'Abba,' Father (Gal

39. Wesley's conception of the experience of justification as but the "porch" of the Christian religion, with the experience of sanctification as itself the "house" contributed to this problem, which influenced pietism in general and Methodism in particular. His teaching on perfection furthered the same tendency. See sec. 17 below.

40. Berkhof, *Christian Faith*, 327.

41. One's ethic is hereby much influenced by gratitude, rather than by mere duty or the pursuit of goals.

42. Berkhof, *Christian Faith*, 453.

43. See chap. 19.

44. A reference to Luther's dichotomized two kingdom teaching.

45. Barth, *CD* 4/2:505, 504. Both Barth and Berkhof agreed with Luther's emphasis on the ongoing need for divine forgiveness, but disagreed with one-sidedly stressing that.

46. Barth, *CD* 4/2:507-8.

4:5-7; Rom 8:14-17). The Spirit turns ordinary men and women into children of God who live in His power and bear His fruit, adopted children, whose adoption now anticipates the full adoption of the future (cf. Rom 8:15a with v. 23)."[47]

Though discipleship is essential, to conceive the ongoing work of Christ entirely in terms of our becoming more sanctified is to distort Christianity: Ongoing moral empowerment is isolated from the pardoning renewal that helps to make that possible. Justification and sanctification do not describe different spiritual stages, but point from the justifying *basis* for becoming a disciple to the sanctifying *effect of ever becoming a more faithful disciple*.

9. Sanctification as Grounded in God's Holiness and His Action in Christ and through Holy Spirit
Issues in Moral Renewal

In biblical word usage, "there are two [primary] senses of the word *sanctification*, which are related to two meanings of holiness. In the first sense, which will alone be dealt with in this section,[48] . . . holiness refers to a state of being separate, set apart from the ordinary or mundane and dedicated to a particular purpose or use." With this meaning of the word, because God's holiness signifies his self-existent purity, our holiness consists in being called out and set apart for relationship with and service on behalf of God. Thus the author of 1 Peter refers to his readers as "a chosen race, a royal priesthood, a holy nation, God's own people" (2:9). "Here, being sanctified means 'to belong to the Lord.' Sanctification in this sense . . . begins at the very beginning of the Christian life, at the point of conversion, regeneration and [the experiencing of] justification. It is in this sense that the New Testament so frequently refers to Christians as 'saints,' though we are far from perfect. Paul, for example, addresses the persons in the church at Corinth in this way, though it was . . . a most imperfect church. 'To the church of God which is at Corinth, to those sanctified in Christ Jesus, called to be saints together with all those who in every place call on the name of our Lord Jesus Christ, both their Lord and ours' (1 Cor 1:2). They were not called to be saints only at some time in the future, but . . . from the very moment of their call."

Far too often the matter of Christ's relation to our experience of justification and sanctification has been conceived as though Christ's representative death for our justification was His own act, but our corresponding counter-movement of sanctification is to be accomplished just by us. To the contrary "Jesus who lived and died for the forgiveness of our sins does not wait as though with tied arms for us to act in accordance with the freedom achieved for us," as though our becoming more holy were independent of Him. "It is natural that He would be thought of in this way when it is overlooked and forgotten that He is not only the suffering Son of God but also [our risen and active Lord]." "As we are not asked to justify ourselves, we are also not asked to sanctify ourselves."[49] Our sanctification consists in our responding to His sanctifying work in our lives.

---

47. Ziesler, *Pauline Christianity*, 95.
48. Sec. 10 explains a less common meaning.
49. Barth, *CD* 4/2:517.

As a work of God and of the Risen Christ, sanctification is also a work of the Holy Spirit. Christians are to live from the power of the Spirit (Rom 8:9, 13) and set our minds upon the things of the Spirit (Rom 8:5). We are to walk according to the Spirit (Gal 5:16, 25), be led by the Spirit (Rom 8:14), and thereby be children of God (Rom 8:16).[50]

The classical sanctification formula from the OT (Lev 19:2; cf. 11:44; 20:7) is quoted in 1 Peter. "As he who called you is holy, be holy yourselves in all your conduct; since it is written, 'You shall be holy, for I am holy'" (1:16). Human holiness flows from relationship with God who alone is holy in Himself. God's active presence as required for human sanctification is stressed by Ephesians 5:26 and Titus 2:14. The author of Hebrews closes his epistle with the prayer that God may equip Christians with everything good, that we may do His will, working in us what is pleasing in His sight (13:20–21).[51]

"The Holy Spirit . . . imparts and writes on our hearts and consciences the will of God as it applies to us concretely here and now, the command of God in the individual and specific form in which we have to respect it in our own situation."[52] Moral application is not a matter of mere repetition of past commands, but of Spirit-led guidance that helps to relate past commands to concrete obedience today. *God is a Living Reality and we are directly responsible to Him.*

We are not our own masters but belong to Christ, are grafted into Christ (Rom 11:17), and have "put on Christ" (Gal 3:27). Christ is the vine, we the branches. Insofar as we abide in Him we can bear much fruit, but apart from Him we can do nothing (John 15:5). "None of us lives to himself, and none of us dies to himself. If we live, we live to the Lord, and if we die, we die to the Lord; so then, whether we live or die, we are the Lord's. For to this end Christ died and lived again, that he might be Lord both of the dead and of the Living" (Rom 14:7–9; see also 12:1–2).

10. Sanctification Involves Cross-Bearing

As the Spirit works to form Christ in us (Gal 4:19) we more truly become Christ's disciples, carrying our crosses (Luke 9:23) and becoming like Him in His suffering and thereby sharing in His risen reality (Phil 3:10). "Conformity with the exalted Christ can come about only [as we seek to correspond] to the way of the suffering Christ."[53] "We have this treasure in earthen vessels, to show that the transcendent power belongs to God and not to us. We are afflicted in every way, but not crushed; perplexed, but not driven to despair; persecuted, but not forsaken; struck down, but not destroyed; always carrying in the body the [dying] of Jesus, so that the life of Jesus may also be manifested in our bodies" (2 Cor 4:7–10). Living at the overlap of the two ages and carrying the cross of discipleship, we

---

50. Erickson, *Christian Theology*, 970–71.

51. And Paul: "Just as you once yielded your members to impurity and to greater and greater iniquity, so now yield your members to righteousness for sanctification. . . . When you were slaves of sin, you were free in regard to righteousness. . . . But . . . what return did you get from the things on which you are now ashamed? . . . But now that you have been set free from sin and have become [servants] of God, the return you get is sanctification and its end, eternal life" (Rom 6:19b, 20–21a, 22; see also 2 Cor 7:1; 1 Thess 3:13).

52. Barth, *CD* 4/2:372.

53. Berkhof, *Christian Faith*, 427; see 2 Cor 6:4–10; Phil 2:1–7; 3:10.

even now can begin to correspond to the New Adam. "As was the man of dust, so are those who are of the dust; and as is the man of heaven, so are those who are of heaven."[54]

Though in some churches there is a loveless discipline, which casts off offenders against the common rule, a more common sin is the opposite: *a loveless lack of discipline*. We have brought into our churches many who have no personal commitment to the Lord and to His cause. The gospel has been made too easy. No hard decisions, no continual self-denial, and no surrender of the whole self to Christ have been expected, reminding one of Bonhoeffer's words concerning "cheap grace."

11. Substitutionary Sanctification in Christ as Aspect of Objective Atonement

The NT most commonly thinks of sanctification in terms of the present working of the Holy Spirit in believers' lives which results in moral transformation. Yet the NT also uses sanctification language to refer to the reality of Christ's atoning victory achieved prior to human appropriation. In effect it says that while we were yet sinners the Holy One died for the unholy ones, and so God sees us in the light of Christ's holiness. Paul attests that God is the source of our life in Christ Jesus, "whom God made our wisdom, our righteousness and *sanctification* and redemption" (1 Cor 1:30, my emphasis).[55] Hebrews speaks similarly of sanctification as having occurred in the Christ event, saying that "we *have been sanctified* through the offering of the body of Christ Jesus once for all" (10:10, my emphasis).

Through a God-initiated substitutionary exchange Christ the Holy One stood forth in place of sinners, God thereby clothing us in Christ's righteousness. Furthermore, we can participate in Christ and seek to conform to Him because the Spirit enables us to respond to Christ's representation on our behalf. Though our righteousness is small compared with Christ's, we seek to show forth our thankfulness for reconciliation by morally striving to correspond to Christ. Personal sanctification thus consists not only in participation in Christ, but in sharing in the representative sanctification that He has already achieved on our behalf.

Christ's representative obedience has reestablished the covenant by fulfilling both the divine and human sides. Sanctification terminology can thus be used to affirm the Gospel of God's outreaching love for sinners. "It belongs to the distinctive essence of the Jesus Christ of the New Testament that as the One He alone is He is not alone, but the royal Representative, the Lord and Head of many."[56] Through His representative obedience, "Jesus is the Mediator through whom God has come to us and through whom we [go] to God."[57]

---

54. 1 Cor 15:48; see also Rom 8:29; 1 Cor 4:16; 2 Cor 3:18.

55. "By a single offering [Christ] has perfected for all time those who are sanctified" (Heb 10:14). Colossians hints concerning the same idea, but as with the 1 Corinthians 1:30 text, quickly relates objectively achieved sanctification to its applied meaning. Because believers have already been raised up with Christ (Col 3:1a), objectively sanctified, they are to "seek the things that are above, where Christ is, seated at the right hand of God" (Col 3:1b).

56. Barth, *CD* 4/2:271, 275; Barth, *Humanity of God*, 46. Jesus's obedience was on our behalf because it occurred within what God regards as a representative history. See chap. 18, sec. 6.

57. Presbyterian Church of Canada, *Living Faith*, Article 3.4.1.

Though the NT occasionally refers to objectively achieved sanctification, the major ways it speaks of objective atonement do not utilize sanctification language. Thus representational sanctification was not considered when discussing the atonement, but is placed with other aspects of sanctification. One thing is certain, Christ's representative obedience cannot take the place of our obedience—nor does the NT at any point assert otherwise.

12. Freedom from Bondage to Sin: Becoming Adult Children of God or Friends of God

According to much of the NT people are *considerably bound* either to God or to what opposes God. However, sometimes this is put in ways that oversimplify the difference between those sinners who are seeking to be responsible disciples and those who have no such commitment. The Fourth Gospel and 1 John are the great over-simplifiers in this regard. As we will also see in section sixteen, unlike the major aspects of the Pauline tradition, the *Johannine traditions do not* consistently attest that though the redeemed Christian is freed from captivity to sin, he nevertheless *lives at the overlap of the two ages*.

Sometimes the Fourth Gospel supposes that to commit sin involves being completely captivated by it, the main text being this one: "Everyone who commits sin is a slave of sin" (8:34).[58] Such simplistic rhetoric seems to imply that *the redeemed vacillate between being unambiguously Christian at one moment and being in bondage to sin the next*. Yet the Fourth Gospel has some fine teaching related to gaining the freedom to serve God: "If you continue in my word, you are truly my disciples, and you will know the truth, and the truth will make you free" (John 8:31–32). "If the Son makes you free, you will be free indeed" (John 8:36). "No longer do I call you servants, for the servant does not know what his master is doing; but I have called you friends, for all that I have heard from my Father I have made known to you" (John 15:15). "To all who received him, who believed in his name, he gave power to become children of God, who were born, not of blood nor of the will of the flesh nor of the will of man but of God" (John 1:12–13).

Paul recognizes that the unrepentant person is considerably bound by "the elemental spirits of the universe" (Gal 4:3). He attests that what is done by unconverted sinners is heavily influenced by sin (Rom 7:20) and thus is done with great unfreedom. But Paul's rhetoric is generally more nuanced (Rom 6:12, 17, 20; 8:15–17) than is the Johannine sharp alternating, this because *Paul recognizes* that Christians live at the intersection of the two ages.[59] In consequence of Christ's atoning victory and kingly rule at God's right hand and through participation in His holiness, Christians can gain freedom from the compulsion to sin. Through sanctification Christians stand with captivity behind them and freedom for obedience to God before them, obedience to God being "implicated freedom."[60] Where the Lord as Spirit is, there and there alone is genuine freedom (2 Cor 3:17). "For freedom Christ has set us free; stand fast therefore, and do not submit again to the yoke of slavery"

---

58. First John attests this even more. See sec. 16.
59. Barth, *CD* 2/2:589.
60. Weber, *Foundations of Dogmatics*, 2:272.

(Gal 5:1; see Rom 6:12–14, 16–18). *Christians are still sinners, but are no longer in bondage to sin.*

Christian freedom results from the gift of God's power and equips us to represent His ways. *Freedom, grace, and obedience have meaning only in interrelationship with one another.* Freed by the Lord, Christians have become His servants (1 Cor 7:22),[61] but are not *mere* servants. Since obedience to the Living Christ enables true freedom and authentic selfhood, servanthood is not dehumanizing. Christ's sharing with His disciples establishes us as His friends, adult children of God.

"All who are led by the Spirit of God are sons [or daughters] of God. For you did not receive the spirit of slavery to fall back into fear, but you have received the spirit of sonship. When we cry, 'Abba! Father!' it is the Spirit himself bearing witness with our spirit that we are children of God, and if children, then heirs, heirs of God and fellow heirs with Christ, provided we suffer with him in order that we may also be glorified with him" (Rom 8:14–17).

13. Teleological Understanding of Christian Life

Though Christians have come under the dominion of the God who is stronger than sin and evil, between here and eternity we are in process, and will achieve fullness of relationship with God only beyond this world of sin and death. Using the analogy of running a race Paul wrote, "Not that I have already obtained this or am already perfect; but I press on to make it my own, because Christ Jesus has made me his own. Brethren, I do not consider that I have made it my own; but one thing I do, forgetting what lies behind and straining forward to what lies ahead, I press on toward the goal for the prize of the upward call of God in Christ Jesus" (Phil 3:12–14). Since in this life we always have much further to go, we are not to waste time congratulating ourselves on how far we have come, but are to struggle to be more faithful. Nor are we to weaken discipleship by flatteringly comparing ourselves with others.

We should think of the old and new ages *conflictually* and *dynamically*. Thus the Christian life involves ever turning from sinfulness to faithfulness. Christ is the way from the one to the other. Through Him is the turning—the crisis—the sanctification.

14. The Moral Growth Involved in Sanctification and the Struggle Sometimes Entailed

According to Ephesians 4:11–16 a goal of individual Christians is to advance toward "mature [personhood]," toward "the measure of the stature of the fullness of Christ" (vs. 13b). Such advances occur as Christians learn to "speak the truth in love" (vs. 15a) and are no

---

61. "In the New Testament the person who belongs to Jesus Christ and obeys him is often called a 'slave'; Paul's self-designation as a 'slave' of Jesus Christ is a title of honor, and Paul [2 Cor 4:5, and Paul's likely student, Col 4:12] are not the only ones who used it. Believers are often compared to 'slaves' (as in Matt 25:14–28; 21:33–41; even more clearly in Matt 24:45–51; Luke 17:10), as those who owe servitude not only to their Lord (as in the Synoptic passages and John 13:16; 15:20), but also to each other (Gal 5:13; indirectly Phil 2:22 and in Eph 6:7)" (Weber, *Foundations of Dogmatics*, 2:272).

longer being tossed to and fro by every wind of doctrine (vs. 14). Every Christian should strive to pass from spiritual childhood (Heb 5:12-14) by gaining heightened knowledge of God (Col 1:10), by increasing in righteousness (2 Cor 9:10b) and by growing in faith,[62] love (Phil 1:9; 1 Thess 3:12) and in the manifestation of the fruits of righteousness (2 Cor 9:10).

The question arises as to how we are to conceive of progress that involves ongoing struggle. If the struggle continues, how can we be progressing? If we are progressing, in what sense are we still struggling? To answer ponder four considerations.

> (1) Only in the brokenness of the conflict does the believer really get to know himself in his opposition against God.... The struggle is thus an advancing in self-knowledge. (2) Consequently the struggle also implies [progress] in [depending on God].... The better we get to know ourselves, the less we expect from ourselves, and the more we fall back on God's grace as the decisive foundation of our lives. (3) But precisely [the growing sense of dependence on God] inspires to fresh and greater efforts, making the struggle more intense. (4) And coupled with that ... we discover new areas of conduct and thought which so far were not involved in the process of renewal and where new opportunities await us. For example, in the use of our charismata for the upbuilding of the church, in respect to our political insights, in fresh conciliatory approaches to one's enemies, in changes in how we spend our income [and time], and in the struggle against discriminatory practices and situations.[63]

In understanding our own growth or lack of growth in sanctification we can err either by claiming too much or expecting too little moral transformation. If we claim too much improvement we become unrealistic concerning our own continuing sinfulness, and less self-critical than we should be. If we expect too little moral transformation we remain content with our imperfections, rather than allowing Christ to lead us toward new levels of faithfulness. Though these two errors differ greatly, the effects in both cases are a lack of moral energy and enthusiasm. Our understanding of others and of society face the same double-sided possibility of error: If we regard others and society too positively we become unrealistic in helping to deal with personal and social problems. Yet if we regard individuals or society as morally hopeless, we lose motivation for helping both to live up to their potentials.

15. Sanctification and Empirical Righteousness: Luther and Wesley Compared

According to Luther, Christians must not trust in any achieved purity, but constantly undergo purification. Utilizing a medical analogy, "the daily process of healing takes place when the ill [person] commits himself over and over again into the hands of the physician

---

62. Rom 14:1; 15:13-15; 2 Cor 10:15; 1 Thess 3:10; 2 Thess 1:3.

63. Berkhof, *Christian Faith*, 471. "Calvin emphasized not only the struggle, but also the [progress] that can be made.... More and more is a favorite expression with him" (Ibid., 472). Wesley also believed that Christians could continue to grow in moral faithfulness, though in this regard he sometimes became unrealistically optimistic. See secs. 14-15.

and does not trust in his own health just starting."[64] "It may sound paradoxical, but it is nonetheless a real fact that empirical piety can exist only within the sphere of the Spirit, where there is a constant flight away from [trusting in] one's empirical piety, to Christ as one's alien righteousness."[65]

Wesley shared Luther's understanding of sanctification as grounded in relationship with Christ. Though Luther recognized that moral growth can occur, that Christ's righteousness is imparted (not just imputed), he did not accentuate imparted righteousness. Wesley, while recognizing imputed righteousness, stressed the imparted—insisting that recipients of grace are not merely declared righteous, but are renewed in the image of God. Like Augustine, Wesley characteristically spoke of sanctification as a process in which the physician begins to heal the patient.

16. Biblical Teachings concerning Attainment of Perfection in this World

Several biblical texts support the idea that in this life Christians can attain perfection, a claim that contradicts central NT beliefs. There is massive NT evidence that argues against perfectionistic teachings. Such comes from the Synoptics, from Paul and from Pauline writers, all attesting the radical sinfulness of humankind.

As for perfection verses in 1 John: "No one who abides in him sins; no one who sins has either seen him or known him" (3:6). "No one born of God commits sin; for God's nature abides in him, and he cannot sin because he is born of God" (3:9). "We know that any one born of God does not sin" (5:18a). "If we say we have no sin, we deceive ourselves, and the truth is not in us. If we confess our sins, he is faithful and just, and will forgive our sins and cleanse us *from all unrighteousness*" (1:8–9, my emphasis). "He who fears is not perfected in love" (4:18c), which seems to imply that with the overcoming of such fear one could be perfected in love.

A key element in 1 John's perfectionist teaching is a defective conception of *sin* that understands it as only the conscious transgressing of a known law of God. This involves confusing sin with sins, and thus isolating sins from an accurate understanding of sin. Not surprisingly, just prior to one of 1 John's affirmations that perfection can be attained in this life he attests this weakened and confused understanding of sin: "Everyone who commits sin is guilty of lawlessness; *sin is lawlessness*. You know that he appeared *to take away sins, and in him there is no sin*" (1 John 3:4–5, my emphases). The author does not seem to understand that "sins" manifest a sinful state of being that lies behind the committing of sins. Because the author seems oblivious concerning the pull of self-centeredness (eloquently described in Romans 7) he manifests a defective understanding of what most of the NT means by sin. And in the light of the broader NT understanding his merely law-centered perspective concerning what God requires is equally defective.

---

64. Prenter, *Spiritus Creator*, 77.
65. Prenter, *Spiritus Creator*, 98–99. See the Beatitudes (Matt 5:3–6).

If we restate 1 John 3:9[66] in the light of broader NT teachings we could say: *Insofar as one is born of God one has access to God's power for dealing with sin*. Such an assertion can be consistently combined with the numerous places in the NT that are frank concerning the ongoing reality of sin in all lives—Christians included.

Matthew 5:48 is also a perfectionistic text: "You ... must be perfect, as your heavenly Father is perfect." These words do not likely come from Jesus; the Luke 6:36 parallel writes of being merciful as our Father is merciful.

First Thessalonians 5:23 appears to support the idea that perfection can be realized in this life: "May the God of peace himself sanctify you wholly; and may your spirit and soul and body be kept sound and blameless at the coming of our Lord Jesus Christ."[67] Should a prayer of benediction be interpreted as though it were as precisely intended as a more didactic text? If so, such supposed perfectionism drastically conflicts with much else that Paul wrote.

Concerning the Philippian Christians Paul attests: "It is my prayer that your love may abound more and more, with knowledge and all discernment, so that you may approve what is excellent, and may be pure and blameless for the day of Christ, filled with the fruits of righteousness which come through Jesus Christ, to the glory and praise of God" (Phil 1:9–11). Though describing a prayer and expressing a hope, Paul never claimed that he or any other disciple had realized such perfection.

The author of Ephesians writes of the upbuilding of the church in love through the exercise of charismatic gifts—that Christians may attain mature personhood and fullness of life in Christ (4:11–16, especially vs. 13). Mature personhood and fullness of life do not likely imply achieving a sinless state in this life. This text may only claim that Christians can and should grow in sanctification, and seek greater maturity in Christ. Second Corinthians 7:1 can be interpreted along similar lines.

Another Ephesians text sometimes cited in support of a belief in the attainment of human perfection in this life points instead to eternity: The reference in Ephesians 5:27 to being "without spot or wrinkle," "holy and without blemish" may concern God's *atonement-strengthened* assessment of believers at the final judgment.

17. Assessment of Wesley's Perfection Teaching

Though in some respects going beyond the teaching from 1 John, Wesley similarly affirmed that Christian disciples can in this life be perfected in love. Wesley did not claim to have achieved this nor—for all his squandered time in questioning people—did he find any Christian disciple whom he regarded as perfect. The whole exercise demonstrated Wesley's domineering spirit in thinking that he should pass such judgments.

---

66. "No one born of God commits sin; for God's nature abides in him, and he cannot sin because he is born of God."

67. Verse 24: "He who calls you is faithful, and he will do it"—attests belief in the perseverance of the saints by divine grace, which, as we will see, conflicts with the Arminianism that Wesley assumed in his perfection teaching and elsewhere.

Frustrating to anyone seeking to understand Wesley's perfection teaching is that he contradicted himself several times. Wesley's general Christian ideas concerning sanctification are far superior to his highly imperfect perfection teaching.[68]

The perfection claims we have seen in 1 John were duplicated in Wesley's teaching that sin is *little more than a conscious transgressing of a known law of God*. Though Wesley did not always speak of sin in this way, this was the characteristic understanding exhibited in his deliberations on perfection. And it flawed that discussion. It is not so difficult for one to become "perfect" if imperfection only involves violating known laws of God. But seeking first God's kingship goes far beyond that! Wesley was much the eighteenth-century rationalist in only emphasizing the role of conscious mind. A "perfection" that ignores the corrupting effects of the sub-conscious is highly imperfect.

If perfection as *freedom from conscious or deliberate sin* is all that is required, achieving perfection is relatively easy. This distortion could easily become the parent of hypocrisy, the essence of which is not the failure to respond to the highest we know, but the belief that the highest we know is the highest. The fact that we are not conscious of any willful transgression may only mean that sin has darkened our perception.

Certainly Christians should intend to love God and neighbor, but this is different from perfectly doing so. The double love commandment concerns the fulfillment of the law of love, not merely the conscious intention to do so. Wesley *sometimes* writes of perfection as *having to do only with simplicity of intention and purity of affection in willing to love God, and in consciously resolving to do God's will insofar as one understands that*.[69] At such points he recognizes that having pure motives does not guarantee that one always does what God wills. When speaking this way he admits he does not believe in "sinless perfection," since even perfected Christians are guilty of involuntary transgressions.[70]

At other places in the same book (!) and without seeming to notice the difference (!) Wesley says that perfection consists of fully loving God and neighbors, which suggests sinlessness at the level of behavior, not mere purity of conscious intention. "Question: What is implied in being a perfect Christian? Answer: The loving of God with all our heart, and mind, and soul (Deuteronomy 6:5)."[71] Wesley asserted that a Christian can be "so far perfect as not to commit sin." That "as Christians are freed from evil thoughts, so are they secondly from evil tempers."[72]

God's measurements are more comprehensive than may seem obviously implied by the two-sided law of love. Since God alone is the ultimate judge no one is competent to certify concerning who is or is not measuring up to God's standards, though Wesley spent

---

68. The Holiness Churches (Anabaptists and Quaker) still emphasize Wesley's teaching on perfection. United Methodists candidates for ordination have to publically answer as to whether they are going on to perfection and expect to attain it in this life. They can easily say yes to the former, which may only mean that they will try to be faithful disciples, and can remain silent or say no to the latter and still be ordained. I was.

69. Wesley, *Christian Perfection*, 7. See also Lindstrom, *Wesley and Sanctification*, 143, 186, quoted in Outler, *John Wesley*, 31.

70. Wesley, *Christian Perfection*, 18, 55, 57.

71. Wesley, *Christian Perfection*, 41; see also 5, 7, 11, 13. Also see Lindstrom, *Wesley and Sanctification*, 149.

72. Wesley, *Forty-Four Sermons*, 472, 473; cf. 462–63.

much time doing so! If Wesley had limited his perfection teaching to emphasizing the need for consciously intending to do God's will—"blessed are the pure in heart" (Matt 5:8)—his teaching would be more defensible. Even then, why should such commitment to Christ be posited as something that can only be attained late in life, and as due to a further conversion experience (the "second blessing")?

Wesley's psychological legalism is not found in the NT. I see no NT justification for expecting that Christians should experience one unique second conversion; Wesley seems to have had several such experiences! Nor do I think that the first one must be sudden. Self-conscious—Yes; instantaneous—No. Nor does every Christian require a second conversion experience.

The transformation of one's conscious will may not carry such far-reaching moral effects as Wesley assumed, since God's will far exceeds our perception of it and our faithful discipleship. Purity of intention should be a Christian concern from the beginning, *but seeking to have a pure intention should never involve claiming to possess one, nor avowing that one fully loves God and neighbor.* Wesley confused the subjective sense of seeking to be faithful to God with divinely adjudged perfection, which encouraged hypocritical people to think they are more moral than they are. He thereby contributed to nineteenth-century Liberal Theology, which by-and-large abandoned the NT teaching concerning human sinfulness.

Wesley may have inadvertently led those who claimed to have received "second blessing" perfection to trust in their achieved purity. Against such presumption, we should remember that some of the worst sins in history have been committed by those with unwarranted conviction that they were doing God's will. To the contrary, if one is to grow in sanctification, self-criticism is needed from the beginning and throughout. And self-criticism must include being open to learning from God through the criticisms of others. We are most likely to be righteous if we do not make pretentious claims about our achieved righteousness, but remain open to God's continuing judgment and correction.

Chapter 23

Christian Prayer, Christian Worship, Jesus's Baptism and Believer Baptism Distinguished but Interrelated, the Lord's Supper/Communion

Christian Prayer

WITHOUT PRAYER WE CANNOT live in relationship with God or be sensitive to His will. Prayer is the channel of communication between our Maker and us and us and our Maker. "The prophets of Israel . . . lived not only in converse with their people but primarily, supremely and specifically in converse with their people's God."[1]

1. Some Differing Kinds of Praying

In addition to listening to discern God's will, "prayer can be, and depending on the situation and circumstances will be: thanksgiving for what God does; adoration for who he is; losing oneself in his incomprehensible love; confession of guilt for sinfulness and for offending [against God's] love; prayer for faith and forgiveness; prayer for strength in the fight of the faith; . . . prayer for help in need; for wisdom to make right decisions; for submission and surrender when we see that our wills conflict with God's. And because the believer does not exist only by and for himself, he cannot intercede for himself alone; together with the church and for the sake of the church he prays for the progress of the proclamation of the gospel and for the upbuilding, unity, and expansion of the church in whatever form,"[2] and for much else.

---

1. Barth, *CD* 3/4:49.
2. Berkhof, *Christian Faith*, 291–92.

2. Jesus's Praying in Private

In the moral battle, as in every other, a decisive part of the engagement is not public. Behind His patience in Pilate's court and His fidelity at Calvary, lay the battle in Gethsemane, where a strategy was thought through and issues settled before God. The forthcoming outward conflicts were reverberation of the results of prior inward struggles. In the garden Jesus prayed for release from the appalling cup (Luke 22:42), but received the courage and insight to go on to suffer and to die in an excruciatingly painful way.

"Particularly noteworthy is the consistent emphasis in both Mark and Luke that Jesus liked to get away, to be alone in his praying,[3] either in the desert (Mark 1:35; Luke 5:16), or on a mountain[4] away from the crowds,[5] sometimes going off very early in the morning (Mark 1:35), sometimes spending much or the whole of the night in lonely prayer."[6] It is probable "that *prayer was Jesus's regular response to situations of crisis and decision.*"[7] Mark realistically stresses the fact that important decision-making times were often times of stress and crisis, whereas Luke only emphasizes that these were occasions for important decision making.[8]

We are surely right in saying that the dominant motive in Jesus's life was service. Yet on one occasion we find Him sending a multitude away, some of whom He might never have had another opportunity to address, and retiring to the solitude of the hills to pray (Matt 14:22–23a). Must we not suppose that he sent the people away, sought solitude, and gave himself to prayer and contemplation because he believed that by so doing he would be able to render the greatest service to others? As with us, those who are completely absorbed in action will not be of as much service as those who turn aside to gain direction from God.

3. Asking for God's Forgiveness

The parable of the Pharisee and the tax collector (Luke 18:9–14) attests the frame of mind with which we must approach God in prayer—with a deep sense of our unworthiness and recognition of our need for divine forgiveness. Before God we have no claim to merit, no ground for self-congratulation. We have separated ourselves from the source of true life and this has caused us to walk over others to get to where we have wanted to go. Our trespasses and sins have put us in debt to the holy God before whom we owe total obedience.[9] We would be hopelessly lost were it not that in Jesus Christ God has forgiven us. However

---

3. Matt 14:23; Luke 9:18; cf. Luke 9:28–29 with Mark 9:2.
4. Mark 6:46; Luke 6:12; 9:28–29.
5. Mark 1:35; 6:46; Luke 5:16.
6. Mark 6:46; 14:32–42; Luke 6:12. Dunn, *Jesus and the Spirit*, 20.
7. Dunn, *Jesus and the Spirit*, 20–21.
8. Luke 3:21; 6:12; 9:18, 28–29; 22:41–45.
9. "Forgive us our debts, as we also have forgiven our debtors" (Matt 6:12 RSV). The word "trespasses" became popular because that was the word used in the Anglican Book of Common Prayer. The Anglicans may have derived that word from the usage a few verses later in Matt 6:14–15. The word "debt" is the more literal translation in Matthew 6:12. Luke's version of the Lord's Prayer uses a different word than either of these, the word "sins." All three words, debts, trespasses, and sins are important.

forgiving others is essential for receiving God's ongoing forgiveness (cf. Matt 6:14–15). If we are sincere in our receipt of divine forgiveness we also ought to ask for forgiveness from those whom we may have wronged. A strong indication of how forgiving Christians should be, and how important forgiveness is to the Christian life, is that we are to pray for those who have or are currently persecuting us (Matt 5:44). Jesus's reported plea from the cross indicates how forgiving Christians should be: "Father, forgive them; for they know not what they are do" (Luke 23:34).

As we forgive "we spare and pardon all who have in any way injured us, either treating us unjustly in deed or insulting us in word. . . . Our forgiveness [involves the] willingness to cast from the mind wrath, hatred, [and the] desire for revenge . . . If we retain feelings of hatred in our hearts, if we plot revenge and ponder any occasion to cause harm . . . we [in effect] entreat God not to forgive our sins."[10] For we are those who are to do unto others as we want others to do unto us (Matt 7:12a).

4. Lord's Prayer[11]

Christ apparently gave this prayer to His disciples as a model for some of the content that should to be included in Christian praying, not that every prayer involves a reciting of this prayer or repeating the exact content of this prayer. The invocation is addressed to "*our* Father" and the requests are on the behalf of fellow Christians: "Give *us*," "forgive *us*," "lead *us* not," "deliver *us*" or "bring *us* not to the time of trial, but rescue *us* from the evil one" (NRSV, my emphases). These references remind us of the broader Christian fellowship, and join our concerns with those of the universal church.

"Father" is the name of God that Jesus taught us, and which apart from Christ we have no right to use (see John 1:12; Gal 4:6; "Mother" would be equally appropriate). Not only are we granted the right to call upon our Father because of forgiveness through Christ, but also because God's Holy Spirit has been poured into our hearts. Thus Paul wrote, "When we cry 'Abba! Father!' it is the Spirit himself bearing witness with our spirit that we are children of God" (Rom 8:15–16).

"Our Father who art in heaven, hallowed be thy name" (Matt 6:9bc). Hallowing God's name involves recognizing that God is to be worshipped and served for His own sake, in His own right and on His own terms. To hallow God's name is to revere and honor God and to glorify Him by being obedient to His will. Our first and primary petition is that throughout our lives we may show forth the honor that God deserves.

In traditional religion (paganism) or its prosperity gospel kinship people much believe in the power of prayer to get such things for themselves as great wealth and prominence. They ignore the Christian condition put on all petitionary praying, that it must be in Christ's name, that is, in His spirit (John 14:13; 16:23, 24, 26). No hurried addition of "for Jesus's sake" appended to a selfish prayer will satisfy God. Petition must be in accordance

---

10. Calvin, *Institutes*, 2:912.

11. Matthew 6:9–13; only partially contained in Luke 11:2–4. The Matthean version is exposited here. That we do not hear of the Lord's Prayer beyond Matthew and Luke is likely because the Gospels were written long after the other NT writings.

with Christ's disclosure concerning God's will. Prayer is not to be confused with supposed magic.

Thy kingdom come, thy will be done, on earth as it is in heaven" (Matt 6:10). We here pray for the final fulfilment of God's purposes, when God will bring history to fulfilment, when evil will be defeated, and when God will be all-in-all. We also here pray that God's kingship or rule may even now be effective in our lives, that even now God may be our King, and His will be done by us. The petitions for daily sustenance (vs. 11), for forgiveness hinged to our forgiving others (vs. 12; 14–15), and for preservation from the temptation and the power of evil (vs. 13) presuppose our trust in God and commitment to His cause.

5. Petitionary Prayer

Prayer as having much to do with petitions helps to guarantee "that the real person comes before God in prayer. For here we inevitably disclose who we are. In prayer . . . all masks and camouflages may and must fall away."[12]

"God is not deaf, He listens; more than that, He acts. He does not act in the same way whether we pray or not. Prayer exerts an influence upon God [and His] action."[13] To be sure, God knows our needs before we ask, but He desires that we ask, and our asking influences Him.

As God has left some things as dependent on human thought and action, He has left other things as dependent on praying. But we do not receive only "yes" or "no" answers to our petitionary prayers. Sometimes divine guidance is given only after a person has persistently sought an answer. If it is worthwhile to persistently wait for an unjust judge's ruling (Luke 18:1–8), it is much more important to wait patiently for the holy God's guidance. Unfortunately many people become impatient and do not continue to seek divine direction.

Even if people have genuinely sought to live in harmony with God's will God may not answer a person's petition affirmatively. But *God will answer the person*. Consider Paul's one reported petition relating to a need of his own, this pertained to his thorn in the flesh (see 2 Cor 12:7–9). Paul's petition for relief from that distress, whatever it was, was not favourably answered. But Paul was answered. God gave the assurance: "My grace is sufficient for you, for my power is made perfect in weakness" (2 Cor 12:9).

A reason that some people let supposedly unfulfilled petitionary prayers destroy their faith in prayer and even in God is that they fail to see that God often answers our prayers in ways we do not expect, or do not at the time like. God also answers genuine petitions in considerable part by shedding new light on circumstances and supplying us with sufficient insight, strength and wisdom to deal with them. Many of the petitions a Christian has occasion to make are answered by God putting a thought into a person's mind.

Petition is the dominant form of praying and is an aspect of most of the other types. Prayers of thanksgiving, of adoration, of confession, and of surrender almost always turn

---

12. Barth, *CD* 3/4:98.

13. Barth, *Prayer and Preaching*, 21. This is the paging from the original book, but may not be that of the republished book of the same name, which has additional interpretive articles by other authors.

into petition, and should. That happens in the Bible and in our own praying. "Even the most superstitious who came to Jesus asking for bread or healing, he did not send away unanswered. On the contrary, in fellowship with him they learned to ask for *more* than they had begun with, and to ask differently; no longer only from the standpoint of their own needs, but much more *from the perspective of God's purposes* of which their cares were only a part. . . . Their master, Jesus, was not spared this training school either. The words of his agonizing prayer in Gethsemane: 'Yet not what I will, but what [you will]' (Mark 14:36b) . . . is a real prayer, of the same nature as the third petition of the Lord's Prayer ['Thy will be done]."[14]

Jesus's view of prayer has much to do with trustful petition combined with commitment to God's will. Though the first three statements of the Lord's Prayer relate to God's cause and our obedience to God, these are also prayers of petition. "Hallowed by thy name (Matt 6:9b. Thy kingdom come. Thy will be done" (Matt 6:10ab). We need God's help, for only God can lead us in the way of obedience. "Ask and it shall be given; seek and you shall find; knock, and the door shall be opened unto you" (Matt 7:7).

Suppose you are confessing your sin to God. In all honesty you tell it as it really is. Fine. Excellent. But you also need to petition God for forgiveness and renewal. *Every genuine prayer of confession is implicitly or explicitly a prayer of petition.* The fifty-first Psalm is as much a cry for help as a confession of need. It begins like this: "Have mercy on me, O God, according to thy steadfast love; according to thy abundant mercy blot out my transgressions. Wash me thoroughly from my iniquity, and cleanse me from my sin! For I know my transgressions and my sin is ever before me" (Ps 51:1-3). A few verses later it further pleads "Create in me a clean heart, O God, and put a new and right spirit within me. Cast me not away from thy presence, and take not thy holy Spirit from me" (51:10-11). A prayer of confession is a Christian prayer only if it is also a prayer for forgiveness and renewal, asking God for help.

"The penitential prayers in the Psalms are . . . real prayers. That is, they do not remain mere expressions of shame, contrition and repentance, but they always issue in asking, desiring, sighing and crying towards God that He will forgive the one who prays, that He will not let him fall, that He will show him His way and give him a clean heart and a new spirit. A confession of sin without [a] climax petition, i.e., an abstract confession of sin, would not be a prayer at all. Only when it results in the corresponding request is it a prayer."[15]

New Testament Christians believed that the spiritual growth and development of the church depends on the prayer life of its members. It's not merely that prayer affects the attitudes and behaviours of those who pray, though this is true. Prayer also makes a difference in the life of the world. Paul said to members of one of his congregations, "You also must help us by prayers" (2 Cor 1:11). He pleaded to another, "Brethren, pray for us, that the word of the Lord may speed on and triumph" (2 Thess 3:1). Paul believed that his success as an apostle was directly related to the prayers of the church. Else he would not have said, "I appeal to you, brethren . . . strive together with me in your prayers to God on my behalf, that I may be delivered from the unbelievers in Judea, and that my service for Jerusalem may be acceptable to the saints" (Rom 15:30-31). Jesus Himself believed that prayers can

---

14. Berkhof, *Christian Faith*, 493.
15. Barth, *CD* 3/4:99.

help build up another person's faith. He said to Simon: "I have prayed for you that your faith may not fail" (Luke 22:32).

6. The Spirit Can Empower Us to Pray

"The Spirit helps us in our weakness, for we do not know how to pray as we ought, but the Spirit [herself] intercedes for us with sighs too deep for words" (Rom 8:26). God does not just listen to our prayers, but is our helper in praying. Think of a young child trying to express herself to her mother. The mother is willing to listen, but the child has trouble forming the words and expressing the ideas. So the mother helps the child to speak her mind. In a much deeper way, God is like that. We cannot pray to God, except as God leads us by Her Holy Spirit. The miracle of prayer is not only that God listens, but that by Her personal presence influences our inner selves so that prayer is possible. We are not only invited and expected to pray, but empowered to do so. Not only *may* we pray and *should* we pray, but by the Spirit's leading we *can* pray.

7. Line between Prayer and God-Centered Reflection Is Very Thin

During Jesus's times alone on the mountain or in the desert He was seeking spiritual enlightenment concerning the next steps to take. This was also a time of much spiritual reflection—and that is an important aspect of much private praying. The line between contemplation concerning God's will and praying is very thin. Sometimes one may be concerned about a decision or a next step to take, and be seeking God's will at very specific points. In this regard some may even manifest a certain quirkiness: Going to bed with an unresolved issue, one may be awakened in the middle of the night, with the answer or answers to be immediately jotted down, and then back to sleep.

More generally, does not God's leading often consist in a strong intuition or feeling that God is guiding us in a particular way? And after gaining a sense of God's directing, praying that it may be successfully implemented. For example, one may have been intently praying that a certain lady would say yes to a decision to be together for a couple of weeks as camp counsellors, the suitor hoping that decision might lead to a marriage possibility. Then after that time together, praying intently that the fine Christian lady who was considering the proposal would indeed decide to marry the gentleman in question. With both people asking repeatedly that God's will would be done. The point of these examples is to attest that God-centred contemplation and reflection is often an accompaniment of praying, not an antithesis.

8. Christians Care about Relationship with God, Not the Mere Fulfilment of Petitions

Though petitionary praying is an important part of the Christian life, Christians have responded to God's love in Christ, and thus our faith is not contingent on the fulfilment of specific petitions. We can "accept the divine acceptance of [a petitionary] prayer whether its overt content is fulfilled or not. Conversely, a prayer which is only a magical concentration on the desired aim, using God for its realization, does not accept an unfulfilled prayer as an accepted prayer, for the ultimate aim of the magic prayer is not God and the reunion with him but the object of the prayer, for example, health."[16]

9. Thanksgiving as an Essential Aspect of Prayer

"Have no anxiety about anything, but in everything by prayer and supplication with thanksgiving let your requests be made known to God" (Phil 4:6b). For Paul gratitude for God's saving action in Jesus Christ (Rom 7:25; 1 Cor 15:57) is the context of all Christian prayer.

Christian Worship

"We know next to nothing about Jesus's appreciation and experience of corporate worship. We are told that he attended the synagogue and may assume that this was His regular practice—although according to our evidence His primary purpose in so doing was to teach and proclaim His message.[17] His zeal for the functioning of the Temple as a place of prayer is on record (Mark 11:17 pars.),"[18] but "He was not content with the pious custom of liturgical prayer three times a day."[19]

1. Worship as a Means of Grace

"In spite of the regular appeal to Matthew 18:20—['Where two or three are gathered in my name, there am I in the midst of them']—the Reformation has never theoretically acknowledged the mediating character of the church service." "This contrasts . . . strongly with the importance which the churches everywhere attach to church attendance. In fact, for many Christians church attendance is a sacramental event that by itself and in spite of some of its elements . . . can strengthen the faith. This edifying character is fully acknowledged only in the Eastern church."

"The mediating character of the congregational gathering consists in the fact that it articulates and [helps us to] realize the encounter between God and his people. . . . Everything we know about love and friendship needs articulation on the one hand and nurture on the other. The communion with God in Christ also needs both; and it receives both together in the church service."[20]

---

16. Tillich, *Systematic Theology*, 279-80.
17. Mark 1:2-3 and pars.; 1:39 and pars.; 3:1 and pars; 6:2 and pars.; Matt 9:35; Luke 4:15-22; 13:10.
18. Dunn, *Jesus and the Spirit*, 16.
19. Jeremias, *New Testament Theology*, 188.
20. Berkhof, *Christian* Faith, 375, 374, 376.

2. The New Testament Holy Day

"The eschatological connexion and significance of the New Testament holy day . . . are manifest in the fact that it has been put on the day of the resurrection of Jesus . . . And the first Christians saw in the resurrection of Jesus . . . the prophecy of the future general resurrection of the dead."

"To observe the holy day means to keep oneself free for participation in the praise and worship and witness and proclamation of God in His congregation, in common thanksgiving and intercession."[21] Already Hebrews 10:23-25 indicates the mediating character of this meeting together: "Let us hold fast the confession of our hope without wavering, for he who promised is faithful; and let us consider how to stir up one another to love and good works; not neglecting to meet together, . . . but encouraging one another, and all the more as you see the Day drawing near."

3. Edification (Upbuilding in Love) as a Criterion of Church Worship

Though worship focuses upon God, written large over Paul's recommendations and directives for public worship at Corinth is that it upbuild or edify Christians and thereby the church (1 Cor 14:26c).[22] "Paul uses the terms "edification" and "to edify" in 1 Corinthians chapter 14 seven times (the former in 14:3-5,12, 26; the latter twice in 14:4, 17)." Negatively, these terms express the "rejection of self-sufficient religious individualism . . . centered upon itself. Positively, it expresses the helping of others . . . through . . . admonition and consolation (14:3)."[23]

For worship to edify and provide mutual help it must be comprehensible . "It should be noted that Paul does not except even prayer here. He [also] shows how radically he understands this need for the language to be comprehensible by his refusal to allow the speaker to address his words only to those who already are of the same mind and have the same experience and knowledge. . . . Those . . . on the periphery or even [generally] outside the congregation (14:16, 23) must be able to understand, be convinced and have the hidden things of their hearts revealed."

Concern for outsiders and non-believers shows that Paul holds fast to the "missionary function of the word even in the case of the word in worship. It is not by chance that for Paul the same verb, 'to build,' designates both his missionary activity and the teaching and care of the congregations by his successors, even [though] the laying of the foundation [was] reserved to him as [an] Apostle . . . (1 Cor 3:10ff.)."

Congregational upbuilding concern also impacts the dealings of "the 'strong' in relation to the 'weak' (1 Cor 8:11-23), [not just of] speakers . . . in relation to the listeners (chap. 14)."[24] One could call the edification of the church its continuing creation, happen-

---

21. Barth, *CD* 3/4:57, 62.
22. Erickson, *Christian Theology*, 1057.
23. Bornkamm, *Early Christian Experience*, 163.
24. Bornkamm, *Early Christian Experience*, 163.

ing through the practical behavior of the congregants toward one another (cf. Rom 14–15; 1 Cor 8–10) and amid its worship.[25]

Cognizant of Paul's insights mentioned in this section, the author of Ephesians 4:12 indicates that God has given various gifts to the church "for the equipment of the saints, for the work of ministry, for building up the body of Christ." "Speaking the truth in love, we are to grow up in every way into him who is the head, into Christ, from whom the whole body, joined and knit together by every joint with which it is supplied, when each part is working properly, makes bodily growth and upbuilds itself in love" (vss. 15–16).

4. Offering Ourselves for Service to God and Further Meanings of Worship

Worship involves revelation-based sharing in the reality of the new age, that enables us to distinguish God's will from this world's, thereby capacitating us to offer our lives to God and to assist in His reclaiming of the world. As celebration and fellowship the meeting anticipates the day which in the deepest sense will be "the day of the Lord," and so worship gives a foretaste of the eternal Sabbath. But not in such a way that the future makes us forget the present ethical struggle. For sin and guilt are real, but so are God's acquittal and empowering for discipleship.[26]

Without self-surrender worship is an inadequate response to God's offering in Christ. God wants far more than monetary contributions for needy causes, though He also wants that. He desires a humble spirit, a contrite heart (Psalms 51:17), and a relationship involving our love and trust and obedience. Thus Paul wrote, "I appeal to you . . . brethren, by the mercies of God, to present your bodies as a living sacrifice, holy and acceptable, which is your spiritual worship" (Rom 12:1). When Paul speaks of presenting our bodies he is calling for the commitment of the whole person.

5. Worship Variation and Stability

It is not easy to strike a balance between formal orders of worship, which can be in danger of quenching the Spirit, and less formal ones that can be excessively casual or revert to wild ecstasy. As for stable elements in worship, in addition to preaching and general praying and singing, prayers of confession might always be included, but with varying forms. Similarly, there are various affirmations of faith (not just the Nicene or Apostles' Creed) and these others can be chosen or new ones written. And an affirmation of faith is not required in every service.

Three scriptural readings (Old Testament, Epistle, and Gospel) are also not requirements. What is important is that the readings be chosen with reference to their relevance in developing the biblical theme being preached upon. Being slavishly bound by lectionaries may lead to fragmentary approaches to biblical topics. Some systematics and Christian ethics can help to shed light on biblical themes.

---

25. Bornkamm, *Early Christian Experience*, 164.
26. Berkhof, *Christian Faith*, 376.

The Lord's Prayer can be sung and sung more than once, the singing and repetition allowing for more concentration on the words. Some hymn verses can also contribute to congregational prayers. And for something considerably different, at the end of the service let the congregation raise issues related to the sermon, with the pastor responding where helpful.

Jesus's Baptism and Believer Baptism Distinguished but Interrelated

1. Jesus's Baptism by John

Often it is easier to know whether or not an event of the past occurred than to grasp what it meant in its original or even secondary context, though sometimes the opposite is the case. Next to the fact that Jesus was crucified as a Messianic claimant, that He was baptized is as certain as anything historical concerning Jesus can be. Since the fact that Jesus was baptized could easily have been misunderstood, Mark would have had little reason for creating such a tradition from prophecy.

Sensing that Mark's narrative could be misinterpreted, Matthew made additions to attest that Jesus was not a sinner needing to repent, but was baptized "to fulfill all righteousness" (3:15b), i.e. to obediently realize God's plan. Matthew implied that John the Baptizer recognized Jesus's purity and thus protested that He was not worthy to baptize Him (3:14). These uniquely Matthean aspects of the narrative seem added to prevent people from drawing a conclusion not intended by Mark, namely that Jesus needed to repent.

Being baptized usually symbolized the need to receive divine forgiveness. However the common witness of the NT is that Jesus was sinless.[27] Matthew's statement that when baptizing Jesus, John recognized Jesus's greater authority (3:14–15) is historically doubtful, but is Matthew's way of attesting Jesus's authority.[28] Had John the Baptist recognized Jesus's authority it is puzzling why he continued to have his own disciples and was uncertain concerning Jesus's messianic status. From prison just prior to the Baptists' execution *he sent his disciples* to inquire whether or not Jesus was the expected Messiah (Luke 7:18–23), a point also mentioned by Matthew (11:2–6).

Contrary to Matthew and Luke's additions, it is doubtful that the historical purpose of Jesus's baptism was to proclaim publicly who He was. With the baptism reference Matthew and Luke apparently wished at early points in their Gospels to clarify *for their readers* who Christ was and is. This even though they had already affirmed Jesus as the Son of God in their virgin conception legends.

Clarifying Jesus's identity for readers was also likely the purpose of even Mark's recounting of Jesus's baptism (1:1–11). A voice only heard by Jesus and vision only seen by Him would not have been a way of attesting Jesus's authority to those present. According to Mark "when Jesus came up out of the water, immediately *he saw* the heavens opened

---

27. John 8:46; Acts 3:14; 2 Cor 5:21; Heb 7:26; 1 Pet 1:19.

28. "Then Jesus came from Galilee to the Jordan to John, to be baptized by him. John would have prevented him, saying 'I need to be baptized by you, and do you come to me?' But Jesus answered him, 'Let it be so now; for thus it is fitting for us to fulfil all righteousness.' Then he consented" (Matt 3:13–15a).

SYSTEMATICS CRITICAL AND CONSTRUCTIVE 2

and the Spirit descending upon him like a dove; and a voice came from heaven [saying to Him],[29] 'Thou art my beloved Son; with thee I am well pleased'" (1:10–11). Mark's narrative purports to describe an inner experience of Jesus alone; so how did Mark know of these words? He didn't. The reason Mark recorded this story was likely to reaffirm in a narrative way what he said in chapter 1, verse 1, that he was writing a "Gospel of Jesus Christ, the Son of God."

Granted that these narratives may have been told primarily for the readers' edification, it is still legitimate to inquire as to what Jesus' baptism may have meant to Him. But it is hard to answer the question. Mark's Gospel alludes to a religious experience that Jesus had at His baptism, but the words of Mark's text imply Mark's belief that Jesus's sense of identity was then deepened, not that it was then created. The first half of the words from heaven reaffirm those of Psalm 2:7b, "you *are* my son," but add the word "beloved." The second half of the words from heaven *does not* continue quoting from Psalms 2:7, to the effect that God that day beget His unique Son. That is what Mark should have reported were he describing God's present adoption of Jesus as His Son. Rather, God is said to have *reaffirmed* His Son by saying "you are my beloved Son; with you I am well pleased" (Mark 1:11).[30]

Mark apparently thought that God may have reassured Jesus of God's pleasure that His Son was beginning His public ministry of enacting and proclaiming the kingship of God, toward which (according to Mark's interpretation) John the Baptizer had already begun to point. According to Mark's text the words from heaven attest divine approval to Jesus concerning the course to which He had committed himself. To Jesus the ratifying voice avows God's reaffirmation that Jesus was indeed God's unique agent of salvation.

Though in quoting Psalm 2:7 Mark eliminated the "today I have begotten you" aspect, which could have pointed to baptismal adoptionism, it is fitting that the supposed words from heaven at Jesus's baptism are those used by the Psalmist to refer to kingly authority (Mark 1:11b). The paradox is that *God's unique agent of salvation, who later in humble circumstances would confess to being the Messiah, had from the beginning of His ministry tread the path of humility*. Though Jesus must have had a sense of unique authority already, He stepped forward to be baptized with sinners. *He who did not need to undergo a baptism of repentance, establishes a basis for ours.* By kneeling in solidarity with us He who would later be shown to be the Savior began to effect salvation.

According to Mark's account of Jesus's transfiguration a similarly affirmative answer was given—"this is my beloved Son" (Mark 9:7)—and also given in answer to the final question that the Jewish leaders raised at His trial. "Are you the Christ, the Son of the Blessed?' And Jesus said, 'I am; and you will see the Son of man sitting at the right hand of Power, and coming with the clouds of heaven'" (14:61b–62). Jesus's affirmation of who He was and is led to His crucifixion by the Romans as King of the Jews (15:26).

Though the historicity of Jesus's baptism by John in the Jordon is reliable, literary details concerning the event were shaped by post-resurrection christological beliefs. The link between Jesus's baptism in the Jordan and the Spirit-led element in Jesus is a part of

---

29. Again, had the Baptist heard these words he would not have been doubtful even from prison late in his ministry.

30. In place of the second part of the Psalm 2:7 quotation we hear an echo of Isaiah 42:1.

the original core of the tradition relating to Jesus's baptism. Jesus' baptism by John may not only have manifested His decision to begin His public ministry, but contributed toward it. Yet in Jesus's public ministry we have no evidence that He baptized anyone.

2. Spirit Baptism and Its Relation to Believer Water Baptism[31]

The Christian life begins with a decisive and basic change in a person's life, in which one begins to die to mere self-will and starts to truly live. Thus Paul said of himself, "I have been crucified with Christ; it is no longer I who live, but Christ who lives in me; and the life I now live in the flesh I live by faith in the Son of God who loved me and gave himself for me" (Gal 2:20). He elsewhere attests that the Christian's whole existence is as "always carrying in the body the death of Jesus, so that the life of Jesus may also be manifested in our bodies" (2 Cor 4:10). Through "the work of the Holy Spirit . . . the resurrection of Jesus Christ is manifest and present to a specific person as one's own salvation history. . . . That which was truth for all, and hence for him too even without his acceptance, becomes truth that is affirmed by him."[32]

John the Baptist is said to have contrasted water baptism with Spirit baptism: "I have baptized you with *water* for repentance; . . . he will baptize you with the *Holy Spirit and fire*."[33] Though the metaphor for Spirit baptism is drawn from the water baptism rite, Spirit baptism is what is most essential. Acts makes it clear that the same antithesis between Spirit-bestowal and the water-rite continued into the Christian era (1:5; 11:16).

"Baptism with the Spirit is . . . divinely effective, divinely causative, and divinely creative. Here, if anywhere, one might speak of a sacramental happening in the current sense of the term. It cleanses, renews and changes a person truly and totally."[34] "Baptism in [the] Spirit . . . is simply a metaphor which was drawn from John's water-rite and which was chosen primarily with a view to bringing out the contrast with the water-rite most sharply." Paul attests that only the Spirit-led are children of God (Rom 8:14). As strongly emphasized in Acts, "in the earliest days of Christianity possession of the Spirit was a fact of *immediate* [personal] perception, not a logical conclusion to be drawn from the performance of an ecclesiastical rite."[35] The NT regards believer water baptism as the expression of the prior faith that Christians hold, not as a means of awakening that faith. "The *New Testament writers distinguish these two uses carefully and explicitly and never confuse them*."[36]

---

31. Though Paul does not utilize the term "Spirit baptism" he does refer to being baptized into Christ Jesus and into His death, as will be further indicated below.

32. Barth, *CD* 4/4, *Fragment*, 27–28.

33. Matt 3:11, my emphasis; see also Mark 1:8; Luke 3:16.

34. Barth, *CD* 4/4, *Fragment*, 34.

35. Dunn, *Baptism in the Holy Spirit*, 22, 149.

36. Dunn, "Rediscovering the Spirit," 9, my emphasis. Though Jesus was baptized by John the Baptist, the Synoptics indicate that sacraments and rituals were missing from Jesus's ministry. The late Fourth Gospel reinterpretation of Jesus traditions provides contradicting and thus unconvincing evidence that He baptized. John 3:22 attests that he did and 4:2 says that he did not. John 3:5 claims that Jesus said: "Truly, truly, I say to you, unless one is born of water and the Spirit, he cannot enter the kingdom of God." It seems likely that the words "water and" in 3:5 and the whole of 6:51b–59 were inserted by an editor to provide some attestation from Jesus concerning the sacraments. This seems all the more likely since John 3:6–9

Returning to the water baptism issue itself, with believer *water* baptism the primary movement is from people to God, not vice-versa as in Spirit baptism. This becomes clear in the one NT verse that most nearly approaches a definition of water baptism, 1 Peter 3:21. There it is described as a pledge or prayer *to* God, not something *from* God. It is "*the expression of the converts commitment and repentance.*"[37]

For the first Christians believer water baptism *symbolized* the death and rebirth that they had experienced prior to seeking to become members of the church. Paul wrote to the Romans, "Do you not know that all of us who have been baptized into Christ Jesus were baptized into his death? We were buried therefore with him by baptism into death, so that as Christ was raised from the dead by the glory of the Father, we too might walk in newness of life" (Rom 6:3-4).

We become Christians by receiving the Holy Spirit.[38] Believer water baptism should follow from but is not identical with the baptism of the Spirit (John 3:3-8), being born of God. Believer water baptism should be a public profession of one's belief in Christ and act of identifying with His church, taking the place of what is often today called "confirmation."

3. Barth's Agreement with Schleiermacher in Advocating Believer Water Baptism and Rejecting Infant Baptism

Schleiermacher wrote that "every trace of infant baptism which people have professed to find in the New Testament must first be inserted there."[39] From the second century onwards, as seen plainly in Justin and Ignatius, baptism and the Lord's Supper "began to be regarded as cultic re-presentations of the act and revelation of God in the history of Jesus Christ, and consequently as the granting of a share in His grace. They thus began to be described and treated as mysteries."[40] To the contrary, the *mystery*, the *sacrament*, is God's revelation in Jesus Christ as known by the Holy Spirit.

> With some variations in detail, but general agreement in substance, the process as described in Acts 2:37f; 8:12, 38; 10:44f.; 16:14f., 32f. is as follows. Individuals or

---

speaks only of being born of the Spirit: "that which is born of the flesh is flesh, and that which is born of the Spirit is spirit. Do not marvel that I said to you, 'You must be born anew.' The wind blows where it wills, and you hear the sound of it, but you do not know whence it comes or whither it goes; so it is with everyone who is born of the Spirit" (3:6-9).

"There is in the New Testament no transfer of the . . . competence to baptise to a specific circle with a particular ecclesiastical office. Among the gifts of the Holy Spirit mentioned in Rom 12 and 1 Cor 12 there is no specific gift for dispensing baptism, or, for that matter, the Lord's Supper. In practice, of course, not every Christian undertook to administer baptism. As Jesus Himself according to the express statement in John 4:2 did not baptise with water, so the apostle Paul was thankful that he had baptised no one, or only a few, in Corinth (1 Cor 1:14-17). . . . There is in the New Testament no trace of the later bureaucratic concern for validity in the administration of the sacraments, including baptism" (Barth, *CD* 4/4, *Lecture Fragments*, 49-50).

37. Dunn, "Rediscovering the Spirit," 9-10.
38. John 20:20-23; Acts 1:5; 11:16; 1 Cor 12:13.
39. Schleiermacher, *Christian Faith*, 634.
40. Barth, *CD* 4/4, *Fragment*, 109. Mystery religions' worship services were held in secrecy at night and at some distance from the nearest city. Those services involved preliminary purifications and participants had to pay, with the assurance that they would be rewarded in the next life.

groups have been reached by the Word of God, i.e., the apostolic preaching... They want to obey the demand for confession of sins, for faith, for conversion. They do obey it. In keeping with this, in visible execution of this act of obedience, they ask for baptism and have themselves baptized. In all these accounts baptism has the character of an action in which there is a common affirmation by the candidates of the Gospel preached and received, which involves their conscious and voluntary participation, and which rests upon and takes place in an act of free decision. In these accounts it is not even conceivable that infants might be the recipients of baptism. This is certainly possible in other passages to which appeal is often made, namely Acts 16:15, 33; 18:8; 1 Cor 1:16. These verses speak of the baptism of whole households, in which there might have been infants. This is, however, a slender rope, for it should be noted that even in these verses we have the sequence of preaching—faith—baptism. Nor is one faithful to the true sense of the verses if one deduces from them that there could have been baptisms of a different kind, for there is no hint that they were trying to say this or even to include it.[41]

Mark 10:13–16 indicates Jesus's love for and concern about children, but this is not a justification for infant baptism: "And they were bringing children to him, that he might touch them; and the disciples rebuked them. But when Jesus saw it he was indignant, and said to them, 'Let the children come to me, do not hinder them; for to such belongs the kingdom of God. Truly, I say to you, whoever does not receive the kingdom of God like a child shall not enter it.' And he took them in his arms and blessed them, laying his hands upon them."

Referring to these verses Barth writes that Jesus was "already the Savior of these children who are not yet called to decision for Him or capable of it. He already prayed for them, took them in His arms and blessed them. "The text is... [a] powerful witness to the universal scope of the work and word of Jesus Christ. *But it is not a baptismal text.*... Jesus has come and is ready for those who do not yet know, recognize, or confess Him, and who [should not] as yet be baptized."[42]

Infant baptism advocates often unfairly utilize arguments for their position that are not disputed by those who favor believer baptism. I list a few:

- That as the Savior of all Jesus blessed and embraced all children;
- That Christian parents especially owe their Christian witness to those who are closest to them;
- That Christian parents have a duty to give Christian instruction to their children, leading them toward Christian faith.[43]

As for why the post-NT church began baptizing babies, this became widely practiced when nominal Christianity became widespread, and the two trends interrelated. Having been baptized as infants, many people grew up thinking they were already Christians, though they had made no decisive commitment to Christ. Not surprisingly the modern theologian who eventually spoke against infant baptism (Barth)—though doing so

---

41. Barth, *CD* 4/4, *Fragment*, 179–80.
42. Barth, *CD* 4/4, *Fragment*, 182.
43. Barth, *CD* 4/4, *Fragment*, 176.

conflicted with his denominational background—did so as part of his lifelong critique of cultural Christianity.

Barth regarded infant baptism as the attempt of christendom to accommodate to the state, rather than to be in tension with the it and the world. He also regarded infant baptism as both a cause and expression of the denial of radical Christian obedience. For infant baptism had the effect of lowering the standards and integrity of church membership. He insisted that instead of being a passive object of baptism, the person baptized must freely decide and freely affirm their Christian faith. He was clear that the price for changing the practice of baptism in this way was to renounce the form of the national church, and other churches of the masses.[44]

Consistent with Jesus's practice of blessing children, but not baptizing them, are church member parents' and congregants' resolutions that through words and deeds they would seek to provide good Christian examples and guidance. Thereby they would in particular help congregant children to understand and decide for Christ. Such commitment is consistent with the development of dedication ceremonies to this effect, though the NT provides no such examples.

4. New Testament Writers' Believer Baptism Terminologies and Procedures

Though water baptism *accomplishes* nothing it *denotes* much—but only in the case of believer baptism. Paul asks and then asserts: "Do you not know that all of us who have been baptized into Christ Jesus were baptized into his death? We were buried therefore with him by baptism into death, so that as Christ was raised from the dead by the glory of the Father, we too might walk in newness of life" (Rom 6:3–4, my emphasis).

As becoming a Christian involves dying to sin and rising to new life, so baptism by immersion publicly attests what has happened (Acts 8:36–39). *Immersion* as a symbol of drowning testifies that the one being baptized has died to the old life. Rising out of the water avows the new life one has come to have through Christ. Immersion symbolizes that one has put off the old nature, and put on the new nature (Col 3:9–11). To symbolize the transition, early baptismal candidates may also have changed from street clothes to specific baptismal garments.

If baptism by immersion occurs in a river the *immersion* aspect continues to represent dying and rising to new life, whereas the flow of the water signifies the *washing away* of sin that had happened prior to the water baptism. Powerful symbolism if referring to those who have reached years of discretion and have decided for Christ; meaningless (even dangerous) if applied to infants.

Baptismal sprinkling or pouring, immersion, and immersion plus washing away all denote that God in Christ has forgiven our sins. We who in ourselves are unworthy have been cleansed in and through Him (Acts 22:16; Eph 5:26; Heb 10:22; 2 Pet 1:9).

Since the NT can be quoted to justify each of these symbolizing activities it is simplistic, inflexible, and legalistic to insist that only one of these methods is legitimate. It is well

---

44. Barth, *CD* 4/4, *Fragment*, 168.

to permit the various forms the NT attests. What all these denote is that that though the candidates were once lost, *by God's grace and their prior experiencing of that grace* they have been found. They are therefore ready to join the community of faith by publically attesting their faith and by being baptized.

5. Christian Community's Role in Baptizing Believers

That people might baptize themselves is as alien to the NT as that the community could perform more welcoming service than to acknowledge purported faith as entitling church membership.[45] Though instruction should certainly have been given concerning essentials of Christian Faith, the baptizing community does not have to be sure of the faith and spiritual endowments of candidates. But it does need to assess the integrity of free decisions and confessions. "When it baptizes it must say yes to the yes which is responsibly said to it."

There are situations in which a dedicated disciple is not able to experience water baptism. "This may be because there is no community from which he may ask and receive it. It may be because the community, in the form in which he encounters it, is so little recognizable or convincing as a true Christian community that he cannot have the trust or confidence to seek its recognition or to associate himself with it." "In no circumstances will a true Christian cease to desire that his obedience of faith be publicly and bindingly declared and that he be recognized and acknowledged as a true Christian by a true Christian community."[46]

The Lord's Supper/Communion

The Lord's Supper or Communion is a memorial of our past deliverance in Christ, a celebration of our present deliverance as we participant in the Risen Christ, and a foretaste of our future deliverance beyond death. Past, present, and future salvation are all celebrated. This is one of the ways in which we remember Christ's life given on our behalf. Wine remains wine and bread remains bread, but they remind us of Christ's last supper and of His broken body and spilt blood on our behalf.

1. Jesus's Last Meal with His Disciples as His Farewell

In this farewell meal Jesus is recorded as affirming an oath of abstinence: "I shall not drink again of the fruit of the vine until that day when I drink it anew in the kingdom of God" (Mark 14:25). "Jesus's last meal with his disciples was supposed to unite the disciples with Jesus precisely when he took leave of them and to strengthen in them the certainty that they would again sit with Him."[47]

Commenting on the above text, Meyer says:

---

45. Barth, *CD* 4/4, *Fragment*, 183–84, 49.
46. Barth, *CD* 4/4, *Fragment*, 192, 157.
47. Kummel, *Theology of the New Testament*, 93.

Jesus was mocked by his adversaries because, in contrast to the ascetic John, [Jesus] was seen as an "eater and drinker, a friend of tax collectors and sinners" (Matt 11:19 par.). In the eyes of the stringently pious, Jesus's table fellowship with the ritually or morally unclean communicated uncleanliness to Jesus Himself. Jesus, of course, saw it the other way round: he was communicating salvation to religious outcasts. His meals with sinners and the disreputable were celebrations of the lost being found, of God's eschatological mercy reaching out and embracing the prodigal son returning home (see, e.g., Mark 2:13–17; Luke 15:1–32). His banquets with sinful Israelites were a preparation and foretaste of the coming banquet in the kingdom of God—a metaphor that appears in various sayings and parables.[48] Thus the Last Supper does not stand in splendid isolation. It is instead quite literally the "last" of a whole series of meals symbolizing the final feast in the kingdom of God. There is therefore nothing strange about Jesus's holding a special symbolic meal with his disciples (especially if he senses his approaching arrest or death) or about his connecting the meal with the ... kingdom of God. ... For Jesus to affirm that he would never again drink wine [Mark 14:25] (the sign of a special festive meal) until he does so in the kingdom of God is to affirm *ipso facto* that this is the last festive meal of his life in the present world.

As for the historicity of Jesus's farewell meal with His disciples, in Meyer's "view, the ... telling criterion is that of discontinuity. Mark 14:25 reflects christological, soteriological, and eschatological ideas—or the startling lack thereof—that are at variance with almost any stream of early Christian tradition, but are perfectly understandable in the mouth of the historical Jesus."[49]

2. Exegetical Examination of Pre-Gospels' Attestings of Lord's Supper Passages

Paul speaks of the Lord's Supper not only as a remembrance of Christ's self-giving, but also as a "communion" or "participation" in Christ. Paul assumes as self-evident that the Lord's Supper points to Christ's self-sacrifice, but is also a means that leads to present participation in the power of the crucified and risen Lord.

"The cup of blessing which we bless, is it not a participation in the blood of Christ? The bread which we break, is it not a participation in the body of Christ. Because there is one loaf, we who are many are one body, for we all partake of the same loaf" (1 Cor 10:16–17). "For I received from the Lord what I also delivered to you, that the Lord Jesus on the night when he was betrayed took bread, and when he had given thanks, he broke it, and said, 'This is my body which is for you. Do this in remembrance of me.' In the same way also the cup, after supper, saying, 'This cup is the new covenant in my blood. Do this, as often as you drink it, in remembrance of me.' For as often as you eat this bread and drink the cup, you proclaim the Lord's death until he comes" (1 Cor 11:23–26).

Paul criticized rich church members for expressing contempt for poor members by not waiting to receive the Lord's Supper, *which when it was an aspect of the worship service was part of a meal.* Paul insisted that all members must receive the Lord's Supper together

---

48. See, e.g., Mark 2:19; Luke 13:28–29 and par.; 14:15–24 and par.
49. Meier, *A Marginal Jew*, 2:303, 305.

(1 Cor 11:17–22, 27–34), arguing that those members who would be too hungry to wait should eat at home before the service (vs. 11:34). "The probability is that . . . the poor (slaves, etc.), having to work that day, were usually able to arrive only [late, and in this case, only] in time for the Lord's Supper (11:21). Hence the rebukes in 11:27, 29; 'not discerning the body' probably means an eating and drinking which does not express fellowship with poor and weak"[50] church members.

"Whoever eats the bread and drinks the cup of the Lord in an unworthy manner will be guilty of profaning the body and blood of the Lord. Let a man examine himself, and so eat of the bread and drink of the cup. For anyone who eats and drinks without discerning the body eats and drinks judgment upon himself" (1 Cor 11:27–29).

3. Mood of Penitence, Joy, and Thankful Rededication

The proper mood for the celebration of Communion or non-Communion worship includes both penitence and joy, sadness for our sin, yet thankfulness that in Jesus Christ our sin has been forgiven. Such double-sidedness is not only the proper mood for such celebrations and re-dedications, but is also the right attitude for our entire Christian lives. As we daily repent of our sin and are thankful for Christ's self-sacrifice, His fellowship with us, and His promise of eternal life we are enabled to become obedient to His will. As with general Christian worship, to celebrate the Lord's Supper should mean that we leave in a mood of thankful rededication to the life of service and love. The Gospel is not like an abstract idea that we can master and that's it. The Gospel is Christ living and present, whom we ever again encounter as we respond to Christian preaching and teaching, as we worship together, as we celebrate the supper of our Lord, and as we seek to live the Christian life.

4. Remembering God's Sacrifice in Jesus and Jesus's Self-Giving

Christ's broken body and spilt blood reflect *God's sacrificial giving of Himself in the life and death of Jesus Christ*. As Jesus broke the bread, so the next day, His body was broken for us sinners. As He poured the wine, so the next day His blood was shed on our behalf. In Jesus Christ, God in His priestly role made a sacrifice, and Christ on God's behalf was the sacrifice that was made.

God's self-giving in Christ's sacrificial death is central to the UMC Communion service. For example, it affirms that God "made there, by the one offering of Himself, a full, perfect, and sufficient sacrifice for the sins of the whole world." "Christ has died for you." "Christ's blood was shed for you."

The New Testament does not refer to the Eucharist as involving Christ's self-offering. However they are means of participation in Christ's self-offering achieved once and for all through Christ (1 Cor 10:16; Heb 9:12). The Lord's Supper and Christian worship services

---

50. Dunn, *Unity and Diversity*, 164. In 1 Corinthians 8:7–13, Paul criticized Christians who were insensitive in their criticisms of Christians who had only recently broken ranks with traditional religion and its superstitions concerning eating food that had been dedicated to idols.

5. Bread and Wine, Body and Blood Issue

Many Protestants regard Christ as not present in the elements, but in the action of the Eucharist, as He is present in the action of other of regular worship services. Bread broken and distributed reminds us of Christ's body broken for our sin; wine poured and received reminds us of Christ's blood shed for us. These elements and actions call to mind the extent of Christ's self-sacrifice. God is present in living relationship with us, but not in the bread and wine.

"This is my body. . . . This is my blood" (Mark 14:22b, 24b). In Aramaic (which was likely Jesus's main language) the words of institution would have to have been formulated without the word "is." This because Aramaic does not have the verb form *estin* [is].[51] It would have read "This—my body"; "This—my blood"; with a purely associational connection. "We might render Jesus's statements as 'This represents [or signifies] my body' and 'This represents [or signifies] my blood.' This [understanding] spares us from the type of difficulties incurred by the view that Christ is physically present in the elements."[52]

"To Jews the drinking of blood is so offensive that it is inconceivable that the saying would have been uttered in Jewish circles without an explanation of the necessity for such a shocking action (cf. Gen 9:4; Lev 17:10ff) *unless it was always considered nothing more than a metaphor.*"[53] Drinking human blood and eating human flesh is also repulsive to modern people.

No one at the first Lord's Supper could have confused the bread and wine with Christ because He was there saying the words! Furthermore, if we take 'This is my body' and 'This is my blood' literally, a [further] absurdity results." It would mean that at that upper room receiving of the elements "his flesh and his blood were at two places simultaneously." To so believe "is something of a denial of the incarnation, which limited his physical human [presence] to one location."

"There are conceptual difficulties for those who declare that Christ has been bodily present in the subsequent occurrences of the Lord's Supper. While the preceding paragraph introduced the problem of how Christ's [body] could *have been* in two places simultaneously, here we face the problem of *how two substances* (e.g., flesh and bread) *can be in the same space simultaneously* (the Lutheran conception) or of *how a particular substance (e.g., blood) can exist without any of its customary characteristics* (the Catholic view)."[54]

---

51. Weber, *Foundations of Dogmatics*, 2:623.
52. Erickson, *Christian Theology*, 1122.
53. Schweizer, *Good News according to Mark*, 301, my emphasis.
54. Erickson, *Christian Theology*, 1121.

6. Frequency of Early Eucharistic Celebrations

The NT says nothing about how frequently worship services were expected to include Eucharistic celebrations. In view of the expensiveness of wine and the poorness of the early congregations, Eucharistic celebrations are unlikely to have been frequent. Infrequent Communion services would not have raised problems, since the focus on Christ's self-offering for our sake was and still should be an integral aspect of all worship services.

7. Zwingli and Zwinglian Understandings of the Lord's Supper

"Zwingli's name is attached to a view of the Lord's Supper that is directed primarily against transubstantiation": the belief in the conversion of the Eucharistic elements into the body and blood of Christ at their consecration, with only the appearance of the bread and wine still remaining. (Of course a chemist would find that the elements of the bread and the wine remain the same!) "In reaction to every attempt to ascribe [effectiveness] to the 'elements,' Zwingli . . . knew that faith lives . . . by the passion, death, and resurrection of Christ"[55] as received through the Spirit.

The Lord's Supper is a commemorative event, with bread and wine as signs helping us to remember and understand the unique work of God through Christ. The elements point backward to the Crucified One, inward to the participant's faith,[56] and upward to the transcendent God. Zwingli's concern was to safeguard the spirituality of faith and preserve the character of faith as pure trust in God through Christ.[57]

Zwingli did not regard the Lord's Supper as the norm of Christian worship, and therefore did not favor frequent Communion. He confined Communion to four times a year. In both matters he stood alone among the continental reformers, though both Calvinists and Lutherans later came to adopt infrequent Communion.

8. Catholic Eucharistic Understanding

According to Catholic teaching the supposed miracle of the transformation of the bread and wine into the body and blood of Christ explains and justifies the understanding of worship as a mass, a re-sacrificing of Christ. Catholics are to believe that with the consecration of the two elements they become the body of Christ that was sacrificed for our sin, the priest receiving both elements and the congregants these days receiving only the bread.

Since the mass is regarded as a repetition or extension of Christ's sacrifice at Calvary, it implies that the original was not sufficient. To Protestants the belief in the re-sacrifice of Christ conflicts with the explicit and repeated NT insistence that Christ has made the once-and-for-all sacrifice for the sin of the world. Protestants believe that Christ's Calvary sacrifice need not and cannot be repeated.[58]

---

55. Weber, *Foundations of Dogmatics*, 2:629.
56. Weber, *Foundations of Dogmatics*, 2:629–30.
57. Lohse, *A Short History of Christian Doctrine*, 174.
58. Schroeder, *Worship in the Reformed Tradition*.

From the Catholic perspective instead of people receiving the assurance that sin has been divinely forgiven in Christ, the Sunday by Sunday Eucharist enables sin to be divinely forgiven, with priestly action causing this to happen, priests being secondary saviors. In recent years Catholics have reformulated their interpretation of the Mass to make it less objectionable to Protestants. Such as that through priestly mediation the church pleads to the Father, which still implies that Christ's atoning sacrifice was not sufficient and thus requires such clerical intercessions. Priests still remain secondary saviors and the once-for-all sufficiency of God's atoning action in Christ is negated. Is it not self-contradictory to speak simultaneously of the need for ongoing pleading and of an "accomplished and effectual sacrifice"?[59] Of course we are to confess our sin, ask for our forgiveness, and seek to be more faithful, but neither priests nor we ourselves can provide salvation.

Instead of the Mass repeating, renewing or continuing the work of Christ's atoning life, death and resurrection, the priest can be seen as re-presenting it. If this only entails being reminded and thereby sharing in the once-and-for-all victory in Christ this is acceptable to Protestants. *If it means more than this—which it likely does, else the concept of the mass as a re-sacrifice is negated—it is little different from the traditional Catholic view.*[60]

9. Exegetical Examination of Fourth Gospel's Drastically Reinterpreted Lord's Supper Teachings

Unlike the Fourth Gospel's regular Lord's Supper teachings, *its redactions/versional additions* widely diverge from its regular teaching and from the earlier Synoptic sources. Though the Gospel of John is an historically inaccurate apologetic re-writing, its varying Lord's Supper teachings are noted because its later redactions appear to have contributed to some aspects of the Catholic understanding concerning the Eucharist.

Unlike Catholicism this Gospel does not say that Christ is re-sacrificed Sunday by Sunday, and only in a few places contains the seeds of the transubstantiation idea, though not as dependent on particular priestly verbalizing. But, as with Catholicism, the Fourth Gospel's redacted additions say that without receiving the Lord's Supper and being baptized one cannot be saved: So Jesus is reported to have said "Truly, truly, I say to you, unless you eat the flesh of the Son of man and drink his blood, you have no life in you; he who eats my flesh and drinks my blood has eternal life, and I will raise him up at the last day" (John 6:53–54; the current Catholic practice of only the priest receiving the wine not being in sync). The redacted additions to the Fourth Gospel also attest that water baptism is required for salvation. "Truly, truly, I say to you, unless one is born of *water* [baptism] and the Spirit, he cannot enter the kingdom of God" (John 3:5, my emphasis).

The original Fourth Gospel author likely attested Jesus as saying "It is the spirit that gives life, the flesh is of no avail; the words that I have spoken to you are spirit and life" (6:63). However the reviser once again differed drastically from the original author! His such verses in large part "refer . . . to the sacramental meal of the Eucharist, where the flesh and blood of the 'Son of Man' are consumed, with the result that . . . meal participants are

---

59. Schroeder, *Worship in the Reformed Tradition*.
60. Schroeder, *Worship in the Reformed Tradition*.

[thereby] assured of the future resurrection."⁶¹ "Thus the Lord's Supper is here [largely] seen as 'the medicine of immortality' (Ignatius). This ... strikes one as strange in relation to the Evangelist's thought in general.... For there the bread of life which the Father gives by sending the Son from heaven (6:32f.) *is the Son himself*, the Revealer. *He gives* (v. 27) *and is* (vv. 35, 48, 51[a, c] *the bread of life* ... to those ... who 'come' to him (v. 35; cf. 3:20f.; 5:40), who believe in him (v. 35; and cf. 3:20f. with 3:18). [*With the original teaching, sacramental acts are not required for gaining authentic life in the present and eternal life in the future!*] Thus it seems that *verses* 51[b], 52-58 have been added by an ecclesiastical editor, the same editor who [made additions] at the end of vv. 39, 40, 44."⁶² Though employing the style and language of the original author, *the editor considerably undermined the original author's Christocentric and soteriological teachings, substituting water baptism and Eucharistic practice.*

---

61. Bultmann, *The Gospel of John*, 218-19.
62. Bultmann, *The Gospel of John*, 219.

THE CHRISTIAN LIFE

Chapter 24

The Christian as Witness[1]

1. Witnessing to Jesus Christ through Word and Deed, Sometimes at Considerable Cost

LIVING IN RELATIONSHIP WITH Christ is important, but the further goal is to be ambassadors for Christ in the world. The new characteristic of the church—knowledge of God in Christ—leads toward the goal of the church: bearing witness to God's love disclosed in Him. We must not hoard the good news about Christ, as though God cared only about us. As we read in 1 Peter, "[We] are a chosen race, a royal priesthood, a holy nation, God's own people, that [we] may declare the wonderful deeds of him who called [us] out of darkness into his marvelous light" (2:9). We certainly believe that "all authority in heaven and on earth has been given to [Christ]' and therefore we must seek to 'make disciples of all nations" (Matt 28:18–19a).

"The Spirit . . . empowers our new life in Christ (Rom 8:11) and motivates and equips us for discipleship and service (Rom 8:14)."[2] Having been called to an inward journey and discovered the Living Savior, we are also sent on an outward journey of responsive behavioral and verbal witnessing. Because the Head of the church "came not to be ministered unto, but to minister" (Mark 10:45), the church through word and deed must be actively involved in attesting Christ.[3]

The Spirit gives Christians courage to witness among all peoples. "We get the word 'martyr' from the Greek word for witness. To witness means to bear public testimony to someone or something, to go on record . . . about the truth of something. That does not mean that every form of Christian witnessing entails what has come to be understood as martyrdom."[4]

"During the Roman persecutions, if a person chose to insist on calling Jesus the Christ, Lord and Savior, he or she (or worse, his or her children) would be put to death,

---

1. See chap. 5, sec. 10.
2. Migliore, *Faith Seeking Understanding*, 171.
3. Barth, *CD* 4/2:690.
4. Placher and Willis-Watkins, *Belonging to God*, 163.

often after torture. Or if Christians refused to hand over the church's sacred writings, they faced the same consequences. All a person had to do to escape torture and death was to betray the faith, turn over the Scriptures to the authorities, and reveal the names of other hunted Christians. One of the miracles of the church's continued existence . . . is that [many] believers, ancient and modern, . . . stand up and [are] counted in the face of enormous persecution, blatant or subtle; choose to [proclaim] the gospel to others (including their persecutors) as good news for them rather than betray the gospel for apparent personal (or familial, or racial, or national, or class) gain"[5]

2. Agents of Reconciliation

In 2 Corinthians 5:18–20 behind the distinction Paul makes between "them" and "us" is a dynamic for mission. "God was in Christ reconciling the world to himself, not counting their trespasses against them, and entrusting to us the message of reconciliation" (5:19; see 5:14–15). "God does not provide a potential salvation and then retire from the scene to observe how creative his followers can be in getting individuals to accept it. He leads his followers (2:14), and his followers derive their authority and authenticity from being drawn into his ministry of reconciliation."[6]

Christian witnesses cannot cause the Holy Spirit to reveal Herself to others and thereby disclose the meaning of the revelation in Christ. Christians, however, can and should actively cooperate with God by clarifying the nature of the choice for God through Christ, that God in His own time and way may use our witnessing to elicit Christian faith.

Accounts of the calling of some of the prophets help us to avoid pragmatically distorting the purpose of witnessing. Such pre-Christian accounts of God calling others show that witnessing does not have to do with the human achievement of positive results, but with being faithful. When God called Ezekiel, God did not guarantee that he would have "successful" results, so that large numbers of people would turn to the Lord (Ezek 1–3). Ezekiel's task was only to faithfully re-present the Word that the Lord had spoken to him, avow God's defiance of their defiance, and stand like a rock among them.[7] Through Ezekiel's attestation they would "know that there had been a prophet among them" (2:5; see also 2:7; 3:11), and therefore would recognize that God is a Living Force with whom to be reckoned.

3. Witnesses as Servants: Beyond Egocentric Christianity

Christian witnessing necessarily involves humble service, as the root meaning of the word "minister" indicates: one who waits upon those at table. Who "is the greater, one who sits at table, or one who serves? Is it not [according to the world's way of thinking] the one who

---

5. Placher and Willis-Watkins, *Belonging to God*, 164.
6. Cousar, "Second Corinthians 5:17–21," 183.
7. Barth, *CD* 4/3, *Second Half*, 582.

sits at table? But I am among you as one who serves" (Luke 22:27). One is reminded of the Fourth Gospel story of Jesus washing of His disciples' feet (13:2–16).[8]

As called into fellowship with Christ and discipleship on His behalf we are to call others into such fellowship and discipleship. If the goal of the Christian life were merely to have fellowship with Christ, with no word and deed obligations to others, Christian existence would be selfish and self-centered. "Is not every form of egocentricity excused and even confirmed and sanctified, if egocentricity in this sacred form is the divinely willed meaning of Christian existence, and the Christian song of praise consists finally only in a many-tongued but monotonous pro me, pro me[9] and similarly possessive expressions?"[10]

4. The Breadth of Verbal Christian Witnessing

As Calvin said of his own experience, when God converts a person He makes him teachable. The Holy Spirit who enables us to learn of Christ also bids us to teach others of Him. "Every [rational] Christian—in however primitive and rudimentary way—can and must be a theologian, and . . . can and must be a good theologian, having a true vision of the One in whom he believes, having true thoughts concerning Him, and finding the right words to express those thoughts. Of course, if what he feels and wants is something without form, then he is not a theologian, but he is also not a Christian. For Jesus Christ is not without form, but in the sphere in which He encounter[s] [us] He is both form and object."[11]

Verbal witnessing to Jesus Christ occurs in a wide variety of ways: Not just in congregational preaching and teaching but in informal conversation, in the interaction that occurs in churchly and extra-churchly educational contexts, in formal and informal pastoral care, through publications, and in numerous other ways.[12] An activity of witnessing much needed today is to show the significance of the Christian Faith for daily moral decisions.

In verbal witnessing and interpreting we need to be discerning, for we "can easily fail, by keeping silent as well as by speaking at the wrong time, by being unnecessarily apologetic [or reluctant to speak] as well as by forcing our views on others. . . . A testimony concerning God's love remains ineffective if that same love has no influence on the [timing] and nature of that testimony."[13] *What is needed is the right words spoken in the right way at the right time.*

5. Witnessing through Actions and Attitudes

Morally faithful actions and attitudes can point others to Christ. As Jesus's conduct in healing the sick and in associating with outcasts showed forth God's kingship and witnessed to

---

8. In regarding Himself as a servant (Rom 1:1; 2 Cor 4:5; Gal 1:10; Phil 1:1), Paul was loyal to Christ and reflected to His ways.

9. Or the monotonous "I am saved, I am saved."

10. Barth, *CD* 4/3, *Second Half*, 567.

11. Barth, *CD* 4/1:765.

12. Berkhof, *Christian Faith*, 417.

13. Berkhof, *Christian Faith*, 417.

God's love, our conduct can attest the Father's love disclosed in the Son. Because the message we seek to proclaim centers upon God's loving action in Christ, loving lives can point to that Gospel. Words of interpretation are hypocritical unless backed by consistent actions and attitudes. "If my words and acts are a real witness to Jesus Christ, then in, with and under them there is [evidence of] . . . my own subjection to the lordship of Jesus Christ, of the comfort of forgiveness, by which I myself live, and of the liberty of the children of God in which I myself move. [The neighbor] . . . notices that I myself look and listen where my words and deeds seem to invite him to look and listen."[14]

6. God Gives Courage and Strength to His Witnesses

Though God calls Christians to difficult missional tasks, He provides the strength that enables us to fulfill our assignments. The Risen Lord who sends forth His witnesses to make disciples of all nations promises to give us the power to fulfill our difficult callings. He says to us, "'Lo, I am with you always, to the close of the age'" (Matt 28:20b). Paul spoke of the confidence that Christians can have through Christ toward God: "Not that we are sufficient of ourselves to claim anything as coming from us; our sufficiency is from God, who has qualified us to be ministers of the new covenant" (2 Cor 3:5-6a). Paul told of a perplexing discouragement of his own—his "thorn in the flesh" "to keep him from being too elated" (2 Cor 12:7)—and of the God who renewed his spirit and empowered him anew. "Three times I besought the Lord about this, that it should leave me; but he said to me, 'My grace is sufficient for you, for my power is made perfect in weakness.' I will all the more gladly boast of my weakness, that the power of Christ may rest upon me. For the sake of Christ, then, I am content with weaknesses, insults, hardships, persecutions, and calamities; for when I am weak, then I am strong" (2 Cor 12:8-10). Strength and courage for Christian mission come from God—not from us (2 Cor 4:7-11).[15]

---

14. Barth, *CD* 1/2:447-48.

15. The Spirit who calls Christians to bear witness to Jesus Christ in the world also endows us with various charismatic gifts for service within the church (Rom 12:6-8; 1 Cor 12:28-31; Eph 4:11; 1 Pet 4:10-11).

Chapter 25

Christian Witnessing Entails Suffering

1. Our Non-Atoning but Responsive Suffering in Correspondence with Christ; Sharing in the Prophetic Work of the Risen Christ

SOMETIMES THE NT REFERS to the disciplining function of general suffering willingly borne by Christians (Heb 12:8; 1 Pet 4:14).[1] "For the moment all discipline seems painful rather than pleasant; later it yields the peaceful fruit of righteousness to those who have been trained by it" (Heb 12:11).

More specifically, costly witnessing to Christ can have the effect of upbuilding the church and advancing the Gospel (Phil 1:12–18). Since a Christian privilege and duty is to point to Jesus Christ, we are to receive whatever suffering that entails. However, our suffering—even to the point of martyrdom—does not atone for our sins or the world's. But occurs in grateful response to Christ's redeeming life, death, and resurrection.

Faithful witnessing can have reconciling effects in that it can clarify Christian faith, that the Holy Spirit may draw others to Christ and help to make the world more livable. Christians' willingness to suffer for the sake of testifying to Jesus Christ is a sign of faith's integrity and sincerity. It reflects lives that bear consistent testimony concerning the One whose faithfulness led to the cross. Negatively speaking, if Christians are unwilling to take up and bear their crosses, they do not genuinely share in Christian faith.[2]

Christ lived and died and rose for our sake and that of the world, and we do not carry His cross. Nor is our carrying of our crosses a reenactment of His suffering, but takes place in correspondence to His work, with the similarity proper to a disciple following his Master. As those who have experienced reconciliation through God's action in Christ, we can and should carry our crosses by gratefully following in Christ's steps (1 Pet 2:21).

Paul neared the edge of mysticism (and overstated his own position) when in Galatians 2:20a he affirmed that because he had been crucified with Christ he no longer lived,

---

1. Such disciplining function of suffering applies both to Christians' general suffering and to that which occurs because of faithful witnessing to Christ.
2. Barth, *CD* 4/3, *Second Half*, 602.

but Christ in him. However, in the next verse he corrected himself by saying "the life I now live in the flesh I live by faith in the Son of God, who loved me and gave himself for me" (Gal 2:20b). He thus attested that his own faith pointed away from itself to Jesus Christ as the object of faith, and to reconciliation already enacted. Paul most certainly did not think that what Christ had done is nothing until we die to sin and take up our crosses and follow Him.

There is a complication related to Christ's suffering: Though He has already lived, died and risen, in considerable part He continues to suffer amid the abuse and mistreatment that occur to His disciples as they witness on His behalf. Unlike the atonement, Christ's suffering is ongoing, linking in part with that of His faithful disciples.[3] The author of Colossians writes, "Now I rejoice in my sufferings for your sake, and in my flesh complete what is lacking in Christ's afflictions for the sake of his body, that is, the church" (1:24).

Enduring the affliction that comes because one is loyal to Christ and faithfully attests to Him is the price of participation in the new existence that Jesus Christ has made possible and is not the same as the general suffering common to all people. "The provisionalness and alienation that mark our human existence unleash a flood of misery in which the whole human race involuntarily shares." By comparison, the suffering that occurs insofar as Christians remain faithful to Christ and bear witness to Him even at cost to themselves is "voluntary."[4]

Between Christ's Easter victory and the consummation of that victory, Christians can and should share in the prophetic work of the Risen Lord. They do so insofar as through word and deed they faithfully point to Christ and thereby continue to call the world to repentance.

"Jesus Christ Himself leads those who are called by Him into the situation in which they come into collision with the world, in which they expose themselves to this collision, and in which they have thus to suffer the pressure brought to bear on them. Christ Himself leaves the Christian no other choice than to accept this [possibly] mortal risk."[5]

The [genuine] Christian is the messenger who tells the world the truth [concerning Jesus Christ] to its face. . . . One thing it will certainly hear and understand. And that is the supremely provoking No pronounced against it in and with the Yes. . . . What it hears is merely the painfully wounding word of a [person] who presumes to contradict its self-understanding and . . . speaks of sin and guilt instead of imperfection; who contests its . . . attitudes in relation to God, who resolutely questions its progress . . ., who tells it quite plainly that it has erroneous views of itself; who proclaims its end as the judgment which comes upon it, and who insists—and this is the most galling thing of all—that a man who lived and died in the years AD 1–30 is the new thing in which alone there is enclosed all salvation and hope. . . . What the world perceives when it hears the witness of the Christian is the opinion of a fanatic who has obviously [burned his bridges] behind him, and demands that it should do the same.[6]

3. Barth, *CD* 4/3, *Second Half*, 636.
4. Berkhof, *Christian Faith*, 463.
5. Barth, *CD* 4/3, *Second Half*, 634.
6. Barth, *CD* 4/3, *Second Half*, 622–23. See also 2 Cor 4:1–6. Though Paul was an educated person who in his writing utilized his knowledge of rhetoric, he nevertheless wrote, "Christ did not send me to baptize

Unless people enter into a new relationship with God through Christ, unless they receive God's judgment and live from His forgiveness, they will continue to oppose Christ and oppress His messengers.

2. Enduring World's Resistance

Jesus pictures the future awaiting His disciples: "If any man would come after me, let him deny himself and take up his cross and follow me. For whoever would save his life will lose it; and whoever loses his life for my sake and the gospel's will save it" (Mark 8:34b–35)." "Blessed are you when men revile you and persecute you and utter all kinds of evil against you falsely on my account. Rejoice and be glad, for your reward is great in heaven, for so people persecuted the prophets who were before you" (Matt 5:11–12). "A disciple is not above his teacher, nor a servant above his master; it is enough for the disciple to be like his teacher, and the servant like his master. If they have called the master of the house Beelzebub, how much more will they malign those of his household" (Matt 10:24–25). Jesus prepared His messengers for being defenseless and unprotected, like sheep among wolves (Matt 10:16; Luke 10:3).[7] "The Christian . . . *is hated as the bearer and representative of a specific claim and cause*. . . . [He] represents . . . the alien and intolerable cause of the kingdom, the coup d'état of God."[8]

The possible price of faithfully pointing to Christ is clearly stated in the Fourth Gospel's highly interpreted words. "If the world hates you, know that it has hated me before it hated you. If you were of the world, the world would love its own; but because you are not of the world . . . the world hates you. Remember the word that I said to you, 'A servant is not greater than his master. If they persecuted me, they will persecute you' . . . All this they will do to you on my account, because they do not know him who sent me" (15:18–21). "The hatred that falls on the disciples . . . corresponds to the general rule: 'I have given them thy word; and the world has hated them because they are not of the world, even as I am not of the world'" (17:14).

"At least five books of the New Testament were written in prison . . . Many were addressed to congregations that were even then undergoing severe ordeals. It can be said without exaggeration that every writing during the first or second generation . . . either recalls or anticipates periods of severe stress. The injunction of 1 Peter is typical: 'Beloved,

---

but to preach the gospel, and not with eloquent wisdom, lest the cross of Christ be emptied of its power. For the word of the cross is folly to those who are perishing, but to us who are being saved it is the power of God. For it is written, 'I will destroy the wisdom of the wise, and the cleverness of the clever I will thwart.' Where is the wise [person]? Where is the scribe? Where is the debater of this age? Has not God made foolish the wisdom of the world? For since, in the wisdom of God, the world did not know God through wisdom, it pleased God through the folly of what we preach to save those who believe" (1 Cor 1:17–21; see also 1 Cor 2:1–5).

7. "As for yourselves, beware for they will hand you over to councils; and you will be beaten in synagogues; and you will stand before governors and kings because of me, as a testimony to them. . . . Brother will betray brother to death, and a father his child, and children will rise against parents and have them put to death; and you will be hated by all because of my name. But one who endures to the end will be saved" (Mark 13:9, 12–13 NRSV).

8. Barth, *CD* 4/3, *Second Half*, 625, my emphasis.

do not be surprised at the fiery ordeal which comes upon you to prove you, as though something strange were happening to you'"(4:12). "The earliest document from Ephesus speaks clearly of the many adversaries Paul had encountered there" (1 Cor 16:9).[9]

Paul's understanding of suffering as a testimony to Christ stems from his experience, that to an extent his converts shared with him. Paul did not endure suffering stoically. He welcomed it[10] because he regarded it as a sign of Christian faithfulness (see 2 Cor 4:7–5:5). "For while we live we are always being given up to death for Jesus's sake, so that the life of Jesus may be manifested in our mortal flesh" (2 Cor 4:11). "So we do not lose heart. Though our outer nature is wasting away, our inner nature is being renewed every day" (2 Cor 4:16). We are "fellow heirs with Christ, provided we suffer with him in order that we may also be glorified with him"[11]

Much of Paul's suffering came from his authority being challenged by fellow "Christians." As seen in 2 Corinthians 10–13 Paul's opponents based their claims to apostolic authority on their impressive charismatic experiences—"signs and wonders and mighty works" (12:12)—which Paul exhibited only to an extent. Not only did they think that Paul was deficient in such areas, but they regarded him as of no account (10:10; 11:21), being physically weak, lacking in "presence" (NEB), oratorical capacity, and power. Paul's response was that divine empowerment is *power amid weakness*.[12] Referring to his first visit to Corinth, Paul wrote, "I was with you in weakness and in much fear and trembling; and my speech and my message were not in plausible words of wisdom, but in demonstration of the Spirit and power, that your faith might not rest in the wisdom of men but in the power of God" (1 Cor 2:3–5). "For the foolishness of God is wiser than men, and the weakness of God is stronger than men" (1 Cor 1:25). Similarly, in response to a prayer for deliverance from a vaguely indicated "thorn in the flesh" (2 Cor 12:7b), Paul attested that divine power "is made perfect in weakness" (2 Cor 12:9). "Power without weakness is destructive; only charismata [spiritual gifts] that manifest power in weakness build up the community . . . This is clearly why Paul *never* boasts of his charismata, but rather of his weakness (2 Cor 11:30). For it is only when we are conscious of our own weakness, that is, when we are not seeking to manipulate or direct the power of God in any way, only then can God's grace and power fully rest upon us and manifest itself through us (12:9)."[13] Thus he affirmed that when we are weak, then we are strong. (2 Cor 12:10).

"*The character of the experience in which Christ speaks through a [person] is determined by the character of the Christ who speaks.* And the key fact here is that Christ remains the Crucified even though He now lives by the power of God (v. 4a). *To experience the exalted Christ therefore is to experience not merely new life but new life which is life through death, life out of death, and which always retains that character.* As soon as the exalted Christ is separated from the crucified Jesus, charismatic experience loses its distinctive Christian [character]. . . . In Paul's view, religious experience for the Christian is not a matter of Christ taking him out of his weakness and leaving it behind in experiences of

---

9. Minear, *I Saw a New Earth*, 203, 207.
10. Rom 5:3; 2 Cor 12:9.
11. Rom 8:17; see also 2 Cor 4:17–18; 2 Thess 1:4–5.
12. 2 Cor 4:7; 12:9; 13:3–4.
13. Dunn, *Jesus and the Spirit*, 329–30.

inspiration and ecstasy; on the contrary, Christ is present in [the disciple's] weakness—*his weakness is part of his experience of Christ.*"[14] "We rejoice in our sufferings, knowing that suffering produces endurance, and endurance produces character, and character produces hope, and hope does not disappoint us, because God's love has been poured into our hearts through the Holy Spirit which has been given to us" (Rom 5:3–5).

3. Human Defenselessness of Christian Witnesses

An aspect of the responsibility of witnessing and enduring whatever opposition occurs is the obligation to love even those who react in antagonistic ways to our testimony. "The command issued to the disciples that they should do good to those who hate them (Luke 6:27),[15] that they should love their enemies, that they should bless those who curse them [is] . . . the marching order never to allow the rejection and opposition that [we] encounter to divert [us] from [our] role as witnesses of the kingdom in which [we] cannot cease to love."[16]

Jesus said, "Behold, I send you out as sheep in the midst of wolves; so be wise as serpents and innocent as doves" (Matt 10:16; see also Luke 10:3). Being "wise as serpents" includes being prudently concerned about effective ways of witnessing. Being "innocent as doves" entails being faithful disciples and not trying to protect ourselves from suffering, possible injury, or even martyrdom.

To avoid being persecuted or humiliated or even being regarded as a bit odd, some "Christians" seek to eliminate the Christian Faith's offensiveness and present it as innocuous human wisdom, that for its reception requires no human transformation.[17] Do we who call ourselves Christians recognize ourselves in the NT descriptions of the suffering that Christian witnessing entails? If not, it may be a symptom of the unreality of our "Christianity," that has become so comfortable that it no longer resembles the NT's exemplification. In contrast, where Christians have taken seriously their existence as disciples and witnesses, they have had to suffer considerably, and for some of the reasons described in the NT.[18] "Real Christians are . . . oppressed by the surrounding world." "For the Christian nature of [our] existence . . . [is] doubtful to the degree [we] experienced no affliction, . . . coming to terms with the world by means of appeasing compromises."[19]

God not only humbled Himself to come to earth, but the Son suffered for His witness and was crucified as a condemned criminal. It is this Jesus who was and is the Christ, and we dare not falsify the gospel for the sake of gaining smooth acceptance for an easier one.

---

14. Dunn, *Jesus and the Spirit*, 331.
15. See Matt 5:43–48; Luke 6:27–36.
16. Barth, *CD* 4/3, *Second Half*, 625.
17. Much philosophical theology proceeds in this way.
18. Barth, *CD* 4/3, *Second Half*, 640.
19. Barth, *CD* 4/3, *Second Half*, 618–19.

4. Fulfillment through the Suffering Discipleship of Christian Witnessing

The Risen Christ edifies and upbuilds His disciples as they endure the suffering occasioned by their faithful witnessing. Having to suffer for attesting Christ thus results in no pitiable state of affairs. Amid the world's persecution or even just its laughter Christians can realize that God stands at our side and upholds us.[20] "Paul could not possibly be ashamed of the Gospel in a hostile world (Rom 1:16). He could only glory in [all] that [befell] him (Rom 5:3) and could say that in all his afflictions he abounded in joy (2 Cor 7:4)."[21]

Distress in witnessing to Christ is one of the ways in which we participate in Christ's dying and rising and in His grace.[22] "If we share abundantly in Christ's sufferings, so through Christ we share abundantly in comfort too."[23] Thereby we live in hope. "The saying is sure: If we have died with him, we shall also live with him; if we endure with him, we shall also reign with him" (2 Tim 2:11-12a). "Rejoice insofar as you share in Christ's sufferings, that you may also rejoice and be glad when his glory is revealed" (1 Pet 4:13). The adversity that occurs because of faithful witnessing to Christ points us away from present preoccupations—that we may take confidence in Christ's final victory. "Blessed are those who are persecuted for righteousness sake, for theirs is the kingdom of heaven. Blessed are you when [people] revile you and persecute you and utter all kinds of evil against you falsely on my account. Rejoice and be glad, for your reward is great in heaven, for so [people] persecuted the prophets who were before you" (Matt 5:10-12).

"The Christian in affliction is a [person] who is absolutely secured by the goal appointed for him in Christ. This is not because the world [that] afflicts him is not powerful enough to shake and even vanquish him. It is not because he himself is strong enough to resist it. The security of the Christian is not that fancied by the Stoics. The Christian is secure, absolutely and essentially secure, because his life is hid with the risen Christ in God, i.e., with the One who was not overcome by the world but overcame it (Col 3:3).... 'If God is for us, who can be against us?' (Rom 8:31). This is the existential determination given to the oppressed Christian by the resurrection of Christ.... No one and nothing can ... do us true and serious harm, or finally overcome us—not even the last thing ..., namely, death."[24]

The NT reminds Christians that the Risen Christ will minister unto us in our affliction, upbuild our trust and hope in God and thereby our moral character, and give us increasing strength to persevere. "Therefore, since we are surrounded by so great a cloud of witnesses, let us also lay aside every weight, and sin which clings so closely, and let us run with perseverance the race that is set before us, looking to Jesus the pioneer and perfecter of our faith, who for the joy that was set before him endured the cross, despising the shame, and is seated at the right hand of the throne of God. Consider him who endured from

---

20. Barth, *CD* 4/3, *Second Half*, 640-41.
21. Barth, *CD* 4/3, *Second Half*, 641.
22. Also see chap. 22, secs. 10 and 14.
23. 2 Cor 1:5; see also Rom 8:15-18; Phil 3:10.
24. Barth, *CD* 4/3, *Second Half*, 645.

sinners such hostility against himself, so that you may not grow weary or fainthearted" (Heb 12:1–3).

The upbuilding of Christians in steadfastness can be occasioned by suffering. "Count it all joy, my brethren, when you meet various trials, for you know that the testing of your faith produces steadfastness" (Jas 1:2–3). "In this you rejoice, though now for a little while you may have to suffer various trials, so that the genuineness of your faith, more precious than gold which though perishable is tested by fire, may redound to praise and glory and honor at the revelation of Jesus Christ" (1 Pet 1:6–7).

5. Though Others Have Suffered for Their Testimonies, Why We Do We Suffer So Little for Ours?

Particular individuals have often vicariously borne oppression. Isaiah's mission was to proclaim the Word that the Lord had spoken to him, and God foretold Isaiah that the people would have a negative response to his preaching, but that God would judge His people (Isa 6:9–13). And Isaiah remained faithful to his calling. Jeremiah's task was to proclaim the fall of Jerusalem, of the temple, and of the house of David, and God also warned him that the people would react negatively to his message and to him (1:4–19). Though the Word of the Lord became to Jeremiah a cause of daily reproach and derision, he remained true to his calling.

"Even as Israel's prophets and Jesus got the strongest persecution from the side of the religious institutions and officials, so through the centuries ecclesiastical institutions have [often] functioned as focal points and instruments of the world's persecution of individuals who [have] sought to follow Christ."[25] "More than many others, Kierkegaard [experienced such persecution], . . . especially in his conflict with Bishop Martensen.[26] That this suffering was caused by the established church is something that makes one stop and think."[27]

Those reading this chapter may wish to point out that in this era of tolerance, many Christians, and even most, do not often suffer for their Christian witnessing, and do not need to. My counter is that having already accommodated to the world, perhaps the reason so few of us suffer for our testimonies is that ours may be muted by self-censorship. Were we more intent on being faithful to Christ we would likely suffer more.

---

25. Berkhof, *Christian Faith*, 456.

26. See especially the nine issues of *The Moment* (1855), later published as part of *Attach upon Christendom*.

27. Berkhof, *Christian Faith*, 467.

Chapter 26

A Mini Theology of Christian Ethics[1]

1. Living from the Power of God's Grace in Christ and through the Spirit; Learning from Dialogue with Fellow-Hearers of God's Word

FROM THE CHRISTIAN PERSPECTIVE human conduct is good insofar as people live from the Holy God, being obedient hearers of God's living command. Such obedience is good because it derives from divine guidance and because the divine source is good.[2] Even Jesus's goodness derived from participation in that of God (Mark 10:18; Luke 18:19); all the more must that of sinners. Goodness in the Christian sense is a relational concept, no mere matter of moral deeds. It has to do with faithfully living in relationship with and serving the God who has come to us in Jesus Christ and is known through the Spirit.

One of the ways the NT speaks of grace is as God's power in believers' lives that works against bondage to sin (Rom 6:1–14) Not surprisingly, with such usage the meaning of "grace" approaches identity with that of "Spirit."[3] As in our relationship with the Spirit, the Christian is called to grace (Gal 1:6), so stands (Rom 5:2), and must beware of falling out of it (Gal 5:4).[4]

"What are we to do? We are to accept as right, and to live as those who accept as right the fact that we do not belong to ourselves, that we therefore do not have our lives in our own hands and at our own disposal, and that we are made a divine possession in Jesus Christ." "The good is to cleave to God. Every [Christian] ethic that is at least half serious aims consciously or unconsciously to say this." "There is no escaping the [living] command

---

1. For related material see chap. 22 above, especially secs. 8–15, mainly on sanctification.
Systematics's direct contribution to Christian Ethics, what is summarized in this chapter and manifested throughout, *is here limited to indicating some of the biblically and theologically mandated norms and guidelines for the Christian Ethics discipline.* That Christian Ethics may be truly *Christian*. Though it is yet to be published, I have written a Christian Ethic consistent with the theological convictions articulated in this book.

2. Barth, *CD* 2/2:546; 3/4:4.

3. See Rom 8:4–5, 14; 2 Cor 3:6; Gal 5:16, 18, 25.

4. Bultmann, *Theology of the New Testament*, 1:290.

of God because, when it confronts us, it immediately and at the same time places itself behind us."[5]

Being empowered by the Spirit is the inner source from which the fulfilling of divine commands becomes possible. The Fourth Gospel speaks of the abiding in God that the Holy Spirit enables and through which we can bear fruit (15:4–5; see 1 John 3:24). God as Spirit contemporizes and applies God's revelation in Jesus Christ, helping us to understand and assess various biblical and post-biblical perspectives concerning God's disclosure in Christ.

The Living God is with us and makes specific demands consistent with His nature and commanding activity as revealed in Christ. *That God remains the Living Commander is a primary datum from which Christian ethics begin and to which it returns.* The God who spoke in Christ still speaks today. We misconstrue God's moral revelation in the past if we think we have to appraise and apply this in God's absence. However we also "hear God's command . . . in conversation and debate with fellow-hearers of God's Word as attested in Scripture. These fellow-hearers may be contemporary or may not: the church is not only present, but also past. So, readiness to hear God's command requires that we open ourselves, under Scripture, to the traditions of the church."[6]

2. Triunitarian Understanding of Christian Ethic

What has been stated in the first section is consistent with and a moral application of a triunitarian understanding of God. Since God has revealed Himself in Jesus Christ, a memory of that revelation is both theologically and morally essential. What we principally learn from Scripture concerns both the nature of God's reconciling activity and *God's expectations concerning our responses*. Triunitarian faith also affirms that the same God who revealed Himself in Jesus Christ is alive today and did not cease speaking when the Bible was canonized. *The Christian life is thus lived from the power and guidance of God as Holy Spirit and in the light of God's revelation in Jesus Christ.*

3. The Living Commander Bestows Freedom

"The form by which the command of God is distinguished from all other commands . . . consists in the fact that it is an [enabling][7]—the granting of a very definite freedom."[8] The spiritually received command of the Holy Spirit empowers Christians to be free for God. Though God lays moral burdens on Christians, by the gift of His Holy Spirit He releases us from having to fulfill His commands on our own. In this respect Christ's holy requirements can even be said to be light and easy (Matt 11:30). We do not find genuine freedom or true

---

5. Barth, *CD* 2/2:580, 552, 596.

6. Biggar, "Hearing God's Command," 109, describing Barth's position.

7. That God "enables" better describes what Barth intends than his word "permits," which need not imply personal interaction with God.

8. Barth, *CD* 2/2:585.

4. The Otherness of God's Living Command

A test of whether we sinners are dealing with the Holy and Living God or only with our own subjectivity is whether we experience considerable conflict between our wills and God's will—and thus confront God as judging and redirecting us. "An imperative to which I owe absolute obedience must necessarily come in the most radical sense from within, in order that it may claim me most radically within. [But the command of the transcendent God cannot be] a command which I have given myself on the basis of what I myself have seen and experienced and felt and judged of the good and the true and the beautiful. It must come to me as something alien, as the command of another, demanding as such that I should make its content the law of my life. If there is [such] an *ought*, it must not be the product of my own will, but touch from outside the whole area of what I can will of myself. . . . *The essence of the idea of obligation is not that I demand something from myself but that, with all that I can demand of myself, I am myself demanded.*"[9]

5. Sinner's Misuse of Legitimate Biblical Law

Paul attests that Christian disciples are no longer *captive* to the old written codes, and serve with newness of life under the Spirit (Rom 7:6). "For now the law of the Spirit of life in Christ Jesus has set us free from the law of sin and death" (Rom 8:2). Having gained freedom from bondage to the law, we now live for God (Gal 2:19). Though critical of much old covenant law, Paul attests that the primary problem is not with commandments such as that we should not covet (Exod 20:17; Deut 5:21). But granted our sinfulness, even such commandments entice us to do what has been forbidden (Rom 7:7–11). This unless the Spirit of God empowers us to do otherwise.

Paul seemed to think that people are held in bondage not primarily by the law, but by their autonomous use of it to hold themselves away from God. The attempt which is constantly made in many forms, to put God's commandments to the service of people's own wishes, makes the law what it is not inherently, the damning, killing law. Jesus died at the hands of sinners who had surrounded themselves with laws.[10]

Having to a degree relativized even biblical law and certainly other types, Paul regarded people as so much in bondage to sin as to require divine forgiveness and liberation if they are to serve God. "We know that the law is spiritual; but I am carnal, sold under sin. I do not understand my own actions. For I do not do what I want, but the very thing I hate. . . . Now if I do what I do not want . . . it is no longer I that do it, but sin which dwells within me. . . . Wretched man that I am! Who will deliver me from this body of death? Thanks be to God through Jesus Christ our Lord!" (Rom 7:14–15, 16a, 17, 24–25a). Apart from such deliverance, our enslavement to sin co-opts biblical law.

---

9. Barth, *CD* 2/2:651, my emphasis.
10. Weber, *Foundations of Dogmatics*, 2:197–98, my emphasis.

It is characteristic of the OT to say what Paul also attests, that what are truly God's commandments are "holy and just and good" (Rom 7:12). But unlike the NT the OT does not attest that the law has fallen under the "power of sin." We search in vain in the OT for either the wording or the sense that we find in many Pauline statements. Such as that the law does not make alive and cannot create righteousness (Gal 3:21), is subordinate to the "elemental spirits of the universe" (Gal 4:3), has becomes the "law" of sin and death (Rom 8:2), and [astonishingly] that it was created by angels, rather than by God (Gal 3:19).

6. Glorifying God by Corresponding to the Shape of His Reconciling Deed in Christ

To take our bearings from the biblical witness to Jesus Christ is to seek to respond faithfully to God's reconciling deed in Christ, corresponding (with some flexibility) to the moral pattern seen in Christ, and thereby glorifying God. Utilizing biblical material in this way involves recognizing similarities applicable to us in actions that are in many respects unique. Jesus Christ has alone realized the good, doing so in a representative and atoning sense. God calls His people to endorse Christ's free forgiveness and substitutionary obedience by reflecting *pattern similarities* to what God in Christ has manifested on our behalf. For example, Paul referred to the Son's act of humility in being willing to become incarnate as exhibiting not only a unique action of God, but more generally the importance of humble Christian living (Phil 2:3–11).

7. Relationship of the Living Command of God to Study of Christian Ethics

Comprehending God's command requires focusing on revelation-based, scripturally informed understandings concerning what is good and right. "We must come to the place of hearing, penitently and prayerfully, but with our heads nevertheless full of biblically informed norms and principles and rules. We must expect God's command *through* our normative biblically informed ethics, not outside them." "The purpose of Christian ethics is to provide general guidelines as to the [revelation-informed] content of God's command. It cannot predict the exact nature of what will pass from God to [us] in the event of that encounter, but it can prepare [us] to recognize the sound of the divine voice. I cannot, therefore, extrapolate from a given set of principles or rules exactly what God will command. The role of normative ethics is, then, strictly preparatory and preliminary."[11]

---

11. Biggar, "Hearing God's Command," 112, 113. "When Barth equates ethics with original sin, he means by it a closed, rationalist system that moves with inexorable logic from first principles through rules to particular cases [and which thus utterly denies divine and Christian freedom]. By sinful ethics he [means] an absolutist form of casuistry" (Biggar, "Hearing God's Command," 113).

What Barth says in the following is a good critique of only rationalistic and legalistic casuistry, not of all types: "Casuistry destroys the freedom of . . . obedience. It openly interposes something other and alien between the command of God and the [person] who is called to obey Him." "It conceals from him the character of his conduct as his own direct responsibility. It spares him what he should not be spared—the knowledge that it is not merely his external conduct, nor his will, purpose and intention, but himself that is demanded" (*CD* 3/4:13, 14).

God's present commands particularizing His past commands can cause Christian ethicists to reinterpret biblically informed principles and reformulate the rules derived from them. Flexibility also comes because Christian ethicists should keep their reasoning open to development and correction in the light of new knowledge of morally significant empirical data. Such new moral data may not only require the modification of specific rules, but may demand a radical reformation of basic principles (though seldom their outright rejection).[12] One thinks, for example, of the necessary Christian rethinking of homosexuality and lesbianism in recent decades.

8. Implications of Understanding Christian Ethics in Context of Belief in God as Living Commander

To describe our apprehension of what is moral in terms of hearing the Living God's command is to deny that our relationship to the good is that of active subjects to a passive object. To the contrary, we need to respond to past biblical revelation with openness to the Living God. Doing so through prayer and worship, with penitence, humility, and gratitude to God, while taking account of the impact of events. "Our freedom is only true freedom when the Holy Spirit intercedes for us to enable us to accomplish what of our own resources we certainly cannot do."[13]

The concept of apprehending what is right by hearing God's command demands an active willingness to review and revise moral assumptions and convictions.[14] Holding firmly to the moral stances one has taken in the past is less essential than being "continually reformed," subjecting all decisions and actions to God's scrutiny—that we may hear God more faithfully today than yesterday.[15]

9. Summary of the Bases of Christian Love[16]

The NT speaks of the *agape* (self-giving love) that came down from God to the world and in which we can share. The God known in Jesus is the God of sacrificial love, who offered Himself in the Son and through the Son's death on the cross. "In this the love of God was manifested among us, that God sent His only Son into the world, so that we might live through him. In this is love, not that we loved God, but that He loved us and sent His Son to be the expiation for our sins" (1 John 4:9–10).

"Love in the Christian sense . . . has its starting point in the reality of God on whom faith relies and which forms the basis of its hope." "Love is a force that radiates from God, . . . [laying] hold of us in such a way as to make us active, too."[17]

---

12. Biggar, "Hearing God's Command," 115, 117–18.
13. Barth, *CD* 1/2:698.
14. Biggar, "Hearing God's Command," 106.
15. The parallel with general learning is that it should also have much to do with being prepared to do serious rethinking, so as not to hold any ideas out of mere habit, intellectual inertia or laziness.
16. See chap. 4, sec. 4, for a additional discussion of agape.
17. Pannenberg, *ST*, 3:183.

"Far truer than the one statement, 'Man is what he thinks,' is . . . 'Man is what he loves.'"[18] "As we come to faith we begin to love. . . . If we believe, the fact that we do so means that every ground which is not that of our being with love to God in Christ is cut away from us."[19] Christians' love occurs in grateful response to God's deed of love in coming forth in Christ, in corresponding to the pattern of love fulfilled in Christ, and through participating in the power of the Holy Spirit. We are to do unto others in response to what God in Christ and through the Holy Spirit has done for us and is doing. We are to love not only because we have responded to Him who first loved us (1 John 4:19), but also because the Spirit has enabled us to share in God's love. "God's love has been poured into our hearts through the Holy Spirit which has been given to us (Rom 5:5b).

Natural love tends to be restrictive. We are prone to love others only if we have something thereby to gain. We, for example, love others if they attract us and/or are likely to love us in return. We admire Christ's example of sacrificial and boundary-shattering love, but of ourselves are not capable of even approximating such. We could not escape restrictive kinds of love were not *the Calvary God with us today*. The Crucified and Risen Lord as Holy Spirit can lead us beyond ourselves, by opening our hearts to receive self-giving agape as the fruit of the Spirit (Gal 5:22–23) and then with gratitude to embody it.

10. Love as Forgiveness Helps to Capacitate Love of Neighbor and of Former Enemy

"*The love which Jesus called for can be measured by its readiness to forgive*. Love of neighbor includes genuine forgiveness of the wrong experienced at the hand of the neighbor or anyone else. And Jesus clearly saw such readiness to forgive as the mark of discipleship and of the community of disciples."[20] "Then Peter came up to him and said to him, 'Lord, how often shall my brother sin against me, and I forgive him? As many as seven times?' Jesus said to him, 'I do not say to you seven times, but seventy times seven'" (Matt 18:2–22)—that is, limitlessly.

---

18. Brunner, *Revelation and Reason*, 428.

19. Barth, *CD* 1/2:371. I have placed Brunner and Barth side by side here, having learned much from both, and from many others. However, I cited them in separate notes, though Barth might not have been too pleased to be listed second after Brunner. I think they both now realize that they were pulling in the same direction. Besides, even in this life they went horseback riding together.

20. Dunn, *Jesus' Call to Discipleship*, 85.

CHRISTIAN HOPE

Chapter 27

Bases for the Hope of Eternal Life and Considerations concerning Its Scope and Nature[1]

Death and Eternal Life

1. Various Reasons for Thinking Seriously about Death

ATTEMPTS TO GIVE MEANING to life entirely from within the context of earthly existence come to grief on the fact of death. Humans alone go to meet death fully aware that one's existence could itself to be lost. From a merely human perspective, "the shadow of [an] inevitable end is thrown backwards over our entire human experience. 'In the midst of life we are in death'—and [some modern] philosophies like that of Heidegger read off the deepest meaning of our life as an 'existence-unto-death.'"[2]

"Apart from hope, every Christian doctrine becomes distorted. A doctrine of revelation would be flawed if it did not acknowledge that we now see through a glass dimly and not yet face to face; a doctrine of God would be deficient if it did not recognize the inexhaustible mystery of the triune God whose love is extended to the world in creation, redemption, and consummation; a doctrine of creation would be incomplete if it failed to emphasize that the creation still groans for its liberation and completion; a Christology would be misleading if it did not stress that the Lord is not simply a memory or a present experience but also the One [who will consummate history]."[3]

Because people live much longer now, the sociology of dying has changed drastically since earlier times. Today people often die in hospitals and are not fully conscious at the time of death, and thus may die without family and friends by their side. "But the basic circumstance, namely the death rate (in the crude sense of the proportion of each generation who die), has remained constant throughout human history at one hundred per cent!"

---

1. The issue of eternal life arises at various points in this systematics, not just in chapters dealing more directly with this topic. For example, in discussing Jesus's resurrection and the meaning of reconciliation.
2. Cocks, "Death," 76.
3. Fergusson, "Eschatology," 231–32.

"Death comes impartially to everyone; there are no privileged or underprivileged in this matter; we are all in the end in the same boat, together not only with all our contemporaries but also with all our ancestors and all our descendants."[4]

Though as organisms we share in a common mortality, unlike other organisms *we know* we are destined to die and recognize death as natural: "Everywhere in nature plants and animals die. Without death there would be no room for new life. These two, life and death, keep nature in balance. Thus speaks our intellect. But . . . our hearts . . . revolt against death."[5]

2. Rejection of Utopianism and Affirmation of Social Realism

Since sin's morally corrupting tendencies are integral aspects of this world, only God in His liberty can bring history to fulfillment. Human history does not usher in God's kingdom, but is dissolved when God consummates history. The coming of the kingdom is not the outworking of a this-worldly process. Such would have involved taking confidence in the power of the Gospel to permeate society.

The apostles would have looked forward to a progressive immanent development of the new life opened up by the resurrection, and then of the state of human and creaturely things generally in the direction of an ideal of good and happy humanity, . . . to be attained approximately in this world and perfectly in a better hereafter, and identifiable with the kingdom of God. Indeed, there have been whole periods in the history of the church when this version of Christian hope has been regarded as necessary both in theory and in practice. The New Testament does not contain a single shred of evidence to support this view. Compared with what the New Testament calls hope, this utopian version can only be described as a fabrication, however well-meaning and attractive. The salient feature about it is that it can do without Jesus. It may know Him as the Jesus of yesterday and today, but it knows nothing of Him . . . as [connected with the consummation]. . . . And this raises the question of whether there is any real understanding of His yesterday and today.[6]

The NT expects the end and new beginning of the cosmos. This anti-utopian realism should not be understood as an argument against social activism, but as encouraging social realism, as well articulated by Reinhold Niebuhr. "Niebuhr argued that history after Christ is an interim between the revelation and the fulfilment of its meaning. In this eschatological tension the kingdom can be revealed but [in part because of our ongoing sinfulness] can never triumph until the end of history. This creates an eschatological reserve whereby no possible state of affairs prior to the [consummation] can be invested with ultimate value or can command absolute allegiance. The other-worldliness of apocalyptic thought, with its claim that the kingdom can only be brought about by the irruption of God at the end of history, prevents one from investing any political program or form of social organization with ultimate significance. At the same time, the possibility remains for protest and reform

---

4. Hick, *Death and Eternal Life*, 81, 87. Though we will all die, the poor die earlier and under worse circumstances.

5. Berkhof, *Well-Founded Hope*, 64.

6. Barth, *CD* 3/2:486.

in the time that God has graciously given us between the resurrection of Jesus and the end of the world."[7]

3. Jesus's Resurrection Presupposes Possibility of General Human Resurrection

In a passage where Paul addressed people *who believed in Jesus's resurrection*, but not in the future resurrection of the dead, he wrote: "Now if Christ is preached as raised from the dead [as you concede], how can some of you say that there is no [general] resurrection of the dead? But if there is no [general] resurrection of the dead, then Christ has not been raised" (1 Cor 15:12–13). These two sentences are circular, but the second sentence is the point here: *Belief that Christ was raised from the dead is not credible if resurrection is otherwise impossible.* To Paul the resurrection of Christ attested the divinely-based reality of human resurrection.

4. Some Characteristics of Eternal Life

In the light of God's revelation in Christ and in human hearts various expectations concerning eternal life can be summarized:

(1) Christ is the forerunner of divinely intended humanity. Because of God's will and Jesus's work we can reach our destiny and be fully sons or daughters of God.

(2) The final salvation hoped for by Paul involves never-ending and never-imperiled communion "with Christ" (1 Thess 4:16b, 17) and through Him with the Father. "We shall live with [Christ] by the power of God."[8] Amid renewed humankind Christ will have the central place. "For he is the root and first fruits of divinely intended humanity and we will be conformed to his image. He is the forerunner who pulls us along. Because of his work . . . we shall at last reach our destiny, at last be fully sons [or daughters] of God ourselves."[9]

(3) Eternal life will involve the removal of sin, which will be absent because love will govern all relationships. "God will come to glory in the realization of a people who . . . love God as God wants to be loved."[10] The Christian hope of resurrection is *not egoistical*, for the real objective of the resurrection of the dead is "that God may be everything *to everyone*" (1 Cor 15:28, my emphasis).

(4) Whereas our old world is full of dark shadows, natural catastrophes, sickness, and dying, the new world will be "fully permeated with the light of God" and "free from pain, sadness, and mourning."

(5) "Eternal life will also mean that the bond with God is no longer wrapped in veils. In the earthliness of our existence this bond is present everywhere only in concealment and brokenness, . . . and hence subject to doubt and unbelief. In eternal life, God will be

---

7. Fergusson, "Eschatology," 236.
8. 2 Cor 13:4; cf. Phil 1:23; Col 3:4; 1 Thess 4:15; 5:10.
9. Berkhof, *Christian Faith*, 535.
10. Migliore, "Karl Barth's First Lectures in Dogmatics," in Barth, *Gottingen Dogmatics*, lix.

fully present and knowable.... The immediate presence of God and the concomitant certainty and joy that will mark this consummated relationship to God ... will be filled with loving, praising, and service."[11]

Paul said that at the present "our knowledge is imperfect and our prophecy is imperfect; but when the perfect comes, the imperfect will pass away.... For now we see in a mirror dimly, but then face to face. Now I know in part; then I shall understand fully, even as I have been fully understood. So faith, hope, love abide, these three; but the greatest of these is love" (1 Cor 13:9-13).

(6) Eternal life will involve perfected relationships with others, and the love of fellow humans and of God will be united.[12] "The biblical images of eternal life are profoundly communal—the kingdom of God, the New Jerusalem, the great banquet. Eternal life is no endless extension of the existence of isolated selves, no perpetuation of individualism into infinity."[13]

(7) Then people will reach their destiny "in the absolute unity of freedom and love that God has in mind for [us] ... and for which the Spirit now trains us in our sanctification."[14]

(8) Life in eternity can be described as "entering into rest" (Heb 4:1a, 11), but only from all the frustrations, tensions, conflicts and self-contradictions of our present struggle. It means coming to peace with our true selves, so that we are free to live creative and active lives in the image of the Living God. "Everlasting life [with God and others will be] inexhaustibly rich. We will never be satiated or bored by it, never feel we have gotten to the bottom of it. In praise and service of the triune God there will be ever new surprises and adventures as God's gift of life and love 'goes on unfolding boundlessly.'"[15]

(9) "What is certain is that one day the relation between [our] entire cultural development and eternity will be disclosed and shown to be meaningful. But we are not able to look beyond the great leap. It is wonderful enough to know that all the true, the good, and the beautiful we receive and achieve in our cultural development is a distant foretaste of the fullness of the life and the world which God has in store for us."[16]

(10) "Looking to what lies ahead, we may hope that what we call 'nature' will share in this future." "We do not expect a realm of pure spirits but one of real people, which will be a harmonious part and crown of a larger world."[17]

---

11. Berkhof, *Christian Faith*, 534.
12. Berkhof, *Christian Faith*, 534.
13. Migliore, *Faith Seeking Understanding*, 246.
14. Berkhof, *Christian Faith*, 535.
15. Migliore, *Faith Seeking Understanding*, 246, quoting Hans Urs von Balthasar, *Credo*, 103.
16. Berkhof, *Christian Faith*, 539. "The Bible, not only in its Old Testament eschatology but also in the New Testament, speaks quite matter of factly about the continuation of culture and human society in the city of God. But these images are matched by no less vivid images" that put the matter quite differently, or so Berkhof thinks. He supposes that Revelation 21:2 refers to "the destruction of the present world," but "the New Jerusalem descending out of heaven" can at most only imply that interpretation. Revelation 21:24, 26, "the cultural treasures of the nations being brought in" certainly contradicts that understanding (ibid., 539). But this is perhaps a dispute in a teapot, since even if the transcendent realm contains elements of our life on this planet, it must vastly transcend these.
17. Berkhof, *Christian Faith*, 535.

(11) Presupposed by the previous characteristics is that in the eternal realm "children [may] grow older in personality and adults [may] grow younger in spirit." "If all who pass into heaven continued forever at the stage of development [previously] reached, a child would remain a child, but also the middle-aged would be permanently fixed at their stage of development, and the old at theirs."[18] And those who died of Alzheimer's would be stuck with that mental incapacity for all eternity.

Universal Salvation and Eschatological Peril Teachings[19]

5. Paul and Pauline-Influenced Writings Often Attest Universal Salvation

As affirming that Christ's representative obedience benefits everyone eschatologically, Paul writes "*God has consigned all [people] to disobedience that he may have mercy upon all*" (Rom 11:32, my emphasis). "While we were yet helpless, at the right time Christ died for the ungodly. . . . For while we were enemies we were reconciled to God by the death of his son, much more, now that we are reconciled, shall we be saved by his life. Not only so, but we also rejoice in God through our Lord Jesus Christ, through whom we have now received our reconciliation" (Rom 5:6, 10–11).

In Romans 9–11 Paul raised the question of Israel as within God's purposes and concluded that, except for a faithful remnant (11:5), she had been disobedient (10:21), had not heeded the gospel (10:16), and had been enemies of God (11:28). Yet on the basis of God's election and mercy (11:25–31) Paul concluded that all Israel will be saved (11:26). "For God's gifts and call are irrevocable" (see Rom 11:29). Paul then extended universal salvation expectation to include everyone: "*For God has consigned all persons to disobedience, that he may have mercy on all*" (Rom 11:32).[20]

An essential theological affirmation utilizes an archaic historical assumption concerning the historicity of Adam: As in Adam all die, so also "in Christ shall *all* be made alive" (1 Cor 15:22, my emphasis). In the verses that follow, Paul speaks of God "destroying every rule and every authority and power" (vs. 24b), bringing all things into subjection to himself (vs. 27a), that "God may be everything *to everyone*" (vs. 28, my emphasis).

As in 1 Corinthians 15:22–27, Romans 5:12–21 writes, "as one person's trespasses led to condemnation for all people, so one person's righteousness leads to acquittal and life for all people" (5:18). "However great the effects of Adam, the effects of Christ are greater" (Rom 5:15, 17).[21]

---

18. Bretherton, *Progress in Heaven*, 161, 155.

19. Passages attesting universal salvation cannot be found in the teachings of Jesus, but this may be only because He did know of the full implications of His own life, death, resurrection, and post-resurrection outpouring of the Spirit. Numerous passages could be cited concerning His non-universalistic perspective, but see Matt 7:13–14, 21–23; 25:41–46; Mark 8:38.

20. Hultgren, *Paul's Gospel and Mission*, 103, my emphases. "Paul does not mean here that the salvation of Israel depends on the conversion of Jews individually or collectively in history" (Hultgren, *Paul's Gospel and Mission*, 117).

21. Hultgren, *Paul's Gospel and Mission*, 104, 53.

As for the Adam-Christ typologies of the last two paragraphs, Paul in my opinion wrongfully assumed two things: that Adam was an historical figure and that he brought sin and death into the world (Rom 5:15). But even a non-literal version of Paul's Adam-Christ typology attests that our disobedience has been countered by Christ's righteous obedience on our behalf, pointing toward universal salvation.

In Philippians 2:5–11, and likely utilizing pre-Pauline poetry, the apostle envisions the consummation of all things, when every knee shall bow and every tongue confess that "Jesus Christ is Lord" (vs. 11b). Verses 10–11 "speak of the eschatological future when the cosmic lordship of Christ will be recognized by all ('in heaven and on earth and under the earth')." "In addition to these statements . . . there are [additional] passages in which Paul looks to the future manifestation of the lordship of God over his entire creation at the Parousia [second coming] of Christ." "The creation itself will be set free from its bondage to decay and obtain the glorious liberty of the children of God" (Rom 8:21).

"When we consider that Paul wrote [universalistic statements] in the pre-Constantinian world of the first century, when far less than one percent of the world he knew was Christian. And wrote them in light of an imminent expectation of the Parousia—which would hardly allow for the triumph of Christianity over the face of the globe, we cannot think of these expressions as idle talk. They are surely rooted in the prior theological conviction of Paul concerning the righteousness [covenant faithfulness] of God, which has now been revealed (Rom 3:21), [because of which God] reaches out to reclaim the fallen creation, no longer computing the trespasses of humanity (2 Cor 5:19; cf. Rom 3:25)."[22] "For the love of Christ controls us, because we are convinced that one has died for all; therefore all have died. And he died for all, that those who live might live no longer for themselves but for him who for their sake died and was raised" (2 Cor 5:14–15). "As surely as God is faithful, our word to you has not been Yes and No. For the Son of God, Jesus Christ, whom we preached among you . . . was not Yes and No; but in him it is always Yes. For all the promises of God find their Yes in him" (2 Cor 1:18–20a).

The author of Colossians wrote that in Christ "all the fullness of God was pleased to dwell, and through him to reconcile all things, whether on earth or in heaven, making peace by the blood of the cross."[23] Also the author of Ephesians refers to God's expansive plan "to unite all things in him, things in heaven and things on earth" (1:10). First Timothy insists that Christ in taking up the divine cause "gave himself as a ransom for all" (2:6a), and "desires all [persons] to be saved" (2:4). And 2 Timothy declares that Christ "abolished death and brought life and immortality to light" (1:10b).

6. Eschatological Peril as Also Attested by Paul

Presenting a challenge to his own universal salvation teachings, Paul writes on various occasions of eschatological peril not only for non-Christians but also for Christians who do not remain faithful.[24] He warns "Christians" of danger "if they become slaves of sin" (Rom

---

22. Hultgren, *Paul's Gospel and Mission*, 84–85.
23. Col 1:19–20; see also 2 Cor 5:18–19; cf. Rom 5:10.
24. See 1 Cor 1:18; 6:9–10; 2 Cor 2:15–16; Gal 6:7–8; Phil 1:28; 3:18–19.

6:16), have a sense of false security (1 Thess 5:3), and continue in immorality (Gal 5:21). But he goes much further.

Focusing on the book of Romans, 1:18—2:16 surprisingly affirms *a natural knowledge of God* from which many have turned aside to worship idols, "exchanging the truth about God for a lie" (1:25a), and worshiping and serving "the creature rather than the Creator" (1:25b). And in some cases thereby giving themselves up to what Paul regards as lustful and impure behavior (1:24).

As for the 1:26–27 related discussion of homosexuality/lesbianism he assumes that heterosexual sexual instincts are for all people natural, which is not the case. In so presuming he may in some cases have had in mind the common Roman practice of heterosexual military men having homosexual relations with younger military men to bind them together as comrades in arms. That would be wrong. But that is not the same as a homosexual having a lifelong committed relationship with a homosexual, or a lesbian having a lifelong committed relationship with a lesbian. This though many homosexual males tend to be highly promiscuous. But these days a large percentage of heterosexual marriages also do not last. So both those with homosexual and heterosexual orientations have much to learn from Christian commitment to lifelong marital fidelity. Except that these days many Christian marriages are also not doing well, perhaps because the partners are not really Christian or because they entered marriages without adequate forethought and prayer.

In Romans 1:28–32 Paul offers a long list of other behaviors he regards as deserving of everlasting death. Among the practices is not only murder, but deceit, malice, envy, covetousness, gossiping and even disobeying parents! Also to be condemned are those who approve such practices! (vs. 32) This is Paul at his worst! Utilizing supposed natural theology sets the whole discussion on a wrong footing.

Some other examples of Paul's moral warnings are seen as only possibly affecting eschatological peril. In 1 Corinthians 11:27–32 Paul takes up the issue of eating and drinking at the Lord's Supper in an "unworthy manner" (11:27). In this regard he speaks of divine judgment being exercised upon Christians by Christians in the present, the effect of which is to chastise offenders toward behaving better "that they may not be condemned" (11:32). "Here condemnation is not held out as a perilous eschatological prospect, but as something [to be] precluded by judgment in the present. A similar motif appears in 1 Corinthians 5:1–5 where Paul 'pronounced judgment in the name of the Lord Jesus' (5:3–4) upon an immoral person. [Strangely put] this person was to be delivered 'to Satan for the destruction of the flesh' precisely 'in order that his spirit may be saved on the day of the Lord' (5:5). [Here] judgment by the community is [regarded as] purgative in its effects; by passing judgment the person is 'prepared' for salvation."[25]

As for other 1 Corinthian particulars, Paul refers to a man cohabiting with his stepmother, likely after his father had died or had divorced the wife. "What raised Paul's ire was not merely that Corinthian Christians had allowed the perpetrator to remain in the community, but had trumpeted that permission as a badge of its freedom. 'And you have been puffed up, and did not rather mourn, so that the one who did this deed be removed from your midst.' [5:2] . . . Paul had expected excommunication, not reception, much less

---

25. Hultgren, *Paul's Gospel and Mission*, 108.

celebration."²⁶ Against that church's inaction and for the sake of the integrity of church membership, Paul demanded that person's excommunication (deliverance to Satan's realm), away from the corrupting effects of remaining in the church. But Paul did not rule out the possibility of his eternal salvation (5:3–5).

7. First Peter as Also Teaching Both Universal Salvation and Eschatological Peril

According to this author, though Christ was put to death, He was made alive in the Spirit and went to preach to "the spirits in prison, who formerly did not obey" (3:19). Doing so, that "they might live in the spirit like God" (4:6c). This could be the author's way of affirming that there are no limitations to the redemptive effects of Christ's having died "once for all, the righteous for the unrighteous" (3:18b).²⁷ Unfortunately the author also writes that "the time has come for judgment to begin with the household of God; and if it begins with us, what will be the end of *those who do not obey the Gospel of God*? 'If the righteous person is scarcely saved, where will the impious and sinner appear?'" (4:18, quoting Prov 11:31 LXX) Here the author asserts that those who purport to be Christians, but "do not obey the gospel of God" face an unfortunate eschatological future. If so, what of the author's descent into hell teaching? Or is that only applicable to those who never came close to being pious?!

8. Fourth Gospel's Basis of Christian Hope in Contrast with 1 John

The Fourth Gospel has several inconsistencies related to our theme. It can seldom be said of this Gospel "that in Christ God has already reconciled the world to himself or that the sins of the world have been borne by Christ. . . . Here the overarching message is that *whoever believes the Son to be what the message declares him to be*—thus authenticating the message for oneself—receives the [eternal] life he brings."²⁸ "He who believes in him is not condemned; he who does not believe is condemned already, because he has not believed in the name of the only Son of God" (John 3:18).

In contrast to the above, the Fourth Gospel also manifests the "disconcerting [predestinarian] idea that mankind *is already irrevocably divided into children of God and children of the devil*, the former . . . to enjoy eternal life and the latter to undergo eternal death. This is expressed at several points. For example, Jesus says to 'the Jews,' 'He who is of God hears the words of God; the reason why you do not hear them is that you are not of God' (8:47). Again, 'the works that I do in my Father's name, they bear witness to me; but you do not believe, because you do not belong to my sheep'" (John 10:25)²⁹

---

26. Harrisville, *1 Corinthians*, 80–81.
27. Harrisville, *1 Corinthians*, 115.
28. Hultgren, *Christ and His Benefits*, 162, my emphasis.
29. Hick, *Death and Eternal Life*, 246, my emphasis.

Unlike the Fourth Gospel, the author of 1 John sometimes attests that "Jesus bore sin/sins and their consequences for the benefit of others" (1 John 1:7; 2:2; 3:5; 4:9-10).[30] *First John 4:9-10* reads as follows: "In this the love of God was made manifest among us, that God sent his only Son into the world, so that we might live through him. In this is love, not that we loved God but that he loved us and sent the Son to be the expiation for our sins." And the corollary of this is that the good news of Christ's redemptive work now seems to be more fully integrated with the summons to believe.

Strangely enough the same author contradicts the above texts by humanistically conceiving God's relationship with us as a function of our moral behavior. "No one has ever seen God; if we love one another, God abides in us and his love is perfected in us" (1 John 4:12). "Those who abide in love abide in God, and God abides in them" (1 John 4:16).

9. Theological Thinking concerning Universal Salvation: Schleiermacher, Barth, and Newbigin as Inclusivists

Because of what God in Christ has done on the behalf of all people Christians are called to an outreaching "ministry of reconciliation" (2 Cor 5:19), which among other things is to help expand the circle of those who profess faith in Jesus Christ and become His disciples. By word and deed we are "to declare the wonderful deeds of him who called us out of darkness into his marvelous light" (1 Pet 2:9). Yet in view of the fact that to the present most people have either lived before Christ or outside the borders of Christianity's influence, can we believe that the God of love wills to damn most people?

"If we attribute to the [eternally] blessed knowledge of the state of the damned, it cannot be a knowledge unmixed with sympathy. If the perfecting of our nature is not to move backwards, sympathy must be such as to embrace the whole human race, and when extended to the damned must of necessity be a disturbing element in bliss, all the more that, unlike similar feelings in this life, it [would be] untouched by hope. . . . Sympathy will be all the stronger because in that earlier time there was a point when we were as little regenerated as they."[31]

"Strange Christianity, whose most pressing anxiety seems to be that God's grace might prove to be all too free . . . , that hell, instead of being populated with so many people, might someday prove to be empty. "[32] "This much is certain, that we have no theological right to set any sort of limits to the loving-kindness of God which has appeared in Jesus Christ."[33]

Newbigin agrees with Barth in affirming the unique truth of the revelation in Jesus Christ, in acknowledging the gracious work of God in the lives of all people, and in attesting the possible salvation of non-Christians. That is, he is exclusivist in not regarding

---

30. Hultgren, *Christ and His Benefits*, 163-64. First John seems to confuse sins with sin, the state of being from which sins occur.

31. Schleiermacher, *The Christian Faith*, 721.

32. Barth, *God Here and Now*, 34.

33. Barth, *Humanity of God*, 62.

non-Christian religions as vehicles of salvation, but inclusivist in refusing to limit the saving grace of God here and beyond to the members of the Christian church.[34]

"As a human race we are on a journey and we need to know the road. It is not true that all roads lead to the top of the same mountain. There are roads which lead over the precipice. In Christ we have been shown the road. We cannot treat this knowledge as a private matter for ourselves. It concerns the whole human family. We do not presume to limit the might and mercy of God for the ultimate salvation of all people, but the same costly act of revelation and reconciliation that gives us that assurance also requires us to share with our fellow pilgrims the vision that God has given us as the route we must follow and the goal to which we must press forward."[35]

10. The Great Importance of the Hope of Eternal Life

If Christian hope applies only to this life we are of all people most to be pitied (1 Cor 15:19). What oxygen is for the lungs, [eternal] hope is for the meaning of human life.[36] To sever present meaning from ultimate hope is to threaten present meaning! We live in and by our ultimate hope. If the final goal of life is to rot in the ground or to be burned up in an incinerator, the rest of life may seem hopeless and absurd.

What happens to Christian morality when Christian hope is lost? It too begins to crumble. It may be no coincidence that we live in an age that on a widespread basis denies eternal hope *and* Christian morality. The denial of Christian hope is a step toward the total disintegration of the Christian life. Paul knew this well. He said, "If the dead are not raised, 'let us eat and drink, for tomorrow we die'" (1 Cor 15:32). The person who believes that this world is the only one will live as though the things of this world are all that matter. If death is the end, there is little left to do but pluck the pleasures of the passing moment. Not all who deny the resurrection draw this conclusion; Paul suggests that it would be reasonable if they did. If death is the end, all moral standards are relativized, and can be totally ignored. People are free to do as they please on their sad little journey toward non-existence.

In contrast to those who deny Christian hope, some for social, political or other improper motives may glibly and superficially "affirm" Christian faith and hope. Some others may latch onto a wishful thinking, free-standing universal salvation idea. They may even say that since everyone is going to be saved, it doesn't matter whether we believe in Christ or not. It also doesn't matter whether we seek to lead Christian lives or even moral ones.

To the contrary, it here and now makes a tremendous difference whether or not a person has *genuine* faith in Christ, for what is at stake is the integrity of one's Christian discipleship. Whether directly denied or superficially affirmed, the attitudes just criticized are impossible for authentic Christians, who have biblical and experiential bases for believing in eternal life.

---

34. Newbigin, *The Gospel in a Pluralist Society*, 182–83.

35. Newbigin, *The Gospel in a Pluralist Society*, 183.

36. Brunner, *Eternal Hope*, 7. As for hopes that fall short of the hope of eternal life, there is always a certain degree of relativity. Though our smaller hopes in life are meaningful, we dare not stake everything on them. For example, some medical students may flunk out of medical school, not because they did not try, but because they did not have what it took to be doctors. But other careers could prove very promising.

For sincere disciples one function of the belief in the triumph of grace through Christ is to comfort believers. We need not despair at the graveside of our beloved friends, even if they have not come to genuine faith in Christ. Their resistance may have been too much for us to successfully challenge, but will not finally be too much for God. We can trust our loved ones into God's care, all of our loved ones. As Christians God can keep us from discouragement at a time when to be a sincere disciple is not as common as it once was. Though the vast majority of people have not come to authentic faith in Christ, we nevertheless believe that Christ is not only our Savior but theirs. The Gospel of God's love in Christ is true and is true for the whole world.

Death does not have the last word. God's incarnate love met humankind's incarnate hatred on the battlefield. But when the sound and fury of the battle cleared away what was left was not an ugly cross and a lifeless body—but the Risen Christ. Jesus's resurrection calls us to joyous and confident hope that stretches beyond death. To worship this God is to celebrate and rejoice—even in the face of all that life has to offer—including death. To live on the resurrection side of Easter morning is to know and believe that death has died. Nothing in all creation will be able to separate us from the love of God in Christ Jesus our Lord (Rom 8:39).

THE CHURCH AND CHRISTIAN TRADITION; TRUE RELIGION AND SOME OTHER RELIGIONS; CHRISTIAN FREEDOM

Chapter 28

The Church; Conflicting Ways of Understanding Christian Tradition

"If the [church] exists visibly ... it exists in a form. But if it exists in a form, the question of the rightness of this form cannot be ignored and we are forced to attempt an answer."[1]

1. Foundation of the Church: Jesus Christ and God's Eliciting of Our Responsive Entrance

"THE CHURCH AS [A] social and historical movement is at the same time [a] movement toward God, which is itself utterly dependent upon the movement of God to man.... The church *exists* just in this relation."[2] The church is only because of God's forgiveness and costly love shown in Jesus's life and teaching, His death on the cross, and declared with resounding firmness with His resurrection. The church is called to be Christ-centered, with His influencing at every point.

Though unworthy we are sisters and brothers in Christ because God through Christ forgave our sin and inspires our confession that He is the Son of the Living God. Flesh and blood has not revealed this to us, but our transcendent Father (Matt 16:17b). The church's one foundation is God's coming in Christ and the Spirit-inspired confession that this has happened.

Because the church stands under God's judgment the institutional structure of the church should be evaluated in the light of the biblically understood nature and purpose of the church. Because our faith involves corporate interpretation of historical traditions we must not abandon the church. "The possibility of a Christianity outside the church and aloof from its common worship could only be the object of bewilderment to the New Testament community.... [According to the New Testament,] assembling for divine

---

1. Barth, *CD* 4/2:685.
2. Welch, *Reality of the Church*, 70–71.

worship . . . is the center and presupposition of the whole Christian life, the atmosphere in which it is lived".[3]

Faith's object is God alone as Father, Son and Spirit. We do not so much believe in the church, but because through the Spirit we believe in Jesus Christ, we are set within the church. Such necessary placement need not and should not result in giving our denomination and/or local or regional church a clean bill of health. But "the legitimate, prophetic, reformation attack upon the church and its doctrine and order and life and attitudes can be conducted only on its own ground, in the name of Jesus Christ, and with the intention of re-establishing it more firmly on this ground."[4]

The only path to the true church is through some form of the organized church however imperfect. Certainly one can switch denominations and/or identify with a local church that has less or more structure, better preaching, a better educational program, more active outreach, etc., but we cannot abandon the institutional side of Christianity without turning aside from the Christian God. Certainly Christianity cannot be defined by institutional structures, but neither can it exist without them.

2. Necessity of Preaching and Teaching[5]

For the Gospel to be powerfully real it has to be interpreted. A significant part of worship involves seeking to understand the meaning of God's disclosure in Christ. Thus preaching and teaching are vitally significant for the life of the church. These are efforts to understand the meaning of Jesus Christ and to perceive His relevance for life today. Paul asked, "How are [people] to call upon him in whom they have not believed? And how are they to believe in him of whom they have never heard? And how are they to hear without a preacher? And how can [people] preach unless they are sent? . . . So faith comes from what is heard, and what is heard comes by the preaching of Christ" (Rom 10:14–15a). "We are ambassadors for Christ, God making His appeal through us. We beseech you on behalf of Christ, be reconciled to God" (2 Cor 5:20).

"In 1 Corinthians teachers [who were also likely preachers] are expressly mentioned in the third place after apostles and prophets.[6] They work within a community[7] to hand on and interpret the message of Christ. . . . They too have authority through the particular spiritual gift accorded to them. . . . But their teaching is not like that of the prophets, founded directly on revelation (1 Cor 14:26–30), but [to a degree] on tradition. . . . Rather than proclaiming intuitively, the teachers expound systematically."[8]

God uses preaching and teaching witnessing concerning His Son to address us today and to show us His will and way. This is a high doctrine of preaching and teaching, but this is not to exalt these workers, but to venerate the God who wills to use the brokenness of

---

3. Barth, *CD* 4/2:640.
4. Barth, *CD* 4/1:692.
5. See Ray, *Systematics Critical & Constructive 1*, 257–63.
6. 1 Cor 12:28–29; cf. Acts 13:1; Eph 4:1.
7. Rom 12:7; 1 Cor 14:26; cf. 1 Tim 1:11–12.
8. Kung, *The Church*, 506–7.

human words to witness to His Word. To take Jesus Christ seriously we need to take the Bible seriously and through preaching and teaching learn the meaning of our faith.[9]

3. Paul's Leadership within Churches He Founded

"There are varieties of gifts, but the same Spirit; and there are varieties of service, but the same Lord; and there are varieties of working, but it is the same God who inspires them all in every one" (1 Cor 12:4–5). These verses and some others could give "a quick impression . . . of a leaderless mob; but it is a false impression. As long as Paul lived his churches had a remarkably strong leader, who was not content to found societies and leave them to themselves, but kept a close eye on them, writing letters and sending colleagues when he could not visit them himself, well aware of an authority that had been committed to him with his apostleship. It was a positive authority, 'for building . . . up and not for casting down (2 Cor 10:8; 13:10), but that meant an authority to do precisely what he was commissioned to do. . . . He did not hesitate to give instructions in his letters, and could promise to set matters in order when he was able to pay a visit (1 Cor 11:34)."[10] He wrote "What would you prefer? Am I to come to you with a stick, or with love in a spirit of gentleness?" (1 Cor 4:21 NRSV)

"Paul had assistants who travelled with him, joined him in writing letters, and could be sent on their own to carry out tasks that Paul would have done had it been possible for him to be in several places at once. . . . He commended them; he expected them to be well treated and respected (1 Cor 16:11). There were other travellers who, though they were not like Selvanus, Timothy, or Titus, members of the team, must have contributed to the success."[11]

4. Spirit-Guided Ministries within Paul's Churches[12]

Spiritual gifts/charisms signify *"the call of God, addressed to an individual, to a particular ministry in the community, which brings with it the ability to fulfil that ministry."* "Charisms are the revelations, in concrete and individual form, of the charis, the power of God's grace, which takes hold of us, leads us to our appointed service and gives us an individual share in the reign of Christ. And to the extent that we have a present share in the grace and reign of Christ in the Spirit, our charisms express . . . 'the manifestation of the Spirit' (1 Cor 12:7.): 'All these are inspired by one and the same Spirit, who apportions to each one individually as he wills'"[13] (1 Cor 12:11).

"There is no divine gift which does not bring with it a task, . . . no grace which does not move to action. Service is not merely the consequence but the outward form and the

---

9. Preaching can and should involve teaching, but teaching should also occur in other contexts.
10. Barrett, *Church*, 34–35.
11. Barrett, *Church*, 35.
12. Like the book of Acts, the Pauline Epistles use the word "church" both for the whole people of God and also for the concrete manifestation in a particular place.
13. Kung, *The Church*, 247, 248.

realization of grace." "No spiritual endowment has value, rights or privileges on its own account. It is validated only by the service it renders."[14] "More than the 'fruits' of the 'Spirit' (Gal 5:22), which [to an extent] are directed towards the sanctification of the individual (love, joy, peace, patience, kindness, goodness, faithfulness, gentleness, self-control), the charisims exist for the 'edification of the church' (1 Cor 14:12; cf. Eph 4:12f)."[15]

5 Criteria That Help Community to Evaluate Charismatic Contributions

"In the course of the three chapters given over to the discussion of the charismata (1 Cor 12–14) Paul highlights three criteria which should enable the community to evaluate charismatic contributions to its life and worship."[16] "One test is provided by the kerygmatic and Jesus traditions [though Paul knew few of the latter] which [Paul] passed on to his converts. . . . It is to these traditions that he turns again and again in 1 Corinthians to provide the basis for rulings on matters of controversy involving the Corinthian enthusiasts.[17] . . . For Paul only that experience was to be recognized as experience of the Spirit which accorded with the founding traditions. The Spirit of Christ must accord with 'the law of Christ' (1 Cor 9:21; Gal 6:2)."[18]

"Another test is provided by love. First Corinthians 13:1–13 is obviously directed against a kind of enthusiasm, where zeal for the more spectacular charismata, particularly prophecy, glossolalia [speaking in tongues] and knowledge, had provoked jealously, arrogance, irritability, and kindred sins. Love had been the loser, and love provided the test (13:4–7). No matter how outstanding the gifts exercised, if they produce a loveless character, Paul counts them of no value whatsoever. By the same criterion in 1 Cor 2–3 he turns his back on all elitism; those who claim to be 'the spiritual ones' but provoke only jealousy and strife and have no concern for others show thereby their unspirituality (3:1–4; 8:1). For Paul 'the [truly] spiritual ones' are all those who have received the Spirit and walk by the Spirit, not giving way to self-conceit, unkind criticism or envy (Gal 5:25—6:3). The criterion of spirituality is not the degree of inspiration but love."[19]

Finally, all charismatic gifts must benefit others, and are to be judged thereby (1 Cor 12:7).[20] *Community benefit (oikodome)* promotes others' upuilding or edification and "Paul uses the verb and noun seven times in 1 Cor 14 (vv. 3–5, 12, 17, 26). This is the criterion which shows clearly for Paul the superiority of prophecy over glossolalia. . . . For Paul charismatic experience is characterized less by ecstasy . . . (cf. 2 Cor 12:2–4) and more by the intelligible word spoken through one believer which brings understanding and guidance to another (1 Cor 14:3–5, 16–19, 24f.). This is why acts of service, however uninspired they

---

14. Kasemann, *Essays on New Testament Themes*, 65, 67.
15. Kung, *The Church*, 248.
16. Dunn, *Jesus and the Spirit*, 293.
17. See particularly 1 Cor 9:14; 11:23; 12:3; 15:3.
18. Dunn, *Unity and Diversity*, 192–93.
19. Dunn, *Unity and Diversity*, 193.
20. Dunn, *Unity and Diversity*, 193.

appear, may well have higher claim to be recognized as charismata than the most manifestly inspired utterance (Rom 12:6–8). ['Having gifts that differ according to the grace given to us, let us use them: if prophecy, in proportion to our faith; if service, in our serving; he who teaches, in his teaching; he who exhorts, in his exhortation; he who contributes, in liberality; he who gives aid, with zeal; he who does acts of mercy, with cheerfulness.'] What does not benefit others cannot be for the good of the church."[21]

6. Ministry according to Post-Pauline Pastorals

"With the *Pastorals* we move into a different world completely. . . . (1) Presbyters or elders appear for the first and only time . . . (1 Tim 5:1f., 17, 19; Titus 1:5). Here we probably see the merging of Jewish Christian Church order with the more formal order which emerged in the Pauline churches in the early Catholicism of second and third generation Christianity. (2) 'Overseers' (1 Tim 3:1–7; Titus 1:7ff.) and 'deacons' (1 Tim 3:8–13) appear now as descriptions of established offices ('offices of overseers,' 1 Tim 3:1). 'Overseers' may be another name for [elders or] 'presbyters' (early catholic synonyms), otherwise the absence of any mention of presbyters in 1 Tim 3 would be rather odd (see also Titus 1:5ff.)."

"(3) Not least to be considered is the position of Timothy and Titus. Their precise relation to the community of Ephesus and Crete is not clear, but certainly they rank above presbyters, overseers and deacons. Perhaps most striking of all is the fact that these letters *[honorably attributed to Paul]* are addressed solely to them, so that the primary responsibility for regulating the community's affairs seems to lie with them. In particular, [these letters] envisage Timothy and Titus exercising an authority which Paul himself never exercised either directly or through his immediate co-workers."[22]

"The fellowship [and] collegiality of all believers, of all those who had charisms and fulfilled their own ministries . . . gave place to the *collegiality* of a special ministry within the community: the collegiality of the leaders of the community, the *episkopoi* or elders, who increasingly began to see themselves as distinct from the community, from the 'people'; this is where the division between 'clergy' and 'laity' begins."[23] This development may reflect some administrative gains, but at the cost of participatory loss on the part of the "laity."

7. Pastoral Epistles Modifications of Pauline Understanding of Charisma

As for the way in which the Pauline concept of *charisma* has been modified in the Pastoral Epistles, "Grau noted three points worthy of comment. (a) *Charisma* no longer seems to denote a great variety of services, the particular utterances and deeds which different believers may be called upon to contribute for the benefit

---

21. Dunn, *Unity and Diversity*, 193–94.

22. 1 Tim 5:17–22; Titus 1:5–6; cf. 2 Tim 2:2; contrast 1 Cor 4:17; 16:15–18; Col 4:7–8; 1 Thess 5:12–15. Dunn, *Jesus and the Spirit*, 347, 348.

23. Kung, *The Church*, 523.

of all. In the Pastorals *charisma* is used only with reference to Timothy (1 Tim 4:14; 2 Tim 1:6); it is a single gift once given which equips him for different responsibilities and gives him his position and authority. Exhortation and teaching [and even reading Scripture] are no longer themselves charismata, but simply part of Timothy's regular responsibilities (1 Tim 4:13). In short, *charisma has become power of office*.[24] (b) In the Pastorals *charisma* has lost its dynamic character. It is no longer the individual manifestation of grace but a power or ability which Timothy *possesses*, which he *has within him* (1 Tim 4:14; 2 Tim 1:6), and which he himself can stir into activity. (c) Charisma is no longer the wholly free gift of the Spirit, as were the charismata of the early Pauline literature. Rather it is a gift given once for all in the course of an act of ordination—"through prophecy along with the laying on of hands for ordination as an elder" (1 Tim 4:14), [or as stated in 2 Tim 1:6] "through the laying on of my hands." In addition [to Grau's contribution], we must note (d) that the finely tensed balance Paul had achieved between prophecy and teaching, that is between new revelations of the ever present eschatological Spirit and the passing on and interpretation of established tradition, seems to have gone. Wholly dominant is the concern to preserve the doctrinal statements of the past—the "sound teaching doctrine," the "faithful sayings," the "sound words," "the faith." The Spirit has become the power to guard the heritage of tradition handed on from the past (2 Tim 1:14). . . . And even Paul himself is depicted more as the keeper of tradition than as its author (2 Tim 1:12).[25]

"Clearly then the vision of charismatic community has faded, ministry and authority have become the prerogative of the few, the experience of the Christ Spirit has lost its vitality, and the preservation of the past has become more important than openness to the present and future. *Spirit and charisma have become in effect subordinate to office, to ritual, to tradition*—early Catholicism indeed! . . . The only way the author of the Pastorals felt able to maintain Christianity was by the formalization of faith and institutionalization of church. But in so doing has he not fallen into the very error he himself warns against—maintaining the outward form of piety but denying its inner power? (2 Tim 3:5) Certainly it would seem that the great distinctives in Paul's handling of religious experience have almost wholly disappeared."[26]

"Perhaps the Pastorals are the first example of that progressive institutionalizing which seems to affect so many movements of spiritual renewal in the second (or third) generations, when the flexibility of fresh religious experience begins to harden into set forms. The lesser men of the second (or third) generation, unable to live creatively out of their own experience of God, have to treat the faith of the founding era as 'the faith.' Teaching which was the living expression of the first generation's spiritual experience becomes sacred word, hallowed heritage to be preserved, guarded, handed on, but not re-interpreted. The springs of present religion are confined almost wholly to the past; the present becomes in effect only a channel whereby the religion of the past can be transmitted to the future in good order. In a word, the vitality of first generation religious experience largely disappears, and

---

24. "No one is sure whether bishops and elders were identical or different, though the prevailing view is that they were identical," Ziesler, *Paul's Letter to the Romans*, 131–32.

25. Dunn, *Jesus and the Spirit*, 348–49, a, b, and c points drawing from F. Grau's unpublished Tubingen dissertation (1946), my emphases.

26. Dunn, *Jesus and the Spirit*, 349.

the second generation begins to attempt what is not possible—that is, to live in the present out of the religious experience of the past. This has not yet fully happened in the Pastorals, but the process is already well advanced."[27]

8. The Twelve Apostles and the Others

"At the transition from the Palestinian apostolic community to the later Gentile Christian [community] stands Paul, according to his own estimate the 'least of the apostles' (1 Cor 15:9) and yet the first theologian of Gentile Christianity."[28] According to Paul, people otherwise unknown, like the Jewish Christians Andronicus and Junias (Rom 16:7) and the "five hundred brethren" of 1 Cor 15:6 were and yet were not apostles! This because to Paul the distinguishing mark of an apostle was *not just encountering the Risen Christ, but also being called to church founding missionary activity* (1 Cor 9:1; 15:9–10; Gal:16–17).

"Paul on the basis of the call that had come to him through the resurrected One, places himself on an equal footing with the Jerusalem apostles, and hence he emphasizes that he did not at first go to see the Jerusalem apostles. But then after three years he did go to Jerusalem and visited Peter for two weeks and, in addition, met James, the Lord's brother . . . (Gal 1:18). . . . When Paul relates in Gal 2:2 that fourteen years later he [once again] laid his preaching to the Gentiles before 'those who were of repute' (RSV) in the Jerusalem community, among whom in addition to James the Lord's brother were also Jesus's disciples Peter and John (Gal 2:9), [he did so] 'lest [he] . . . run in vain.' This account was found in the context of a statement in which Paul [attests that he] wished to prove the essential independence of his apostolic office from men and above all from the Jerusalem apostles (Gal 1:1, 11; 2:8–9, 11)."[29]

9. Hiddenness of Church

There is always a sense in which the true church is hidden within the institutional church and not identical with it. "We cannot see and understand the community of Jesus Christ as a monolithic block, as a collective of which the individual [members], as mere parts of the whole, are all equally and in the same way blessed, endowed and determined . . . to the same degree."[30]

The problem was already present in NT times. We see from Jesus's parables that there are many weeds among the wheat (Matt 13:24–30, 36–43) and many bad fish among those that come into the net (Matt 13:47–50). Even among the apostles there was Judas and after Jesus's crucifixion the remaining apostles deserted Him. Later "there were 'false brethren' (2 Cor 11:26), . . . a companion of the Apostles who 'loved this present world' (2 Tim 4:10), and . . . Gnostic teachers of heresy (1 John 2:19) who had gone out from the community but did not belong to it. These factors and others lead to the question whether the

---

27. Dunn, *Jesus and the Spirit*, 157–58.
28. Kummel, *Theology of the New Testament*, 136.
29. Kummel, *Theology of the New Testament*, 135.
30. Barth, *CD* 4/3, Second Half, 784.

Community can be fully the Community. The answer found to this question in 2 Timothy 2:19, 'The Lord knows those who are his,' makes plain that the [early] Community and the subsequent tradition did not think that the problem could be done away with."[31]

10. Inward and Outward Church Growth

"The body of Christ grows *inwardly*, in the growth of faith, knowledge, love and in 'sufferings,' which 'complete what is lacking in Christ's afflictions for the sake of his body, that is, the church' (Col 1:24). And the body grows *outwardly*, through new members who have been incorporated by [Spirit] baptism [sometimes in response to] the preaching of the Gospel. In this way the church is 'the fullness of him who fills all in all' (Eph 1:23). . . . Given that Christ is the head of the church and hence the origin and goal of its growth, growth is only possible in *obedience* to its head."[32] However, mere numerical growth can be attained in less faithful ways.

"Growth is impossible if we are not at the same time prepared to humbly allow ourselves to be served by gifts of grace which we lack. And that in turn is not possible unless we are aware that the truth we wish to defend is the truth of the love which surpasses our knowledge and which we can only comprehend in company with all the saints (Eph 3:1–18f.), so that there is no room left for contempt, jealously, or competition."[33]

11. Criticism of Church

"The church stands in the fire of criticism [from] its Lord. . . . It has always needed and it always will need self-examination and self-correction. It cannot exist except as [a church being reformed]." "The legitimate prophetic reformation attack upon the church and its doctrine and order and life and attitudes can be conducted only . . . in the name of Jesus Christ, and with the intention of [helping the church to be] re-established more firmly on this ground." "Therefore no matter how well-grounded and necessary and sharp may be the criticism brought against [the church], that [should] never harden into absolute condemnation and rejection. Ultimately it can have only the character of penetrating questions addressed to it."[34]

---

31. Weber, *Foundations of Dogmatics*, 2:540–41. Contrary to Weber, 2 Timothy's congregation or congregations would not have reflected "the oldest community," which would have been Paul's congregations. Thus the bracketed change.

32. Kung, *The Church*, 309. See also Eph 4:15–16; Col 2:19.

33. Kung, *The Church*, 404.

34. Barth, *CD* 4/1:690, 692.

12. Conflicting Ways of Understanding Post-New Testament Christian Tradition[35]

Early Catholic Supposed Apostolic Succession as Guaranteeing Genuineness of Tradition and Then Roman Catholic Understandings of Tradition. The post-NT church sought to "create a means of guaranteeing the genuineness of tradition [through its expanded understanding of] the office of bishop." Even supposing that the uninterrupted apostolic succession of bishops could be proven—which it can't—bishops ordained in supposed unbroken succession were not necessarily the bearers of the original apostolic doctrine.

With this Early Roman Catholic understanding the principle of tradition as consisting in the supposed continuity of truth "was replaced by the notion that tradition consisted in the continuity of [bishops's] succession in office. . . . The further the church became removed in time from its historical origin, the less likely was the continuity of mere succession in office to assure the continuity of . . . the message handed down from the apostles . . . , [and as a result] dogma *did* change."[36]

"The church could not altogether fail to recognize this fact. But sought to justify itself both in its own eyes and in those of the world . . . by combining . . . a quite different conception, one which . . . is . . . present in notions of tradition prevalent among Catholics today: the thought of *the unfolding of something which was originally only latent into its fully explicit and . . . mature form.* By means of this notion it became possible to identify the new with the old, without being compelled to deny the element of newness."[37]

This conception of development is not without its dangers. For with the aid of such a theory that which is incompatible easily gets equated, and thereby transformations and distortions occur. Side by side with the process of legitimate development, incompatible alteration took place in the early church.[38] "This fact is intimately connected with . . . the tendency to equate unbroken succession in office or legitimacy with continuity in the sense of preserving the original deposit. The apparent continuity of the succession . . . produced the appearance of a real and substantial continuity. . . . The *office* became an unproved and unprovable guarantee of truth."[39]

The Neo-Roman Catholic Idea of Tradition. Until the middle of the twelfth-century canon law was in the hands of the theologians and their knowledge was not juridical but theological. Then lawyers schooled in the science of Roman law entered the Curia and the church thereby ceased being represented by bishops, and began to be ruled by the Pope. This happened at the same time that secular law came to be wielded by the power of the state.[40]

At the Council of Trent (1545–63) what is without scriptural basis was placed on the same level of importance as Scripture, and from 1918 both faith and morals were

---

35. Here will be no discussion of Vatican 2 changes because those did not occur in the areas discussed in this sec.
36. Brunner, *Misunderstanding of the Church*, 36–37, my emphases.
37. Brunner, *Misunderstanding of the Church*, 37–38, my emphasis.
38. Brunner, *Misunderstanding of the Church*, 39–40.
39. Brunner, *Misunderstanding of the Church*, 40.
40. Brunner, *Misunderstanding of the Church*, 42.

determined by the Pope, he being no longer bound by the consensus in the church as reflected by the bishops. Thus he was able to create dogmas concerning faith and morals, tradition being superseded by the development of a supposed infallible administrative and teaching office.[41] Thus Pope Pius IX declared, "'I, the Pope, am tradition.' What the Pope declares to be tradition *is* tradition . . . though no trace of such a tradition [may] exist."

"From these considerations it may be seen how hopeless it is for Protestants, [other] non-Roman Catholics and Roman Catholics to discuss the rights and wrongs of tradition, since each means by tradition something quite different. . . . The laxest notion of tradition is that characteristic of Roman Catholics; by their system of canon law and ecclesiastical jurisdiction they reject the idea of any need to test received authoritative doctrine by the touchstone of apostolic teaching."[42]

---

41. Brunner, *Misunderstanding of the Church*, 43–44.
42. Brunner, *Misunderstanding of the Church*, 44, 45.

Chapter 29

Christ the Source of True Religion with Nine Comparisons

1. Brunner and Barth on Priority of Revelation over Religion

"The relativistic conception of religion has been represented within Continental theology and the science of comparative religion, particularly in connection with Schleiermacher's theory of religion. According to him there is an 'essence of religion'—'the religion in the religions'—which lies at the basis of all particular religions; this 'essence,' however, only manifests itself in a concrete and living way in definite historical and individual forms. According to Schleiermacher, a 'natural religion' does not exist in addition to the various religions (as people used to think at the time of the Enlightenment); but 'natural religion'—the 'religion within the religions' lies beneath all religions as their foundation, and as their 'essence.' . . . [Against this perspective] it is impossible to be a Christian in the New Testament sense and at the same time to accept the view that there is a universal 'essence of religion' of which Christianity has a predominant share. The Christian revelation and these 'relative' theories of religion are mutually exclusive."[1]

"For whereas the 'relative' theory of religion regards the basic element in all religions as 'the *essence* of religion,' and all that distinguishes them from one another as nonessential, as far as biblical faith is concerned the exact opposite is true. It is the distinctive element that is [most important]. . . . The Christian understanding of revelation . . . is absolute, not relative. God's revelation in Jesus Christ is related to that which 'the other religions' claim as their revelation, not as an individual formulation of something common to all—such as . . . the mystical element or reverence for the Holy [or as with Schleiermacher, the feeling of absolute dependence]—but as the special revelation of salvation." "Christian faith . . . [does not agree] that its faith is one species of the genus 'religion.'"[2] For with that understanding

---

1. Brunner, *Revelation and Reason*, 219–20.
2. Brunner, *Revelation and Reason*, 220, 258.

the religious person becomes his own master, rather than Jesus Christ ruling over even the pious. "The modern relativist theory of gradation, according to which the Christian religion is merely a phase, though perhaps the climax, of the general history of religion, is irreconcilable with the Christian belief in revelation." "By revelation the Christian believer means something fundamentally different from an individually unique expression of the universal essence of religion."[3] Christian faith is of another genus, not a different species within the same genus.

"All the more or less radical and destructive movements in the history of theology in the last two centuries are simply variations on one simple theme, and [following Schleiermacher] that theme was clearly [manifested] by van Til and Buddeus: that *religion has not to be understood in the light of revelation, but revelation in the light of religion*. To this common denominator the aims and the programs of all the more important tendencies of [nineteenth and early twentieth-century] theology can be reduced. Neo-Protestantism means 'religionism.'" "We [were] defenceless against the 'German Christians' . . . [until] we [knew] how to guard against the development which took place in van Til and Buddeus, and even earlier." "Protestant theology would never have conceived of reversing the relationship between revelation and religion if it had not shared with the whole church of the time in a widespread vacillation concerning something which the Reformers had so clearly perceived and confessed. This was that the decision about man had been taken once and for all in . . . Jesus Christ."[4]

A related question arises: "Might it not be possible for a non-biblical religion to point toward Christ in the same way as the Old Testament points to Him? [This depends upon whether there is in a particular religion] a similar beginning that points toward Jesus Christ as its goal and its fulfilment, as there was under [some aspects of] the Old Covenant. All through the centuries, down to the present day, the Christian church has clearly answered this question in the negative by undertaking the work of missions. The Christian church does not regard . . . [even Judaism as reflecting the] Old Testament prophecy of Christ."[5] Though particular religions may overlap with Christian Faith at some points, they all disagree in not being grounded in God's once-and-for-all revelation in Jesus Christ.

2. Biblical Examples of Christian Unfaithfulness; Need for Focusing on Revelation in Christ and Deliverance through Christ

"When the disciples are seen as men, independent . . . of their commission, and of the directing and sustaining word of Jesus . . . they at once enter that peculiar shadow-world where their religion is seen to be . . . unbelief. The chief exemplary figure in this respect is the apostle Peter. When Peter stands on his own feet, he is the man who does not mean the things of God, but the things of men (Matt 16:23). He is the doubter who ventures, and then immediately withdraws (Matt 14:28ff). He can cut off the right ear of Malchus (John 18:10), but then deny Jesus thrice. . . . But what strange figures the rest of the disciples also

---

3. Brunner, *Philosophy of Religion*, 128, 129.
4. Barth, *CD* 1/2:290-91, my emphasis.
5. Brunner, *Revelation and Reason*, 221.

cut. . . . We remember the sons of Zebedee with their wish to sit the one on the right hand of Jesus and the other on the left (Mark 10:35f.). We think of the despair of the disciples in the storm on the lake: 'Why are you so fearful? How is it that you have no faith' (Matt 4:35ff.). We recall their sleeping in the garden of Gethsemane (Mark 14:37). . . . So far as they stand on their own feet, the four Gospels make it quite clear that they . . . have their religion, but it is equally clear that their religion is unbelief."[6]

True religion begins at that point where our spiritual pride is broken, where we fall on our knees and find out who we really are and who God really is. The church is not established with the question "who is the greatest in the kingdom of heaven" (Matt 18:1), but with the knowledge that "our power is made perfect in weakness" (2 Cor 12:9b). For when we are weak—when we are utterly dependent on God, God's forgiveness, and God's leading—then we are uplifted and made strong (2 Cor 12:10b).

Has the church taken seriously Christ's judging and redeeming Word concerning religion? Or has she pursued a religion that is centered elsewhere than in Christ? Have Christians in effect "prayed" "God, I thank you that I am not like other men, extortioners, unjust, adulterers, or even like this tax collector. I fast twice a week, I give tithes of all that I get" (Luke 18:11–12). Or have Christians prayed, "God be merciful to me a sinner"? (Luke 18:13c)

3. God's Grace in Christ Contradicting Our Contradiction; The Christocentric Basis of Christian Religion

"To believe means . . . in the knowledge of our own contradiction against grace to cleave to the grace of God which infinitely contradicts our contradiction. In this knowledge of grace, in the knowledge that it is the justification of the ungodly, grace for the enemies of grace, the Christian faith attains to its knowledge of the truth of the Christian religion."[7]

"If the confession of [Christ] as the sole Savior of the world is to be called 'exclusiveness,' then we must let this charge stand. No one is forced to make this confession. But there is no sense in giving oneself out as a Christian if for any reason one does not think one has the freedom to make this confession. In truth, it is basically a confession which is 'inclusive,' which bears upon, and is open, to every person."[8]

"The universal significance claimed by the church for one human person, Jesus of Nazareth, has been expressed in the famous words of Acts 4:12, attributed to Peter, that 'there is salvation in no one else, for there is no other name under heaven given among men by whom we must be saved.'" Recently, this word has come under attack as a symbol of Christian exclusivism. But in fact it proclaims the core of Christian inclusivism, the source of the church's universal mission. Admittedly, it also excludes something—the charms of other saviors or would-be saviors. It does not necessarily deny salvation to members of other cultures and religious traditions, but it certainly claims that if those persons will

---

6. Barth, *CD* 1/2:229–30.
7. Barth, *CD* 1/2:338.
8. Barth, *God Here and Now*, 107.

obtain salvation, it will be through the grace of Jesus Christ whom perhaps they did not even know; it will not be through the power of their own religion."[9]

4. Christian Faith in Contrast with Mysticism

"Christ does not merge into the Christian nor the Christian into Christ. There is no disappearance or destruction of the one in favour of the other. Christ remains the One who speaks, commands and gives as the Lord. And the Christian remains the one who hears and answers and receives as the [servant] of the Lord. In the fellowship both become and are genuinely what they are, not confounding or exchanging their functions and roles nor losing their totally dissimilar [identities]."[10]

> There can certainly be no question of an experience of union induced by psychical and intellectual concentration, deepening and elevating the human self-consciousness. For though . . . the Christian . . . acts as well as receives, neither one's receiving nor one's acting in this fellowship is the product or work of his own skill, but both can be understood only as the creation of the call of Christ which comes to him. Again there can be no question of a disappearance of the true confrontation of God and man, of the One who addresses and the one who is addressed and answers. There can be no question either on the one side or the other of any depersonalising or reduction to silence. There can be no question of any neutralising of the distinction between Creator and creature or of the antithesis between the Holy One and sinners, nor of any establishment of . . . equilibrium . . . between the divine Jesus Christ and the human person. . . . In this fellowship of encounter there is not merely safeguarded the sovereignty of God, of Jesus Christ and of the Holy Spirit, but also the freedom of the human partner is preserved from dissolution. Indeed, it is genuinely established and validated. Unless we consider, safeguard and expressly state these things, we do better not to speak of "Christ-mysticism" when there is obviously no compelling reason to do so.[11]

5. Evaluating Five Religions

"We must not confuse the problem of toleration with the solution of the question of truth. Tolerance is a human attitude, which respects the personality of the other, but it has nothing to do with the truth or falsity of the other's opinions and ideas."[12]

To evaluate other religions from the Christian perspective is to engage in a theology of other faiths. Such an examination often draws on the results of scientific studies of various religions, but seeks to evaluate the validity of various religions' claims from the perspective of God's revelation in Christ.

Judaism. "It is incorrect to regard Judaism simply as the continuation of the revealed religion of the Old Testament. Through the rejection of Jesus as the Messiah the Jewish

---

9. Pannenberg, *Introduction to Systematic Theology*, 53-54.
10. Barth, *CD* 4/3, Second Half, 539.
11. Barth, *CD* 4/3, Second Half, 539-40.
12. Brunner, *Revelation and Reason*, 219.

religion has taken its stand upon a particular interpretation of the Old Testament, namely, that Jesus cannot have been the Messiah. Pious Jews are still waiting for the Christ who is to come; this means, however, that they are still waiting for the revelation which we Christians believe and confess to be the one who has already come.... Both Jews and Christians maintain the provisional character of the revelation in the Old Testament.... The difference lies in the rejection or acceptance of the fulfilment."[13] "For to this very day, when they read the old covenant, the same veil remains unlifted, because only in Christ is it taken away.... But when a [person] turns to the Lord the veil is removed" (1 Cor 3:14b, 15b).

"The radical conception of sin which is embodied in the New Testament and therefore radical forgiveness as expressed in the justification of the sinner through the reconciling suffering and death of the Savior seems to [Jews] to be unbearable, even blasphemous. As the cross of Christ is foolishness to the Greek, that is to [an exclusively] philosophical mind, it is a scandal or stumbling-block to the Jews.... As Paul has shown again and again, they cannot accept the radical message of free grace."[14]

However much movement towards humankind on God's part there was prior to the incarnation, considerable separation remained. When God became man, He bridged the gulf. "Christian faith alone dares to maintain revelation in the strict, unconditional sense of the word, because it alone dares to assert that 'the Word became flesh'" [John 1:14a]. "The radical claim to revelation is bound up with the knowledge of God who is Himself Revealer, that which is revealed, and the revealing activity, Father, Son, and Holy Spirit."[15]

Islam. According to Islam there is no personal relationship with God here or hereafter. Nor is God regarded as bounded by a righteous will, nor seen as loving and forgiving, but as omnicausality, fate, arbitrary power. As for Muslims exercise of power, force has long been used to prevent conversions from Islam to Christianity.

The illiterate Mohammed, who lived six hundred years after Jesus Christ, is credited with writing the Qur'an, which claims to be a book of divine revelations. "Mohammed teaches ... that before him there were other prophets, among whom, above all, Abraham and Jesus must be reckoned; but he himself is [believed to be] the 'seal of the prophetic,' by whom ... the earlier prophets are superseded. For the faithful the [Qur'an] is [regarded as] the 'eternal, uncreated word of God' and faith in this revelation, and in Mohammed in particular, the [merely human] revealer, is the first article in the creed of Islam: 'There is no God save Allah, and Mohammed is His prophet.' The source of this revelation is [said to be] the Almighty—the [Qur'an] knowing nothing about a holy ... [and] merciful God."

"When we compare the [Qur'an] more closely with the Old and the New Testament we cannot help seeing that its creative originality is nil. Actually we understand it best if we regard it as a blend of Old Testament Judaism plus some secondary Christian elements, with ... a fair amount of ancient Arabian paganism, plus ... elements of personal religious and poetic imagination.... An objective comparison leads to the judgment that the prophetic claim does not seem to be in any way justified by the actual content of the

---

13. Brunner, *Revelation and Reason*, 232.
14. Brunner, *Scandal of Christianity*, 46.
15. Brunner, *Revelation and Reason*, 236.

revelations. 'Islam in its constituent elements and apprehensions must be called a superficial religion, . . . a religion that has almost no questions and no answers'"[16]

"At the point in the Christian faith where the person of the Redeemer is central, there stands in Islam the book, the written doctrine. . . . 'Islam is in the full sense of the word a religion of law; its explicitly political character makes this inevitable.' . . . Islam is [also] a religion of the 'righteousness of works,' [and] of moralism. . . . Here there is no revelation of the gracious mystery that the holy God loves sinners."[17]

"The idea of divine forgiveness is not entirely foreign to the [Qur'an], but . . . does not have a decisive place within its system of rigid legal moralism. Allah [is asserted to be] a good and holy God, but he is not the holy one who is at the same time the Merciful Father. Jesus's word that God is love is unthinkable here. Islam . . . is a religion of moral legalism with a moralistic eschatology, in which nothing matters but the norm of obedience to the law."[18]

"Islam's ethical commands correspond to its relatively narrow formulation of the divine essence. It requires the faithful to fight for the honor of the faith, to practice prayer, and to treat one another humanly, but . . . the grandiose concept of [God's] will overwhelms everything. Before this will, there can be only fear, sacrifice, and uncritical acceptance. . . . [God's will overwhelms] everything; but his directions make no sense; and hence Islam forfeits all warmth and life. It is the starkest monotheism on earth; it judges Christianity to be somewhat polytheistic due to its doctrine of the Trinity and the [Roman Catholic] veneration of Mary. Islam's starkness is expressed in the doctrine of the absolute omnipotence of God over everything, which renders the concept of the divine essence weak and insignificant."[19]

Original Buddhism. "The teaching of the Buddha consists in instructions on the 'right path' which man has to tread in order to enter into the passionless state of nirvana. If by revelation is meant the disclosure of a divine will of the Lord who, through His self-disclosure, claims man for Himself, and works out His will in him, Buddhism is the exact opposite; both in origin and aim it is purely anthropocentric; it [supposedly!] is the doctrine of the way to [tranquillity]."[20] But according to Buddhism the eschatological goal is to lose one's self! "Such a religion, in which all that remains is this blessed annihilation, is pessimistic to the core; for it engulfs [and overwhelms] . . . in every respect whatsoever."[21]

Pure Land Buddhism differs from classical Buddhism only in looking to *a mythical figure* called Amita Buddha and the legend that after he had already entered into nirvana he out of pity helps us to be absorbed into nothingness. But why should we need any help? And how could his consciousness have survived the transition and who is he to help us

---

16. Brunner, *Revelation and Reason*, 229-30; 230, quoting Hendrik Kraemer, *Christian Message in a Non-Christian World*, 217.

17. Brunner, *Revelation and Reason*, 231.

18. Brunner, *Scandal of Christianity*, 45.

19. Troeltsch, *Christian Faith*, 132.

20. Brunner, *Revelation and Reason*, 225. Brunner says "happiness," not tranquillity, but I think that is less accurate. Another point: If you believe that the goal of life is to escape from the desires of the world you may be willing to do as the first Buddha did, leave your spouse and family to pursue a career of meditation.

21. Troeltsch, *Christian Faith*, 134.

to achieve the nothingness he has not achieved? And why do we need any help, since nothingness is supposedly the inevitable result anyway? And since this is only a myth why should anyone pay attention to it?

"Behind all this lies the same impersonal outlook as in ancient Indian Buddhism, only here everything has [*supposedly*] been transformed from a pessimistic world-denying view into a more pantheistic world-affirming understanding of life. But what is given to the dead . . . [is only the goal] of nirvana, the fusion of the self with the all."[22]

African Traditional Religion (ATR).[23] African Christians in Nigeria and some other African nations *are tempted* to incorporate into their thinking the worship of ancestors and of nature gods, to accept a prescientific understanding of the causation of misfortunes and illnesses, and to think that morality is identical with following tribal customs.[24] Such beliefs should be challenged by Christians. Since Christians believe in immortality through God's love disclosed in Christ, we should disbelieve that the dead can only live on for a time as shadowy and malevolent spirits on earth; such that offerings need to be made to appease their malicious intentions.

ATR seeks to avoid the very cross carrying that Christianity regards as of the essence of Christian discipleship. Christianity certainly teaches that we are to strive to overcome needless suffering for ourselves and for others, suffering as due to such misfortunes as poverty, hunger, sickness, and the absence of education. But Christianity also teaches that discipleship inevitably involves cross-bearing. For ATR, for Islam, and for general secular thinking, success is a much less ambiguous concept than for genuine Christianity. In many respects authentic Christian faith stands alone, and Christian dialogue with non-Christians can occur only as we honestly recognize this fact.

6. Evaluating the Jehovah's Witnesses and Noting Their Similarities with Other Sectarians[25]

In this section the Jehovah's Witnesses will be briefly described and will be used to highlight tendencies common to other sects/cults. Everyone in a sect/cult is tightly controlled by a small elite at the top. For example, the authoritarian nature of the JWs is obvious from the fact that the articles in the Watch Tower Magazine are never signed, and the members

---

22. Brunner, *Revelation and Reason*, 226.

23. See sec. 8 on African Separatist Churches. Having taught Systematic Theology, Christian Ethics and multiple other subjects at a Nigerian Theological College for fifteen years, I describe the background from which most of our students came. The students I taught for eleven years at Saint Paul's United Theological College (now University), Kenya did not come from such African Traditional Religion contexts.

24. Many of the students had tribal marks on their faces, which could forever be used to establish which side they would be presumed to be on in tribal fights.

25. Davies, *Christian Deviations*, influenced the content of this section. When working on the material for this chapter I discovered that I don't own the book or it is in hiding. Working from South Africa amid a pandemic and not currently having access to the book, I am not in a position to be more specific concerning my utilization of Davies' book.

Though the Mormons are discussed in the next section, and African Separatist Churches in sec. 8, such distortions as Christian Science will not be appraised.

have no idea who wrote them. Yet Witnesses claim that such anonymous pamphlets declare the ultimate truth.

One sect's doctrine may differ from another, but the goal is to establish a convert who is incapable of critical thought, and unable to consider ideas that disagree with the ideology of the group. That is why discussion efforts with such people about their religions are usually a non-conversations. They do the talking and even if we manage to squeeze in a word or two they don't seem to think about what we say—unless they are very new to the sect—which I once discovered with a Jehovah Witness.

If we are to help people to remain free from cults, critical thinking must be encouraged. If pastors expect church members to always agree with them, pastors should not be surprised if those congregants become easy candidates for sects and cults. Having a dialogue period following sermons is one way to encourage critical thinking on the part of church members, and indirectly helps them to avoid falling prey to cults.

In cults such as the Jehovah's Witnesses and the Mormons Greek/Hebrew incompetents control their "translating" of the Bible. They "translate" in such ways as to modify the Bible's teachings to bring them into line with their sect's beliefs. The gullible rank-and-file have no idea that their "Bible's" translation is inaccurate. For example, JW members are "biblically" led to believe that before Jesus's incarnation He was the Archangel Michael, which they claim is taught in Daniel 12:1, and perhaps it is in their "translation"!

A whole lot is at stake with false biblical "translations." Charles Taze Russell, the conman founder of the Jehovah's Witnesses, taught that being saved by Christ's atonement only means that sinners receive another chance to earn their salvation. As with Islam the only chance of being saved is by fulfilling a list of commandments. Regarding salvation as based on works, I suspect that many Jehovah's Witnesses have painful doubts as to whether they will be saved. Can sinners ever do enough to *earn* God's favor?

Salvation is regarded as even less likely because of the JW teaching that only Jehovah Witnesses and only 144,000 of them will be saved *for eternal fellowship with God*. Other Jehovah's Witnesses will receive the losers' prize of living forever on earth, but that is a small consolation since it is to be without fellowship with God.

In accounting for the beliefs of the Witnesses we cannot omit their condemnation of Christian churches as devil-controlled. A group claiming to be Christian, yet so vicious in rejecting others who believe in Christ, manifests a loveless spirit that negates their profession of being Christians! (see 1 Cor 13:13)

The Jehovah's Witnesses are subject to additional criticisms, some of which also apply to Mormons. Firstly, their doctrine is largely based on obscure passages from such apocalyptic books as Daniel and Revelation. The implication is that the revelation of God is a tangled skein only to be unravelled by speculation from those at the top of this sect. Secondly, to use the Bible as an almanac of predictions is to misunderstand its purpose and to claim to know more than Jesus Himself, who confessed that He did not know the time of the consummation (Matt 24:36). Thirdly, their creed must be rejected because it offers salvation on the basis of human worthiness, not because of God's victory in Christ. The entire Christ event can be omitted from such a theology without noticeably affecting the substance of belief. This is why the Jehovah's Witnesses are best understood as a Jewish sect. They do not know Jesus Christ as their Savior, and thus they are left to work out their own salvation.

Whatever we may think of the JW's particular teachings and methods, like the Mormons they have succeeded in convincing their members that every member must be a witness. Like the Mormons in not having an educated and trained clergy or clergy of any kind necessitated their recognition that each member must attest the faith. In many denominations the mistaken idea has developed that the clergy alone are the evangelists, since they get paid to witness. Yet in contrast with Jehovah Witnesses and Mormons we see how badly churches needs formally educated leadership. This is not to displace the laity from the missionary task, but that through the clergy's study, preaching and teaching the church may avoid the gross interpretive distortions that are so glaring in "Christian" groups that lack theologically trained leaders.

Perhaps an even greater asset than JW's zeal for evangelism is their capacity for sacrifice. For many of them are willing to give up friends and family, to work without ceasing, to give unstintingly, to withstand bitter persecution, and to remain loyal to their convictions even unto death. Without imitating the JW's quality of loveless rigidity and their renouncing of biblical scholarship, we who look more truly to the Christ of the NT need to be as devoted to the Father who is known in the Son by the Spirit, as many sects and cults are to their dubious leaders.

7. Evaluating the Teachings of the Church of Jesus Christ of the Latter Day Saints (Mormons)[26]

Opposing thesis: "No other foundation can anyone lay than that which is laid, which is Jesus Christ" (1 Cor 3:11).

Early Mormon History and Legends. Joseph Smith, the founder of Mormonism, was born in Vermont in 1805, and though having received no formal education and being completely unlearned, professed to desire the learning of heaven alone. At the age of fifteen Smith claimed to have seen a vision and received a call to become a prophet of the Most High God. In 1823 in Manchester, New York he further avowed that an angelic messenger told him that he would find a precious religious document buried on a hill, and that this volume was written on plates of gold. He also claimed to have been told that it contained

---

26. The word "Mormon" is derived from the Book of Mormon, which forms one part of their supplements to the Scriptures of the OT and NT.

Most of the material in this section comes from a sermon given as pastor of the University Park United Methodist Church, in Portland, Oregon on January 22, 1978, where we later unsuccessfully attempted to have dialogue with members of The Church of Jesus Christ of the Latter Day Saints. (The invitees from other sects met with us; the Mormons did not.) *Some the insights in this section may have come from Horton Davies' Christian Deviations*, so I cannot identify that influence.

The Community of Christ Latter Day Saints are not under discussion in this section. Though both Mormon groups accept the book of Mormon, the Community of Christ rejects baptisms for the dead and celestial marriages, and purports to be monotheistic, though the latter is hard to square with its acceptance of the Book of Mormon. But they may read that book with more critical eyes. Members of the Community of Christ believe in the Trinity, do not claim to be the only true church, allow visitors to their tabernacle and even accept female priests. All of which the Church of Jesus Christ of the Latter Day Saints do not.

the history of the early inhabitants of the North American continent, as well as an account of the gospel as delivered by the Risen Christ to the ancient inhabitants of America.

In 1827 Smith attested that an angel of God told him where to look for the golden volume, and Smith claimed that he found it. He maintained that these golden plates were inscribed in a strange form of writing the Mormons later labelled "Reformed Egyptian." With the aid of promised crystals and the assistance of God, the illiterate Smith was supposedly enabled to translate the plates. Smith claimed that the golden tablets are the Book of Mormon.

Smith later asserted that the golden plates Book of Mormon just happened to get lost. One wonders how heavy and valuable golden plates that would have firmed up the historical basis of the religion were mislaid, along with the original translation that the illiterate Smith had made.

There being no credible evidence to substantiate any of these assertions, these claims were probably Smith's way of sanctifying America, and endorsing his linking of American patriotism with his truncated and distorted version of Christian Faith.

Mormon history in America. Keep in mind that though the Old Testament patriarchs practiced polygamy, that practice was rejected by Jesus with His teaching concerning monogamous marriage.

The Mormon religious community became increasingly unpopular among its neighbors because of the Mormon conviction that God had commanded the practice of polygamy. (A conservative estimate is that Joseph Smith had seventeen wives and forty-seven children!) Because the neighbors did not take kindly to polygamy, it became necessary for the Mormons to move on from Ohio. More objections in Missouri, where folks have always been a little hard to convince, on to Illinois, where they again faced persecution. At the request of the governor of the state, Joseph Smith and his brother Hyrum were imprisoned. On June 27, 1844, a mob with faces blackened to prevent their recognition broke into the prison and shot and killed the two brothers. The effect of that atrocious and cowardly act transformed Joseph Smith into a martyr and legend.

The prophet's mantle fell upon the shoulders of Brigham Young, who became the second father of the Mormon people. He led a large party into the promised land of Utah. Unfortunate for Mormon polygamous practicing men, in 1862 Congress passed a law prohibiting polygamy. Though the Mormons resisted the law for some time, they increasingly fell afoul of the law in Utah, Idaho, and Arizona. And so in 1890 the Mormon leader, President Woodruff, just happened to receive a new revelation that set aside Joseph Smith's previous revelation. God no longer favored polygamy.

Teachings of the Book of Mormon. The Book of Mormon falsely claims to describe the inhabitants of the Western hemisphere during the years from 600 BC to AD 400. No evidence is given concerning authorship or authorships covering such a wide time period. (The Bible reflects a broad time period, but it had multiple authors of its books.) The first theme of the book is the arrival and settlement of *Israelites* on the continent of America before the Christian era. This is introduced to explain the origin of the American Indians whose tribes scatter across the current boundaries of the lower States! (Why just the lower states?) It's hard to believe that ancient members of Jewish groups ventured across the ocean centuries before Columbus sailed the ocean blue and did not fall off the edge. If Jews had the needed navigational knowledge, had gathered vast provisions, and set off for they knew not where, it seems some people of those earlier centuries would have passed on the information concerning that event.

Archaeologists and linguists have found no evidence of Egyptian writing in ancient America. One also ponders how an ancient Egyptian language could have been used in the U.S. without any traces of such an early foreign language having been spoken, nor any Native Americans passing the story on to descendants. Even more crucially it's odd that an ancient Egyptian language could have been translated into perfect King James English. The Book of Mormon contains twenty-seven thousand words taken directly from the King James Bible.

It happens that a nineteenth century Presbyterian minister named Spaulding wrote just such a piece of fiction. And it is fascinating to learn that it was stolen before it got to the publisher. *And most fascinating of all—that that minister's helper happened to be named Joseph Smith.* Also intriguing, in the Book of Mormon, Nephi, who was purportedly a pre-Christian prophet, uses verbatim quotations from the seventeenth century Westminster Confession of Faith. A nineteenth-century Presbyterian Minister might have done just that. The Book of Mormon also includes an excerpt from a Methodist Book of Discipline and a quotation from Shakespeare.

Mormons don't get along well with historians or anyone who is trying to be honest concerning evidence. Historical criticism indicates that the Book of Mormon is not an ancient document, but an anthology of quotations from Joseph Smith's day. The Book of Mormon is full of anachronisms and discrepancies. For example, Labon is given a steel sword in 600 BC (Nephi 4:9). Jaredites (the early Jewish settlers/American Indians) are said to have eaten pork (Ether 9:18) though the Mosaic Law prohibits it. Even less plausible is the fact that in the Book of Mormon prophets and seers refer to "Jesus Christ," "the Son of God," and to the details of His death and resurrection centuries before those events would have transpired. What can a reasonable person do but shake one's head. Or laugh if all this represents a nineteenth-century Presbyterian minister having a little fun.

Additional teachings of the Book of Mormon. It tells us that our Savior made his appearances upon the American continent after his resurrection, planting the Gospel there in all its fullness before ascending to heaven. This legend helps to explain the popularity of Mormonism in America, since it links American history directly to biblical salvation history. More generally, Mormonism regards America as the land of promise, "a land which is the choice above all other lands" (II Nephi 1:5).

The fact that the Mormon religion is asserted to have been founded on American soil is appealing to those with tendencies toward uncritical patriotism. The Mormon religion is also distinctively American in that many Americans have had an optimistic understanding of human nature. But neither super-patriotism nor optimism concerning human nature are true to the NT. For a rejection of the latter see Rom 7:7–25. One more Mormon legend: with the publication of the Book of Doctrine and Covenants the *illiterate* Smith was no longer regarded as only a passive God-guided translator, but a prophetic writer.

Analyses of some Mormon documents. The first selected items with their original numbers are from the *"Articles of Faith,"* purportedly written by Joseph Smith, with my emphases and bracketed theological criticisms and corrections.

"3. We believe that through *the atonement of Christ*, all mankind may be saved, *by obedience* to the laws and ordinances of the Gospel." [Against the atonement as giving us the opportunity to earn our salvation, we are saved by the grace that leads us in the way of obedience.]

"4. We believe that the principles and ordinances of the Gospel are first, Faith in the Lord Jesus Christ; second, repentance; third, baptism by immersion for the remission of sins; fourth, laying on of Hands for the Gift of the Holy Ghost." [Certainly some Christians might put the words this way, but better put would be this: Without needing any laying on of hands, the receipt of the Spirit leads to the repentance by which we come to have faith in the Lord. Baptism by immersion or otherwise, not being a causative factor leading to faith in the Lord, only symbolizes having received the Spirit.]

"8. We believe the Bible to be the word of God *as far as it is translated correctly*" [which should be by textual scholars, not by Mormons trying to prop up doctrines]; "we also believe the Book of Mormon to be the word of God." [Jesus Christ is the Word of God, and the Book of Mormon is not a responsible testimony to Jesus Christ.]

"10. We believe in the literal gathering of Israel and in the restoration of the Ten Tribes: that Zion will be built upon this (the American) continent; that Christ will reign personally upon the earth; and that the earth will be renewed and receive its paradisiacal glory."[27] [To the contrary, eternal fellowship with the triune God will be realized beyond the dimensions of the United States, this planet, and this universe.]

Joseph Smith is supposed to have written that "Man is *of the family of the Gods.*" [This is unchristian polytheism, a divinizing of humans, a rejection of human sinfulness and of divine Triunity.] In the same sentence Smith is supposed to have immediately went on to write that [man] "was *begotten in his pre-existent state* by his Heavenly Father." [No. We are created and in this world and not begotten; we are not divine!] "*God himself was once as we are now; and is an exalted man.*"[28] [No! No! No! What an indirect attesting of the need for a theologically educated ministry! Which the Church of Jesus Christ of that Latter Day Saints does not have.]

Mormons believe that God *in His eternal dimension inhabits a body of flesh and bone*! They also believe that Mormon men can in the afterlife become gods! Why only men? They also believe that Jesus will not only return but will establish his kingdom's capital in Independence, Missouri. [What blather!]

The Mormon movement features a finite god, a perfectible humanity, and works-righteousness. They have stressed the process of human exaltation rather than the need for reconciliation and redemption. Among Smith's followers he ended the belief that the revelation of God through Jesus Christ is definitive.

More on Mormon Teaching. After Joseph Smith's death the source of continuing revelation came to be the Twelve Elders and the Mormon president, but the president had, and still has the final say. His official word, when spoken in the name of the Lord, is received by the church as the Word of God. The Pope looks like a non-directive counsellor compared with the President of the Mormon religion. The Mormon belief in supplementary scriptures, alternatively translated biblical Scriptures and continuing revelation devalues the

---

27. Smith, *Thirteen Articles of Faith.*
28. Widtsoe, *The Divine Mission of Joseph Smith,* supposing to be quoting Joseph Smith, 15.

finality of Christ's revelation. In Mormon theology salvation is not seen to be on the basis of God's love revealed in Christ.

It's not just the Mormon concept of progressive revelation that creates problems, but the content of the Mormon additions, which contradict biblical teachings. Mormons teach not only tritheism, but polytheism, since they believe that humans can become gods. Having an astonishingly optimistic view of human nature, Mormons deny the biblical belief that we humans are sinful.

Mormonism believes that the gods have bodies and that Jesus Christ lived in the flesh in heaven before becoming incarnate on earth. Human beings are also regarded as having existed as souls in heaven prior to their existence on earth. No one can be truly created if everyone who is born has already pre-existed in heaven. And can an originating god be distinguished from divinized humans? If so he could perhaps be regarded as the organizer of creation, rather than as the creator.

Mormons believe that they comprise the only true church, and that all others are in varying degrees heretical and false. Heretical groups commonly regard everyone else as heretical!

Mormonism long had little appeal to black people, since it propounded a preposterous interpretation of the OT, to the effect that black people are an inferior race. Until recently black men could not become priests (which every Mormon male must be). However, in 1978 the President had another convenient revelation that rejected that doctrine.

As for offensive customs not previously mentioned, consider the "baptism for the dead." That ritual supposedly helps dead ancestors who might otherwise miss the joys of heaven or suffer delays. Getting one's family tree sorted out is believed to have a good deal to do with one's future possibilities. Another distinctive belief is "celestial marriage." Apart from ordinary marriage vows which are believed to last only until death, "celestial marriages" are believed to survive death. Since earlier Mormon men had many wives this could have gotten very complicated for them—including Joseph Smith. Maybe they were thought to get a heavenly harem, as they had on earth.

An essential tenet of Mormon belief and practice is that there are various sources of doctrine: the written word of God (i.e., selected passages from Mormon-translated Scripture), unrelated and even contradicting revelations as declared by the Book of Mormon and in Mormon Doctrines and Covenants, additional Mormon writings, and most of all in the rulings from the Mormon President. Though biblical writings are recognized as having some ill-defined importance, other writings are regarded as more important. To the contrary the Protestant Reformation insisted on the centrality of Jesus Christ and thus on the authority of the Bible in general and the NT in particular, through which we come to know of God's revelation in Christ through the power of the Spirit.

Because of the Mormon's distorted and highly selective use of the NT, they seem to end up judging Christ instead of submitting to Him. The obedience of faith in Christ becomes obedience to the dictates of Mormon traditions and to the Mormon president. The Mormon theory of progressive revelations destroys the finality and uniqueness of the revelation brought by the incarnate, crucified, and risen Lord. Furthermore, the Mormon President and the Twelve Apostles of the Mormon Church have unbridled authority.

Conclusion. This author believes (and I'm on good terms with him) that Rev. Spaulding was the true author of what is now called the Book of Mormon. As a piece of humorous fiction written by a Presbyterian minister wanting to entertain, the Book of Mormon may have some merit. As for serious Christian theology the book of Mormon with its fantastic tales is a hoax.

Opposing thesis again: There is no other true foundation than that which is laid in Christ Jesus (1 Cor 3:11).

8. Evaluating African Separatist "Churches" and Noting the Similarity with Western Prosperity Gospel "Churches"[29]

First a clarification: African Separatist churches name and appeal to the Christian God, whereas in African Traditional Religion various deities and other supernatural forces are recognized and addressed.

The separatist "churches" (non-members of the World Council of Churches) lean heavily on the strong personalities of their leaders,[30] many of whom are regarded as prophets. Though such churches profess some relationship with Christian belief, what they teach and practice often has little connection with that. *"The Christianity offered by the separatist churches may be described as a power for overcoming the ills of the secular aspect of life," as is the purpose of African traditional religion.* Though such terms as 'sin,' 'grace,' 'the blood of our Lord and Savior Jesus Christ,' and other Christian themes are constantly spoken of [in the separationist churches], the central preoccupation is and remains how to cope effectively with the ills of worldly life."[31]

The "gospel" here may be summed up in the words of a typical separatist church invitation—which represents a theology of glory out of balance with a theology of the cross. The invitation reads: "Bring all your worries of unemployment, poverty, witch troubles, ill-luck, enemies, barrenness, sickness, blindness, lameness, or sorrow. Jesus is ready to save [by overcoming such problems] for all who come to him in belief and faith."[32] Faith is regarded as having no doubt that the particular help sought will be supplied. Like African traditional religion and the western prosperity gospel, members of African separatist churches have little consciousness of sin, and regard that only as it is a cause of bodily, mental, or social disorder.

In many African separatist churches holy water plays a supposed magical role. Sometimes congregants are asked to bring "one white bottle filled with water. This is blessed in the course of the service and then taken home for use." "Church services of 'witnessing' are regularly held in which members give testimonies concerning God's granting of their requests. The nature of the hopes held provides an answer to those who wonder why historical churches are not able to attract such large crowds as the separatists draw. But . . . is

---

29. For related background see sec. 5 above where the final part deals with African Traditional Religion. In the current section, Christian G. Baeta refers to a 1957 incident in which two indigenous churches wanted to join the Council of Churches in Ghana. At the time Baeta was a senior lecturer in Divinity at the University College of Ghana, and was the chairman of the Ghana Christian Council and of the International Missionary Council.

30. Baeta, "Conflict in Mission," 291.

31. Baeta, "Conflict in Mission," 293, my emphasis.

32. Baeta, "Conflict in Mission," 293–94.

this the true essence of Christianity? Is it legitimate to present what are merely some beneficial by-products as the whole thing?"[33] Is Christianity merely a primitive technology for attaining our secular desires or is it essentially something else? Does God determine the purpose of Christianity, or does humankind establish the goals, such as becoming rich and/or famous, using "Christianity" to attain such goals?

As in African traditional religion the separatist churches observe a large number of special rites and ceremonies, particularly ecstatic dancing and various fasts and honoring of taboos. Such actions are looked upon as necessary techniques whereby the coveted blessings are secured. Ecstasy is seen as necessary because it is believed that in this condition contact is made with the supernatural power and the desired result obtained. The dance that induces ecstasy is therefore no mere jubilation before the Lord, but a calculated means of obtaining the benefits sought. These ideas, familiar in African Traditional Religion, are regarded by the African historical churches as heretical. In African Traditional Religion and with the separatist churches divine power is seen as at the beck and call of the natural person, at least if the natural person knows the correct techniques. God is created in the image of natural person and is turned to as a way of satisfying natural desires.

In African Traditional Religion and Separatist Religion the blame for failure to obtain requests is firmly fixed on some fault in the petitioner himself, in the performances of the prescribed observances, or in failing to believe that the desired results would accrue. But it is confidently taught that if all is in order on the petitioner's side his wish cannot fail to be granted. Such an assumption assumes that people have the power to manipulate God. Quite obviously this is not the NT understanding, or else Jesus would not have died on a cross! For if He was sinless and did not desire to suffer and die, that event would not have occurred. Against such thinking, suffering can be seen as an integral aspect of the Christian life.

A final stumbling block to fellowship between the two groups of churches was the question of polygamy. This was a sore point when Christianity was first preached in sub-Saharan Africa and is still a sore point today. As far back as 1938, on the occasion of the Tambaran Conference of the International Missionary Council, the Historical Churches in Africa asked the delegates for a clear ruling on this burning issue: Is monogamy a mere factor of civilisation or is it so vital to the life of the church that it has to be realised in its own experience as "was taught by the Lord Himself and [which has other] New Testament authority behind it (Eph 5:31–33; 1 Tim 3:12; 5:9)?" The judgment given was that for both men and women "polygamy mitigates against the attainment of the fullness of life which is in Christ."[34]

"All of the separatist churches recognize polygamy, not indeed as a concession or in order to seduce members from the historical churches, but because they believe that the position of historical churches in this regard, and within the African context, is entirely mistaken. In a statement of faith one of the separatist churches, the Musama Disco Christo Church declared: 'We believe that polygamy is not a moral sin.'"[35] There can be no reasonable doubt that the welcoming of the separatist churches into the National Council of

---

33. Baeta, "Conflict in Mission," 294; no source of African Separatist Church quotations were indicated.
34. Baeta, "Conflict in Mission," 295.
35. Baeta, "Conflict in Mission," 296.

Churches would mean the acceptance of the practice of polygamy for all church members. How could there be an association of churches in the same council, in which some approved polygamy and others did not permit it?

Considering the whole of this section the general conclusion is that "the divergence between the positions of the two groups, both in religious belief and in morality, is very serious indeed. Doctrinally it is not merely a matter of holding different views on certain particular aspects of fundamentally the same faith (for example, different interpretations of ministry or of the sacraments). The issue is rather that of two totally different understandings of what the Christian religion is, and of what people are attempting to accomplish through the practice of religion. In other words, it is not a case of parting company somewhere along the road and coming together again further on, but one of separating from two entirely different points and never really meeting at all."[36]

---

36. Baeta, "Conflict in Mission," 298.

Chapter 30

Freedom within Limitation

1. Our Unique Opportunity

"So teach us to number our days that we may gain a heart of wisdom" (Ps 90:12).

If we are to best accomplish Christian purposes we need to learn to number our days and to prioritize. Such in part involves taking account of our limited time-span and placement in this world—basic realities we all face. God calls us to responsibly receive our restricted time and specific geographical contexts and to take account of their implications.

In becoming incarnate as a particular person at a particular time and place God dignified temporal placement, and showed that human life has meaning and purpose precisely within such boundedness.[1] Limited opportunities and specific time spans: such "was the decree and arrangement of the creative and overruling will of God."[2] To be responsible to God is to recognize, take seriously, and occupy our context as our own, to be used responsibly in service to God and others.

By the Son's coming and by His life, death, and resurrection God has injected new possibilities into history. Jesus came in the fullness of time and enables those who look to Him to share in time's fullness (Mark 1:15; Gal 4:4). As Christ's disciples we exist here and now in transition between "no longer" and "not yet," and between here and eternity. We can thus participate in God's revolution and become people of the future.

The NT encourages us to focus on the need for ongoing moral preparedness in the face of uncertainty as to when we will die or when God will consummate the world. We do not know the day nor the hour, nor did Jesus (Mark 13:32), but we are always to remain ready. The householder did not know when the thief would come, and was unprepared (Matt 24:43–44). The wicked servant was not only unaware when his master would return, but behaved irresponsibly and was in no position to meet him (Matt 24:45–51). And the foolish bridesmaids got tired and fell asleep (Matt 25:1–13). Like these people, we do not know when our end or the end will be; unlike them, we are to remain morally ready in the face of timing uncertainty.

1. Barth, *CD* 3/4:569–72.
2. Barth, *CD* 3/4:571.

That we do not know the day or the hour gives the command and warning in the NT its character of extreme urgency, its eschatological character.³ With the present as always the time for preparing, the NT insists that "now is the acceptable time, now is the day of salvation" (2 Cor 6:2c). What is required is to be constantly faithful, knowing that *our* end or *the* end may come at any time (see Matt 24:45—25:13).

We cannot locate eternity on maps or charts of the created cosmos. But we know with whom we will share life eternal. It will be like going to an unknown place, but knowing that our well beloved Friend will welcome us and others. Meanwhile we should remember that time is running out. "Whether used or misused, it will suddenly be gone. As the thief comes in the night (1 Thess 5:2), as a landlord returns to his house, as the bridegroom arrives for the celebration, so at the hour chosen by the Lord but not previously intimated, the end will be suddenly revealed to those who wait."

"The summons of the New Testament ethic is urgent. Everywhere it emphasizes that the time loaned to us is important because everywhere it sees concretely, not merely that this time has a limit, but that God is its limit." "Every act, therefore, must be measured and tested by the question of whether it is a seizing or neglecting of *the unique opportunity* presented [to us in our] time. When put from this standpoint the question of obedience has a distinctive and critical edge. We can think of decisions, acts and attitudes that may seem to be blameless, right and good from other angles, and yet we are startled if we ask what is their significance as an accomplishment of what is fitting for [our] particular existence in [our] particular time. We have perhaps done too little, or too much, or acted too differently, to be able to say responsibly that what we have done is really 'timely' for us."⁴

Each of us is unique. Yet we all feel a good deal of pressure to conform to what other people want us to be and to do, which usually consists of becoming more like those others. The time is short and we waste a lot of time trying to live other people's lives, rather than our own. Though we can and should receive guidance from others, to be directly accountable to God within our own restricted span is to be the unique person God has called and is calling us to be.

To be responsible to God within the boundaries of our own temporal placement involves making *hard choices as to how we will or will not spend our time.* "With all the demands that crowd upon us we must know how to give preference to one thing and to set aside another. We must know how to concentrate and therefore how to separate the center from the periphery, or from the many peripheries in question."⁵ There is much work that is intrinsically good and beautiful, but which we must leave to others because we must concentrate on what God wants *us* to do. "It is simply a relic of the delusion of infinity, or a sign that we have made a bad and disobedient selection, if we have a bad conscience in relation to what we cannot undertake for lack of time, or if we allow side-glances at that to disturb or unsettle us in what we can and should do."⁶

The struggle to perceive God's concrete will should be equally intense for all Christians, though some conditions may be limiting. If we have any choice in the matter, an

---

3. Barth, *CD* 3/4:583.
4. Barth, *CD* 3/4:583, 584.
5. Barth, *CD* 3/4:587–88.
6. Barth, *CD* 3/4:588.

employed Christian must seek to know how much time to spend in financially remunerative work. But even if we are not employed we are still responsible to God concerning how to fulfill our specific callings. How much time to spend in activity within the organized church and how much with Christian outreach within the broader community. How much with our nuclear family, how much with our extended family, how much with friends. *We must prioritize if we are to have focus and best accomplish Christian purposes.*

We might be tempted to think that retired people (of both the younger and older varieties) would not need to stay so focused, and for many there may be some truth to this. But even at such stages unless people seek to remain faithful to God they may trivialize their later years by watching too much TV or too many films, doing too much "face-booking," or too much tweeting or otherwise treating this period as entertainment time. At most stages of life we can be of some service to others and such service helps us to be less preoccupied with ourselves. Also, as we have more free time we may be able to deepen our relationship with God.

Christian boldness in living from God within our own duration and in seeking to be the unique people God is calling us to be is aided by contemplating our own deathwardness. Christians who do not face up to their finiteness are not living from the full resources that the Gospel makes available. Though we should habitually remind ourselves that we will die, if we stand in awe of the God who in Christ has conquered death we need not fear.

Those who do not take confidence in God's forgiveness will try to cover over death by using a variety of techniques of evasion or denial. Some may pretend that they are inherently immortal. Belief in the inherent immortality of the soul is a mere projection or wishful thought—as though imagining can make it so. A popular American means of denial or evasion of death is to keep oneself so busy that one does not stop long enough to think about the final and ultimate mystery of life in this world—that it ends at the grave.

An old German proverb went this way: "I come and know not whence. I go and know not wither. I marvel that I am still so happy."[7] If secular people really faced their finitude they might not be so happy. But until people have reason for genuine confidence in God's love, most will keep distracting and deceiving themselves.

"It is indeed unpleasant to think that some day I shall be a corpse whom others will leave behind and go home chatting [about], after they have heaped wreaths and flowers and poured out kind words and music upon me. It is indeed unpleasant to think that my [earthly] place will then be in a coffin [or my ashes be in a urn or in a niche in a wall or tossed to the wind]. It is indeed an unpleasant thought that though for a time I will be missed, . . . I will be finally be extinguished from human memory when the last of those who knew me has gone the same way. This is undoubtedly the kind of death which awaits us with absolute certainty."[8] Yes and no. For example, Barth's writings could be long remembered, and Barth insofar as he shines through his writings, which indeed he does (!), but the time will come when no one will have directly known him.

A heart of wisdom in the face of death comes from trusting in the God whose love was revealed in Christ. "That which in death we shall always fear without God, namely, the fact that we shall cease to exist, that it will be too late, that there is an implied threat of

---

7. Barth, *CD* 3/2:572.
8. Barth, *CD* 3/4:589.

annihilation [or even of never-ending judgment], we shall now fear no longer." "The real reason why we need not . . . and must not fear death any longer is that, at the point where we [would] cease to be, God the Lord . . . comes to meet us." Our Lord is at the beginning of our time, within our time, and also at its end. "He is the frontier ahead and it is to Him that we move."⁹

Since we can trust that God will forever be for us, we need no longer be for ourselves. Here and now we can participate in the future kingdom, and do so by grappling with the specific way in which God wills that each of us live out our particular calling within our own limited timespan.

9. Barth, *CD* 3/4:593, 591.

Bibliography

Allen, Diogenes. *Christian Belief in a Postmodern World: The Full Wealth of Conviction*. Louisville: Westminster/John Knox, 1989.
Althaus, Paul. *The Theology of Martin Luther*. Translated by Robert C. Shultz. Philadelphia: Fortress, 1975.
Aulen, Gustaf. *The Faith of the Christian Church*. Philadelphia: Muhlenberg, 1960.
Badham, Paul. "The Meaning of the Resurrection of Jesus." In *The Resurrection of Jesus Christ*, edited by Paul Avis, 23–38. London: Darton, Longman, & Todd, 1993.
Baeta, Christian G. "Conflict in Mission: Historical and Separatist Churches." In *The Theology of Christian Mission*, edited by Gerald H. Anderson, 290–99. New York: McGraw-Hill, 1961.
Baillie, D. M. *God Was in Christ: An Essay On Incarnation and Atonement*. London: Faber and Faber, 1961.
Barbour, Ian G. *Religion in an Age of Science*. London: SCM, 1990.
Barrett, C. K. *Church, Ministry, and Sacraments in the New Testament*. Grand Rapids: Eerdmans, 1985.
———. *The First Epistle to the Corinthians*. London: Adam & Charles Black, 1968.
Barth, Karl. *Church Dogmatics*. Vol. 1/1, *The Doctrine of the Word of God: Prolegomena to Church Dogmatics*. Edited by Geoffrey W. Bromiley and T. F. Torrance. Translated by G. T. Thompson. Edinburgh: T. & T. Clark, 1936.
———. *Church Dogmatics*. Vol. 1/2, *The Doctrine of the Word of God*. Translated by G. T. Thompson and Harold Knight. Edinburgh: T. & T. Clark, 1956.
———. *Church Dogmatics*. Vol. 2/1, *The Doctrine of God*. Translated by T. H. L. Parker et al. Edinburgh: T. & T. Clark, 1957.
———. *Church Dogmatics*. Vol. 2/2, *The Doctrine of God*. Translated by Geoffrey W. Bromiley et al. Edinburgh: T. & T. Clark, 1957.
———. *Church Dogmatics*. Vol. 3/1, *The Doctrine of Creation*. Translated by J. W. Edwards et al. Edinburgh: T. & T. Clark, 1958.
———. *Church Dogmatics*. Vol. 3/2, *The Doctrine of Creation*. Translated by H. Knight et al. Edinburgh: T. & T. Clark, 1960.
———. *Church Dogmatics*. Vol. 3/3, *The Doctrine of Creation*. Translated by Geoffrey W. Bromiley and R. Ehrlich. Edinburgh: T. & T. Clark, 1960.
———. *Church Dogmatics*. Vol. 3/4, *The Doctrine of Creation*. Translated by A. T. Mackay et al. Edinburgh: T. & T. Clark, 1961.
———. *Church Dogmatics*. Vol. 4/1, *The Doctrine of Reconciliation*. Translated by Geoffrey W. Bromiley. Edinburgh: T. & T. Clark, 1956.
———. *Church Dogmatics*. Vol. 4/2, *The Doctrine of Reconciliation*. Translated by Geoffrey W. Bromiley. Edinburgh: T. & T. Clark, 1958.
———. *Church Dogmatics*. Vol. 4/3, *First Half, The Doctrine of Reconciliation*. Translated by Geoffrey W. Bromiley and R. Ehrlich. Edinburgh: T. & T. Clark, 1961.
———. *Church Dogmatics*. Vol. 4/3, *Second Half, The Doctrine of Reconciliation*. Translated by Geoffrey W. Bromiley. Edinburgh: T. & T. Clark, 1962.
———. *Church Dogmatics*. Vol. 4/4, *The Christian Life (Fragment), Baptism as the Foundation of the Christian Life*. Translated by Geoffrey W. Bromiley. Edinburgh: T. & T. Clark, 1969.
———. *Church Dogmatics*. Vol. 4/4, *The Christian Life, (Lecture Fragments)*. Translated by Geoffrey W. Bromiley. Grand Rapids: Eerdmans, 1981.
———. *Credo*. Translated by J. S. McNab. New York: Scribner's Sons, 1962.

BIBLIOGRAPHY

———. *Evangelical Theology*. Translated by Grover Foley. New York: Holt, Rinehart, and Winston, 1963.

———. *God Here and Now*. Translated by Paul M. Van Buren. New York: Harper and Row, 1964.

———. *Gottingen Dogmatics*. Vol. 1. Edited by Hannelotte Reiffen. Translated by Geoffrey W. Bromiley. Grand Rapids: Eerdmans, 1991.

———. *The Humanity of God*. Translated by Thomas Wieser and John Newton Thomas. Richmond: John Knox, 1963.

———. *Prayer and Preaching*. Translated by Sara F. Terrien and by B. E. Hooke. London: SCM, 1964.

———. *Protestant Theology in the Nineteenth Century*. Translated by Brian Cozens and John Bowden. London: SCM, 1972.

———. "Rudolf Bultmann—An Attempt to Understand Him." In *Kerygma and Myth*, edited by Hans Werner Bartsch, 2:83–132. London: SPCK, 1962.

———. *The Word of God and the Word of Man*. Translated by Douglas Horton. New York: Harper & Row, 1928.

Beare, Francis Wright. The *First Epistle of Peter*. Oxford: Blackwell, 1961.

Berkhof, Hendrikus. *Christian Faith: An Introduction to the Study of Faith*. Translated by Sierd Woudstra. Grand Rapids: Eerdmans, 1979.

———. *The Doctrine of the Holy Spirit*. Atlanta: John Knox, 1977.

———. *Well-Founded Hope*. Richmond: John Knox, 1969.

Bicknell, E. J. *A Theological Introduction to the Thirty-Nine Articles of the Church of England*. 3rd ed. London: Longmans, 1963.

Biggar, Nigel. "Hearing God's Command and Thinking about What's Right: With and Beyond Barth." In *Reckoning with Barth*, edited by Nigel Bigger, 101–18. London: Mowbray, 1988.

Bornkamm, Gunther. *Early Christian Experience*. Translated by Paul L. Hammer. New York: Harper and Row, 1969.

Braaten, Carl E. "The Christian Doctrine of Salvation." *Interpretation* 35.2 (1981) 117–31.

———. "The Person of Jesus Christ." In *Christian Dogmatics*, edited by Carl E. Braaten and Robert W. Jenson, 1:465–550. Philadelphia: Fortress, 1984.

Bretherton, John. *Progress in Heaven*. London: Epworth, 1934.

Brosnan, Sarah and de Waal, Frans. "Female Brown Capuchin Monkeys' Sense of Grievance and Individual Rights." *The Economist* (Sept 20, 2003), 83.

Brunner, Emil. *Dogmatics*. Vol. 1, *Christian Doctrine of God*. Translated by Olive Wyon. Philadelphia: Westminster, 1950.

———. *Dogmatics*. Vol. 2, *The Christian Doctrine of Creation and Redemption*. Translated by Olive Wyon. Philadelphia: Westminster, 1952.

———. *Eternal Hope*. Translated by Harold Knight. Philadelphia: Westminster, 1954.

———. *The Misunderstanding of the Church*. Translated by Harold Knight. Philadelphia: Westminster, 1953.

———. *Revelation and Reason*. Translated by Olive Wyon. Philadelphia: Westminster, 1956.

———. *The Scandal of Christianity*. Translated by M. E. Bratcher. Richmond: John Knox, 1965.

———. *Theology of Crisis*. New York: Scribner's Sons, 1931.

Bultmann, Rudolf. *Essays Philosophical and Theological*. Translated by James C. G. Greig. New York: Macmillan, 1955.

———. *Existence and Faith*. Translated by Shubert M. Ogden. Cleveland: World, 1966.

———. *The Gospel of John: A Commentary*. Translated by G. R. Beasley-Murray et al. Oxford: Blackwell, 1971.

———. *Primitive Christianity*. Translated by R. H. Fuller. Cleveland: World, 1956.

———. *Theology of the New Testament, Vol. 1*. Translated by Kendrick Grobel. New York: Scribner's Sons, 1951.

———. *Theology of the New Testament, Vol. 2*. Translated by Kendrick Grobel. New York: Scribner's Sons, 1955.

Calhoun, Robert Lowry. *Lectures on the History of Christian Doctrine*. New Haven: Yale Divinity School, 1949.

Calvin, John. *Institutes of the Christian Religion*. Vols. 1 and 2. Translated by John T. McNeill and Ford Lewis Battles. Library of Christian Classics. Philadelphia: Westminster, 1960.

Camfield, F. W. "The Doctrine of God: (3) God's Election of Grace." In *Reformation Old and New*, edited by F. W. Camfield, 71–85. London: Lutterworth, 1947.

Clark, William Newton. *An Outline of Christian Theology*. New York: Scribner's Sons, 1908.
Cocks, H. F. Lovell. "Death." In *A Handbook of Christian Theology*, edited by Marvin Halverson and Arthur Cohen, 76–79. London: Meridian, 1962.
Cousar, Charles B. "2 Corinthians 5:17–21." *Interpretation* 35.2 (1981) 180–83.
———. *A Theology of the Cross*. Minneapolis: Fortress, 1990.
Croxall, T. H. *Kierkegaard Studies*. London: Lutterworth, 1948.
Dahl, Nils Alstrup. *The Crucified Messiah*. Minneapolis: Augsburg, 1974.
———. *Jesus the Christ*. Edited by Donald H. Juel. Minneapolis: Fortress, 1991.
———. *Studies in Paul*. Minneapolis: Augsburg, 1977.
Darwin, Charles. *The Origin of Species*. In *The World's Great Thinkers: The Philosophies of Science*, edited by Saxe Commins and Robert N. Linscott. New York: Norton, 1977.
Davies, Horton. *Christian Deviations*. London: SCM, 1974.
Dawe, Donald G. "The Divinity of the Holy Spirit." *Interpretation* 34.1 (1979) 13–31.
———. *The Form of the Servant: A Historical Analysis of the Kenotic Motif*. Philadelphia: Westminster, 1963.
Dunn, James D. G. *Baptism in the Holy Spirit*. Studies in Biblical Theology, Second Series. London: SCM, 1970.
———. *The Evidence for Jesus*. London: SCM, 1985.
———. *Jesus and the Spirit*. Philadelphia: Westminster, 1975.
———. *Jesus' Call to Discipleship*. Cambridge: Cambridge University Press, 1992.
———. *Jesus Remembered*. Grand Rapids: Eerdmans, 2003.
———. "Rediscovering the Spirit." *Expository Times* 84.1 (1972) 7–12.
———. *The Theology of Paul the Apostle*. Grand Rapids: Eerdmans, 1998.
———. *Unity and Diversity in the New Testament: An Inquiry into the Character of Earliest Christianity*. Philadelphia: Westminster, 1977.
Eddy, G. T. "The Resurrection of Jesus Christ: A Consideration of Professor Cranfield's Argument." *Expository Times* 101.11 (1990) 327–29.
Edwards, Jonathan. *Representative Selections, with Introduction, Bibliography, and Notes by Clarence H. Faust and Thomas H. Johnson*. New York: Hill and Wang, 1962.
Eichrodt, Walther. *Theology of the Old Testament, Vol. 2*. Translated by J. A. Baker. London: SCM, 1967.
Erickson, Millard J. *Christian Theology*. Grand Rapids: Baker, 1985.
Fergusson, David. "Eschatology." In *Cambridge Companion to Christian Doctrine*, edited by Colon E. Gunton, 226–44. Cambridge: Cambridge University Press, 1998.
Fiddes, Paul S. *The Creative Suffering of God*. Oxford: Oxford University Press, 1988.
———. *Past Event and Present Salvation: The Christian Idea of Atonement*. London: Darton, Longman and Todd, 1989.
Fitzmyer, Joseph A. "Pauline Theology." In *The New Jerome Biblical Commentary*, edited by Raymond E. Brown et al., 1382–416. Englewood Cliffs, NJ: Prentice Hall, 1990.
Fosdick, Harry Emerson. *A Guide to Understanding the Bible: The Development of Ideas within the Old and New Testaments*. New York: Harper and Row, 1967.
Fretheim, Terence E. *The Suffering of God*. Philadelphia: Fortress, 1984.
Fuller, Reginald H. *The Foundations of New Testament Christology*. London: Collins, 1972.
Gartner, Bertil E. "The Person of Jesus and the Kingdom of God." *Theology Today* 27 (1970) 32–43.
Geering, Lloyd. *Resurrection: A Symbol of Hope*. London: Hodder and Stoughton, 1971.
Geyer, Hans-Georg. "The Resurrection of Jesus Christ: A Survey of the Debate in Present Day Theology." In *The Significance of the Message of the Resurrection for Faith in Jesus Christ*, edited by C. F. D. Moule, 105–35. London: SCM, 1968.
Gould, Stephen Jay. *Ever Since Darwin: Reflections on Natural History*. New York: Norton, 1979.
Griffin, David Ray. *God, Power, and Evil: A Process Theodicy*. Philadelphia: Westminster, 1976.
Gunton, Colin E. *The Actuality of the Atonement: A Study of Metaphor, Rationality, and the Christian Tradition*. Edinburgh: T. & T. Clark, 1988.
———. *Yesterday & Today: A Study of Continuities in Christology*. Grand Rapids: Eerdmans, 1983.
Harker, Joseph. *A Cow's Grieving Capacity*. Notes and Queries compiled by Joseph Harker. *The Guardian Weekly* (date and paging lost).
Harrisville, Roy A. *1 Corinthians*. Minneapolis: Augsburg, 1987.
Hick, John. *Death and Eternal Life*. London: Collins, 1976.

BIBLIOGRAPHY

Hillerbrand, Hans J. "Anabaptism and the Reformation: Another Look." *Church History* 29.4 (1960), 404–23.

Houlden, J. L. *Paul's Letters from Prison: Philippians, Colossians, Philemon, and Ephesians.* Hammondsworth: Penguin, 1970.

Hultgren, Arland J. *Christ and His Benefits.* Philadelphia: Fortress, 1987.

———. *Paul's Gospel and Mission.* Philadelphia: Fortress, 1985.

Hunter, A. M. *Paul and His Predecessors*, London: SCM, 1961.

Jablonka, Eva, and Marion J. Lamb. *Evolution in Four Dimensions.* Cambridge: MIT Press, 2005.

Jays and Ravens Understand That Others Have Minds and are Capable of Empathizing and Deceiving. *The Economist* (May 15, 2004), 77.

Jeremias, Joachim. *New Testament Theology.* Vol. 1, *The Proclamation of Jesus.* Translated by John Bowden. London: SCM, 1971.

———. *The Parables of Jesus.* Translated by S. H. Hooke. New York: Scribner's Sons, 1963.

Kasemann, Ernst. *Essays on New Testament Themes: Studies in Biblical Theology.* Translated by W. J. Montague. London: SCM, 1964.

———. "The Pauline Theology of the Cross." *Interpretation* 24.2 (1970) 151–77.

Keller, Ernst, and Marie-Louise Keller. *Miracles in Dispute.* Translated by Margaret Kohl. London: SCM, 1969.

Kierkegaard, Soren. *Philosophical Fragments; or, A Fragment of Philosophy.* Translated by David F. Swenson. Princeton: Princeton University Press, 1962.

———. *Sickness unto Death.* Copenhagen, 1849.

———. *Training in Christianity.* Translated by Walter Lowrie. Princeton: Princeton University Press, 1960.

Kselman, John S., and Ronald D. Witherup. "Modern New Testament Criticism." In *The New Jerome Biblical Commentary*, edited by Raymond E. Brown et al., 1130–45. Englewood Cliffs, NJ: Prentice Hall, 1990.

Kummel, Werner Georg. *The Theology of the New Testament.* Translated by John E. Steely. Nashville: Abingdon, 1973.

Kung, Hans. *The Church.* Translated by Ray and Rosaleen Ockenden. Garden City, NY: Doubleday, 1976.

Lampe, G. W. H. and D. M. MacKinnon. *The Resurrection: A Dialogue.* Philadelphia: Westminster, 1966.

Lindstrom, Harold. *Wesley and Sanctification.* Nashville: Abingdon, 1946.

Lohse, Bernhard. *A Short History of Christian Doctrine.* Translated by F. Ernest Stoeffler. Philadelphia: Fortress, 1966.

Marshall, I. Howard. *Jesus the Savior.* Studies in New Testament Theology. London: SPCK, 1990.

Martin, Ralph P. *Worship in the Early Church.* Grand Rapids: Eerdmans, 1974.

McCormack, Bruce. *Karl Barth's Critically Realistic Dialectical Theology: Its Genesis and Development, 1909–1936.* Oxford: Oxford University Press, 1997.

McGrath, Alister. *Justification by Faith.* Basingstoke: Marshall, Morgan and Scott, 1988.

McKenzie, John L. *Vital Concepts of the Bible.* Denville, NJ: Dimension, 1969.

Mealand, David L. "The Christology of the Fourth Gospel." *Scottish Journal of Theology* 31 (1978) 449–67.

Mehl, R. "God, NT." In *A Companion to the Bible*, edited by J. J. Von Allmen, 146–51. New York: Oxford University Press, 1958.

Meier, John P. "Jesus." In *The New Jerome Biblical Commentary*, edited by Raymond E. Brown et al., 1316–28. Englewood Cliffs, NJ: Prentice Hall, 1990.

———. *A Marginal Jew: Rethinking the Historical Jesus.* Vol. 1, *The Roots of the Problem and the Person.* New York: Doubleday, 1991.

———. *A Marginal Jew: Rethinking the Historical Jesus.* Vol. 2, *Mentor, Message, and Miracles.* New York: Doubleday, 1994.

Members of the Crow Family Can Learn from Their Experience and Perceive the Intentions of Others. *The Economist* (November 24, 2001), 83.

Midgley, Mary. *Beast and Man: The Roots of Human Nature.* London: Routledge, 1995.

Migliore, Daniel L. *Faith Seeking Understanding.* Grand Rapids: Eerdmans, 1991.

Minear, Paul S. *I Saw a New Earth: An Introduction to the Visions of the Apocalypse.* Eugene, OR: Wipf & Stock, 2003.

———. *To Die and Live.* New York: Seabury, 1977.

Morris, Leon. *The Cross in the New Testament.* Exeter: Paternoster, 1967.

Newbigin, Lesslie. *The Gospel in a Pluralist Society.* Grand Rapids: Eerdmans, 1989.

Niebuhr, H. Richard. *The Responsible Self.* New York: Macmillan, 1962.

Niebuhr, Reinhold. *The Irony of American History*. New York: Scribner's Sons, 1952.

———. *Moral Man and Immoral Society: A Study in Ethics and Politics*. New York: Scribner's Sons, 1960.

———. *The Nature and Destiny of Man*. New York: Scribner's Sons, 1949.

Nineham, D. E. *Saint Mark*. Harmondsworth: Penguin, 1964.

O'Collins, Gerald. *The Resurrection of Jesus*. Valley Forge, PA: Judson, 1973.

Outler, Albert C., ed. *John Wesley*. Oxford: Oxford University Press, 1964.

Pannenberg, Wolfhart. *Apostles' Creed in Light of Today's Questions*. Translated by Margaret Kohl. London: SCM, 1972.

———. *An Introduction to Systematic Theology*. Grand Rapids: Eerdmans. 1991.

———. *Jesus—God and Man*. Translated by Lewis L. Wilkins and Duane A. Priebe. Philadelphia: Westminster, 1968.

———. *Systematic Theology*. 3 vols. Translated by Geoffrey W. Bromiley. Grand Rapids: Eerdmans, 1991–98.

Placher, William C. *Jesus the Savior*. Louisville: Westminster John Knox, 2001.

———. *Narratives of a Vulnerable God*. Louisville: Westminster John Knox, 1994.

Placher, William C., and David Willis-Watkins. *Belonging to God: A Commentary on A Brief Statement of Faith*. Louisville: Westminster John Knox, 1992.

Polanyi, Michael. *Science, Faith, and Society*. Chicago: University of Chicago Press, 1964.

Prenter, Regin. *Spiritus Creator*. Philadelphia: Muhlenberg, 1953.

Presbyterian Church of Canada. *Living Faith: A Statement of Christian Belief*. Winfield: Wood Lake, 1984.

Ray, Ronald R. *Systematics Critical and Constructive 1: Biblical-Interpretive-Theological-Interdisciplinary*. Eugene, OR: Pickwick, 2018.

Reasoning Capacity of Smart German Shepherd. *Washington Post* (June 10, 2004), paging lost.

Ritschl, Albrecht. *The Christian Doctrine of Justification and Reconciliation*. Edited by H. R. Mackintosh and A. B. Macaulay. Edinburgh: T. & T. Clark, 1902.

Rosato, Philip J. *The Lord as Spirit: The Pneumatology of Karl Barth*. Edinburgh: T. & T. Clark, 1981.

Ruef, John. *Paul's First Letter to Corinth*. Harmondsworth: Penguin, 1971.

Schleiermacher, Friedrich. *The Christian Faith, Vol. 2*. Edited by H. R. Mackintosh and J. S. Stewart. New York: Harper and Row, 1963.

Schroeder, Frederick W. *Worship in the Reformed Tradition*. Philadelphia: United Church, 1966.

Schweizer, Eduard. *The Good News according to Mark*. Translated by Donald H. Madvig. Atlanta: John Knox, 1970.

Smith, J. Weldon, III. "Some Notes on Wesley's Doctrine of Prevenient Grace." *Religion in Life* 34.1 (1964–65) 68–80.

Smith, Joseph. *Thirteen Articles of Faith of the Church of Jesus Christ of the Latter-Day Saints*. https://www.churchofjesuschrist.org/comeuntochrist/article/articles-of-faith.

Thomas, George F. *Religious Philosophies of the West*. New York: Scribner's Sons, 1965.

Tillich, Paul. *Systematic Theology, Vol. 3*. Chicago: University of Chicago Press, 1963.

Troeltsch, Ernst. *The Christian Faith*. Translated by Garrett E. Paul. Minneapolis: Fortress, 1991.

Trueblood, David Elton. *General Philosophy*. Grand Rapids: Baker, 1963.

United Presbyterian Church in the U.S.A. *Book of Confessions*. Philadelphia: Office of the General Assembly of the United Presbyterian Church in the United States of America, 1967.

Wainwright, Geoffrey. "The Doctrine of the Trinity: Where the Church Stands or Falls." *Interpretation* 45.2 (1991) 117–32.

Weatherhead, Leslie D. *The Will of God*. London: Epworth, 1944.

Weber, Otto. *Foundations of Dogmatics*. 2 vols. Translated and annotated by Darrell L. Guder. Grand Rapids: Eerdmans, 1981–83.

Wedderburn, A. J. M. *Beyond Resurrection*. Peabody, MA: Hendrickson, 1999.

Weiss, Rich, quoting C. Randy Gallistel. Monkeys Have Pre-Mathematical Reasoning Capacities. *Washington Post* (October 22, 1998), paging lost.

Welch, Claude. *In This Name*. Eugene, OR: Wipf & Stock, 2005.

———. *The Reality of the Church*. New York: Scribner's Sons, 1958.

Wendel, Francois. *Calvin*. Translated by Philip Mairet. New York: Harper and Row, 1950.

Wesley, John. *Christian Perfection*. Edited and Introduced by Thomas S. Kepler. Cleveland: World, 1954.

———. *Forty-Four Sermons*. London: Epworth, 1961.

Widtsoe, John A. *The Divine Mission of Joseph Smith*. Independence, MO: Zion, n.d..

BIBLIOGRAPHY

Ziesler, Paul. *Pauline Christianity*. Oxford: Oxford University Press, 1983.
———. *Paul's Letter to the Romans*. London: SCM, 1989.

www.ingramcontent.com/pod-product-compliance
Lightning Source LLC
Chambersburg PA
CBHW080934300426
44115CB00017B/2811